COMING OF AGE
IN THE
GLOBAL VILLAGE

The Science & Technology,
Politics, Economics,
Environment & Ethics
Literacy Book

by Stephen P. Cook

with contributions
by Donella H. Meadows

Parthenon Books

This book is dedicated to my children.

copyright 1990   by Stephen P. Cook

printed in the United States of America
First Printing
Library of Congress Catalogue Card Number: 90-62089
ISBN 0-9627349-0-X

Acknowledgments

copyrighted articles by Donella H. Meadows originally
appeared in the Lebanon N.H. Valley News and are used here
with her permission.

photo credit: cover photo of child provided by Foster Parents
Plan International, Sulawesi, Selatan, Indonesia Office.

Grateful acknowledgment is made for permission to reprint
excerpts from the following copyrighted works:
"Ideologies and Science Teaching" by Gérard Fourez copyright
1988 by STS Press.
Science for All Americans copyright 1989 by the American
Association for the Advancement of Science.
No More Plastic Jesus by Adam Daniel Finnerty, copyright 1977
by Orbis Books.

I wish to thank my past and present academic colleagues
Robert Allen, Leo Bowman, Laurie Cook, and Frank Reuter for
reading parts of the manuscript and offering suggestions, and
ATU Dean Richard Cohoon for granting my request for a shortened work week.

Parthenon Books
PO Box 822
Russellville, AR 72801

TABLE OF CONTENTS

PREFACE

I am indebted to hundreds of people for their contributions to this book. I hope that I have adequately acknowledged their efforts. I wish to apologize for my use of certain male gender terms ("kings", "masters", "mankind", "brotherhood" and so on). I found it impossible to convey the intended neutral gender meaning without sounding cumbersome.

To protect the privacy of friends and loved ones, certain people, organizations, and places in Part C have been given fictitious names. While there are (usually clearly indicated in Part C) fictional scenes, otherwise the book contains as good an approximation of reality as I can provide.

Yet, this book is a compromise. It paints a portrait of reality as seen from many different viewpoints. If one viewpoint dominates, it is that of a global citizen valuing fair play and holding a science-based perspective. While this worldview eventually prevails, where controversy is involved both sides are even-handedly presented. While the book's orientation is global, given its intended American audience, many illustrations are focused in the U.S.

As a compromise, this book contains something to offend nearly everyone. Patriotic, freedom-loving Americans won't like the book's global (rather than "Americanism") stance and its environmentally-inspired calls for restraint. Those embracing economic growth will recoil from the book's ultimate promotion of "enoughness". Yet some "deep ecology, anti-technologist" types may be turned off by the pro "science for the people, technology with a human face" attitude. Despite its typically rational thrust, many scientists won't like its occasional spiritual, anti-materialistic moments. Even so, religious people who view God in personal, moralistic terms--may disapprove of how God is ultimately depicted.

This book is offered as a jumping off place for educational exploration--a quest to make connections and find meaning in life. While suitable for use in some classroom settings, teachers used to dry, less readable, compartmentalized, de-politicized texts may shy away from it given its scope, and wholistic, controversial and personal nature.

Despite these perceived offenses, people in the above categories--and all intelligent, concerned people--will find much of value in these pages. My intention is not to provoke or offend, but to encourage independent thinking, discussion and learning. I do not pretend to have all the answers. My hope is that together we can find some of them.

PART A :

BACKGROUND, HISTORY, WORLDVIEWS

Until recently, indeed, science had little relevance with respect to the global education of the youth, while today it is in science classes that most structure their worldview. Science teaching is not merely specific instruction. It is the place where the youth is educated to understand the universe, society, and relationships among science, technology, politics, and ethics.

Gérard Fourez,
Universitaires de Namur,
Belgium

"Ideologies and Science Teaching"
Bulletin of Science, Technology & Society
vol. 8, #3 1988, p.270

LETTERS

I. TO THE READER

Stable, peaceful village communities exist throughout the world. Some are hundreds of years old. While technological developments have brought changes, the traditions and values, the humanity and close ties to the natural world characteristic of such places have been preserved.

Elsewhere in the last two centuries, untold numbers of communities have succumbed to impacts associated with the accelerating pace of technological change. Machines have dehumanized workplaces. Medical and public health advances have helped trigger population explosions. Electronic images and voices have replaced written and spoken words. Ethical concerns and questions--many never before considered--have arisen. Biotechnologists have begun playing God and creating life. If nuclear tools of destruction are employed, war threatens Homo Sapiens with everlasting death. In the last decade, evidence has mounted that human activities are compromising the integrity of Earth's life support biosphere.

"What can we do to maintain our planetary home as a healthy place to live?" many wonder. Some envision a prosperous, sustainable world and look to the creation of the global village.

What is "the global village"? The phrase often creeps into discussions about the ultimate role of computers and communications in society. "Wiring the planet has begun. Eventually an information network and global marketplace interactions will interconnect all people," some proclaim. Others--leery of the selfish perpetuating injustices and leaving the have-nots of a fragmented humanity out of the supposed new order --embrace the "one world" connotations of "the global village". They envision the individuals of a new species-- a more caring Homo Sapiens --empathically wedded to each other--all part of a collective consciousness. Still others, recalling Gandhi's "production by the masses, not mass production" or Schumacher's "small is beautiful, technology with a human face" themes, look to village-scale, appropriate technologies in an integrated, but culturally diverse, decentralized world.

Unfortunately, a majority take no part in such discussions. Many in developed countries--while avid consumers of corporate technologists' offerings--lack the scientific and technological literacy necessary to participate in technology assessment debates. In the "have-not" world, hundreds of millions are struggling to survive in their technologically-impoverished, information deficient world. Undeniably the movement toward the global village has begun. In mid-1985 an estimated three billion people watched televised pictures of The Live Aid for Africa concert. Perhaps as a result, the lyrics, "We are the world, we are the children" live inside many human heads. Some may also recall Burt Lancaster saying,

> If mankind can learn to live as one family, we can do a lot more than end the African famine. We might just grow up.

What is the global village? Perhaps nothing more than many possibilities yet to be realized. But it can become what we want it to be. Coming of Age in the Global Village was written with its creation in mind.

Originally, this book was entitled "The Global Education of My Children". This title seemed appropriate for two reasons. First, it embodies the book's chief purpose: the education of tomorrow's global citizens. Second, one can argue that "we are all children" and only our collective growing up can solve humanity's most challenging problems.

Nevertheless, this title was abandoned because I feared it would be misunderstood. I cannot easily explain use of "my children" in that context. The explanation goes beyond my writing the book for my own two children. It goes beyond my writing this book. (Only a foolish author fails to recognize his debt to others!) It goes beyond me period. By the end of the book perhaps you will understand.

Still, I suppose some explanation is needed as you begin this initial chapter. Consider what follows to be a generic, collective letter written by globally concerned, caring parents for their children everywhere.

II. TO THE CHILDREN

Dear Children: Once you were not here, but I was. Out of the ecstasy of love your mother and I shared, you were conceived. You began as a microscopic cellular union, but those cells packed millions of years of genetic wisdom and you grew steadily. With my hand or ear resting on your mother's tummy I gauged your development as best I could. I felt your kick, listened to your heartbeat, suspected a hiccup--then one day you wanted out and your mother labored. It was me she turned to in her anguish before the moment of birth. Minutes later you heard my voice saying "It's a boy" or "It's a girl". I lifted you to your mother's breast and could not hide my joy at seeing you.

With your mother, I was up in the night to comfort you when you cried. I saw the smile of accomplishment when you first stood without help. I watched your first uncertain steps and helped cushion your falls. When you tired I carried you up hills, and later cautioned you about running down them. You learned to talk by imitating me. I taught you the alphabet, counting, and encouraged your pictures and creativity. I helped you understand the world and "soft wire" your brain. Your mother and I have been "God" to you.

Now you are older. You do not need my hugs, my help arbitrating disputes, or my instruction nearly so often. And your education has entered another phase.

Both education and growing up never really end--they are ongoing processes. As Gail Sheehy noted in her 1976 best-seller Passages, "Men and women continue growing up adult from 18 to 50. There are predictable crises at each step."

Sheehy represents forces influencing human behavior in terms of an inner custodian, which protects and controls us embodying parental cautions, and two different inner selves. The Merger Self longs to bond with others, express tenderness, empathize, share unselfishly and love intimately. In contrast, the Seeker Self is more independent and self-centered. It drives us to explore, develop our own unique individuality and become our own master.

A first step into the adult world comes with moving away from home and parents, first physically and gradually emotionally. Sheehy places this transition as extending from ages 18 to 22 and writes,

> The tasks during this time are to locate ourselves in
> a peer group, a sex role, an anticipated occupation,
> an ideology or worldview...Each time we master an under-
> taking that replaces the parental view of the world with
> our own evolving perspective, we overtake another inch
> or so from our inner custodian.

I encourage your exploration and questioning. Many of the answers to be found and values to be clarified are ones you have to arrive at yourself: they will mean more if they are truly yours. I can only guide you, not make your choices.

But I shall caution you. As you shop in "The Reality Marketplace" avoid spending your "reality cash" too early, before you have seen everything. Many people get stuck with attitudes and desires that do not bring happiness nor promote planetary well being. Also, recognize the tug of war going on inside you in light of Sheehy's caution,

> While our Seeker Self urges us to confront the unknown and take chances--pushing the young person to all manner of extremes--our Merger Self beckons us back toward the comforts of safety and the known--and the possibility of locking in prematurely.

This is a book for your future, for growing up and leading happy, meaningful, ethical lives. It can be your handbook for understanding and caring. Long hours and much inspiration went into creating it. As its creator I think of it as "a holy book". Indeed, at times I live again as "God" in these pages. For you, I hope it becomes a family bible that you seek out when the imperfections and complexities of human society threaten to overwhelm you.

III. THE BOOK'S ORGANIZATION & WORLDVIEW THEMES

I have told you in general terms what this volume is about--now I shall be more specific. I will characterize the book in three different ways.

First, I will outline the book's organization, general themes, and settings employed. The book is divided into three parts. Part A contains six chapters, Part B seven chapters, and Part C six chapters.

Parts A and B immerse you in the "what was" and "what is" world of facts and knowledge. This is the world of history and science. The central question addressed here is, "What is the nature of things?"

The word that best summarizes the complex and diverse possible answers to this question is the German word Weltanschauung. This refers to an individual's or society's comprehensive conception of the world as a whole. This conception includes all things and events in the world, and encompasses past, present, and future. Besides incorporating a purpose or "raison d'etre", it also provides an outlook or expectation for the world as it exists or is perceived to exist. In place of "Weltanschauung", which has no exact English equivalent, I shall use the term "worldview" to mean the same thing.

This book is a tool to aid your search for something important: a healthy worldview. You are a thinking, doing, and feeling human being. Without denying the other two aspects of human nature, as a thinking animal I value basing worldviews on reason. So Part A begins by looking at the foundations and methods of science. As you read about the development of the modern scientific conceptual framework (in CONCEPTS), realize that you are still building your own worldview framework.

Part A continues with a chronological review of both the roots of and the human experience itself. As we proceed, I will discuss several worldview themes that have shaped and continue to shape human history in a significant way. Many of these will be formally identified, numbered for later reference and succinctly summarized (Fig. #1).

```
+------------------------------------------------------------+
|              FIG. #1   WORLDVIEW THEMES                     |
|                                        page in text        |
|    #1  The Humble Skeptic Worldview         16             |
|    #2  The True Believer Worldview          16             |
|    #3  Tunnel Vision: The Small Picture     18             |
|    #4  Global Vision: The Big Picture       18             |
|    #5  Mechanistic Worldview                26             |
|    #6  The Classical Scientific Worldview   36             |
|    #7  Mystical / Eastern / New Age Worldview  45          |
|    #8  The Vitalist Doctrine                51             |
|    #9  The Christian Fundamentalist Worldview  54          |
|   #10  Humanism                             55             |
|   #11  The Fatalist Worldview               56             |
|   #12  The Free Will Worldview              56             |
|   #13  Scientism                            58             |
|   #14  The Spiritual / Moralistic Worldview  68            |
|   #15  The Collective Cognitive Imperative  75             |
|   #16  Family of Man / Other People Orientation  77        |
|   #17  The Wronged, The Vengeful Orientation  77           |
|   #18  The Emotional Ungovernable Person    80             |
|   #19  The Economic Man                     84             |
|   #20  The Elitist Worldview                86             |
|   #21  The Populist Worldview               86             |
|   #22  The Expansionist Worldview           89             |
|   #23  The Sustainable Worldview            90             |
|   #24  The Survival-Oriented Worldview     106             |
|   #25  Anthropocentrism                    111             |
|   #26  The Consumerist Mentality           112             |
+------------------------------------------------------------+
```

Seldom does just one of these worldview themes dominate an individual's behavior. Typically several together comprise a major part of the framework that represents an individual's actual worldview. Of course there are as many worldviews as there are individuals. In looking for the major worldview themes behind the human experience, we are simplifying a very complex history. This has been done to aid your rationally putting together a healthy worldview.

Parts A and B are set in The Reality Marketplace--where important ideas, central values, worldview themes, and interpretations of reality are bought and sold. In GENESIS, I make this setting explicitly clear; elsewhere you will have to imagine it since I focus on what I learned.

After reviewing science and human history in Part A, in Part B I take you to various neighborhoods in The Reality Marketplace. In some of these neighborhoods I provide the people we meet with aptly titled characterizations (Grabbers, Pushers, Technologists, etc.) Keep in mind that the shops and neighborhoods we visit are not necessarily good or bad ones --just important places many people never adequately explore. Thus, few seriously consider certain arguments or viewpoints which could be valuable. I believe in fairness and an even-handed educational approach. If it seems I am avoiding certain shops --for example, I spend little time in either "The 'America is Great' Shop" or "The Corporate Good Guy Shop"--it is because I think you have been in them before. If you have not, seek them out. Wise decisions are made when you have all the facts.

As we explore these neighborhoods and shops, we meet the principal players in the problem-plagued human drama of the late 20th century. Our interest is in the dominant themes of future acts in this drama. In particular, we investigate five such possible dominant themes, "Liberalism", "Environmental and Social Decay", "Heightened Corporate State", "Techno-logical Fixes", and "Attitudinal Fixes".

IV. THE BOOK AND VALUES

Part C is set in "The School of Hard Knocks" and in "The World of My Imagination"--although there are brief returns to The Reality Marketplace. In Part C, we bridge the gap between the "what was" and "what is" worlds (where Parts A and B are predominantly focused), and the "what ought to be" world. This jump can only be made by inserting value judgements after one's worldview has been articulated.

Understanding your own values and their origin is critical to living the life you want to live --the "what ought to be" as far as your personal future is concerned. In Part C I illustrate this process by tracing the development of my own worldview and values, and describing the steering of my life toward desired goals.

Mixing science and human values makes some --including many scientists --uncomfortable. Why must human values no longer be considered "off limits" to science? Responding to this question Roger Sperry, professor of psychobiology at Caltech, wrote[1]

> I tend to rate the problems of human values Number One
> for science...above...problems like poverty, population,
> energy, or pollution on the following grounds: First,
> all these crisis conditions are man-made and very large-
> ly products of human values. Further, they are not cor-
> rectable on any long-term basis without first changing
> the underlying human value priorities involved.

In classroom discussion of values, teachers often adopt a "neutral observer" role or employ strategies in which students clarify their own values. Recently, scholars have attacked these approaches --one critic being University of Chicago ethics and society professor Robin Lovin. Such orientations are unsatisfactory "because they separate too sharply the reasoning that governs knowledge of facts from the reasoning that we use to order and express values" he writes. Lovin notes that value choices "are not absolutely unique products of individual experience. They are formulated by religions, political traditions, family folklore, local customs, and the current wisdom of popular culture." Of course these factors, along with genetics, parents, socioeconomic class, race, relationship with siblings, and friends/role models, shape a person's identity, attitudes, and worldview.

Lovin suggests a new approach in which students not only clarify their own values but learn to affirm them in terms that are meaningful to others. He calls this strategy "values articulation" and writes,[2]

> To be articulate about one's values is to be able to
> locate them within these traditions and systems of
> belief and to be able to explore the implications that
> these larger contexts have for how values are to be
> applied and practiced. To be articulate is also to

understand which of the several systems that may support
a specific value position is decisive for one's own
affirmation of the value and to be able to explain how
that tradition relates one both to others who affirm the
same value for different reasons and to those who deny
it.

Coming of Age in the Global Village embraces this values
articulation approach. Parts A and B--with their background,
history, worldview themes, and depiction of western culture-
-provide a framework for students to draw on in articulating
values. Part C --besides documenting a quest for "a way of
doing that seems right" i.e. the ethical--provides a detailed
example of an individual's articulation of values.

```
+-----------------------------------------------------------------+
|             FIG. #2  THIS BOOK'S LEARNING OBJECTIVES            |
|      Reading this book will help you,                          |
|      1) appreciate the heritage of our planet and your own     |
|         unique place in its web of life,                       |
|      2) feel like a member of the world community of five      |
|         billion plus humans,                                   |
|      3) to think globally but act locally,                     |
|      4) understand global economic, political, ecological,     |
|         and technological systems,                             |
|      5) understand the causes of global problems and get       |
|         involved in the search for solutions to them,          |
|      6) consider the effect of your actions on the Earth's     |
|         biosphere,                                             |
|      7) understand the rapid, ongoing transformation of        |
|         the world into a global society,                       |
|      8) understand your own life support and higher needs,     |
|         and thus the needs and aspirations of all people,      |
|      9) develop skills and knowledge for living in and         |
|         solving problems in an increasingly complex and        |
|         changing world, and                                    |
|     10) understand the evolution of universal and diverse      |
|         human values and articulate your own values.           |
+-----------------------------------------------------------------+
```

For teachers, leading discussions about ethical behavior
is a risky proposition for detractors may hurl "mind control"
charges at them. In response, Gunn and Vesilind, in their
book, Environmental Ethics for Engineers, write,

...there is a very significant difference between
teaching what to think and how to think. Teaching

ethics in the classroom involves the expanding of the
mind's horizons to encompass the wisdom of the ages, and
to bring these methods of thinking about difficult
topics to bear on contemporary problems. Teaching ethics
is the exact opposite of mind control; it is the
unshackling of the mind and making it free to understand
other ideas and other values. (emphasis theirs)

V. THE BOOK AND GLOBAL EDUCATION

As a second way to characterize this book, consider it a
rather unusual text in global education. In Fig. #2, I list
its global education learning objectives.[3]

How does my global education approach differ from the
usual high school or college treatment? First, such wholistic
education emphasizes the interconnections and interdependencies traditional, reductionist education --which divides
knowledge up piecemeal fashion into discrete subjects --often
overlooks. Global education focuses on whole systems--as in
Fig. #3 [4] --rather than on individual subjects. It also extends boundaries. A topic's past, present, future and relationship to the rest of the world --not just its here and now
aspects--are scrutinized.

```
+-------------------------------------------------------------+
|                                                             |
|        FIG. #3   THE LEARNER AT THE WORLD'S CENTER          |
|                                                             |
|     The Global Village          The World as a              |
|     Social, Political &         Physical System             |
|     Economic Systems                                        |
|                                                             |
|                                                             |
|                                                             |
|                                                             |
|                         +----------+                        |
|     The Human           |INDIVIDUAL|         The World as a  |
|     Species             |LEARNER   |         Biological System|
|                         +----------+                        |
|                                                             |
|                                                             |
|                                                             |
|     Communicative &             Evaluative &                |
|     Expressive Systems          Belief Systems              |
|                                                             |
+-------------------------------------------------------------+
```

Similarly, global education involves the <u>whole</u> person. It recognizes that you are a thinking, doing, and feeling human being. An education that stresses one of these three aspects to the relative neglect of the others may have un-healthy consequences. Critics charge that conventional higher education --where students attend either analytical-thinking dominated colleges or vo-tech schools--produces "thinkers who can't do and doers who can't think". Others view science ed-ucation as emphasizing thinking to the extent of ignoring feelings. Such people find science and technology dehumaniz-ing. Global education and related Science, Technology, and Society (STS) approaches can restore humanity to these sub-jects by connecting them to real people and problems whose solutions lead to a better human existence.

Second, the perspectives adopted in global education are different. Most fundamentally, students are encouraged to think like world citizens rather than U.S. citizens. In this book I express viewpoints and put you into situations that will arouse your feelings and get you to think. Elsewhere I have sought to frame a topic so squarely in a real-world set-ting that I have brought all the tensions, conflicts, uncer-tainties, and hassles along also. I have tried to help you see other viewpoints where a choice is involved or how issues that you could not relate to touch your life.

VI. THE STORY WITHIN

To describe the third way I have of characterizing this book, I must overview the story which enfolds within it. It is a story about growing up and searching --searching for a simple lifestyle, for small pleasures derived from the nat-ural world, and for a community where people join hands. It is also about experiencing "the highest high" and trying to "save" the planet. It is a story about valuing common sense, fair play, empathy, and humility, and a tale of seeking fun-damental truths and aspiring to greatness.

If these descriptions of roles I play in this book seem contradictory, they are. Still, there is a simple explanation for my behavior: my life is the practical integration of two opposing worldview themes. What are these themes? I think <u>Limits to Growth</u> co-author and global citizen Donella H. Meadows --whose contributions are sprinkled throughout this book --describes them well. (I have added the word "humble" otherwise the words are hers):

* #1 THE HUMBLE SKEPTIC WORLDVIEW *

Skeptics never forget the complexity of the world or the smallness and ignorance of any one person. They aren't sure enough of anything to lay it on everyone else. They trust not in high principles, but in small experiences.

* #2 THE TRUE BELIEVER WORLDVIEW *

I understand what it is to be a Believer. I like to think of myself as devoted to noble causes. I too can overcome obstacles through courage, persistence, and Shining Purity. I define who I am, magnify my identity, and recognize my enemies through my crusades.

My worldview pendulum has long swung back and forth between "what is" and "what ought to be" orientations. Meadows also realizes the need for moderation. She writes, "Only people out at the dangerous extremes of True Believerdom fail to respect holders of other beliefs." She notes that, "Every-time Europe has been reduced to rubble, it has been in the name of some glorious cause --Jesus, Mohammed, the King, the Pope, the Fatherland, the Proletariat." And she quotes great American writer and always skeptical E.B. White, who found it "sobering to encounter the idealists at work, for they seem to live in a realm of their own, making their plans for the world in much the same way that any common tyrant does."

Clearly, there are all sorts of extreme ideals to hold and extreme ways to live. I have decided there is only one path to personal <u>and</u> global happiness: it is the path of moderation, the golden mean. To define this path and encourage you to wander down it, I have adopted a most unusual viewpoint. Perhaps you have already guessed it : I have written this book <u>as if</u> I were a great prophet, a Messiah, a saviour of Mankind. But that does not mean that I am such a person-- this is an important distinction. Before you dismiss my pretending as irrelevant, consider information that bears on my claim to be an ethical person.

Scientists, in their investigations of the development of moral behavior in humans, have constructed schemes that portray moral development as a sequence of stages. Over time, an individual, society, or whole species may evolve out of the initial, egocentric, self-interest stage, and through stages which involve increasing concern for others. Ultimately a universal principle orientation is adopted where justice, equality, and human reciprocity guide behavior.

Similarly, others conceive of human ethics as evolving

over time via an inverted pyramid scheme. Amongst precivilization humans, ethics applied only to small groups or perhaps only to specific important individuals (close relatives). Under pressure to survive, a person might even cannibalize his own offspring or mate. Eventually, as culture developed and pressures eased, ethical behavior broadened to include tribes, regions, nations, and races. Today, at the top of the pyramid, are a few individuals who have made an ethical leap. Their behavior reflects a family of man orientation.

I think of myself as such a global citizen. I have long applied universal principles in fashioning ethically acceptable behavior. For 10 years I conducted socially-relevant research (at The School of Hard Knocks!) by living according to the ethics of a philosophy called Ecosharing. Part C describes and documents this experiment --in which a family of four lives with no more than its fair ecoshare. I think your global education will benefit from an exploration of all the ramifications of this adventure. (i.e. Could all humans maintain a similar standard of living? Would such families be "poverty-stricken" or "materially and spiritually well-off"? Should such Ecosharing ethics be a goal for humanity?)

VII. GROWING UP, SEEING THE BIG PICTURE

You have started Coming of Age in the Global Village at the beginning. Perhaps you are now ready for the subtle and sophisticated things I want to teach you --but maybe you are offended that I keep treating you like a child. To make you feel better, I could argue that, "We are all children." In his Operating Manual for Spaceship Earth , Buckminster Fuller advanced this position.

> My own picture of humanity today finds us just about to step out from amongst the pieces of our just one-second-ago broken eggshell. Our innocent, trial-and-error nutriment is exhausted. We are faced with an entirely new relationship to the universe. We are going to have to spread our wings of intellect and fly or perish.

How should we do this? Fuller suggests we "think big". Thinking big is more lastingly effective, but it is not easy and neither is growing up. Consider the following characterization[5] of a whole generation's difficulties in moving in those directions.

> Without anything about which to feel secure, the post boom generation has had a hard time planting our

feet on the ground....Post-boomers live in the present
because our future seems so ominous....Because we cannot
visualize our collective future, we have narrowed our
scope of vision to the small picture--our lives, our
homes, our careers, our bodies, and our hobbies.

It is this self-centered, "small picture" worldview that I
find childish. I shall help you find an alternative to it.

To contrast this orientation with another diametrically
opposed to it, I formalize these worldviews as follows:

* #3 TUNNEL VISION: THE SMALL PICTURE *

*The world you visualize in your mind's eye revolves
around yourself. This self-centered small picture depicts
your immediate concerns. Spatially, this picture is confined
to your home, school, work, and recreation locale, and temporally focused on the "here and now".*

* #4 GLOBAL VISION: THE BIG PICTURE *

*You recognize that increasing global interdependencies
tie your own future and that of loved ones to the well being
of the entire planet. So the world you visualize in your
mind's eye extends to include events in remote lands. Similarly, you look into the past for causes to today's problems,
and assess future consequences of today's actions. While
your actions are undertaken locally, you recognize their effects may have broader consequences so you think globally.*

In the pages to come, I shall paint a "big picture", offer lessons in what it means to be a member of the global
village community of five billion humans, and provide a
vision of our collective future. I hope this global education will culminate in your growing up. Let us begin.

Questions & Projects

1. As children grow, they shift from feeling, to feeling and
   doing, to thinking, feeling, and doing creatures. Discuss.
2. Analyze yourself in terms of feeling, doing, and thinking.
3. Is the imagined conflict between the Merger Self and the
   Seeker Self relevant to you at this time in your life? If
   so, where does it stand? If not, why not? Discuss.
4. Think back on your education. Provide specific examples
   where reading or listening could have been supplemented by
   doing to enhance your understanding of a topic.
5. Gérard Fourez distinguishes textbooks which present an
   image of science which emphasizes "truth" from those which
   emphasize "social usefulness". Which type is this book?

6. Describe a personal experience involving a dehumanizing aspect of science and technology.

7. In his 1943 book <u>Liberal Education</u> , Mark Van Doren wrote, "The connectedness of things is what the educator contemplates...the student who can begin early in life to think of things as connected, even if he revises his view with every succeeding year, has begun the life of learning." Relate this to building a worldview.

8. Contrast the educational approach behind Fig. #3 with colleges insisting freshmen choose a major (this is like shoving students into mailroom pigeon-hole slots!)

9. Relate the word "ideologist" to "true believer".

10. Identify the True Believer and the Humble Skeptic in these conversations. a) person 1 --Have you been saved ? person 2 -- Saved from what ? b) person 1--Oil is becoming scarce and valuable. person 2 --If so, its price should have increased. The market wouldn't undervalue it. Make up another such conversation and interpret it so that others can understand.

11. Suppose you're leading a discussion on a controversial values-laden issue. Two people with narrow worldviews -- one a true believer, the other a strong skeptic--threaten to disrupt the event. How might you defuse tension?

12. How are science and technology helping to make possible trading worldview theme #3 for worldview theme #4?

13. After noting biblical book names in the Table of Contents, and reading its initial chapter, is this book to be a sort of bible? (Consider the following phrases from definitions of "Bible" and "bible" : "a tremendous sweep of its histories", "preeminent especially in authoritativeness", "a holy guide of faith and conduct", "written under the guidance of God".)

Notes

1. Sperry, R.W. quoted in Pugh, G.E. "Human Values, Free Will and the Conscious Mind" <u>Zygon</u> 11, 1 1976 pp.2-24

2. Lovin, R. "The School and the Articulation of Values", <u>American Journal of Education</u> , February, 1988

3. list inspired by Kniep, W. M. "Defining A Global Education By Its Content", <u>Social Education</u> , October, 1986

4. a simplified version of a drawing in Boulding, K.E. <u>The World as a Total System</u> , Sage, Beverly Hills, CA 1985.

5. Urbanski, W. <u>The Singular Generation: Young Americans in the 1980s</u> , Doubleday, New York 1986

CONCEPTS

I. CHILDREN, SCIENTISTS, AND BUILDING BLOCKS

In the beginning there was you. As a small child the world seemed mysterious and your understanding of its workings came slowly. At first you did not separate yourself from the external world and thought that many non-living objects were living and conscious. Your interpretations of happenings involved animism and magic. As your awareness of a separate self grew, you began seeing relationships, categorizing, discriminating and generalizing about what your senses revealed. In this way you replaced sensory experiences and memories of them with abstract generalized ideas and understanding: concepts.

At first your conceptualization was hindered by magical thinking and your egocentric point of view. Still, by the time you reached a certain age --perhaps as early as three, perhaps not until age seven --you had acquired hundreds of concepts.

As you grew you gradually put these concepts together into a framework for understanding your environment. New experiences or problems provided lessons that necessitated revising or adding to your conceptual framework. You were naturally curious. At a very young age you started gathering information by experimenting and testing. At first you did this to establish limits important to your well being, to gain understanding or solve problems. You are still acquiring new concepts and your conceptual framework is still changing as new experiences provide new insights.

Like children, scientists are curious. They also gather information--albeit sometimes as numerical data --perform experiments, test hypotheses, and solve problems. Similarly they fit what they have learned into conceptual schemes and fit many such schemes into a conceptual framework.

Obviously child's play and scientific investigations are quite different. Science can be defined as a methodical quest for reality and truth. The problems scientists work on and the systematic methods they use are beyond the realm of most people's everyday pursuits. The methods involve planning, preliminary library research, careful observation--often using instruments that extend the range of ordinary human senses--testing, and refining. Their conceptual schemes typically are shrouded in mathematical abstractions and sometimes employ things that no one has actually ever seen. Unlike children, scientists are quick to catch and long remember the occasional phenomenon that does not fit into their conceptual framework.

The problems scientists work on--which can be contrasted with a child's here and now preoccupation with fixing a toy or climbing to a better vantage point--may involve searches that will eventually lead to greater comfort for many human beings. Or they may be removed from any human motive except understanding by many orders of magnitude in time or space.

Despite these differences, frequently both children and scientists humbly and innocently stand in awe of the natural world. At least one scientist has likened questing for better scientific conceptual schemes to child's play:[1]

> We are like children making a house out of a variety of
> blocks. The constraint is that each block has to fit
> with the ones under it and over it and the whole
> structure has to stand up. But there may be more than
> one way to build the house.

If you have ever played with children's building sets, maybe you've felt that you could build anything from the various small pieces by putting them together properly. You can appreciate a related scientific effort, one aimed at taking things apart rather than putting them together. This ongoing quest is for the fundamental building blocks that make up all matter. This search began over 2000 years ago, perhaps in response to some child's question, "What is everything made out of?"

II. THE ARISTOTELIAN CONCEPTUAL FRAMEWORK

Greek philosopher Aristotle (384-322 BC) had his conceptual framework widely adopted by others. He supposed a fundamental difference between matter found in the heavens and that found on earth. Objects in the celestial realm were made of a pure, most noble element: the quintessence. In the terrestrial domain everything was supposedly composed in various proportions of one or more of four basic elements:earth, water, air, and fire. Movement in the terrestrial region was in straight lines, whereas heavenly bodies possessed a natural circular motion.

The Greeks had long recognized certain objects that appeared to wander amongst the fixed stars --objects called planets for the Greek word for wanderer. Aristotle held that each of them --Sun, Moon, Mercury, Venus, Mars, Jupiter, and Saturn --revolved in a concentric circle (fastened to a rotating sphere) about the fixed Earth. Beyond the planets lay the outermost sphere of the fixed stars. Beyond that was the hand of the Prime Mover --who kept the whole clockwork-type system turning.

Hundreds of years later, the "official" conceptual framework of the Middle Ages was largely based on Aristotle's. The Catholic Church identified the Prime Mover with the hand of God, added a hell and heaven, and enshrined the whole hierarchical system. Some Church scholars realized that a related, but more complex system possessed some advantages in making sense of celestial motions. By employing small circles (called epicycles) on top of large circles --as in Fig. # 4a --the system originated by Claudius Ptolemy (85-165 AD), explained the (sometimes) observed, irregular, retrograde motion of the planets. Despite that, the simpler Aristotelian system was more widely taught.

Not until the latter 18th century did the last visages of the Aristotelian worldview disappear. Why did it take so long to replace it with something better? For a millennium Western people put their faith in the unquestioned authority of the Catholic Church. The Church authorities --instead of doing independent thinking and analysis --mostly depended on scholars from antiquity--like Aristotle--when wisdom from the Bible was lacking.

Aristotle attempted to explain both the motions and composition of matter. We shall now consider these topics separately, starting with the former and tracing the development of the scientific method.

III. COPERNICUS AND KEPLER

Both Aristotle's and Ptolemy's planetary models shared four incorrect beliefs/flaws:
1) the universe was geocentric with the massive, immobile Earth at the center,
2) the celestial bodies moved in uniform circular paths,
3) different physical laws governed the terrestrial and celestial regions, and
4) the mathematics used was not modeling physical reality.
In addition, determinations of planetary positions, which might be used to make improvements in these models, were seldom made and plagued by inaccuracies.

The first of these obstacles was removed with the introduction of a new, sun-centered system by a Polish monk, Nicholas Copernicus (1473-1543). This appeared in his classic,
<u>Revolutions</u> <u>of</u> <u>the</u> <u>Celestial</u> <u>Orbs</u>, which Copernicus delayed
publishing until he was on his deathbed to avoid conflict
with the Church. In his system, the Earth was given a daily
spin on its axis and placed in an annual circular orbit
around the sun. He assigned similar motions to the other
planets. But his simple system (Fig. #4b) could hardly account for the complex irregularities in observed planetary
motions, which were in fact due to the true elliptical nature
of their orbits.

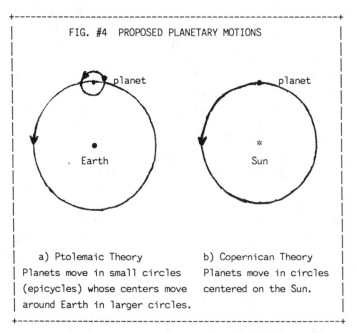

```
+--------------------------------------------------------------+
|            FIG. #4   PROPOSED PLANETARY MOTIONS              |
|                                                              |
|                                                              |
|                  planet                    planet            |
|                                                              |
|                                                              |
|                                                              |
|              Earth                     Sun                   |
|                                                              |
|                                                              |
|                                                              |
|                                                              |
|     a) Ptolemaic Theory        b) Copernican Theory          |
|    Planets move in small circles   Planets move in circles   |
|    (epicycles) whose centers move  centered on the Sun.      |
|    around Earth in larger circles.                           |
+--------------------------------------------------------------+
```

Copernicus made few planetary observations, his system
was largely based on the observed planetary positions of ancient astronomers. These observations of 1500 years earlier
were accurate to only 1/6 degree. In order to choose between
rival Copernican and Ptolemaic systems--or develop a new sys-
tem-- more observations were needed. For over 20 years the
Dane, Tycho Brahe (1546-1601), carefully charted planetary
positions to an accuracy seldom in error of 1/30 degree. To
analyze his observations, Tycho hired a young German math-
ematician Johann Kepler (1571-1630).

Kepler is a pivotal figure in Western history. He stands squarely on the boundary between the ancient and modern worlds. This was reflected in his own personality, which had both pseudoscientific and scientific facets. He cast astrological horoscopes, dabbled in alchemy, had a mother who practiced witchcraft, was fascinated by numerology, and attached mystical importance to geometrically perfect solids. Yet Kepler was one of the first to utilize an analytical problem solving approach.

Kepler's problem was: Can a model be devised that will successfully predict planetary positions? For data he used Tycho's observations of the planet Mars. Kepler had two models or theories he wished to test. Did the old Ptolemaic or the new Copernican system provide predictions consistent with Tycho's data? After much mathematical analysis of the competing theories, he realized that neither framework could accurately represent the Mars data. So both were discarded. New models were constructed mathematically, tested and--given this feedback --appropriately modified, rejected, or accepted as a solution. (Note use of underlining to highlight steps in scientific methodology.)

Finding a satisfactory representation for the Mars data caused Kepler great headaches. After years of work, he arrived at a complex scheme of epicycles that represented the Mars observations to within 1/7 degree accuracy. Yet, believing in the greater precision of Tycho's observations, he discarded this system and started afresh. He began trying oval curves. He soon found to his delight that the ellipse was the shape which would fit the data. After testing this elliptical model against Tycho's observations of other planets, he reached a conclusion: Planets move about the sun in elliptical orbits. The result, published in 1609, came to be known as Kepler's 1st Law of Planetary Motion.

IV. GALILEO AND NEWTON

Kepler was successful partly because he reduced a more complex problem to a simpler one. Instead of asking why planets move the way they do, he merely found a model that would allow predictions of future planetary positions (without regard to why). This reductionist approach, which Frenchman Rene DesCartes (1596-1650) later championed, of seeking understanding by continually breaking things into simpler parts, would characterize modern science.

While Kepler in Protestant Germany did not run afoul of the Church for his support and refinement of Copernicus' sun-centered system, his contemporary Galileo (1564-1642) in Catholic Italy did. Galileo's much publicized telescopic observations of Venus' phases and Jupiter's moons did much to establish the basic validity of the Copernican system. But his book <u>Dialogue</u> <u>Concerning</u> <u>the</u> <u>Two</u> <u>Chief</u> <u>Systems</u> <u>of</u> <u>the</u> <u>World,</u> <u>Ptolemaic</u> <u>and</u> <u>Copernican</u> got him into trouble. In 1633 he was arrested and put on trial for heresy by the Catholic Church. A casualty of the science vs. religion clash, Galileo was convicted and forced to recant his previous teachings. While he escaped the fate of Giordano Bruno, who was burned at the stake thirty years earlier by the Catholic Inquisition for similar divergent views, Galileo spent his last years under house arrest.

While Kepler suggested that some magnetic attraction existed between the sun and planet, and Galileo corrected Aristotelian ideas about terrestrial motion and falling objects, it was Issac Newton (1642-1727) in England who cast universal physical laws in modern form. He did this by using mathematics to model the world in terms of forces acting on matter.

According to legend, Newton was sitting in an orchard when an apple fell. He began wondering whether the same force that caused the apple to fall could also make the moon fall around the Earth. The problem of the moon's motion plagued him for 20 years. In fact, he had to invent a new branch of mathematics --calculus--to fully understand it. Nonetheless, by 1687 with the publication of his monumental <u>Mathematical</u> <u>Principles</u> <u>of</u> <u>Physics</u>, Newton showed that gravity not only pulled the moon and falling bodies toward the massive Earth, but also held Earth and planets in elliptical orbits around the much more massive sun.

Newton's book laid the foundation upon which modern science was built. In toppling Aristotle's conceptual scheme, Newton showed that the same physical laws applied to both terrestrial and celestial domains. Likewise there was no reason to assume that celestial bodies fundamentally differed in composition from those found on Earth.

V. DESCARTES AND THE MECHANISTIC WORLDVIEW

While Kepler, Galileo, and Newton were uncovering "the laws of nature", DesCartes was speculating that God ruled the universe through these laws. He suggested that once the Deity created the universe and decided on the natural laws, He had left it alone to function as a self-running machine.

By the 18th century a mechanistic worldview had emerged in nearly modern form.

* #5 MECHANISTIC WORLDVIEW *

The material world, with all of its different objects -- including living things and the human body --can be considered to be a huge machine. One can understand the functioning of this machine by studying its component structures and mechanisms --all of which are subject to the same natural laws.

DesCartes fostered this worldview in another way. His philosophy divided nature into two independent realms: matter and mind / spiritual. He did this to banish spirits and non-material entities from the material realm --his world of extension --which he saw as the proper domain for scientific investigation. Since DesCartes' time, this notion of dualism has become imbedded in Western thinking. DesCartes' system opposed the traditional Aristotelian / Church scheme in which nature was ordered in hierarchical fashion --a great chain stretching from God and angels in heaven, and progressively down through the ranks of men, animals, plants, and minerals on Earth.

In contrast to the observation and experiment-based empirical inquiry methods employed by Kepler, Galileo, and Newton, DesCartes embraced rationalism. This emphasizes deduction and logic. "I think, therefore I am", was the hallmark of this philosopher who believed he had deduced the existence of God. Along with the large scale organization and workings of the universe, DesCartes also pondered the very small. As to fundamental building blocks, he wrote,

> We also see the impossibility of atoms--pieces of matter that are by nature indivisible....Even if God made it not to be divisible by any creatures, he could not take away his own power of dividing it; for it is quite impossible for God to diminish his own power.

VI. 18TH CENTURY CHEMISTRY

Physics and astronomy had cast off Aristotelian misconceptions and were emerging as modern sciences as the 18th century began. Chemistry remained saddled with the ancient doctrine that substances were made of earth, water, air, and

fire. For example, Robert Boyle (1627-1691) , after noting
that tin heated in an open flask gained weight, explained
that it absorbed fire particles. As late as the 1760s, most
chemists identified something called phlogistan with the
element of fire. Phlogistan was supposedly present in com-
bustible materials and released upon burning. Experiments
like Boyle's were explained as due to phlogistan's "positive
lightness". One investigator wrote,

> Phlogistan is not attracted towards the center of the
> Earth but tends to rise: thence comes the increase in
> weight in the formation of metallic calces.

Supposedly phlogistan had a negative mass and getting rid of
it produced a weight increase!

With the 1789 publication in France of LaVoissier's
(1743-1794) Elements of Chemistry, the situation changed.
LaVoissier repeated many experiments under carefully controlled conditions. He demonstrated that burning a substance
involves its rapid combining with something in the air. Util-
izing experimental findings of Steele (1742-1786) in Sweden
and Priestly (1733-1804) in England, LaVoissier identified
oxygen as the component of air which supported combustion.
He realized that air is a mixture -- containing about 20 %
oxygen and 80 % of a more inert gas, nitrogen. Based on work
by Priestly and Cavendish (1731-1810), his book similarly
identified water, not as an element, but as a compound of
hydrogen and oxygen.

In place of the ancient's four elements, LaVoissier's
book correctly listed 23 elementary substances which could
not be broken down into simpler things by chemical means.
However, his list also incorrectly included a substance called "caloric". This he thought was the matter of heat.

LaVoissier is credited with formulating The Law of Conservation of Mass, which states that there is no change in
mass during the course of a chemical reaction. Another em-
pirically-derived law --The Law of Definite Proportions of
Compounds, was put forward in 1797 by Proust (1755-1826) in
France. Efforts to explain these laws led to the next important conceptual advance: the atomic theory. John Dalton
(1766-1844), a Scottish schoolteacher, modified older atomic
schemes to do this. He used his new theory to predict a third
law -- The Law of Multiple Proportions --which was soon verified.

In modernized form, Dalton's atomic theory states:

1) All matter is composed of extremely minute particles called atoms.
2) Atoms of a particular element have the same size, shape, and form, but differ from atoms of other elements.
3) A chemical reaction is the separation and / or union of atoms. Atoms unite to form molecules. When atoms of different elements combine into molecules, compounds result.
4) In a given pure compound, the relative numbers of atoms of the elements present will be definite and constant.

Dalton utilized colored balls representing different atoms to make molecular models. For example, two black balls (representing hydrogen atoms) and a white ball (an oxygen atom) could together represent a molecule of water -- symbolically written as H_2O. Fig. #5 shows a chemical reaction in which hydrogen is burned producing water. All of the atoms in the reactants (on the left hand side) are accounted for in the products formed (the right hand side). No atoms are created or destroyed in the reaction --another way of describing The Law of Conservation of Mass.

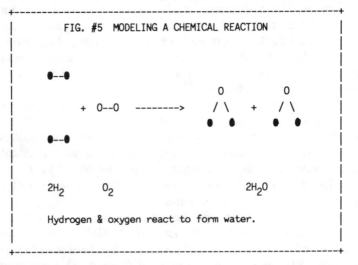

FIG. #5 MODELING A CHEMICAL REACTION

2H$_2$ O$_2$ 2H$_2$O

Hydrogen & oxygen react to form water.

Despite making advances, Dalton labored under a misconception. He thought that two identical atoms --two oxygen atoms for example --could not combine to form molecules. We know that oxygen in air is actually O_2. Dalton imagined atoms surrounded by an atmosphere of heat. This supposedly produced a repulsion which prevented identical atoms from combining, but did not interfere with unlike atoms forming compounds.

VII. HEAT AND ENERGY

LaVoissier and Dalton helped lay the cornerstones of modern chemistry. Due in part to the conceptual revolution they wrought, during the 19th century many more fundamental building blocks were identified. However, both men were confused about the true nature of heat.

Eventually, a few men realized that heat was not a substance but a form of energy. In 1837, German chemist Friedrich Mohr (1806-1879) would write,

> Besides the known fifty-four chemical elements, there exists in Nature only one agent more...it can under suitable conditions appear as motion, cohesion, electricity, light, heat, and magnetism...Heat is thus not a particular kind of matter, but an oscillatory motion of the smallest parts of bodies.

Five years later his countryman, Robert Mayer (1814-1878) wrote,

> Motion in many cases has no other effect than to produce heat and thus the origin of heat has no other cause than motion.

Today we understand that as a gas like air heats up, its many molecules (one cubic centimeter contains over ten billion billion molecules!) move faster and faster. The same is true for liquids and solids. Since the atoms and molecules which make up these two other states of matter are closer together and more rigidly bound (particularly in solids) than those in gases, the effect is not as pronounced. We also know that as gas molecules move faster, the number of collisions they experience, either with each other or with the walls of a container, increases. Thus gas pressure increases as the gas heats.

Energy is generally defined as the ability to do work--that is overcome an opposing force and move something. By the mid-19th century, many physicists understood that energy could be transformed from one form to another. Using the set-up shown in Fig. #6, Englishman James Joule's (1818-1879) measurements showed that the mechanical energy of a moving paddle-wheel was converted into heat energy. Joule also investigated the conversion of electrical energy into heat. One such 1843 experiment helped disprove the caloric theory of heat. Joule's work paved the way for The Law of Conservation of Energy: Energy can neither be created nor destroyed only transformed from one type to another.

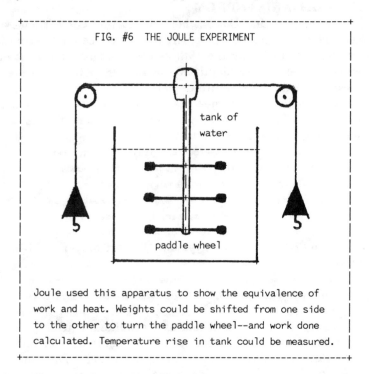

FIG. #6   THE JOULE EXPERIMENT

tank of water

paddle wheel

Joule used this apparatus to show the equivalence of work and heat. Weights could be shifted from one side to the other to turn the paddle wheel--and work done calculated. Temperature rise in tank could be measured.

Efforts to improve the efficiency of steam engines spurred the understanding of heat energy and heat transfer.   The quest for the ultimate machine --a perpetual motion machine-- proved futile, however. Out of such failure came the realization that one can't get something for nothing --to paraphrase the energy conservation law.

VIII. 19TH CENTURY BIOLOGY

Herman Helmholtz (1821-1894) argued that if living organisms obtained their energy, not just from foodstuffs but from a special vital life force, they would be perpetual motion machines. He knew this wasn't so. Helmholtz popularized the idea that the phenomena of life are explained solely by chemical and physical processes.   This view has become a cornerstone of modern biology.

Today, biologists maintain that, although living organisms are much more complex than non-living systems,   they can be understood without postulating some unique vital force. Both living organisms and the cells they are made of are considered to be transducers which convert chemical energy stored in food (which ultimately comes from solar energy) into electrical, mechanical, and other forms of energy capable of doing work.

The preparation from inorganic materials of compounds that previously had been obtained only from living things -- such as German chemist Friedrich Wohler's 1828 preparation of urea -- weakened the vitalists' position. By Helmholtz' time the central role in the structure of organic compounds played by the element carbon was appreciated. Similarly, scientists were realizing that all living things are composed of cells and cell products.

While living things are built of atoms and molecules -- just as non-living substances are --organic molecules are carbon-based and the cell is the simplest unit considered to be alive. In higher life forms, groups or layers of specialized cells performing a certain function make up tissue. Groups of different tissues--joined together structurally and functioning as a unit to perform some task --make up organs. Organs group together to form systems. Organisms can studied in terms of their separate systems -- for breathing, digesting food, reproducing, etc.

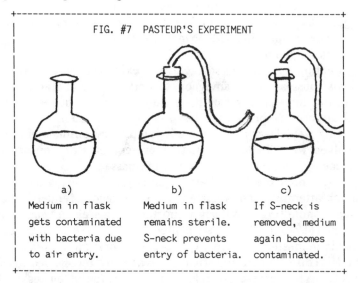

FIG. #7 PASTEUR'S EXPERIMENT

a)
Medium in flask gets contaminated with bacteria due to air entry.

b)
Medium in flask remains sterile. S-neck prevents entry of bacteria.

c)
If S-neck is removed, medium again becomes contaminated.

1859 was a pivotal year in the understanding of how liv-

ing things originate. In France, F.A. Pouchet supposedly offered experimental proof of the ancient idea that living
things could arise through spontaneous generation. His work
aroused French chemist Louis Pasteur (1822-1895), who repeated many of Pouchet's experiments with opposite results.
Pasteur devised a simple, elegant experiment (Fig. #7) to
convincingly disprove spontaneous generation --and force even
Pouchet to retire from the debate.

    1859 also marked the publication in England of Charles
Darwin's (1809-1882) classic On The Origin of Species. This
contains detailed evidence Darwin gathered from field studies
supporting his theory of natural selection. The essence of
Darwin's theory --as biologist Julian Huxley pointed out a
century later--can be deduced from three simple facts.

Fact #1: As Thomas Robert Malthus noted in his 1798 Essay on
Population, plant and animal populations tend to increase in
a geometric manner --1,2,4,8,16,32 rather than in an arith-
metic manner--1,2,3,4,5.

Fact #2: Populations of particular species are observed to
remain more or less constant over long periods of time.

On the basis of these two facts one can deduce the following:

Deduction #1: There must be a struggle for existence since
not all members of a species that are produced can survive to
become reproducing adults.

Combining this with another observation,

Fact #3: Every species of plants or animals tends to show a
variation among individual members,

one can conclude,

Deduction #2: In the struggle for existence, those individuals possessing advantageous adaptations or characteristics
win out in a "survival of the fittest". They thus leave behind more offspring than less favored individuals.

In this way, Darwin postulated, plants and animals gradually
evolved with better-adapted, more complex organisms slowly
replacing simpler organisms as time passed.

    At about the time Pasteur and Darwin were attracting so
much attention, an Austrian monk, Gregor Mendel (1822-1884)
was conducting similarly important research in anonymity.
From 1857-1868 he experimented with cross-breeding pea plants
in his monastery garden. Out of this work came Mendel's Laws
of Heredity. Their significance was fully recognized around
1900. They offered insight into a question often asked by
late 19th century biologists, "How are parental character-

istics transmitted to offspring?"

Today, we know that all living things come from living things. New individual organisms begin as single cells -- typically resulting from the union of an egg and a sperm from parents. The organism grows as old cells divide to form new ones. Rod-shaped bodies in a cell's nucleus called chromosomes contain the structures by which heredity is handed down from one generation to another: genes.

IX. SEARCH FOR FUNDAMENTAL BUILDING BLOCKS

By the 1860s, the search for the fundamental building blocks involved a Russian chemist, Dmitri Mendeleev (1834-1907). Mendeleev, after spending countless hours in libraries throughout Europe, assembled information about the then 63 known chemical elements. He proceeded to summarize the properties of each element on a small card and fit the cards into a meaningful classification scheme. When he arranged the elements in order of increasing atomic weight, he found a pattern: properties tended to repeat every eight elements.

On the basis of this periodic law, Mendeleev was able to recognize gaps in his array. In 1869 he boldly predicted that three new chemical elements would be found and described the properties they would possess. By 1888, all three of these missing puzzle pieces had been found and Mendeleev's prediction dramatically confirmed. Despite his successes, Mendeleev never understood why his periodic law worked.

Throughout the 19th century evidence had been accumulating that Dalton's conception of atoms as indivisible, impenetrable, structureless, incredibly tiny spheres needed modification. For example, many of the elements in Mendeleev's periodic chart had been discovered by using electricity to decompose various compounds. In the 1830s, English chemist Michael Faraday (1791-1867) studied relationships between the amount of electricity used and the amount of compound decomposed. On the basis of this work it was proposed that electric charges were associated with atoms. In 1881 Helmholtz wrote,

Now the most startling result of Faraday's laws is perhaps this: if we accept the hypothesis that elementary substances are composed of atoms, we cannot avoid concluding that electricity also, positive as well as negative, is divided into elementary portions which behave like atoms of electricity.

Somewhat later, the negatively charged "particles of electricity" were named electrons.

By 1900, many physicists conceived of atoms as having nearly uniform density throughout, with the electrons buried in a glob of positive charge much like raisins in a pudding. Then, in 1909, Ernest Rutherford (1871-1937) and Ernest Marsden (1889-1970) conducted a famous experiment (Fig. #8).

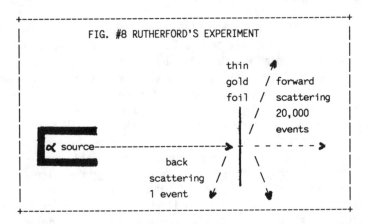

They bombarded an incredibly thin sheet of gold foil with alpha particles --which we now recognize as the positively charged nuclei of helium atoms. Most of the alpha particles passed through the foil. However, a few--around one in 20,000 --experienced large deflections, with some bouncing nearly straight back. The results were unexpected. Contrary to prevailing conceptions, they seemed to indicate that the atom was mostly empty space --except for a massive, tiny, central nucleus.

On the basis of this experiment and studies of emission spectra of light, Danish physicist Neils Bohr (1885-1962) proposed a new model of the atom. Bohr atoms are miniature solar systems -- with the heavy, positively-charged nucleus playing the role of the Sun. Like planets orbiting the Sun, electrons revolve about the nucleus in orbits of varying distances. The force --analogous to gravity-- that holds the atom together is the electromagnetic attraction between positive charges--called protons--and negative charges.

Using this model it is possible to explain many phenomena. Mendeleev's periodic law is understood on the basis of the number of electrons atoms have in their outermost or-

bital levels. Atoms possessing the same number of outermost --
or valence -- electrons, have similar properties. Likewise,
the emission of light and other electromagnetic radiation can
also be understood (Fig. #9). When an electron jumps from a
higher to lower energy level (or orbit) it releases the energy difference as a photon of electromagnetic energy. If the
energy jump is a small one, infra-red light is produced; a
bigger jump produces visible light; a still larger change
produces ultraviolet light.

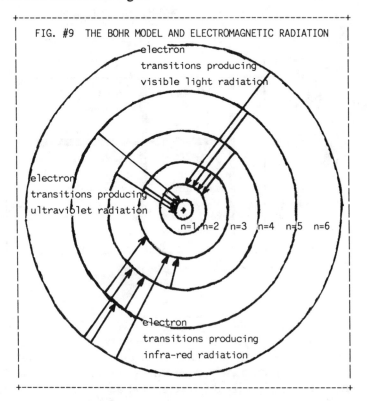

FIG. #9   THE BOHR MODEL AND ELECTROMAGNETIC RADIATION

electron transitions producing visible light radiation

electron transitions producing ultraviolet radiation

$n=1$ $n=2$ $n=3$ $n=4$ $n=5$ $n=6$

electron transitions producing infra-red radiation

   Despite its successes, the Bohr atom proved flawed.
Nonetheless, given its conceptual advantages, it is still
often used as a teaching aid. It seems that many people --
grasping its perceived link to classical physics--are reluctant to abandon it in favor of a more accurate--and much more
complex--representation of reality.

X. CLASSICAL VS. MODERN PHYSICS
   Classical physics -- Newtonian physics supplemented by

James Clerk Maxwell's (1831-1879) equations describing electromagnetic forces --proved inadequate for explaining phenomena that occur in the realms of the very small, very fast,
very energetic, and very massive. Between 1900 and 1930 two
revolutionary theories, meant for just these realms (Fig.#10)
were developed. The first -- formulated by Albert Einstein
(1879-1955) --was the theory of relativity; the second, quantum mechanics.

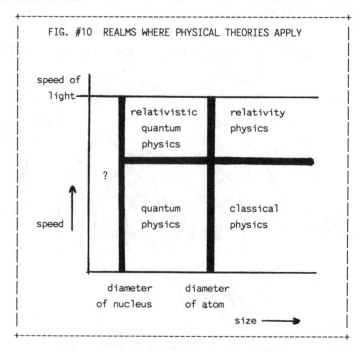

FIG. #10   REALMS WHERE PHYSICAL THEORIES APPLY

In classical physics, particular events or effects are
associated with a definite cause. For example, using Newton's
Laws one can completely determine the resulting path and velocity of an object if the forces that act on it are known.
Quantum mechanics replaced this causal determinism with statistical laws about events, laws cloaked in probabilities not
certainties.

Before leaving the "nice" world of classical physics for
the more mysterious world of modern physics, let us summarize
the worldview the former was built on.

* #6 THE CLASSICAL SCIENTIFIC WORLDVIEW *
***Reality is completely explained by the existence of mat-
ter alone (materialism). The world is made up of discrete,***

separate things. Events are caused by interactions--described by natural laws -- between the things, interactions which precede or occur simultaneously with the events (causality). Scientists study these events in a detached, objective manner --safe in assuming that they have no effect whatsoever on what they are observing (objectivism). To understand complex systems or phenomena spread out over space or time, one needs to simply reduce them to their component parts and order them. The ordering can be done according to spatial, temporal, or functional relationships (reductionism).

The quantum world is full of what seem to be paradoxes. Light can be considered to be <u>either</u> an energy wave or a stream of particles called photons --but, in explaining any one effect, not simultaneously both. Likewise energy can be created or destroyed by seemingly random events --but this violation of The Law of Conservation of Energy can only happen for time intervals which are impossible to observe. Similarly, it is impossible to perfectly specify <u>both</u> the position and velocity of a particle --as Werner Heisenberg (1901 -1976) first pointed out.

This fundamental uncertainty can be appreciated by considering how one might measure these quantities: any act to view or detect the particle disturbs it. In the macroscopic world of everyday experience the disturbance is so slight that it can be ignored, i.e. photons striking (in comparison) huge, massive objects do not effect the object's position or velocity. In the atomic or subatomic world however, the impact of photons can dramatically alter the very state one sought information about.

By the mid-1920s, conceptual schemes based on relativity and quantum mechanics --not classical physics-- aided physicists in their continuing quest for fundamental building blocks. By then the periodic chart had nearly assumed its modern form, so the search progressed beyond finding more chemical elements. Physicists began probing the nuclei of atoms. In 1932 the discovery of a neutral particle (possessing neither positive or negative charge) constituent of the nucleus--the neutron--was announced.

Typically, physicists hunt for new particles by shooting particle beams at nuclei in an effort to dislodge elementary particles otherwise bound by nuclear forces. These nuclear forces are much stronger than the electromagnetic forces which must be overcome before electrons can leave the atoms they are bound to. Thus nuclear reactions--like the splitting apart of uranium nuclei involved in nuclear power plants or bombs-- unleash far more energy than chemical reactions--like the burning of coal. They also require a great deal of energy to induce. As the decades passed, physicists found themselves building increasingly powerful particle accelerators to smash nuclei with.

XI. THE SEARCH FOR THE FUNDAMENTAL STUFF OF LIFE

While physicists were probing the atom, biologists, in their search for the fundamental "stuff of life", were looking inside the cell's nucleus at chromosomes. By the first decade of the 20th century, W.S. Sutton and T.H. Morgan had stated that the units of inheritance--associated with genes-- were arranged in linear fashion in the chromosomes. Chromosomes were known to consist of proteins and nucleic acid.

Proteins are large molecules composed of several hundred amino acids -- compounds containing an amino NH_2 group and a carboxyl COOH group. Since there are twenty plus amino acids, various combinations and permutations of these permit abundant diversity. By contrast, nucleic acids--which are present in all living things --seemed rather monotonous. These large molecules were known to consist of but four nucleotides-- compounds composed of a phosphate (PO_4) group, a five-carbon based sugar, and purines and pyrimidines (which are built of rings of carbon and nitrogen atoms). These four nucleotides can be identified by their initials A,T,C,G reflecting their adenine, thymine, cytosine, and guanine constituents --all found in DNA. (In RNA, uracil replaces thymine.)

In their quest for the language of heredity -- that is, how genetic instructions are passed from one generation to the next --early researchers dismissed the role of nucleic acids. They felt these compounds lacked the potential for producing the abundant variation genetic material fostered. Instead they believed genes to be messages coded in protein.

By 1944, experiments conducted at the Rockefeller Institute for Medical Research involving viruses parasitic to bacteria altered this view. Avery, MacLeod, and McCarty found these viruses possessed genes in which cores of deoxyribonucleic acid (DNA) were covered by protein coats. By using radioactive isotopes to label the sulfur found in the protein and the phosphorus found in the DNA, and tracing them through the life cycle of the multiplying viruses infecting the bacteria, it was found that bacterial cells were imparted with phosphorus but not sulfur. This established that DNA carried the genetic instructions. <u>How</u> it did this remained a mystery.

Shortly thereafter, using X-ray diffraction techniques, Rosalind Franklin and Maurice Wilkins in London showed that the DNA molecule was most likely a large coil known as a helix. Building on this work, and the studies of chemical bonding by Linus Pauling and others, in 1953 James Watson and Francis Crick proposed a model for DNA. The model explained DNA's ability to replicate itself and eventually led to an understanding of how genetic instructions are transmitted.

Watson and Crick pictured the DNA molecule as two poly-nucleotide chains wrapped around each other and making up a double helix sort of spiral staircase or ladder. Each rung of this ladder (Fig. #11) consists of a pair of nucleotides. Only four kinds of pairs are possible: AT, TA, CG, and GC, the initials specifying nucleotides on left and right sides respectively. When these chains (and thus pairs of nucleo-tides) separate, each one can then form a new chain comple-mentary to it. Created are two new double chains in which the nucleotide pair sequences are identical. With each cell divi-sion, DNA chains replicate and daughter cells receive a copy of the genetic code.

```
+-------------------------------------------------------------+
|                                                             |
|     FIG. #11 A SECTION OF A DNA DOUBLE HELIX MOLECULE        |
|                                                             |
|                                                             |
|        "antisense"                    "sense"               |
|        DNA strand         C--G        DNA strand            |
|                           T---A                             |
|                           A---T                             |
|                           G--C                              |
|                           C--G                              |
|                           A---T                             |
|                           T---A                             |
|                           G--C                              |
|                           G--C                              |
|                           A---T                             |
|                           T---A                             |
|                           C--G                              |
|                                                             |
|                                                             |
+-------------------------------------------------------------+
```

Genes determine the character of an organism by over-seeing the putting together of key proteins called enzymes--catalysts which speed up and regulate biochemical processes. A gene is a recipe for a particular protein synthesis -- the recipe coded in the nucleotide pair sequence of DNA. The DNA acts as a pattern or template and transcribes its four letter code to a smaller nucleic acid, RNA. This RNA functions as a messenger, passing out of the nucleus and acting as a blue-print to synthesize proteins.

As the 1960s began, biologists recognized the most im-portant function of cells: building proteins using instruc-tions coded in DNA molecules. By that decade's end, molecular geneticists had learned to artificially manipulate and change DNA by experimental means. The first fully functional manmade gene -- a bacterial gene of 126 nucleotide units--was chemi-cally synthesized in 1976 by a team at the Massachusetts In-stitute of Technology. By the 1980s work had begun on mapping the 100,000 or so genes found on the 23 pairs of human chrom-osomes. At the decade's end, preliminary maps had been com-pleted for most of these chromosomes. In the works was a plan that would transform human genetic makeup from unknown to well-charted territory: an effort to map the complete nucleo-tide pair sequence (believed to number in the millions) of human DNA.

XII. PHYSICISTS' STANDARD MODEL

While molecular biologists probed DNA in their search for the fundamental makeup of life, physicists were smashing the nuclei of atoms and looking for the fundamental building blocks of everything. By the 1970s, they had detected dozens of seemingly elementary particles. Throughout that decade, physicists were confused by all the denizens in the "ele-mentary particle zoo". By the 1980s however, many seemed sat-isfied with one coherent picture--called the Standard Model--which emerged out of all the experimental and theoretical research.

Physicists know of four fundamental forces in nature: gravity, electromagnetism, plus strong and weak nuclear forces. They believe that whenever one of these forces acts, the interaction is mediated by the exchange of a particular particle. The type of particle exchanged depends on the force involved. Gravity is thought to be mediated by gravitons, electromagnetic forces by photons, and so on. Efforts to understand these separate forces as but different manifestations of the same universal interaction continue. The goal is a so-called Grand Unified Field Theory.

The Standard Model attempts to unify three of the four forces -- gravity being the interaction excluded. This model explains these forces in terms of particles called gluons. Gluons, as their name implies, help the postulated fundamental building blocks of matter--called quarks and leptons-- to stick together. Physicists believe there are six types of quarks. Protons are thought to be made of two "up" quarks, and one "down" quark, neutrons of one "up" quark and two "down" quarks. Similarly, six types of leptons are postulated -- the electron being one of them.

In refining The Standard Model and seeking a Grand Unified Field Theory, some physicists feel they need accelerators with even more energy. Other physicists are now looking elsewhere, however, for energetic events. Instead of attempting to produce such events in the laboratory, they are looking to nature as a laboratory. They are studying an event 15 billion years ago when the observable universe was born. By looking deep into space--and thus far back into time--they can test their models by investigating the ultimate energy event: The Big Bang.

Questions & Projects

1. Define animism. Construct a worldview theme based on it. Investigate: are there cultures which embrace animism?

2. When Kepler's mathematics revealed the true nature of Mars' orbit, he wrote, "I felt as if I had been awakened from a sleep." Describe some unexpected insight you've had in terms of the changes it affected in your worldview.

3. Many Catholic priests refused to look through Galileo's telescope. Some of those who did -- instead of accepting logical conclusions --claimed the telescopes were bewitched. Provide modern day examples where people only see what they want to and see nothing that challenges pre-conceived notions.

4. Late in his life, Issac Newton wrote, "If I have seen farther than others, it was by standing on the shoulders of giants." Relate this to a) scientific advances since Newton's time, b) wisdom is associated more with older people than young people.

5. Put together a description of the human body as a machine

consistent with worldview theme #5. Extend your description by factoring in human participation in the " mind / spiritual" realm.

6. Specify which of the four aspects of worldview theme #6 would be inconsistent with a) ghosts, b) seeing the animal fall dead, then hearing the gunshot, c) if no one is there to see it, it doesn't really happen, d) intuitive problem-solving leaps.

7. Discuss "the criterion of repeatibility is the cornerstone of science". Use it to define a miracle in a way that puts it outside the realm of scientific investigation.

8. Contrast deduction (note example involving evolution) with induction (see dictionary). Which did Darwin actually use?

9. In 1960, only 13 % of staphylococci infections were resistant to penicillin. A dramatic increase in antibiotic use (particularly in animal feed destined for human consumption) followed. By 1988, 91 % of such infections were resistant. Explain in terms of natural selection.

10. Some scientific insights have resulted from unusual creative insights rather than analytical / experimental approaches. Two examples include Kekule's work on the benzene ring structure, and Glaser's development of the bubble chamber. Report on the circumstances of these and find other examples.

11. Report on recent work involving a) physicists' quest for a Grand Unified Field Theory, b) biologists' human genome mapping project.

Notes

1. Press, F. and Siever, R. Earth , W. H. Freeman, San Francisco, 1982 p. 16.

GENESIS

I. "LET THERE BE DOUBT"

In the beginning, there was no solid ground. There was nothing we can comprehend, no voices, no clouds, no stars, only the unknowable. We can postulate God. Poets can write of the great calm on the all pervading ocean or the perfection of the interwoven fabric. Physicists can distinguish between the underlying, timeless, unchanging implicate order and the dynamic explicate world we live in. But all descriptions of the beginning are built on a footing of uncertainty.

If God spoke, perhaps those first words were, "Let there be doubt !" Suddenly the pristine serenity poets would later describe gave way to chaotic, hurried vibration. Random creation and annihilation entered the world of the infinitesimal to the later dismay of physicists. Perhaps this doubt, this fundamental uncertainty, began a vibrant cosmic dance in which each moment is created, cherished, destroyed, and then created anew, a process which continually restructures as bits of the implicate condense into explicate configurations, evaporate into the underlying implicate fluid, and condense again. Time as we know it began.

Maybe then God said, "Let there be light!" With that, a wave disturbed the poetic ocean, a thread pulled out of the divine tapestry, a quantum instability ignited the physicist's primeval fireball with a "big bang".

II. MYSTICS AND THE IMPLICATE ORDER

It seems the implicate order, that separate reality whose description defies words, symbols, and reason itself, makes people uncomfortable --and why not ? The unknown is frightening but also alluring. Some identify this cosmic ocean with the kingdom of heaven and long to dwell there, if not in life, then in death. History records both lamentations over "paradise lost" and successful attempts to topple frameworks for making sense out of the world. In recent years, the desire to sail the implicate ocean has led many to seek altered states of consciousness and a few renegade physicists to rebellion. These rebels seek to remove conceptual barriers "the uncertainty principle" has erected to accessing the virtual world, and find an explanation for seemingly random transformations.

I was introduced to the implicate world early one morning during a visit to The Reality Marketplace. Here people buy and sell answers to the big questions: "Why am I here?", "How does nature work ?", "How should I live ?", "How can I know God ?". I was curious so I went into "The Implicate Reality Shop", despite the sign outside which said "Welcome Mystics". After the salesman's pitch, I listened to shoppers' conversation.

A woman was talking, "I find the implicate world totally unfathomable, but sometimes even the explicate world which unfolds before my eyes mystifies me. Some say the explicate demands an audience, at least one observer to give it more than a virtual, imagined reality in the implicate. Suppose the wind blows a tree over. If no one watches it or hears it fall, or sees it laying on the ground, did the event happen?" Before anyone can answer her the salesman cuts in. "Even if someone was there to record the event, what interpretation should be given? As the tree fell one could say, 'The tree is moving, not the wind' or 'The wind is moving, not the tree'. I would say, 'The tree is not moving, the wind is not moving, your mind is moving'."

I talked with the salesman and other "mystics" and decided that their worldviews had been shaped by observations made from an "inner space observatory". I heard stories about momentarily losing one's "I-ness" in experiencing the wholeness of the cosmic ocean, locating one's consciousness outside one's body, and about freezing time. All told of the powerful emotions that surrounded these highest states of consciousness. I was interested, but also appreciated the experiential nature of this mystical evidence for the existence of the implicate order. I could not test any of these claims, I could only compare them with my own personal experience.

My thoughts returned to the orderly view of nature behind classical science. I recalled Thomas Huxley's depiction of it,[1]

> The chess-board is the world, the pieces are the
> phenomena of the universe, the rules of the game are
> what we call laws of Nature.

A conversation with an artist strikingly contrasted scientists' quest to uncover natural laws, with the mystical world and what artists do. Many artists and poets, I was told, assume that nature is inherently mysterious, ever changing, in constant turmoil. Given this worldview, their artistic creations attempt to impose a permanent, artificial, orderly structure on this transient chaos.

Before leaving the shop, I talked with a Chinese Buddhist and two people involved in the so-called New Age movement. After leaving, I pieced together what seemed to be the consensus worldview of those inside.

 * #7 MYSTICAL / EASTERN / NEW AGE WORLDVIEW *
One is all and all is one. Although things and events appear to be separate and discrete in space and time, in fact they are all interconnected. Time is an illusion. There is only one universal life force, consciousness, pure undifferentiated energy. Our ordinary conscious minds perceive the ever-changing explicate manifestations of this underlying implicate whole--as the dynamic yang / yin interplay of polar opposites (light / dark, male / female, aggressive / passive, good / evil.) By balancing polarities, one can grow spiritually and ultimately swim in the cosmic ocean.

Down the street I went into two shops: one which advertised "Great Moments in Science and Technology !" on its windows, and another which displayed a sign above the door, "The Big Bang Shop". Here nearly everyone was skeptical of mystical evidence. From the mystics I had just heard one must look inward, not outward, to find God and heaven. The salesman had quoted a scholar of India's philosophies,[2]

> For where dwell the gods to whom we can uplift our
> hands, send forth our prayers, and make oblation?
> Beyond the Milky Way are only island universes, galaxy
> beyond galaxy in the infinitudes of space--no realm of
> angels, no heavenly mansions, no choirs of the blessed
> surrounding a divine throne of the Father...

This talk of island universes, galaxies, and God intrigued me so I lingered in "The Big Bang Shop".

III. "LET THERE BE LIGHT!" / EVOLUTION BEGINS

The universe began with all the radiation, all the matter, everything compacted together inside an incredibly dense primeval fireball. In that first crowded instant, frequent and violent collisions kept elementary particles from sticking together. But expansion brought cooling. After a millionth of a second the temperature dropped to 10,000 billion degrees. Protons and neutrons formed from quarks. After one minute of fireball expansion, the temperature dropped to 1.3

billion degrees, the density plummeted, and the collisions slackened. Whereas combinations of one proton and one neutron had previously been knocked apart by collisions, they could now hold together. The formation of chemical elements-- nucleosynthesis--had begun.

The nucleosynthesis era lasted five minutes. It halted as neutrons were used up and continuing expansion and cooling finally made collisions so infrequent that protons and neutrons were no longer colliding and sticking together. When it ended, the universe was about 76 % hydrogen nuclei --one proton, and 24 % helium nuclei--two protons and two neutrons. The universe continued to expand and cool with nothing really interesting happening for thousands of years.

Throughout this time the radiation component --the photons-- kept colliding with the universe's matter, and these collisions prevented electrons from combining with nuclei to form atoms. At last, after 500,000 years of expansion and cooling, the photons were no longer energetic enough to dislodge electrons from nuclei. Matter and radiation decoupled and the universe's first stable atoms were born. With the radiation flood subsided, matter emerged as the dominant constituent.

This matter was hardly uniformly distributed. In the first instant after The Big Bang, local small-scale differences were enlarged to an astronomical scale by an inflationary process which produced clumps of matter. Over billions of years, turbulence broke these into smaller clumps. After fragmenting into a first generation of billions of protostars, these smaller clumps became individual galaxies. The protostar concentrations of gas and dust fell together under gravity. Eventually their central density and temperature became so great that once again nuclei began colliding and sticking together. With the dawn of stellar nucleosynthesis, protostars became stars.

For eons, stars live as stable configurations, with the inward pull of gravity balanced by the outward push of radiation from stellar nuclear energy production. But finally the nuclear fuel runs low. Massive stars succumb to the squashing force of gravity. Many of these stellar deaths are catastrophic explosions in which the heavy elements formed inside the star are strewn out into space. But even as old stars are dying, a new generation of stars is being born from an enriched interstellar gas and dust medium.

IV. ASTROPHYSICISTS AND THE EXPANDING UNIVERSE

At first I was skeptical that scientists could so as-
suredly give a minute by minute account of what happened some
15 billion years ago, but then I was taken on a video tour by
the salesman inside "The Big Bang Shop". In this way I visited both a great "outer space observatory" and a great astro-
physical cosmology library. Seeing man's collective wisdom on
how the universe began was both humbling and awe-inspiring.
Here were millions of pages, written in a complex, precise
mathematical language, structured so that each new page depended on the previous ones. Since the goal was finding a model, a theoretical framework, an interpretation that best fit
the reality uncovered by observation, the "fit" was being
continually improved.

After seeing the edifice on which this understanding was
built, I began to take seriously the evidence for The Big
Bang that the astronomer/salesman presented. "...In the 1920s
and 30s, astronomers discovered that all galaxies seem to be
moving away from us and away from each other. They deduced
this by using giant telescopes, capable of detecting the
light of a candle thousands of miles away, and spectrographs,
capable of breaking light into component colors and photo-
graphing the resulting rainbow-like spectrum. From such a
photograph --a spectrogram-- one can learn about the physical
conditions and chemical composition which characterize the
light source, in this case a galaxy. Relative motion between
it and the observer can be determined by looking at so-called
doppler shifts in the spectrograms. Just as the siren of an
approaching fire engine has a much higher pitch than that of
a receding one, the light from a galaxy approaching us is
shifted to the blue part of the spectrum, and that of a receding galaxy exhibits a red shift. After thousands of red-
shifted galaxies were found and no blue-shifted ones, the
expanding universe idea was born".

"If the universe is expanding," he continued, "it seems
reasonable to assume that long ago its matter was much closer
together than it is now. Extrapolating even further, one arrives at a time when everything was close together in an extraordinary compact volume. Not surprisingly, a primeval big
bang explosion which started the expansion was theorized, but
no direct evidence for it was found until 1965. Then scientists discovered the background radiation remnant from the
primeval fireball --something theorists predicted should be

observable.

This background radiation has now been subjected to numerous studies. The results indicate that its spectrum, doppler shift, and uniform distribution over the entire sky, all are in accordance with big bang cosmological theory. Likewise, everywhere astronomers point their telescopes and use spectrographs to analyze large-scale chemical composition, there is at least 24 % helium. The five minute long initial era of element-building as described by big bang theory seems consistent with observational evidence." I left that shop appreciating the world in a new way (Fig.#12).

```
+------------------------------------------------------------+
|                                                            |
|        FIG. #12  EVOLUTION -- SINCE THE BIG BANG           |
|                                                            |
|   Billions of Years Ago    Event of Evolutionary Interest  |
|        *                                                   |
|      15          The Big Bang                              |
|      13 ?        Massive stars form in protogalaxies       |
|      10 - 13 ?   Galaxies form                             |
|      4.6         Solar System,  Earth form                 |
|      4.0         Earth differentiates; oceans form         |
|      3.5         Anaerobic photosynthesis                  |
|      2.5         Aerobic photosynthesis                    |
|      1.0         Atmospheric O2 1/10 modern level          |
|       .57        Cambrian Era brings rapid evolution       |
|                  of life as O2 nears modern levels         |
|                  ozone shielding cuts UV radiation         |
|                                                            |
|   * = date of Big Bang uncertain (10-20 billion yrs. ago)  |
+------------------------------------------------------------+
```

Across the street I noticed a store with a big sign, "Biblical Creation Science for Sale". Although I suspected this was old stuff I had once been asked to buy on faith alone, merely dressed up in new clothes, I went in anyway. I might have warmed up more to the salesman's claim that the universe is only a few thousand years old if he had shown me the kind of evidence I had seen in "The Big Bang Shop". I left after only a few minutes. As I neared the door, I was urged to visit certain other shops --apparently all under the same management --including, "The 'Put Your Faith in God, He is Great' Shop", "The Eternal Salvation Shop", and "The House of Original Sin". Instead, I went into a store whose flashing neon sign read "Out of the Organic Soup".

V. THE ORIGIN OF LIFE[3]

Inside this shop, a rude heckler repeatedly interrupted the saleslady's presentation. She had begun by recalling the birth of the sun and how the planets formed from material in the outer regions of the protosun that got left behind.

"The third planet out from the Sun possessed enough gravity to accrete cold, rocky planetesimals in fiery collisions, but not enough to hold the abundant, light gases. So under the onslaught of intense solar radiation Earth lost its primordial hydrogen / helium outer layers. All that survived was a rocky interior. While impacts heated the surface, radioactive decay of uranium, thorium, and heavy potassium atoms heated the interior. After a few hundred million years, temperatures reached the melting point of iron. Molten iron --and other abundant heavy elements like nickel-- sank to the Earth's center, while lighter elements-- oxygen, silicon, calcium, aluminum, etc. and their compounds --floated to the surface forming continents. With this differentiation, came outgassing which produced the oceans and an early atmosphere.

"This primitive atmosphere contained water vapor, carbon dioxide and nitrogen gases. Lightning and unshielded ultraviolet solar radiation broke apart the atmospheric gases and sometimes the fragments recombined into more complex molecules. Rain deposited these into the oceans where they dissolved and created an increasingly complex organic soup. It was a slow process.

"Eventually the oceans filled with amino acids, fatty acids, sugars and other simple organic compounds. In shallow pools along the shores, sand and clay particles provided surfaces for these carbon-based molecules to stick to and evaporation increased their concentrations. Other salts and minerals --leached from the crust and spewed out in volcanos- -joined the mix. Quite by trial and error, after natural recombination experiments spanning millions of years, nitrogen bases, simple sugars, and phosphates formed nucleotides. At some point, a chain of nucleotides arose which was capable of making crude copies of itself.

"This remarkable molecule can simply be called 'The Replicator'. This early ancestor of DNA -- the double-helix nucleic acid master molecule of all life -- functioned as a template in reproducing itself. It produced large numbers of duplicate molecules and ushered in a new era of stability."

"Were these original Replicator molecules the planet's first life ?" She had asked a rhetorical question but the heckler jumped on it. "How could they be? ", he interjected, "They weren't endowed with the life force!" The saleslady was taken aback. I got the feeling she departed from her script, nonetheless she kept her cool.

"In deciding whether something is living or non-living, what it can do--not its makeup or structural properties--must be examined. With 'The Replicator', at least one of the necessary functions of living organisms --<u>self perpetuation</u> was in place. Life must also function to overcome those forces, in particular molecular collisions, which otherwise disorder systems. Energy is required if a complex molecular structure is to avoid decaying into a chaotic collection of individual atoms. So living organisms need a <u>metabolism</u>, a way to make the necessary energy transfers with their environment to maintain steady state control and avoid disintegration. To do this successfully over time requires the ability to <u>adapt</u> to changing environmental conditions.

"The environmental demands on these precursors of life were not severe. Without predators the Earth was a garden of Eden. However, there was competition for increasingly scarce building blocks. This competition could have quickly died out with the production of a stable configuration. Because of imperfection it did not. Undoubtedly the primitive molecules' replication was inefficient compared to the near perfect present-day DNA copying process. Most of the resulting mutations were harmful or gave no advantage. They were selectively weeded out. A few however, were beneficial and their cultivation provided a needed evolutionary driving force..."

She was interrupted again. "What other driving force besides God is needed ? When you should be talking about God breathing life into previously inanimate matter, you're bogged down with mutations !" She could not brush him off this time, but counterattacked skillfully.

"By definition God is unknowable, so one can, with impunity, attribute nearly any unexplained phenomenon to Him...or Her," she added, smiling. "I know of no evidence supporting the notion that God breathes life into matter."

She turned to the heckler. "This notion of yours is an

extreme formulation of the old vitalist doctrine. I can summarize that as follows.

* #8 THE VITALIST DOCTRINE *

*Life processes are not explicable by the laws of physics
and chemistry alone. Complex organisms exhibit unique responses to their environment, responses that can be understood only by postulating some degree of self-determination
for the organism or its possession of some vital spirit.
The Chinese identify this life force with the Ch'i; in India
it is linked to prana or kundalini.*

"Molecular biologists have reasons to suspect that inefficient copying processes, by increasing structural diversity
and thereby increasing otherwise extraordinarily low probabilities, could have been precursors of life. If there are
billions of different molecules --instead of just hundreds--
the odds that one will arise with special functions, i.e.
self-perpetuation, metabolism, and adaptation capabilities,
improve. Like it or not, mutations and erratic copying have
had important ramifications.

"Consider another example[4] from the days when books were
copied by hand, with new copies made from old copies and so
on," she continued. "At first, faithful scribes probably made
just a few errors in copying books of thousands, perhaps hundreds of thousands of words. But these 'first generation'
errors were passed on and joined by new errors down through
the generations. Compounding the problem, important books--
like the Bible--were translated into several languages. Often
a word in the 'source language' had no exact replacement in
the 'destination language'. Look at one Biblical example and
its consequences. The Hebrew word for 'young woman' got
translated into the Greek word for 'virgin' and a prophecy
was born: 'Behold a virgin shall conceive and bear a son!'"

The heckler would not let her continue. "This is blas-
phemy !" he shouted. "The Bible was written by the hand of
God!" The saleslady, in a matter of fact tone, said, "I see",
then added, "This time you're invoking the hand of God. Before it was the breath of God !" He got up muttering and
headed for the door. She went on with her presentation.

VI. BIOLOGICAL EVOLUTION

"Errors from erratic molecular replication were essential for the progressive evolution of life. As time passed, reproduction became more efficient, structures became more specialized, and eventually molecules with specific functions joined together to form the first cell. Sometime before that transition from chemical to biological evolutionary pro- cesses, the march of life, imperceptibly, had begun.

"As the earliest cells reproduced and flourished a pro- blem arose: the ever-increasing multitude of cells was feed- ing on the free organic molecules in the oceans and depleting them faster than they could form. Predators were loose in paradise and the food supply was dwindling. Something had to be done! While one initial response was to feed on each other, the primitive cells needed to develop something more permanent. The evolutionary response to this first major bio- sphere crisis of three and one-half billion years ago set the stage for much to come.

"Single cell plants, able to produce their own food, evolved. Using sunlight, carbon dioxide and water, they made carbohydrate food and oxygen. As the area covered by these photosynthetic plants grew, so did the amount of atmospheric oxygen. While this was happening, evolutionary developments like multicellular organization and cell structure speciali- zation were occurring. Chemical receptors for tasting, smelling and --after enough free oxygen was available-- for a new, efficient form of respiration evolved. Organ systems for breathing, and later for seeing and hearing, followed. Animals joined plants. Life moved out of the ocean onto the land. Flowering plants and insects made faster animal meta- bolisms possible. Vertebrates joined invertebrates.   First fishes and amphibians, then reptiles, and finally mammals-- with the most rapid metabolism of all -- dominated the animal kingdom.

"In piecing together evolutionary history, (Fig.#13), scientists once thought that the metabolically quicker mam- mals may have hastened the demise of the huge, lumbering dinosaurs. Some speculated that the quick, rat-sized mammals of 65 million years ago ate dinosaur eggs faster than they could hatch. Recently, thinking has changed. Now evidence supports another scenario: the so-called Cretaceous Era ended when Earth encountered some space debris --left over from the solar system's birth--resulting in a catastrophic impact. For dinosaurs this asteroid or comet was a 'Lucifer's Hammer' of death, but for surviving mammals it proved a godsend... And one day, but a few million years ago some tree-dwelling mammals left the branches for the ground.

```
+------------------------------------------------------------+
|          FIG. #13  EVOLUTION SINCE THE PRE-CAMBRIAN        |
|                                                            |
|   Period      Millions Years Ago    Highlights            |
|                                                            |
|   Quaternary     0 - 2       humans, glaciation,          |
|                              great mammals extinction     |
|   Tertiary       2 - 65      age of mammals, spread of    |
|                              grasses, flowering plants    |
|   Creataceous   65 - 136     dinosaurs peak, die out      |
|                              first oak, maple forests     |
|   Jurassic     136 - 190     early birds and mammals      |
|                                                            |
|   Triassic     190 - 225     first dinosaurs              |
|                                                            |
|   Permian      225 - 280     modern insects arise,        |
|                              supercontinent breaks up     |
|   Carboniferous 280 - 345    first reptiles, forests      |
|                              of gymnosperms, seed fern    |
|   Devonian     345 - 395     first amphibians             |
|                                                            |
|   Silurian     395 - 430     land plants                  |
|                                                            |
|   Ordovician   430 - 500     primitive fish               |
|                                                            |
|   Cambrian     500 - 570     trilobites, brachipods       |
|                              dominant                     |
|   pre-Cambrian 570 - 4650    multicellular and shelled    |
|                              organisms evolve at end      |
|                                                            |
+------------------------------------------------------------+
```

"Human beings are members of the primate family, which includes lemurs, tarsiers, monkeys, and apes. Modern primates evolved from a common ancestral order dating back 75 million years (Fig. #14). Nearly four million years ago, apelike creatures were walking upright and using crude tools. Anthropologists have found not only the skulls and skeletal remains of these early people, but also their footprints. It took roughly 30 million years for the hominid brain to double

in size, from 350 to 700 cm^3, and but one million years for
it to double again. By then--a scant 30,000 years ago--human
brains attained their current average size of 1400 cm^3 and
began to develop a curious asymmetry. Apparently in response
to the pressure of language acquisition, the right and left
hemispheres became specialized for particular functions..."

```
+-----------------------------------------------------------------+
|                                                                 |
|             FIG. #14  HUMAN EVOLUTIONARY HISTORY                |
|                                                                 |
|      Millions of Years Ago      Highlights / Brain Size cm³     |
|                                                                 |
|         0                 modern-day Homo Sapiens / 1400        |
|         0.4               early Homo Sapiens appears            |
|         1.6               Homo Erectus appears / 750-1200       |
|         2.3               Homo Habillis appears / 650           |
|         3.9               Australopithecus Afarensis / 450      |
|         7                 terrestrial ape-like ancestor         |
|         30                early Hominids (arboreal ape-         |
|                           like ancestors)   / 350              |
|         75                early Primates                        |
+-----------------------------------------------------------------+
```

VII. FUNDAMENTALISTS AND HUMANISTS

I left the "Out of the Organic Soup" shop just as the
point was made that our brains make us really different from
other animals. As I walked, I thought back over the morning.
While the saleslady had identified the heckler's viewpoint
with vitalism, I was fairly sure he was a fundamentalist:

*** #9 THE CHRISTIAN FUNDAMENTALIST WORLDVIEW ***

*Fundamentalists believe that 1) there is a God who can
and has personally intervened in the lives of men and women,
and 2) the Bible is literally true and we should believe
everything it says.*

I recalled fundamentalists I had known. Why was my
worldview so different from theirs? I was so eager to
learn, so enamored with the quest for truth, so anxious to
make connections and behold the beauty of new knowledge.
And they seemed so certain they had found everything of
importance in one book.

I rounded the corner and came upon "The Two Cultures
Shop" -- its name derived from the title of a 1959 book by
C.P. Snow. Inside, humanists and scientists sought to recon-

cile their divergent worldviews and learn from each other.
I soon realized that both humanists and scientists possessed
what fundamentalists seemed to lack --something that Prome-
theus supposedly gave mankind --a spirit kindled by the flame
of knowledge.

Before long, I learned enough about the humanist
worldview to attempt summarizing it.

* #10 HUMANISM *

*While asserting the dignity and worth of man and tol-
erantly embracing human imperfections, Humanists struggle
with ignorance and chaos by pursuing learning concerned with
the human condition. They champion both the capacity for
self-realization through reason, and responsible living
through brotherhood and belonging. Many humanists reject
supernaturalism and embrace secular values, but others hold
that a luminous consciousness (God?) energizes all things and
all lives.*

I also learned that sometimes interactions between scientists
and humanists get quite heated.

A biologist had just finished using arguments similar to
Helmholtz' in debunking vitalism (see CONCEPTS). He was arguing that, "Living organisms exist for the benefit of DNA rather than the other way around" --and a Jesuit priest[5] interrupted him. "When I think about the people who have loved me,
cared for me, sacrificed their own interests for mine--", he
began, "Yet according to your mechanistic reductionistic scientism their actions exist for the sake of a set of complex
molecules. I find it difficult to imagine a more absurd and
pernicious statement."

VIII. FATALISTS, FREE WILL, AND SCIENTISM

I was hungry so I left this debate. I found a bench in a
large courtyard and sat down to eat my lunch. I noticed several shops in the distance and tried to decide where to head
next. A sign pointing to my left said "Human Consciousness
Mall --This Way", while another pointing to my right said
"Quantum Reality Mall--This Way". In front of me was an interesting assortment of shops. At one end of the block was "The
Fatalist's Hangout", while down at the other end was "Free
Will: The Hang Loose Shop". I was about to walk over, when an
affable man who looked like a college professor sat down next
to me and said hello. We exchanged small talk, then he asked
what I sought in The Reality Marketplace ? I told him I was

hunting for Truth with a capital "T" and searching for a meaningful, proper way to live. Just now, I told him, I was puzzling over how to fit God into a scientific worldview. He told me he had just returned from "The Quantum Reality Mall" and suggested I go there and learn about "observer created realities". Later, I decided to heed his advice. First, I ventured across the street.

For the next hour I immersed myself in the centuries old question, "Is there free will or are human actions completely pre-ordained and already determined ?" I reformulated the problem in the context of a timely example. " That second apple I had eaten in finishing lunch, did I eat it because my metabolism demanded it, because I had gotten a pleasant sensation in eating the first one, unconsciously as a psychological defense mechanism in response to feeling uncomfortable with a stranger, because God willed me to, or out of plain capriciousness and free will on my part?"

The fatalists' --who generally prefer to be called determinists-- position can be summarized as follows.

* #11 THE FATALIST WORLDVIEW *

Events are fixed in advance for all time in such a manner that humans are powerless to change them. As such, human behavior is governed by factors beyond human control: natural laws, genetic endowment, the (predictable) response to environmental stimuli, etc. Many include something like "God's plan" in this list.

In contrast, non-determinists claim that arguments for their position began when Adam picked the forbidden fruit from The Tree of Knowledge in the Garden of Eden in defiance of the will of God. This worldview is summarized as follows:

* #12 THE FREE WILL WORLDVIEW *

Humans possess the power to freely choose between alternatives so that choice and action are (to at least some extent) creatively determined voluntarily by their conscious guidance. Human behavior is not entirely governed by factors beyond human control.

After talking with psychologists in both shops, I appreciated that assumptions of determinism and causality must necessarily be behind all studies of human nature that seek laws of behavior. Scientific investigations would be inappropriate if whim and randomness were postulated. Accordingly, perhaps the strongest support a scientist can give the notion of free will is the "feet in both worlds" hedging of Carl Rogers, a humanistic psychologist. According to him[6], a person

> ...wills or chooses to follow the course of action which is the most economical vector in relation to all the internal and external stimuli, because it is that behavior which will be most deeply satisfying. But this is the same course of action which from another vantage point may be said to be determined by all the factors in the existential situation.

Physicists used to side with the determinists on this question, I learned. Around 1900 -- aided by the prevailing mechanistic and classical scientific worldviews --scientists could very simply state the causality / free will problem. According to Sir James Jeans,[7]

> We supposed the world to consist of atoms and radiation; we imagined that precise positions could be assigned, in principle, to every atom and to every element of radiation, and the question of causality was simply whether, knowing these positions, it was possible in principle to predict the future course of events with certainty. The question of free will was whether it was still possible to predict this course when consciousness and human volitions intervened in the picture.

Of course classical physics gave way to quantum mechanics and the uncertainty principle made stating the problem of free will more challenging. So by 1942, Jeans would conclude that arguments for determinism seemed "less compelling" than they were at the turn of the century.

In the half century since Jeans' remarks, quantum mechanics has yet to be replaced by a completely deterministic formulation. Recent work by University of California physiologist Benjamin Libet bolsters the free will position. Libet concludes, "I happen to believe free will exists. If it does exist, our experimental data are pointing toward the brain processes that would be involved." But equally impressive findings -- University of Minnesota studies of identical twins raised apart -- underscore the powerful role genetic endowment plays in shaping even the tiniest details of human behavior.

I left this controversy and headed to "The Quantum Reality Mall". On the way, I visited one other shop, "The

World of Scientism". Lack of knowledge and curiosity aroused by the store-front display, which read, "Scientism-- The True and Ultimate Problem Solving Approach", triggered my entry.

Inside, I learned that science is not scientism and scientism is not science. Expecting to be confronted by salesmen who were scientists, I was surprised by the ideologists who descended on me. These true believers seemed too sure of themselves. To them, there was up to date scientific knowledge and there was nonsense: black and white, but no shades of grey. There was the explicate, material realm, but nothing else. They seemed addicted to an unfeeling, "de-Godized religion" which arrogantly asserted that, unimpeded, the omnipotent powers of science and technology would eventually uncover all knowledge and solve all pressing problems.

Given my state of mind, dominated by an open-minded spirit of inquiry and growing uncertainties, I had to leave. Outside, a man waiting at the street-corner explained that scientism had been popular years ago. Nowadays, he asserted, its dwindling ranks included as many non-scientists as scientists. Increasingly, even scientists shunned it, he said. A lady overheard our conversation and inquired, so we summarized scientism for her.[8]

* #13 SCIENTISM *

An ideology that asserts 1) the methods of the natural sciences should be used in all areas of investigation including philosophy, the humanities and the social sciences, and 2) only these methods can fruitfully be used in the quest for knowledge.

IX. TROUBLING ASPECTS OF QUANTUM MECHANICS

Around two o'clock that afternoon I entered the mall and was surprised to encounter "The Scientific Stumbling Block". A small crowd had gathered outside its shops and a salesman was addressing them. "...Granted, scientific successes in interpreting the workings of the gross, macroscopic world have been astounding--but such methods have their limitations and stumbling blocks. Mystics may have the only access to the implicate reality, although physicists can investigate explicate manifestations from the implicate order.

"In the micro, subatomic explicate world, physicists have run into difficulties. Many, including Albert Einstein, have been troubled that the best scientific tool for understanding this realm, quantum mechanics, provides only a probabilistic picture--not completely deterministic predictions-- of micro events. Einstein could not accept the random events of a God who seemed to roll dice. He spent his last years searching for something to complete what he viewed as an incomplete formulation."

He paused, then continued. "There is another troubling aspect of quantum mechanics: it appears to require an observer to give reality to events. Using a macro world analogy, it seems that unless someone sees the tree fall, the event has no reality ! Yet, experimental tests of its predictions and those of competing theoretical formulations continue to support quantum mechanics. As a tool -- one with important applications in the macro world as well -- quantum mechanics has been highly successful; the problem is one of interpreting the physical reality behind it."

He went on talking, but I decided to walk through the mall and visit the many shops selling different interpretations of the reality behind quantum mechanics and its experimental basis. Inside each of these shops was a physicist / salesman making a pitch and hoping to sell his goods. Some had purchased a quantum reality, others seemed uncomfortable buying any of them.

After I had been in several of these shops, I saw some young physicists gathered around an old man. I moved closer and overheard much of their conversation. As he counseled them, the old physicist admitted that Einstein had left "The Quantum Reality Mall" without purchasing anything, and went searching for, or perhaps hoped to create, another interpretation of reality. "Einstein trusted me," the old physicist said, adding, "he left his reality cash to me". He then described his coming to terms with quantum reality.[9]

These people ...have forgotten ...the principle of complementarity. This principle asserts that in describing reality we must invoke complementary concepts that exclude each other--they cannot both be true...My favorite illustration of complementarity is the picture of a vast made of of two profiles... (Fig.#15) Is it a vase or two profiles...You can see it as either...But you cannot see it as both simultaneously. It is a perfect example of observer-created reality--you decide which reality you are going to see... What is the vase and what is the profile depend on each other--you cannot have one without the other. They are different representations of the same underlying reality...

FIG. #15 IS IT A FACE OR A VASE?

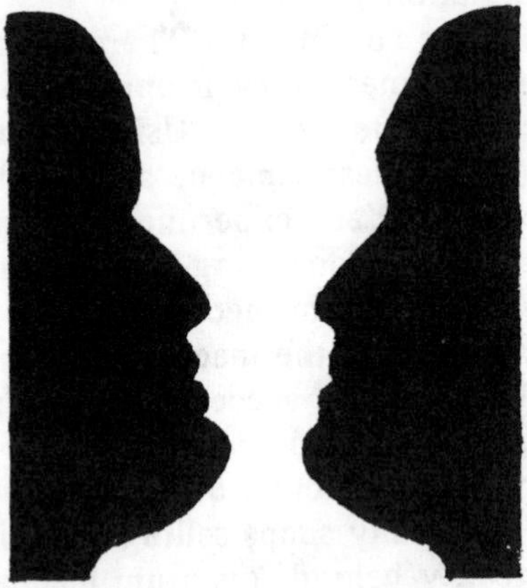

After a pause he concluded,[10] "What quantum reality is, is The Reality Marketplace. The house of a God that plays dice has many rooms. We can live in only one room at a time, but it is the whole house that is reality." After another pause one of the younger listeners spoke. "You mention difficulties understanding how nature works. It seems we must both generate a framework and interpret whether reality fits it. And who is to judge what fits ? We are!" The old physicist nodded as if he agreed.

I spent the rest of the afternoon in "The Quantum Reality Mall". But instead of latching onto some fundamental Truth, I became disturbed and confused. I discovered that the common sense doctrine that the world is made up of objects whose real existence is independent of human consciousness is not supported by quantum mechanics. I learned that most physicists feel this contradiction is only a problem in the quantum mechanical interpretation of the micro world, but a few think it applies to the macro world and the whole universe. Nobel Laureate Eugene Wigner has been puzzled by the existence of trees. John Wheeler has claimed that, of an infinity of expanding and contracting universes, only those finely tuned enough to allow the evolution of conscious minds have a concrete, rather than a paler, virtual, theoretical reality.

When closing time forced me to leave, I thought back to something I heard in "The Scientific Stumbling Block": "After a four century long march of continually refining the frame-work with which they interpret reality, physicists have now become bogged down and run out of solid ground."

Questions & Projects

1. Buddha taught, "The world is going to exist forever...The world was not created by anyone. The world always was." Using the account at the beginning of this chapter, recon-cile the Buddhist position with the Biblical "God created the heavens..." version.

2. According to Jewish myth, only in their mother's womb does a person know the secret of the universe -- but it is for-forgotten at birth. Discuss in terms of implicate / expli-cate realms. Those dominated by which worldview themes might accept or reject this notion?

3. Some adopt a variation of worldview theme #7. They reject a pervasive consciousness or life force, but instead post-ulate that everything is spatially interconnected in high-er dimensional space. Why might some scientists be more comfortable with this interpretation?

4. Carl Sagan has described humans as "the ash of stellar al-chemy". Explain.

5. Some scientists --citing extraordinarily low probabilities -- challenge the trial and error version of the evolution of complex molecules preceding the origin of life. Instead they suggest that comets and meteorites brought life's or-ganic building blocks to Earth long ago. Investigate and report.

6. Loren Eiseley, in The Immense Journey , argued that with-out flowers man would never have existed. Discuss.

7. Investigate the doctrine of teleology. Prepare a worldview theme entitled "Teleologism". How might evolu-tionary history be recast by someone embracing this doctrine? Contrast teleology with causality.

8. A person who envisions a moralistic, judgemental God de-scribes evolution as a ladder culminating with man, instead of as a branching bush. Discuss.

9. Relate the climactic scene in the movie Star Wars -- when Luke destroys the Death Star -- to the mechanistic vs. vi-talist conflict.

10. Identify the extent vitalism dominates a) Right to Life movement, b) natural foods movement, c) homeopathy.
11. A Northern Illinois University professor's ongoing, nationwide survey estimates that around 20 % of college students are fundamentalists (based on the two criteria of worldview theme #9). Discretely sample beliefs at your school. Compare your results with the above. Discuss.
12. Contrast a behavioristic psychologist's position on determinism vs. free will, with Carl Rogers' position.
13. "If free will exists, what social scientists do is not really science." Discuss.
14. In The Emperor's New Mind, Roger Penrose suggests, "The future might be determined by the present in a way that is in principle non-calculable." Discuss.
15. Investigate the "Schrodinger's Cat" thought experiment often mentioned in discussions of the interpretation of quantum mechanics. Explain why it has given those unhappy with "a God who rolls dice" headaches.
16. To appreciate the distance scale of the universe and the use of exponents, look up the size (in meters) of the following: atom, atomic nucleus, blue whale, cell, Earth--nearest star distance, Earth, human being, Milky Way Galaxy, millimeter, observable universe, quark, Sun--Earth distance, Sun. Arrange in order from smallest to largest. By what factor does the largest size exceed the smallest?

Notes

1. Thomas Huxley in A Liberal Education , 1868
2. Zimmer, H. Philosophies of India, Meridian Books, NY 1956
3. for a scientific assessment of uncertainties about the origin of life, see Shapiro, R. Origins: A Skeptic's Guide to the Creation of Life on Earth, Summit Books, NY 1986
4. adapted from Dawkins, R. The Selfish Gene , Oxford University Press, Oxford, 1976
5. Pendergast, R. "Reflections on the Myth of the Machine", Bull. Sci. Tech. Soc., Vol. 8, pp. 163-166 1988
6. Rogers, C. Freedom to Learn , Merrill, Columbus, OH 1969
7. Jeans, J. Physics and Philosophy , Cambridge University Press, 1942
8. adapted from Fischer, R.B. Science, Man, and Society , W.B. Saunders Co., Philadelphia 1975
9. Pagels, H. The Cosmic Code, Simon & Schuster, NY 1982
10. ibid

EXODUS

We now leave the solid footing of science. We journey into the realm of irrationality, superstition, religion, pseudoscience, the paranormal, and the fringes of science.

I. DEBUNKING ASTROLOGY, ATLANTIS

Early humans undoubtedly spent untold hours watching the night sky and some obtained a needed sense of security by noting the orderly workings of the heavens. Occasionally the order was disturbed by totally unpredictable events. The fiery death-dive of a shooting star, the eerie glowing, pulsating curtains of the aurora borealis, the sudden appearance of a new star where none had been before, lunar and solar eclipses, and, most frightening of all, "hairy" stars with tails called comets, all interrupted the usually tranquil and predictable celestial scene.

People tend to fear what they can not understand. Sometimes explanations with no basis in fact are concocted to allay these fears. Superstitions and myths are thus born.

Solar eclipses--the Chinese believed--were caused by a terrible dragon who was trying to eat the Sun. Only by beating on drums and making loud noises could the dragon be frightened away and the Sun saved, they decided.

During the Middle Ages, people associated comets with the fall of mighty kings, death, and havoc. They were believed to be sent by the Devil. Prayers, such as, "Oh Lord, save me from the Devil, the Turks, and the wrath of the comet," were offered as protection.

Throughout history, various peoples have found celestial explanations for events on Earth or personality traits in certain individuals. Astrologers might cast a horoscope that predicted an aggressive personality for someone born when the red planet Mars--associated with blood and the God of War-- was in a prominent position in the night sky.

Today, scientists can predict when eclipses will occur based on the orbits of the Earth and Moon. Comets--now known to be small, rocky cores surrounded by frozen, volatile gases--similarly move in orbits governed by Newtonian physics. As for the influence of Mars, the forces it exerts on you are minuscule. This book held arm's length away, exerts about one billion times stronger a gravitational pull on you than does Mars when it is closest! Similarly, light,

radio signals, or magnetic effects reaching you from planets
are hundreds of millions of times weaker than effects
produced by household lights, transistor radio outputs, or
permanent magnets in loudspeakers.

Of course, astrologers might postulate that forces
unknown to science are involved. As astronomer George Abell
pointed out, such a force would have to have some strange
properties.[1]

> It would have to emanate from some but not all celestial
> bodies, have to affect some but not all things on Earth,
> and its strength could not depend on the distance,
> masses, or other characteristics of those planets giving
> rise to it.

Some New Age fanatics involve similarly mysterious
forces and energies in a tale about the lost "continent" of
Atlantis[2]...Supposedly a great Atlantean civilization flourished from 150,000 B.C. to 9600 B.C. While originally an
agricultural society, later the Atlanteans developed technology based on "the higher dimensional energies of consciousness" and "pranic forces carried by sunlight", which plants
("flower essence") and quartz crystals ("gem elixirs") helped
them control. Alas, Atlantis had problems. Its "great
crystals" used for broadcasting energies were "tuned too
high". This triggered major earthquakes which reduced the
continent to small islands. And there were "wars involving
the perverted use of crystalline and atomic weapons". A
great flood ultimately submerged Atlantis....

Perhaps the gullible, scientifically illiterate will accept this confused account as true, no one else will. Archaeologists have found no evidence of such a long-lived sophisticated civilization. They date the first human agricultural
activities at 7000 B.C. Many archaeologists and geologists
suspect the Atlantis legend sprang from the 1350 B.C. volcanic eruption and subsequent submergence of most of what is
now the island of Thera, off the coast of Greece. Guided by
plate tectonics theory, geophysicists calculate that major
earthquakes release energies which far exceed that released
by detonating all the world's nuclear weapons. To speculate
human tuning of crystals could release such energy is nonsense. Physicists have not found the expected long-lived isotopes ancient atomic weapons should have created. Prana is an
ancient Hindu concept and something not found by astrophysicists as they map the sun's electromagnetic spectrum.

II. SCIENTISTS CONFRONT THE PARANORMAL

As related earlier (see CONCEPTS), the history of science is one of the continual improvement of the conceptual framework for making sense out of the natural world. Sometimes particular phenomena will necessitate tearing down and rebuilding a part of the framework so that the entire structure can remain standing. A few scientists are not sure that certain unexplained parapsychological phenomena are just coincidences. They believe the next great scientific revolution will come when science incorporates mind transcending matter type happenings into its framework. No doubt it will be difficult for this accommodation to occur.

While stories of precognitive dreams, legends of miraculous happenings, and reports of the supernatural abound throughout history, many scientists pay little attention to anecdotal evidence of the paranormal. Instead they prefer to conduct their investigations inside the laboratory. Consider two examples of such research.

For many years, Harold Puthoff and Russell Targ, scientists at the Stanford Research Institute, worked with both "gifted" and ordinary individuals in so-called remote viewing experiments. In one series of experiments, one researcher leaves the laboratory in a car. Along the way, he uses a random number generator to select a destination point. Meanwhile, another researcher stays behind with the subject and asks this person to draw a picture of the site being visited. Reportedly, the correlation between the subject's description and the actual site have been unaccountably high --both for "psychic" and ordinary subjects. Fig. #16 shows one example of line drawings made from a) the subject's remote viewing sketch and b) a photograph of the actual site.[3]

Consider a second example. For many years, Dr. Charles T. Tart, now psychology professor at the University of California, Davis, has investigated out of body experiences. In 1965, he began working with a subject he calls Miss Z. Since childhood, she had numerous experiences in which she awoke for a few seconds during the night and felt she was floating near the ceiling. At those times she looked down and saw her body in bed!

Tart arranged for Miss Z to sleep for four nights in the laboratory. He planned to monitor physiological effects that occurred during an out of the body experience (OOBE) and test if Miss Z was able to read a target number, visible only from

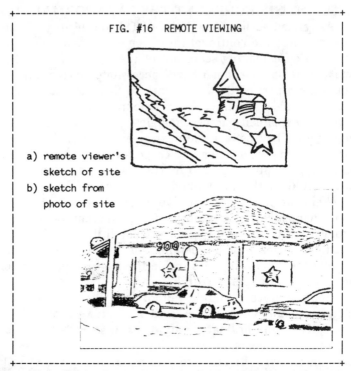

FIG. #16 REMOTE VIEWING

a) remote viewer's sketch of site

b) sketch from photo of site

the ceiling. With electrodes and wires attached to her body, she could not leave the bed without disturbing this hookup.

Over the course of the four nights, Miss Z experienced several OOBEs which she reported within a minute or two of their occurrence. While her heart rate and skin resistance patterns were normal at these times, an unusual and distinct brain wave pattern was recorded. During all of her OOBEs except one, Miss Z did not feel in a position to observe the target number. However, on her last night in the lab, she did float to a position near the ceiling and correctly reported the target number as 25132. The odds of someone guessing this number in one try would be 100,000 to 1!

Tart[4] does not totally rule out cheating or fraud.

> It is conceivable that she might have concealed a mirror and a telescoping rod in her pajamas and used these to inspect the number at a time when she thought I might not be looking through the observation window....I consider this highly unlikely...

In the scientific community those attributing any reality to paranormal phenomena are a tiny minority. At the heart of modern science are four viewpoints: materialism, causality, objectivism, and reductionism. Lumped together, these viewpoints can be used to summarize how most scientists view the world (recall worldview theme #6). As we have seen (CONCEPTS, GENESIS) , quantum mechanics challenges causality and objectivism--so do paranormal phenomena. In addition, certain psychic phenomena (among them OOBEs) seem to challenge materialism. In recent years a few renegade Western physicists have reinterpreted and extended another worldview--one with roots in the ancient tradition of Eastern mystical experience (recall worldview theme #7). Those enmeshed in this worldview focus on the implicate reality behind the explicate world.

In his science fiction classic Childhood's End , Arthur C. Clarke adopts a similar viewpoint to explain mind linkages and telepathy.

> Imagine that every man's mind is an island, surrounded by ocean. Each seems isolated, yet in reality all are linked by the bedrock from which they spring.

In 1976 The Committee for the Scientific Investigation of Claims of the Paranormal (CSICOP) was established. Besides exposing fraudulent claims and combating pseudoscientific nonsense, CSICOP members have investigated the supposedly significant results of controlled research studies involving the paranormal. Recently, one of its members, D.F. Marks, psychology professor at the University of Otago in New Zealand, summarized CSICOP findings.[5] Their conclusion is a thorn in the side of paranormal researchers:

> The failure of paranormal investigators to produce a single repeatable effect despite 100 years of published research is a serious matter. The hoped-for results have been described in thousands of reports, but not one can be repeated in a properly controlled replication.

Consider their analysis of the remote viewing experiments conducted by Puthoff and Targ.

> (They) are also invalid because of the many sensory cues, non-randomization and inappropriate statistics. Tart organized a reanalysis of this research and claimed to have removed all of the sensory cues and obtained the same highly significant results. However, he did not in fact remove all of the cues as he had stated. Attempted replications of the remote viewing research are

either flawed or, in the case of well-controlled
studies, show no evidence of ESP.

Marks suggests that Charles Tart's real motives in doing such research are "religio-spiritual" in nature. In addition he comments,

An immaterial 'soul' has passed out of the formal
language of parapsychology, but anti-materialism is
still the backbone of the underlying philosophy.

III. SOULS, MORALIZING, AND CONSCIOUSNESS

42 % of Americans claim to have been in contact with someone who has died (says the U. of Chicago's National Opinion Research Center). These people believe that part of one's consciousness survives death. This belief--diametrically opposed to the materialism of the classical scientific worldview--is central to Christian and Eastern religions. But Western Judeo-Christian traditions hold that a moralistic, judgemental God decides one's fate upon death.

* #14 SPIRITUAL / MORALISTIC WORLDVIEW *

Human beings have spirits or souls in which resides the seat of consciousness. These are capable of leaving the body, and, although they are like physical bodies in some ways, are not subject to physical laws. They are, however, subject to God's judgement. If one has lived an upright, moral life relatively free of sins, and has affirmed certain religious beliefs, one's soul is rewarded after death. Otherwise, God's verdict may be a harsh punishment.

Those adopting this worldview typically cite Biblical examples of God's rewards or wrath when questioned about their characterization of God as a moralist.

Judeo-Christian religious history, with its prophets and miracles, is traditionally understood by enmeshing oneself in the Spiritual/Moralistic worldview. Most scientists have steered clear of this domain--but not all. Shortly we'll consider how Old Testament "miracles" might be recast by someone with a scientific worldview. The starting point for this exercise is a look at "the seat of consciousness".

Around 1900, psychologist William James wrote, "It is a general principle in psychology that consciousness deserts all processes where it can no longer be of use." For example, athletes, dancers, and those involved in sexual intercourse can be hindered by thinking about what they are doing. In their performances, consciousness, that special form of

mental life in which real things or acts are replaced by
symbols and abstractions and these manipulated in mental
space, is absent. In its place, the brain employs simple
"motor programs" to govern behavior. There is awareness, but
not consciousness.

Just what consciousness is, and whether humans have
always possessed this sophisticated state of awareness or if
it developed during human evolution, are open to speculation.
Some investigators associate the emergence of consciousness
with the development of language and the left hemisphere of
the brain. Others have perceived two different types of con-
sciousness--one associated with the left brain and one with
the right.

IV. THE BRAIN; RIGHT AND LEFT HEMISPHERES

The human brain is extraordinarily complex and
psychologists' understanding of it has come slowly. In
assessing these efforts, Nobel Prize winner Francis Crick
writes,[6]

> The basic difficulty is that psychology attempts to
> treat the brain as a black box. The experimenter studies
> the inputs and outputs and tries from the results to
> deduce the structure and operation of the inside of the
> box....The difficulty with the black box approach is
> that unless the box is inherently very simple a stage is
> soon reached where several rival theories all explain
> the observed results equally well. Attempts to decide
> among them often prove unsuccessful because as more
> experiments are done more complexities are revealed. At
> this point there is no choice but to poke inside the
> box.

Consider one such poking "inside the box" experiment and
where it led.

In the 1960s, Roger Sperry and his co-workers at the
California Institute of Technology performed experiments in
which the cord connecting the right and left brain hemispheres (the corpus callosum) of cats was cut. The cats
seemed to function as if they had two separate, self-con-
tained brains. This work led to Sperry and neurosurgeon
Joseph Bogen performing similar operations to help epileptic
patients. These efforts helped spur a widespread investigation of right/left brain differences.

By the late 1970s, most scientists interested in the

human brain believed that the two brain hemispheres were specialized for performing different functions. Many felt that the worldviews and actions of some individuals might be dominated by one hemisphere or the other. Numerous ways of measuring the extent of such individual brain lateralization--including dichotic listening, visual half-field techniques, dichaptic touching, electroencephalograph (EEG) patterns, cerebral blood flow, skin electrical resistance, lateral eye movements--were developed.

Understanding verbal communication, speaking, reading and writing are left brain centered. The left brain processes information in a sequential, bit by bit, mode. Such an order- ed mentality is crucial for analytic reasoning, number skills and manipulation, and skeptical, critical thinking. The left brain can think abstractly and manipulate symbols.

In contrast, during strenuous physical activities, non- verbal communications, and dreams, the right brain is at work. It processes information not piecemeal but in wholes-- storing and retrieving the pictures which the left brain might break down into individual, ordered pixels. The right brain is also called on for assessing spatial relationships, three-dimensional vision, face and pattern recognition, intuitive and wholistic reasoning. If left brain dominant individuals make good analytical scientists, accountants, and lawyers--then musicians, artists, architects, and poets make use of right brain talents.

Pre-civilization humans possessed something akin to a right brain mentality. However, as language and later writing developed, the situation changed and the left brain began to compete with the right for control. Eventually this mentality replaced the right side's wholistic and intuitive nature in shaping Western civilization.

In understanding this right brain / left brain struggle for dominance two suggestions may prove useful. First, think of both hemispheres as sending information to the human mind's manager and governor, located in the frontal cortex. The frontal brain monitors both of these inputs, synthe- sizing, analyzing, sending to and recalling from memory storage as needed. After interpreting the information pro- vided by these two main channels, plans, strategies, and goals for future behavior are developed. As this behavior is implemented, the body's speech and motor centers are activated. Feedback from these actions is received and used to modify behavior if necessary.

Second, while much human neurological circuitry is fixed by "hard wiring", the brain also employs more flexible "soft wiring". The language and cultural environment young children are raised in appears to initially program the "soft wiring". Research studies show that, in response to brain injury or (temporarily) to certain drugs, reprogramming can occur.

V. THE ORIGIN OF CONSCIOUSNESS--JAYNES' THEORY

Investigating how human consciousness developed can be more of an exercise in human cultural history than in evolutionary biology. Sometimes attempts to fit past reality to different theoretical frameworks lead to dramatically different interpretations of what really happened. Consider the early days of human civilization as recorded in ancient books, the best known being the Old Testament of the Bible. Many biblical events are interpreted by postulating miracles and involving God. A modern framework constructed by Princeton University psychology professor Julian Jaynes can likewise model the reality behind the ancient accounts. Although it may not get us any closer to understanding what happened long ago than postulating religious miracles, this new interpretation may seem just as plausible as the old.

Jaynes, in his book The Origin of Consciousness in the Breakdown of the Bicameral Mind, argues that consciousness didn't fully emerge until the 1st millennium B.C. Before then humans spoke, judged, reasoned, solved problems, and did most things that people do today--only they were not conscious! They possessed an earlier mentality, the "bicameral mind". Unable to introspect, they heard voices just as some schizophrenics do today. These auditory hallucinations coming from the right side of the brain, told them what to do under novel circumstances or in times of stress. The voices, experienced as real sounds, had their origin in the once heard real voices of parents, long-dead relatives, leaders, kings, or other authority figures. The inner voices were believed to be the voices of the gods.

At this time, human nature was split in two, with the executive part called a god, and the follower, a man. Neither of these inhabitants of the mind was conscious. Visual hallucinations, also given divine interpretation, sometimes accompanied the "voices of the gods" (again in times of stress). Temples, statues of idols, small figurines, and even

the corpses of dead leaders, aided the hallucination experience. Human society in those bicameral days was built around
integrating the inner voices into a stable social hierarchical order. That hierarchy often determined whose bicameral
voice was the correct one to obey when a decision affecting a
whole tribe was necessary.

The bicameral mentality, which (supposedly) persisted
from the 9th millennium to the 2nd millennium B.C. was not to
last. Several developments contributed to its demise: 1) The
newly acquired written word helped weaken the authority of
the transitory voices of long dead leaders. 2) Trade between
different cultures, and later forced migrations resulting in
intermingling of peoples with different customs and gods,
brought people into contact with others whose behavior seemed
bewilderingly strange. Perhaps some individuals first postulated a conscious self in others to explain their actions,
then inferred it in themselves by generalization. 3) In times
of conquest by others, war, and upheaval--conditions which
dominated latter 2nd millennium B.C. history--there was
survival value in being able to hide one's true self. For
many, surviving these turbulent times demanded wearing a
false front of acceptance, while actually harboring hatred
and revenge inside. Perhaps the development of such deceit
was an important step toward consciousness. 4) During such
times, those unable to resist internal commands to kill in-
truding strangers were more likely to be killed themselves.

Conceivably, natural selection's last important contribution to shaping human beings, could have been to select for
the genes of the less impulsive, less obedient, more detached
from the will of the internal gods. Those whose brain
physiology and makeup was less fundamentally bicameral may
have endowed the next generation. There is some Biblical
evidence that strongly bicameral children were simply killed.

With a bicameral mind interpretation, the Old Testament
of the Bible becomes a story of the Hebrews' loss of god-like
voices and visions, and their replacement by subjective
consciousness over the 1st millennium B.C. The taking of the
forbidden fruit / fall of man from Eden story can be viewed
as a myth telling of the breakdown of bicameral mentality.
For the serpent promised "your eyes will be opened and you
will be like the elohim, knowing good and evil." Thus after
the fall they were conscious of their nakedness and saw themselves as others saw them.

The bicameral visual component of the hallucinated gods, whose frequency and intensity varied from culture to culture, was the first to change form and be lost. Only once does Moses talk to "He who is" as "face to face, as a man speaketh to his friend." More typically, He is perceived as a burning bush, or a cloud, or a huge pillar of fire. The story of Moses receiving the ten commandments in the wilderness of Mt. Sinai can be seen as a story emphasizing legitimacy--the legitimacy of replacing the bicameral voices' and visions' authority, with the authority of the written word, written in this case on stone tablets.

According to Jaynes, the books of the Old Testament were written "just as the voice of Yahweh (Jehovah) in particular was not being heard with any great clarity or frequency." They were written out of "nostalgic anguish for the lost bicamerality of a subjectively conscious people".

The Greek gods and mythology and their subsequent early literature--particularly the Illiad and the Odyssey--can likewise be understood with a bicameral mind breakdown interpretation. So can the early religious writings of other cultures, according to Jaynes.

VI. THE GENERAL BICAMERAL PARADIGM

Julian Jaynes claims that modern human consciousness couldn't develop until the left brain centered language and writing made it possible. Certainly scientific thinking, which depends critically on analytical skills, wasn't possible during the bicameral era. Similarly, today, strongly right brain dominant people have little use for structured, scientific type methodology. Instead such people rely more on what Julian Jaynes calls "The General Bicameral Paradigm".

Jaynes defines this process as "a hypothesized structure behind a large class of phenomena of diminished consciousness which are interpreted as partial holdovers from an earlier mentality." Like the scientific method of which it is the anti-thesis, it has a few component parts: 1) collective cognitive imperative, a belief system, a culturally agreed on expectancy which defines roles to be acted out, 2) induction, a ritualized procedure to narrow consciousness by focusing on something, 3) the trance, a response to both of the above characterized by the diminishing or loss of consciousness (the analog "I" gives way to a role acceptable to the group), 4) the archaic authorization, to which the trance is directed or related, is usually a god but sometimes a person who is accepted by the individual and the culture as an authority and who, by the collective cognitive imperative, is perceived as being responsible for the trance.

Consider how the bicameral paradigm explains hypnosis. If the authority of the hypnotist tells a person that he or she is about to drink champagne or is about to feel a pleasurable sensation, then hypnotized subjects will taste vinegar as champagne or experience pleasure from a pin prick. Under a hypnotic spell, people live in an "as if" type of reality and totally suppress any "it isn't" skepticism. Investigations have found that the most "easily hypnotized person is one who can 'listen to' and rely on the right hemisphere more than others".

Many modern scholars dispute Jaynes' interpretation of the human past, but manage to temper their criticism with praise. "Even if Jaynes has overstated his case (as most commentators think) he has posed fascinating questions and drawn attention to important facts and problems hitherto unconsidered", comments one. Others are somewhat harder, "Until empirical work is done to satisfactorily corroborate them, these claims will continue to be considered by experts in the field of brain functions as imaginative science fiction."

Jaynes' book appeared in 1977 and a controversy followed its publication. In the next decade, some findings[7] appeared to strengthen his case: 1) a 1983 study reported that 71 % of college students had, at some time, experienced brief verbal hallucinations, 2) studies which indicate that associated with a) children's imaginary playmates are "clearly 'heard' and not imagined" voices, b) a non-verbal population of cerebral palsied quadriplegics hear inner voices, sounding like a relative but identified as God", 3) a 1983[8] study indicated that 1 to 5 % of people in Western cultures "see" vivid hallucination-like images in experiencing fantasies that seem as real as actual life. Reportedly, such people are highly suggestible, easily hypnotized, and report more supposedly paranormal experiences, such as "telepathy, precognition, ghosts, and out of body experiences". Finally, 4) Recognizing that drumming in the four to seven beats per minute range can alter one's consciousness, in 1989 researchers offered an explanation. They noted[9] this frequency is similar to that of the brain's theta waves--active during dreaming. They suggested that drumming blocks left brain activity and allows the right brain to dominate.

Summarizing Jaynes' ideas and related research in a way that makes it relevant to various controversial present day topics (drugs, faith healing, charismatic religion, hypnosis, media manipulation, etc.) leads to the following:

* #15 THE COLLECTIVE COGNITIVE IMPERATIVE *

Under proper environmental stimulation or stress, people of a psychological makeup susceptible to this imperative may suspend analytical thinking, narrow their consciousness and passively transfer control of themselves to some real or imagined authority. In doing this, they put their faith in the authority who they associate with the culturally agreed on expectancy behind the belief system. These experiences typically involve rituals which trigger trance-like behavior, and may involve auditory and / or visual hallucinations. Primitive peoples are more susceptible to this imperative. The mentality this imperative fosters is perhaps a relic of an earlier (bicameral) mentality in which humans were not fully conscious.

VII. RELIGIOUS PROPHETS OF BROTHERHOOD

After the supposed disappearance of the bicameral inner voices of many gods, and perhaps, one could argue, because of it, there was an important advance in religion. The belief in many gods gave way to the belief in just one God. With this unified religious focus, perceiving mankind as one large family became much easier. With that perception, concluding that only what is good for mankind is good for individuals, and what is bad for mankind is bad for individuals naturally followed. Such thinking spawned the great idea of the brotherhood of man.

Actually a kernel of this great idea--the so-called Golden Rule--is much older, perhaps dating back to the first gatherings of people in villages. The Golden Rule is a part of cultural heritages throughout the world, and many prophets have featured it in their teachings. So, in the sixth century B.C. when Confucious was asked, "Is there one word that would cover the whole duty of man?", the great sage replied, "Fellow-feeling, perhaps is that word. Do not do unto others what thou wouldst not they should do unto you."

Jesus, in his Sermon on the Mount, put it in a slightly different way, "Therefore all things whatsoever ye would that

men should do to you, do ye even so to them." He immediately
added, "Every good tree bringeth forth good fruit; but a
corrupt tree bringeth forth evil fruit. A good tree cannot
bring forth evil fruit, neither can a corrupt tree bring
forth good fruit."

Sidhatta Gautama, the Buddha, reached essentially the
same conclusion, after a lifetime search. Sitting under a
tree, the idea came to him and his face lit up with joy. "At
last, I have found the key to wisdom" he said. "This is the
First Law of Life: From good must come good and from evil
must come evil."

Today, Buddhists are taught, "Hurt not others with that
which pains yourself." Jews are reminded, "What is hurtful
to yourself, do not to your fellow man. That is the whole
truth of the Torah and the remainder is but commentary."
Hindus learn, "That is the sum of duty; do naught to others
which if done to thee would cause pain." And Islam concurs,
"No one of you is a believer until he loves for his brother
what he loves for himself."

Similarly, the great religions and prophets echo with
statements regarding human equality. Mohammed taught, "All of
you are of the same equality. You are all of one brotherhood." Likewise, at the Last Supper, Jesus explained,
"Remember, the servant is not greater than his lord; neither
is he that is sent greater than he that sent him."

These great prophets of brotherhood all spoke out
against materialistic greed and excesses. Mohammed preached
against the rich merchants in Mecca who used the Well of
Ishmael and The Temple of the Kabba as sources of profit.
They tried to stop him from preaching against the rich. "Not
even if you set the sun against me on my right hand and the
moon on my left hand would I leave my mission!" was his im-
passioned reply. In responding to a rich young man who asked
what good thing besides obeying Jesus' commandments he could
do, Jesus said, "Go and sell all you have and give the money
to the poor and you will have riches in heaven." Lord
Mahavira, prophet of Jainism, taught that "...the suffering
of the world comes from Desire. People suffer and are unhappy
because they want so many things. No matter how much a man
gets of food and wealth and fame, he always wants more. Only
by doing good can you reach Nirvana. Within yourself lies
salvation." Similarly, Buddhists see the essence of civilization, not in multiplication of wants but in the purifica-

tion of human character. The Chinese book of Tao adds, "The perfect sage is content to give up extravagant comforts and ...set the nation an example of returning to simplicity."

So in the teachings of the world's great religious prophets there are important areas of agreement. Variations on the Golden Rule, the brotherhood of man idea, and an emphasis on spiritual rather than materialistic concerns are themes common to all religions. These teachings are the basis for some universally-endorsed human values regarding the morally right way to treat others. With regard to those values, we summarize traditional religious wisdom as follows:

* #16 FAMILY OF MAN / OTHER PEOPLE ORIENTATION

You are but one member of the family of man. All members of this family are precious and special and The Golden Rule should guide your treatment of them. That is, treat others as you would want them to treat you. If you desire and horde more than your fair share of material wealth, you will be taking from others and some may be left without. Your behavior should take the welfare of the entire family of man into consideration. Remember good can not flow from evil.

VIII. THE DARK SIDE OF HUMAN HISTORY

So much for humanity's noblest teachings. The antithesis of the Golden Rule is to do unto others what you fear and dread someone doing to you. For victims, such acts may preclude obeying the Christian New Testament instructions to love your neighbor and turn the other cheek. They can generate hatred, the need for vengeance, and, if whole tribes or nations feel wronged, lead to war.

The Old Testament God was one of retribution. And Hebrews taught--besides The Golden Rule--"an eye for an eye, a tooth for a tooth". This is an important component of the following worldview.

* #17 THE WRONGED, THE VENGEFUL ORIENTATION *

(Along with my people?) I have been unjustly insulted, persecuted, and injured. I now seek justice. I aim to inflict on those responsible the same pain I have felt. It is my (our?) duty.

In mediating a childish quarrel, parents can rationally inquire as to its origin and establish how it should end. A big picture look at this dark side of humanity can only start with Cain's Biblical murder of Abel, identify hatred as a driving force, and recount a sordid history of suffering and death. Recent chapters in this history would recall the torture of the Catholic Inquisition, countless women accused of witchcraft and burned at the stake, 30 million black bodies tossed overboard by slave traders, Native American children given smallpox-riddled blankets by whites who sought to exterminate them, the Ottoman Empire's liquidation of one million plus Armenians, the Soviet purges of the 1930s, the Nazi genocide of six million Jews, the Cambodian killing fields...

When will the evil end? Is retribution a victim's only recourse? Holy men from Jesus to Gandhi have taught, "Good cannot flow from evil" in advocating non-violent--instead of hateful, vengeful--responses to evil. Always, rational leaders, fearing chaos, have sought order and embraced law.

Questions & Projects

1. A 1984 Gallup poll found that 55 % of American teenagers believe in astrology. Arm yourself with "Your Astrology Defense Kit" (see Sky & Telescope August, 1989), find a vocal proponent of astrology, and arrange a debate.

2. Attempt to explain ESP from a materialist viewpoint.

3. Would you purposely avoid spending a night in a supposedly haunted house if faced with that prospect? Discuss.

4. James Randi is a magician famous for debunking psychics and pseudoscientific deception. Report on his work.

5. Study Fig. #16. Are you convinced that the subject really scored "a hit"? Discuss.

6. French immunologist J. Benveniste's claim, that an extremely dilute (one part in 10^{120}) antiserum against immunoglobulin E retained its effectiveness by imprinting water with a memory of its presence, sparked controversy. Investigate this seeming challenge to science.[10]

7. For philosopher and mystic Martin Buber, human consciousness emerged when the I-YOU was disturbed by an I-IT recognition. Refer to Buber's I and Thou and report.

8. Joseph Campbell, in The Power of Myth , writes, "All the gods, all the heavens, all the worlds are within us. They are magnified dreams...The myth is the public dream." This statement most nearly reflects which worldview theme?

9. Consider two representations of the time: one provided by the numbers on a digital watch, the other by the hands of an old-fashioned watch. a) which do you prefer? b) which might RB dominant people prefer?...LB dominant prefer?

10. News item: a University of Chicago biopsychologist's

research indicates that creative or "right brain thinkers" have innate brain activity patterns making them more likely to be "optimistic, extroverted, and happy" than analytical or "left brain thinkers" . Suppose you wanted to partially confirm this result. What might you do?

11. Out of physical chemist Michael Polanyi's interest in creativity came his concept of "tacit knowing". He illustrates this with an example. "I can pick out the face of an acquaintance in a crowd of thousands, yet I may not be able to explain how I do it." Discuss in LB / RB terms.

12. Recall experiences of people you know-- acquaintances or historical figures--who have heard inner voices.

13. A sign for a rural old-time religious revival reads, "Deliverance Revival: Come Expecting Your Miracle". Relate to the Collective Cognitive Imperative.

14. Discuss the following as to their basis on scientific methodology and/or the Collective Cognitive Imperative: a) rainmaking, b) water witching

15. Suppose worldview themes #16 and #17 both contribute significantly to a person's overall worldview. Imagine what type of person this could be and discuss.

Notes

1. ed. Abell, G. and Singer, B. Science and the Paranormal , Scribner's, New York, 1981

2. see for example Gerber, R. Vibrational Medicine Bear & Co Santa Fe, NM 1988 p.328

3. Targ,R. & Harary, K. The Mind Race , Ballantine, NY 1985

4. Tart, C. "Out of Body Experiences" in Psychic Exploration, ed. White, J. G. P. Putnam's Sons, New York, 1974

5. Marks, D.F., "Investigating the Paranormal", Nature vol. 320, 13 March 1986 p.119

6. Crick, F.H.C. "Thinking About the Brain", in The Brain, a collection of Scientific American off-prints, 1984

7. Jaynes, J. "Hearing Voices and the Bicameral Mind", Behavioral and Brain Sciences, Vol. 9 #3, Sept. 1986

8. Wilson, S.C. and Barber, T.X. in Imagery: Current Theory, Research, and Application (ed. Sheikh, A.A.) J. Wiley, New York, 1983 pp. 340-387

9. see Yoga Journal, Jan. / Feb. 1989 issue

10. see Nature Vol.333 p.816 , June 30, 1988.

LAW, ECONOMISTS & ECOLOGISTS

I. GUARDING AGAINST SOCIETAL BREAKDOWN

Primitive human animals used their brains to overcome "The Law of the Jungle", by which they were easy prey for larger, faster, more powerful predators. To survive in a world of "tooth and claw" ethics, humans 1) used tools to obtain food and protect themselves, 2) created social organization based on co-operation, 3) developed language to further enhance the value of co-operation as a social strategy, and 4) cultivated reason. Eventually, by becoming co-operators and thinkers unequalled by any in the biological world, Homo Sapiens dominated all other species. When reason departs, individual actions based on strong feelings threaten societal stability. Consider the mentality behind this threatening behavior.

* #18 THE EMOTIONAL, UNGOVERNABLE PERSON *

In place of reason, my actions are often guided by primitive urges and intense emotions. These disturbances of my psyche--whether they be feelings of fear, anger, jealousy, frustration, inferiority, hope, sympathy, love, lust or whatever--sometimes build into an intense force which overcomes any restraint imposed by reason. At those times, this irrational force governs my behavior.

If such a person also holds "The Wronged, Vengeful Orientation" (worldview theme #17) and is a true believer (theme #2), he is a leader whose unpredictable and violent nature threatens society. If enough people follow him, societal breakdown and chaos may result.

According to economic historian Robert Heilbroner[1], man has invented only three ways of organizing society to guard against calamitous breakdown. First, tradition can hold society together. The diverse tasks needed for the continuity and well being of the village are handed down from generation to generation according to custom and usage. Religion is frequently the "glue" that holds such societies together. As a reward for co-operative behavior, religion promises "life after death" to the co-operator. Second, "central authoritarian rule" can govern society. The ruler or rulers may be called chief, Pharaoh, king, dictator, Politburo, Big Brother or whatever. Finally, the last solution to be developed was, in Heilbroner's words, "an astonishing game" known as the "market system". Its operation was simple: "the lure of gain steered each man to his task".

It was this last "paradoxical, subtle, and difficult solution to the problem of survival" that spurred the development of the science of economics. And eventually the people caught up in ailing market-based systems came to depend upon economists for the analyses and prescriptions that would restore the economic health. Before the fine-tuned smooth functioning was restored however, people worried. For, as Heilbroner concludes, "unlike the simplicity of custom and command, it was not at all obvious that with each man out only for his own gain, society could in fact endure."

II. THE CHURCH AND MONEY-MAKING

The Middle Ages combination of the first two solutions to the survival problem--feudalism--dominated western civilization for centuries. During this era dominated by the authority of kings and God's apparent agent on Earth--the Catholic Church--social changes came painfully slow. In the countryside peasants and serfs toiled at their lord's estate. In cities apprentices and journeymen served craftsmen and master guildsmen. This labor largely went uncompensated-- these were the expected "duties" of serfs. Likewise land was generally not for sale, forming as it did the core of social life and the basis of a nobleman's status. Similarly, while great private wealth existed, seldom was it manipulated for gain. Any notion of economic growth, progress, or "getting ahead" was lacking.

The Church viewed an individual's money-making and materialistic pursuits as both harmful to society and a barrier to salvation. They prohibited banking or money lending (usury) to discourage such behavior. Prices were fixed by guilds and feudal government as there was no market pricing system. There were inequalities: many feudal noblemen were wealthy and had an easy life compared to serfs. Still, materialistic greed was harshly viewed by most.

With the rational awakening and Protestant Reformation, religious thinking on economic matters changed. Martin Luther's 1517 nailing of his 93 word heretical letter to the Church door in Wittenburg, Germany started another movement which undermined Catholic Church authority. Thirty years later the reformation movement was given another push by John Calvin (1509-1564). His "unceasing activity in the service of God" idea changed not only the era's religious--but also its economic--order. According to this Protestant work ethic, by always laboring at one's optimum in pursuing one's own special "calling" or line of work, one gained God's approval. Economic concepts of efficiency and specialization of labor had their roots here, so did the production of surpluses-- since other religions frowned on such accumulation.

Medieval Catholic workers would rest when their labor produced enough to meet their family's needs. Similarly, Islam taught that any accumulation of wealth beyond that needed by a family was sinful. Moslem traditions required that surplus earnings be given to the community as part of a holy pilgramage. Protestant workers, in contrast, labored on long after their family needs were met.

What was to become of the resulting surplus? Calvin taught that since it was produced to serve God's glory there was nothing sinful about it. It would be sinful to use it to satisfy one's own desires. Therefore the proper use of the surplus was for reinvestment in one's business or special calling to improve productivity and the ability to generate still larger surpluses for God's glory, and so on. In this way, capital formation, another important ingredient of capitalism, was justified.

So the Protestant work ethic helped foster three of four elements needed for capitalism: system efficiency of production, specialization of labor, and capital formation. The fourth, the necessary planning process which precedes production, came with the rational awakening.

The economic revolution that produced capitalism and its characteristic market system had its beginnings in the 13th century. The economic changes came gradually. The market system emerged in an often painful evolutionary process that most notably spanned the three centuries from 1550 to 1850. Commercializing both labor and land meant making workers out of serfs and enclosing lands for sale or profit. These and other changes threatened the entrenched feudal way of life and they were often bitterly resisted. There were riots. Peasants were thrown off heretofore common land. Before factories and the industrial revolution produced jobs in the cities, displaced serfs became unemployed paupers.

As the economic revolution progressed, first the authority of the Church and later the authority of kings diminished. With the changing 17th century economic scene, the Catholic Church reluctantly abandoned its rules against money lending. In doing so they acknowledged the reality that most Christians had become capitalist merchants. The Protestant Reformation clearly had important impacts outside religion. As one historian would later write[2],

> Protestant reformers set out to achieve a radical sanctification of all human behavior before God, but...after a lapse of a couple generations, provoked in parts of Europe a disciplined application to the business of making money such as the world had scarcely seen before.

III. LOCKE ON MONEY & SELF-INTEREST; CAPITALISM

With the waning of the Catholic Church's authority, scholars began re-examining many old religious teachings. In particular, the conclusions of England's John Locke (1632-1704) had important economic ramifications.

Locke began his analysis by conceding that the Earth and its fruits were originally given to mankind in common. As evidence he cited the authority of biblical scriptures and the dictates of natural reason. He went on to postulate 1) that men have a right to preserve their own lives, and 2) that a man's labor is his own, i.e. he can use it to obtain wages and he owes no debt to society for it and its productivity. From these postulates, Locke proceeded to justify the individual acquisition of the Earth's once common wealth.

Initially he realized that his logical argument for individual appropriation had three limitations: 1) A man may take only as much as leaves "enough and as good" for others, 2) a "spoilage" limitation, summarized with Locke's statement, "Nothing was made by God for men to spoil or destroy" and 3) A man's possessions should be limited to what he can acquire with "the labour of his body and the work of his hands." Had Locke's reasoning stopped here, he would have not been advocating such a dramatic break with the religion-dominated economic past.

Locke did not stop. He proceeded to show how each of these limitations could be removed with full consent of men! The key to Locke's seeming turn-around was the introduction of money. He argued that for "the part of mankind that has consented to the use of money" these limitations do not apply. Of the three limitations, the second one was the easiest to overcome for, as Locke put it, surplus "gold and silver...may be hoarded up without injuring anyone; these

metals not spoiling or decaying in the hands of the pos-
sessor". The first limitation was demolished by implication
that use of money is consent to the consequences. Society's
accepting the validity of the wages agreement, whereby one
man may sell "the service he undertakes to do in exchange for
wages he is to receive", was used to get around the third
limitation.

After removing these limitations, Locke advocated each
person act in his own self-interest and ultimately saw this
behavior as the only basis for society. He thereby freed
those pursuing wealth from value judgements others might
make.

Locke's conclusions had wide-ranging effect. In late
17th century England, he gave the growing capitalist movement
the rationally-derived moral basis it needed. His beliefs
dominated English thought for the next century and provided
inspiration for America's founding fathers. The incredible,
unexploited riches of the new continent likewise influenced
Locke. The unmoderated scramble for personal material gain
would not degenerate into savage chaos, he felt, because
people were inherently good. Only poverty made them turn to
evil. With the nearly limitless New World wealth added to
that of the Old, Locke felt that self-interest oriented
individuals would not come in conflict with the interests of
others.

Locke's economic thinking inspired Adam Smith (1723-
1790), whose work laid the foundation for modern capitalist
economics. Smith echoed Locke on self-interest and saw no
conflict between individuals pursuing their own desires and
societal needs. He felt that an individual who "intends only
his own gain...is led by an invisible hand to promote...the
public interest".

To summarize, at the heart of capitalism is the
following.

* #19 THE ECONOMIC MAN WORLDVIEW *

*As a creature in the economic jungle, pursue your own
gain or predators will take advantage of you. The great
market system demands your participation. As you compete, let
self-interest guide your accumulation of wealth and power.
Rationally weigh various options with your own well being in
mind. Don't try to do good. Out of selfishness will naturally
emerge a situation "most agreeable to the interest of the
whole society".*

This provides quite a contrast with the religion-
inspired "The Family of Man / Other People Orientation"
(theme #16). Paradoxically, capitalism was largely created by
deeply religious Christians--Calvinists and Puritans. They
formulated their ideas rationally within the framework of a
moral conscience. As time passed however, their rationality
triumphed and the conscience disappeared, argued German
sociologist Max Weber (1864-1920). Weber prophecized that
while the Puritans had regarded possessions as a "thin coat"
which could easily be cast aside, eventually they would become a "steel cage" from which the spirit had flown. He
wondered what would live in that cage in the future?

IV. AMERICAN HISTORY--ELITISTS VS. POPULISTS

In 1776, Adam Smith's classic The Wealth of Nations was
published. Across the ocean from England another people was
forging a new nation. "We hold these truths to be self-
evident that all men are created equal..." said their declaration of independence from the rule of an English king.
Thomas Paine, in Common Sense , had called on Americans to
cast off kings altogether. "Of more worth is one honest man
to society ...than all the crowned ruffians that ever lived"
he wrote.

Despite such sentiments, many Americans would have
gladly accepted their military leader George Washington as
King. Even in the 1790s, Thomas Jefferson worried that forces
led by Alexander Hamilton sought central authoritarian rule,
either by concentrating power in the chief executive or by
establishing a monarchy. Jefferson feared Hamilton was
grooming bankers, stockjobbers, and merchants for roles in an
"American House of Lords", which would prop up a monarchy.

Hamilton feared democratic elections conducted by
"flattering the prejudices of the people and exciting their
jealousies and apprehensions, to throw affairs into
confusion". Jefferson trusted "the good sense of the people".
Democracy would work, he felt, if people were properly
educated and truthfully informed. Jefferson put his faith in
man as "a rational animal, endowed by nature with rights, and
with an innate sense of justice", laissez faire economics (he
thought highly of Adam Smith), and the land. For him,
happiness was tied to family farming. He joyfully contemplated an America built on people proudly beholding their
land and saying, "This is mine and it will be my children's."

While the Hamilton - Jefferson quarrel is often portrayed as a conflict between advocates of a strong central
government vs. states' rights diehards, or as a battle between big city capitalists and devotees of an agrarian-based
economy, fundamentally it was based on a collision of two
differing worldviews.

* #20 THE ELITIST WORLDVIEW *

*The masses of common people are incapable of deciding
what is best for society. Assemblies of such people are not
to be trusted. Their collective strength is to be feared and
opposed. Society is best served by a select few clear-
sighted, capable masters who direct the masses toward
appropriate ends.*

* #21 THE POPULIST WORLDVIEW *

*Put your confidence in the continuing education of the
people and their collective wisdom. Identify with hard-
working common people, cherish their struggles and aspirations. They are (in Jefferson's words) "the most honest and
safe...depository of the public interests".*

Contrary to Jefferson's hopes, America was not to remain a
nation of predominantly small, agriculturally-based towns and
surrounding farms.

V. THE CONQUEST OF THE AMERICAN ECONOMY

By the mid 19th century, about 50 years behind England,
the Industrial Revolution caught fire in America. Labor
shifted from the agricultural to manufacturing sectors. New
machines and methods increased productivity, and rapid
American economic expansion began. The great cities grew
quickly as people left farms and small towns, and immigrants
left the Old World for the New.

The village community one-to-one human scale of economic
enterprise was slowly replaced. Much larger, impersonal
organizations, with different concerns, moved in. Initially
these corporate endeavors were often guided by one man
pursuing the practical implementation of his own methods or
invention. Later this individual-in-charge nature of American
companies would change. Regardless of who was in charge, the
battle to come would not be a nearly equal meeting of mere
individuals.

Linking efficiency, new technology, and analytical
problem solving skills with the power of American
businessmen, a well-organized corporate army easily defeated

the virtuous but unsophisticated American people on the economic battlefields of the late 19th and early 20th centuries.
Typically these predatory capitalists simply encouraged the
division of any organized opposition into individuals defined
by self-interest and prejudices. This strategy proved effective against big business' opponents. Although many participants in these labor struggles--the Wobblies, the Molly
MacGuires, the Western Federation of Miners, the Haymarket
martyrs, the immigrants, the women's shirtwaistmakers--
inspired millions with their courage and solidarity, these
early unions were often ruthlessly overwhelmed.

The conquest of a previously free economy by a new
aristocracy of "robber barons" brought a new era dominated by
monopoly capitalism. An America of small towns and frontier
villages, one of warm, spontaneous, burgeoning life based on
nature and community, was transformed into an urban, corporate world of time clocks, assembly lines, managers, marketing techniques, and cold, clean, order where a few individuals might "get ahead". The trend was toward ever bigger,
increasingly technologically sophisticated empires, many
built through corporate merger. By 1910, 1 % of all the
country's business firms produced 44 % of its manufactured
goods. This trend was not limited to industrial manufacturing, agriculture was reshaped as farms became bigger and
more mechanized.

The Depression of the 1930s interrupted the growth: in
but four years production fell 50 % and unemployment
increased by eight times. The decade changed the American
economic scene in other ways. A "Big Labor" emerged to
sometimes counterbalance the interests of "Big Business". The
government, which had previously remained in the economic
background, now entered the scene. The "laissez faire" days
were over. Various forms of public insurance and some built-
in stabilizers to protect against future crashes were
legislated. These brought increased business regulation and
new taxation. However, despite much rhetoric, there was
little redistribution of wealth. Instead, the government
intervention precedent would later have another effect: the
government would intercede frequently on behalf of American
corporate interests, both domestically and around the world.

VI. AMERICAN ECONOMY--INTERNATIONALIZATION

American economic activities became increasingly spread

out around the world. American businessmen had pioneered in developing the multinational corporation--a company that operates in several countries but is incorporated in only one country. Its foreign business is conducted through sales offices, subsidiaries, and foreign affiliates. By using various intracompany transfers, playing "tax games", and "exchange rate games", multinationals can maximize profits. These companies are sometimes characterized as making their products in countries where production costs are least and registering their profits in countries where taxes are least.

Around 1900, a few U.S. based multinational companies were engaged primarily in overseas agricultural plantation, railway, or mining operations, but since World War II most foreign investments have been in manufacturing. Between 1945 and 1970, the real value of multinational sales increased by an average 10 % per year. By 1970, of the top hundred U.S. industrial firms, two-thirds had production facilities in at least six nations.

By then many people were viewing these companies with alarm. The charges leveled at multinationals included,
1) They were answerable to no sovereign authority;
2) They were conducting their own foreign policy or unduly influencing U.S. foreign policy;
3) They were exporting American jobs overseas;
4) They were exploiting undeveloped nations;
5) They were helping to precipitate world currency crises.

By the time these concerns were voiced, a quarter century of post war growth had brought America unparalleled material prosperity. By then, Americans--as participants in a highly complex system of interdependencies known as the global economy--both depended on products and were affected by decisions originating in foreign lands. The dramatic price escalation and shortages of gasoline and heating oil in late 1973 (and again in 1979)--partly due to decisions made in the Middle East--taught this lesson in a way people would not soon forget.

VII. ECONOMICS AS SCIENCE / AS IF PEOPLE MATTERED

In 1969, the first Nobel prize for "economic science" was awarded. In justifying the award, the Nobel committee observed that "economic science has developed increasingly in the direction of...mathematical specification and statistical quantification" and pronounced that economic analytical techniques had "proved successful". Few who considered this justification questioned the notion that economics was anything but a rigorous science.

There was one economist with solid credentials who took issue with the views of the Nobel committee. E.F. Schumacher, in his 1973 counterculture classic <u>Small</u> <u>is</u> <u>Beautiful</u> noted that,

> The great majority of economists is still pursuing the absurd ideal of making their "science" as scientific and precise as physics, as if there were no qualitative difference between mindless atoms and men...

His alternative to this trend was best summarized in the subtitle of his book--"Economics as if People Mattered".

Before considering Schumacher's economics and contrasting it with traditional economic thinking, we summarize the latter by spelling out the worldview of those embracing it. Because the key word for most economists is "growth", we identify this viewpoint as "expansionist".

* #22 THE EXPANSIONIST WORLDVIEW *

A healthy economy is one whose production of goods and services, per capita consumption, jobs, and energy use is growing due to proper functioning of market system forces. Because they interfere with these forces, attempts to right wrongs by redistributing wealth are flawed. Instead of dividing the "economic pie", letting it grow will eventually result in everyone getting a big enough piece. While problems posed by environmental degradation, resource depletion, and increasing population are formidable, government and corporate planners--backed by scientific and technological expertise--are up to the challenge. While some economic activities undoubtedly will need to be redirected to address these problems, no fundamental changes are required.

Schumacher faulted economists and entrepreneurs holding this worldview for various reasons, including:

1) They fail to distinguish between fundamentally different types of goods: non-renewable resources (of which no more are being made) and renewable resources (ultimately, solar energy based).

2) They generally ignore what they can not readily assign a monetary value to.

3) They employ whatever technical means available to further their acquisition of wealth--regardless of possible negative social or environmental effects. Little attention is paid to

real needs and aspirations.

4) They fail to consider the most appropriate scale of an activity, presuming always that "bigger is better" and "to prosper one must grow".

The "small is beautiful" philosophy is based on the appreciation of limitations and human needs. Schumacher's book reflected his admiration of Gandhi's philosophy and village-based economics. Gandhi taught, "Earth provides enough to satisfy every man's need, but not enough for every man's greed", and emphasized the value of "production by the masses" instead of mass production.

In a chapter entitled "Buddhist Economics" Schumacher wrote,

> The modern economist...is used to measuring the "standard of living" by the amount of annual consumption, assuming all the time that a man who consumes more is "better off" than a man who consumes less. A Buddhist economist would consider this approach excessively irrational: since consumption is merely a means to human well being, the aim should be to obtain the maximum of well being with the minimum of consumption.

His teachings comprise a philosophy of enoughness. After noting "There are poor societies which have too little", he asked, "Where is the rich society that says 'Halt! We have enough!?'...There is none!" he concluded.

E.F. Schumacher was an important contributor to a worldview diametrically opposed to the "Expansionist" viewpoint. This can be called the "Sustainable Worldview" and summarized as follows:

* #23 SUSTAINABLE WORLDVIEW *

Continued, unrestrained economic growth threatens the integrity of the Earth's biosphere. Ultimately, only economic activities which are sustainable on a long-term basis should be permitted. Restructuring economies into stable steady state systems based on technologies with a human face, renewable energy use, and resource recycling is needed. Redistributing wealth is needed to foster community and long-term stability. These actions are necessary to avert disasters of various types. Making this transition will depend on changes in value systems and lifestyles and fostering long-term global perspectives.

VIII. THE TARNISHING OF THE AMERICAN DREAM

In America, the 1960s and early 1970s were characterized by social upheaval and widespread questioning of fundamental beliefs and entrenched institutions. The Vietnam War raised questions about American meddling in other nations' affairs. Environmentalists worried about ecosystems breaking down under the mounting impact of pollution and waste. Many questioned the need for continued economic growth. One critic charged that, for some, the American Dream was "to convert goods to trash as fast as possible". Another, Yale professor Charles Reich, saw individuals threatened by the environmental, social, and spiritual costs of continued 'economic progress'. He felt Americans no longer found self expression in their work and were alienated "as money, not inner needs, called the tune".

During the same decade that American technological and productive genius put a man on the moon, many pointed out environmental and ethical flaws in technology-based solutions to problems. While those subscribing to the "Expansionist Worldview" possessed a "technological fix" mentality, those adopting the "Sustainable Worldview" typically preferred "attitudinal fixes". Not surprisingly, the two camps differed over the best way to end the Vietnam War. One side sought a military solution, the other a troop withdrawal in recognition of a changing American attitude toward the war.

During these years, millions of Americans traded their faith in technology for faith in people's abilities to choose wisely. Transformations of "Expansionist Worldviews" into "Sustainable Worldviews" were widespread. Some, like Schumacher, built their worldviews on a foundation of traditional religious wisdom. From Jesus' Sermon on the Mount beatitude, "Blessed are those of gentle spirit, they shall have the earth for their possession", he concluded, "We need a gentle approach, a non-violent spirit, and small is beautiful." Others found the "Mystical / Eastern / New Age Worldview" (theme #7) and the "Sustainable Worldview" highly compatible. Many made a break with their former livelihoods and opted out of--as they saw it--the economic jungle in which only the greediest prospered, and pursued a non-materialistic, healthy, non-competitive lifestyle.

In the 1970s, an estimated 5 to 15 million Americans (according to the Stanford Research Institute) were limiting their consumption and either totally or partially practicing "voluntary simplicity". Food co-ops and other worker-owned businesses sprung up in cities, while a "back to the land" movement revitalized rural America. Many of those who fled to the countryside, fearing societal breakdown, embraced small farm self sufficiency and independence. Others found communal living situations.

While some responded to the tarnishing of the American dream with a co-operation-based / respect for the environment and other people orientation, others responded differently. Instead of blaming corporate America, they blamed the welfare state. In place of co-operation and restraint, they embraced "the virtue of selfishness". They worshipped laissez faire capitalism and private property and abhorred socialism.

In socialist nations the government owns all resources. Its planners co-ordinate production and distribute benefits accruing from production according to individual need. Workers labor--not for personal gain--but for the social good.

By the late 1950s, many blamed America's problems on "creeping socialism". Ayn Rand, a popularizer of the libertarian philosophy, attacked "the morality of sacrifice". In her 1957 novel <u>Atlas</u> <u>Shrugged</u> she charged,

> You let them infect you with the worship of need--and
> this country became a giant in body with a mooching
> midget in place of its soul...We will rebuild America's
> system on the moral premise...that man is an end in
> himself, not the means to the ends of others...

Ayn Rand grew up in the Soviet Union and emigrated to the United States in the 1930s. There she became disturbed that many intellectuals considered only Soviet methods to be evil and continued to believe communist ideals were noble. Her books attack these ideals and socialist programs for using private property for the public welfare. By the 1970s, other authors had similarly popularized libertarian thinking, including Robert Ringer's 1977 <u>Looking</u> <u>Out</u> <u>For</u> <u>Number</u> <u>One.</u>

In 1980 a powerful spokesman for the market system and the great law of self-interest upon which it is based was elected U.S. president: Ronald Reagan. Libertarians cheered his election. The nation's mood--at least that conveyed by the national media--changed. One reporter, in a mid-1983 article[3], captured the essence of this change:

> Americans are once again doing their own thing. In the
> late 1970s people in droves were assiduously devoting
> themselves to the simple life, trying to prove

that less is more. In 1981, with the advent of the
Reagan Administration, wealth was back in style. People
who had it were flaunting it, following the latest high
fashions and proving that more is more.

The other-oriented were dismayed. By 1985, one would
report[4],

> Reagan has emerged as the avatar of a new age of
> narcissism, where the pursuit of happiness has been
> reduced to the ruthless pursuit of money. What hedonism
> and unbridled capitalism have in common is the
> repudiation of the social contract. When conservatives
> say "Me"...they mean me, myself, and mine. They don't
> mean anything as altruistic as an interest group, which
> inevitably means others.

Liberal Democrats were upset. By 1987, retired House Speaker
Tip O'Neill would write, "I blame the president for allowing
selfishness to become respectable." Environmentalists were at
times frantic. As one analyst[5] would describe it,

> Socialists, liberals, and conservatives believe that
> unregulated capitalism poses a threat to the natural
> environment in which we live. By contrast, libertarians
> and Reagan Republicans share a kind of utopian faith in
> capitalism's beneficence toward mankind and nature--a
> faith not unrelated to a pre-occupation with the balance
> sheet and the bottom line.

Still, during the Reagan years much of the country was
upbeat. Rebounding from the energy shortages of the 1970s and
the early 1980s recession, Americans who once dreamed of
their own palace of abundance had their hopes renewed.

IX. GLOBAL INTERCONNECTIONS

An American college professor's lesson for the day
centers on a commonplace item: a simple incandescent light
bulb. He begins by naming the various components of the light
bulb--there are seven. Next, he lists the raw materials used
to make these components--his brief summary cites 13--and
specifies where they are obtained. Besides U.S. mining
locations, he cites 27 other countries as sources of the raw
materials. Finally, he considers the energy consumed in
manufacturing and using these light bulbs. His formal lecture
ends. Students are asked to attach meaning to his presentation. Written responses are followed by discussion.

Symbolizing manufactured objects used by our society,

the light bulb is a not so simple product of a complex, globally dispersed technological enterprise. As professor Lynn Brant notes,[6]

> The simple purchase, use, and disposal of a common light bulb involves the person in international trade, world politics, and in the very lives of persons living far away. The user is also responsible for the use of non-renewable resources and the production of waste materials, some of which become pollutants.

His efforts have opened students' eyes to the economic relationships that connect them to people around the world.

As the 1980s began, the United States depended on 25 other nations for more than half of its supply of strategic minerals. By the decade's end, U.S. based multinational corporations were doing 25 % of their manufacturing outside the U.S. The increasingly global economy is aided by an electronic communications grid which links together an ever growing percentage of the world's people. Nearly $100 trillion/year in electronic fund transfers--made via satellite or cable connection--are the life-blood of this global marketplace.

As the world economy grew, driven by the great law of economic self-interest, environmental problems of a global nature arose as the scale of human activities approached limits imposed by natural laws. While conventional economists and corporate planners slowly began factoring environmental impacts into their thinking, a powerful force increasingly demanded this be done: self-interest. So by 1989, radical environmentalists would be photographed demonstrating in front of a multinational timber company with a banner reading, "There are no jobs on a dead planet". And Donella Meadows would pen the following article.

Biodiversity--In Our Own Interest, by Donella H. Meadows
Most of us have grasped the idea that there's a hole in the sky over the South Pole that could give us skin cancer. We are beginning to understand that a global warming could inundate Miami Beach and make New York even more unbearable in summer. There is another environmental problem, however, that doesn't have a catchy name like "ozone hole" or "green-house effect", and that hasn't yet entered the public con-sciousness. It's the loss of biodiversity.
Bio-WHAT?

Biodiversity sounds like it has to do with pandas and tigers and tropical rainforests. It does, but it's bigger than those, bigger than a single species or even a single ecosystem. It's the whole, all of life, the microscopic creepy-crawlies as well as the elephants and condors. It's all the habitats, beautiful or not, that support life--the tundra, prairie, and swamps, as well as the tropical forest.

Why care about tundras and swamps? There's one good reason--self-interest. Preserving biodiversity is not something to do out of the kindness of our hearts, to express our fondness for fuzzy creatures on Sunday mornings when we happen to feel virtuous. It's something to do to maintain the many forms of life we eat and use, and to maintain ourselves.

How would you like the job of pollinating all trillion or so apple blossoms in New York State some sunny afternoon in late May? It's conceivable, maybe, that you could invent a machine to do it, but inconceivable that the machine could work as efficiently, elegantly, and cheaply as the honeybee-- much less make honey.

Suppose you were assigned to turn every bit of dead organic matter, from fallen leaves to urban garbage to road kills, into nutrients that feed new life. Even if you knew how, what would it cost? Uncountable numbers of bacteria, molds, mites, and worms do it for free. If they ever stopped, all life would stop. We would not last long if a few beneficial kinds of soil bacteria stopped turning nitrogen from the air into fertilizer.

Human reckoning cannot put a value on the services performed for us by the millions of species of life on earth. In addition to pollination and recycling, these services include flood control, drought prevention, pest control, temperature regulation, and maintenance of the world's most valuable library--the genes of all living organisms--a library we are just learning to read.

Another thing we are just learning is that both the genetic library and the ecosystem's services depend on the integrity of the entire biological world. All species fit together in an intricate, interdependent, self-sustaining whole. Rips in the biological fabric tend to run. Gaps cause things to fall apart in unexpected ways.

For example, attempts to replant acacia trees in the Sahel have failed, because the degraded soil has lost a bacterium called rhizobium, without which acacia trees can't

grow. Songbirds that eat summer insects in North America are
declining because of deforestation in their Central American
wintering grounds. European forests are more vulnerable to
acid rain than American forests, because they are human-
managed single-species plantations rather than natural
mixtures of many species forming an interknit, resilient
system.

Biodiversity cannot be maintained by protecting a few
favorite animals in a zoo. Nor by preserving a few greenbelts
or even large national parks. Biodiversity can maintain itself, however, without human attention or expense, without
zookeepers, park rangers, foresters, or refrigerated gene
banks. All it needs is to be left alone.

It is not being left alone, of course, which is why biological impoverishment has become a problem of global dimensions. There is hardly a place left on earth where people do
not log, pave, spray, drain, flood, graze, fish, plow, burn,
drill, spill, or dump.

Biologist Paul Ehrlich estimates that human beings
usurp, directly or indirectly, about 40 % of each year's
total biological production (and our population is on its way
to another doubling in 40 years). There is no biome, with the
possible exception of the deep ocean, that we are not degrad-
ing. In poor countries, biodiversity is being nickeled and
dimed to death; in rich countries it is being billion-dol-
lared to death.

To provide their priceless service to us, the honeybees
ask only that we stop saturating the landscape with poisons,
stop paving the meadows and verges where bee-food grows, and
leave them enough honey to get through the winter.

To maintain our planet and our lives, the other species
have similar requests, all of which add up to: Control yourselves. Control your numbers. Control your greed. See yourselves as what you are, part of an interdependent biological
community, the most intelligent part, though you don't often
act that way. Act that way. Do so either out of moral respect
for something wonderful that you did not create and do not
understand, or out of practical interest in your own
survival.

X. RESTORING PLANETARY HEALTH

After much self-indulgent partying, the patient doesn't
feel right. An economist is called in to restore health--but

basically finds nothing wrong. He does suggest fine tuning and prescribes the usual "More of the Same" medication. The patient questions his diagnosis. He replies, "Look, all the indicators suggest that, fundamentally, you're healthy. And when everyone's having a ball, who wants to stop the music?"[7]

The economist is sent away. The patient has a hunch and surmises, "The house I've lived in for so long is now making me sick". An ecologist, one who literally studies organisms in their house, is summoned.

After hearing the ailments described, the ecologist thinks, "My patient knows little about this house." She pulls a bottle out of her doctoring bag and says, "Take two of these and I'll see you in the morning." The patient looks at the medication and its "Control Yourself" label. "I think I know what ails you", the ecologist continues, "but I need to help you understand how your house is built and functions. Then you can do a better job of telling me what's wrong."

Questions & Projects

1. In his 1924 book <u>Religion</u> <u>and</u> <u>the</u> <u>Rise</u> <u>of</u> <u>Capitalism,</u> R.H. Tawney wrote, "If...economic ambitions are good servants they are bad masters." Discuss.

2. Sociologist Amitai Etzioni challenges three assumptions behind the Economic Man worldview that capitalism is based on. He charges that we don't act as individuals, we don't always act rationally, and that our moral convictions can't be collapsed into pleasure seeking. Discuss.

3. According to University of Lowell sociology professor Shirley Kolack[8], Alexander Hamilton's vision of America prospering through manufacturing and trade was first tested in Lowell, Massachusetts. Life in the early 19th century village, where "they lived as Thomas Jefferson extolled people to live--a slow-paced existence tuned to the seasons with every household an independent unit", changed dramatically over the next century as "indus-trialization eroded the social foundations of the rural countryside." Report.

4. The American dream has meant different things to people: to some achieving a dignified human community, to others realizing the full potential of freedom, to many a rags to riches transformation. What does the American dream mean to you?

5. Compose contrasting populist and elitist reactions to the

following news items:
   a) voter participation in the election decreased sharply
   b) a grassroots organization demands a seat on a corporate
      board
   c) critics charge that only the rich will be able to
      attend the private university if a proposed tuition
      hike is approved
   d) a request filed under the Freedom of Information Act
      is denied
   e) a new law limits individual contributions to political
      campaigns
6. Pick a large multinational corporation and investigate the
   extent to which its manufacturing plants, sales offices,
   R & D labs, etc. are spread out around the world.
7. Characterize the following as supporting either
   sustainable or expansionist worldview themes:
   a) She wants something, gets it, isn't really happy, and
      wants something more.
   b) "I'm not concerned with resource depletion--there are
      asteroids out there with $1 trillion of raw materials"
   c) Fearing more drought and declining water tables, the
      county board would not issue permits to drill new wells
      or allow new customers to hook up to municipal water.
8. Does the "Sustainable Worldview" (theme #23) maintain a no
   growth orientation? Discuss.
9. In Home Economics,[9] Wendell Berry writes, "...economics
   has strayed far from any idea of home, either the world or
   the world's natural ecosystems and human households." He
   longs for "an economy that does not leave anything out"--
   a "Great Economy" which, like nature, allows no book-keeping errors and whose end we can not foresee. He notes,
   "The difference between the Great Economy and any human
   economy is pretty much the difference between the goose
   that laid the golden egg and the golden egg." Explain.
10. How the food you eat reaches you provides another example
    of the workings of a complex technological enterprise.
    One study found the "average food molecule" traveled 1300
    miles before it was eaten. Investigate where your food
    comes from. What percentage originates locally? Report.
11. Relate the "who wants to stop the music" quote to
    difficulties American politicians have in confronting the
    budget deficit.
12. Ronald Reagan fan and British Prime Minister Margaret

Thatcher once remarked, "There is no such thing as society--only individuals." Discuss.

13. Virginia Postrel, editor of the libertarian magazine <u>Reason</u>, argues[10] that the future's important political battles will involve growth vs. green--"the proponents of economic dynamism and the advocates of stasis (or sustainability)..."--rather than left vs. right. Discuss.

14. An Earth First! bumpersticker reads "Subvert the dominant paradigm". Explain.

15. During the 1920s and 30s, U.S. foreign policies were generally isolationist. In today's economically and environmentally interrelated world, would such policies be outmoded? Discuss.

16. Less than 1 % of the world's plant species have been investigated as to potential value to humans. Provide examples of pharmaceutical drugs derived from plants.

Notes

1. Heilbroner, Robert, <u>The Worldly Philosophers</u> , Simon and Schuster, New York 1972
2. McNeil, W. <u>The Rise of the West</u>, Doubleday, NY, 1962
3. "Lifestyles of the 1980s: Anything Goes!", <u>U.S. News & World Report</u> , August 1, 1983.
4. Blumenthal, S. "The G.O.P. 'Me Decade'", <u>The New Republic</u> September 17-24, 1984.
5. Judis, J. "Confessions of a Socialist Conservative", <u>New Oxford Review,</u> October, 1987.
6. Brant, L. "The Light Bulb as a Symbol of the Connectedness in STS", <u>Bull. Sci. Tech. Soc.</u> Vol. 8, pp.419-423, 1988.
7. the last sentence appeared in MacLennon, H. <u>Voices in Time</u> MacMillian of Canada, 1980.
8. Kolack, S. "The Impact of Technology on Democratic Values: The Case of Lowell, Massachusetts", <u>Bull. Sci. Tech. Soc.</u> pp.405-410, 1988.
9. Berry, W. <u>Home Economics</u>, North Point Press, San Francisco 1987.
10. <u>Utne Reader</u>, No. 40, pp. 57-58, July / August 1990.

NUMBERS & CYCLES

I. EARTH DAY, 1970

In April, 1970, millions of Americans demonstrated their concern about human activities disrupting planetary life support systems, and participated in the first Earth Day. Throughout the country, speakers offered diverse opinions as to the cause of the environmental crisis and prescriptions for solving it. One theme, common to many Earth Day speakers, might be expressed, "Environmental problems result when man disrupts natural cycles."

Most Americans, caught up in a linear "buy it--use it-- throw it away" mentality, hardly knew what natural cycles were. Scientific American magazine sought to dispel its readers ignorance of such things. Its September, 1970 issue was devoted to Earth's chemical cycles and food chains.

II. EARTH'S BIOSPHERE--AN OVERVIEW

Using simple concepts, the Earth can be characterized as existing in three basic phases--1) a solid lithosphere, 2) a liquid hydrosphere, and 3) a gaseous atmosphere--held together by gravity and depending on the energy input of a medium-sized star 93 million miles away. Life on Earth exists within the thin (about nine mile thick) spherical shell that lies at the intersection of these three phases. This is known as the biosphere.

Within the biosphere are various self-sustaining communities of organisms--microbe, plant, and animal--each related to some unifying environmental factors and functioning as an ecosystem. The various components of an ecosystem are connected by two major processes: chemical cycling and energy flow. Fig. #17 shows a typical example.

As Fig. #17 indicates, roughly one percent of available solar energy is actually utilized by photosynthesis. While the sun's radiant energy builds the molecules--proteins, carbohydrates, lipids-- that make up diverse living things, ultimately this energy dissipates as heat. Whereas the periodic chart contains over 100 chemical elements, ecologists sometimes define the biosphere as the locus of interaction of just six of them: hydrogen, carbon, nitrogen, oxygen, phosphorus, and sulfur. These elements dominate the chemistry important to living things. Life processes depend on the cycling of these elements and the flow of energy

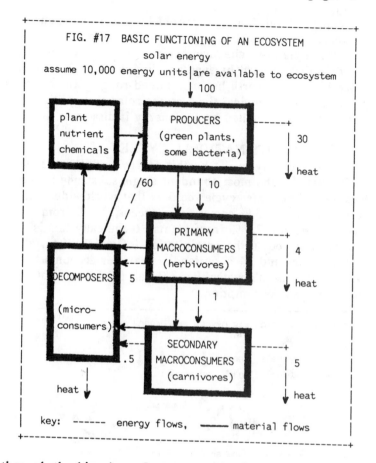

FIG. #17 BASIC FUNCTIONING OF AN ECOSYSTEM

through the biosphere. Let us consider in turn the gross energy flow and each of these chemical cycles.

About 150,000,000 trillion kilowatt-hours of solar energy are intercepted by the Earth each year. About 25 % (depending on cloud cover) never reaches the Earth's surface but is reflected back into space. 25 % of the incident sunshine is absorbed in the atmosphere--including dangerous ultraviolet radiation which is soaked up by an unusual molecular form of oxygen, ozone (O_3). Around 5 % is reflected from the Earth's surface, while the remaining 45 % is absorbed there. Some of this evaporates water and drives the water cycle; the rest is re-radiated as longer wavelength, infra-red heat energy. Some of this escapes to space, some is trapped in the atmosphere (mostly by water vapor and carbon dioxide) producing a mild greenhouse effect. A very small percentage of sunshine is captured by green plants and converted to chemical energy via photosynthesis.

Unlike nature's chemical cycles, energy flows in only one direction: toward its eventual dissipation as low grade, waste heat. The Earth has maintained roughly the same temperature over geological time, so the solar energy it receives must be matched by the energy it dissipates to space.

III. THE EARTH'S NATURAL CYCLES

Linked closely to the Earth's energy budget is its water cycle. Water is the most abundant single substance in the biosphere. The water cycle requires that worldwide evaporation (of which 85 % comes from oceans, 7.5 % from soil / fresh water, and 7.5 % from plants--technically this is transpiration) equal the precipitation (of which 76 % falls on the oceans and 24 % on land). Seawater accounts for about 97 % of the Earth's water. Its .3 % salt (NaCl) content precludes human consumption.

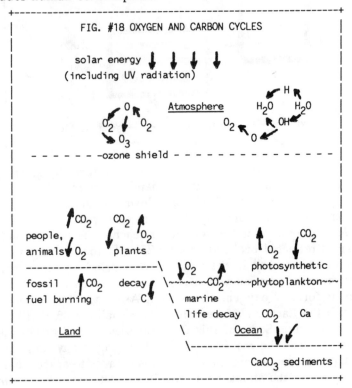

FIG. #18 OXYGEN AND CARBON CYCLES

About one-fourth of the atoms in living matter are oxygen. 21 % of the atmosphere is free oxygen (O_2), a constant percentage maintained as the oxygen consumed by animals, bacteria, and chemical processes is balanced by that released by photosynthetic plants. One can hardly separate the oxygen cycle from the carbon cycle (see Fig. #18), nor can either be considered separate from photosynthesis and respiration. In photosynthesis, plants pull carbon dioxide from the air, water from the ground, and utilize solar energy to form carbohydrates and release oxygen:

$$6CO_2 + 12H_2O + energy ---> C_6H_{12}O_6 + 6H_2O + 6O_2$$

In the opposite process, respiration, carbohydrates are "burned" releasing carbon dioxide and energy while oxygen is consumed:

$$C_6H_{12}O_6 + 6O_2 ---> 6CO_2 + 6H_2O + energy$$

This process is crucial to animals that breathe. Carbon cycling in the biosphere involves two distinct cycles--one on land, another in the ocean (see Fig. #18).

Nitrogen makes up 78 % of the atmosphere, but unlike oxygen it is relatively inert. Despite its seeming abundance, the human food supply is more limited by the availability of nitrogen than any other plant nutrient. This is because

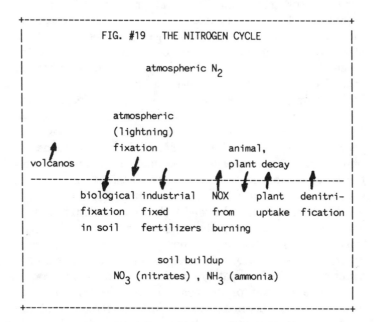

FIG. #19   THE NITROGEN CYCLE

atmospheric N_2

atmospheric (lightning) fixation

animal, plant decay

volcanos

biological fixation in soil   industrial fixed fertilizers   NOX from burning   plant uptake   denitrification

soil buildup
NO_3 (nitrates) , NH_3 (ammonia)

atmospheric nitrogen (N_2) must be converted (or "fixed") into chemical compounds that can be utilized by plants. In nature, micro-organisms and nitrogen fixing legumes are responsible for this biological fixation which produces plant proteins (Fig. #19). These are eaten by animals and ultimately return to the soil, either in animal waste or after death. There, denitrifying bacteria liberate free nitrogen completing the cycle. Both nitrifying and denitrifying bacteria rely on converting nitrogen compounds to other forms for the energy they need to survive. These little-known--but very important-- micro-organisms are crucial to supplying the protein and amino acids people need.

A different group of bacteria can similarly exploit sulfur-containing compounds. These are the basis for the sulfur cycle. Sulfur is essential to the proper functioning of protein molecules since it helps them maintain their three-dimensional shape. There are inorganic contributors to the sulfur cycle. Each year, volcanos, ocean spray, wetlands, and tidal flats release millions of tons of sulfur to the atmosphere. Sulfur's atmospheric presence is in the form of sulfur dioxide (SO_2), and hydrogen sulfide (H_2S).

The last of the six important elements, phosphorus, occurs in soil, rock, and living things as phosphates (containing PO_4). Phosphates from the soil are absorbed by plant roots and converted into organic compounds. These are eaten by animals and returned to the soil--in organic form-- when the animal or plant dies. Also, phosphates which are eroded or dissolved from soil eventually end up in the ocean. While some phosphates are used by marine life, most are incorporated into deep sea sediments and lost from the cycle. Eventually geologic uplift processes, taking millions of years, return them to the surface. In living organisms, phosphorus is an important constituent of both DNA and ATP, the latter critical to cellular energy transfers. Phosphorus shortages are often what constitute soil infertility.

While these six lightweight elements dominate the chemistry of life, other elements are important--if only in trace amounts. Generally, as one proceeds down the periodic chart, the elements become less essential to proper biosphere functioning. Unfortunately, the heaviest elements pose certain dangers. Many of the heavy metals--cadmium, mercury, lead, etc.--are chemically toxic. And the tendency of the very heaviest elements--radium, uranium, plutonium, etc.--to break apart constitutes a radioactive threat. Only in the last half-century, due to human meddling, has the biosphere been threatened with the nuclear fuel cycle.

After reviewing "Mineral Cycles", E.S. Deevey concluded his September, 1970 <u>Scientific</u> <u>American</u> article by recognizing "the necessity of a global view of biochemistry". To underscore the importance of better understanding the chemical cycles of the six key elements, he wrote,

> There is a unique and nearly ubiquitous compound, with the empirical formula $H_{2960}O_{1480}C_{1480}N_{16}P_{1.8}S$. Its synthesis...is the most intricate feat of chemical engineering ever performed--and the most delicate operation that people have ever tampered with.

IV. SPACESHIP EARTH--EARLY 1970S

1973 is ending. Viewed globally from a human perspective, it has been a difficult year. A widespread drought and famine in Africa meant death and misery for millions. Many in developed countries fear oil shortages and projected fuel price increases.

A few people have broadened their perspective and now think of where they live as "Spaceship Earth". One writer[1] uses this metaphor in summarizing the human situation. He imagines a captain giving a report which begins,

> Passengers on Terra I...it is time for you to hear the annual State of the Spaceship report...Let me briefly summarize the state of our passengers and of our life support system. 1/4 of you have occupied the good to luxurious quarters in the tourist and first class sections. You have used about 70 to 80 % (some say 90 %) of all supplies available this past year....I am saddened to say that things have not really improved this year for the 75 % of our passengers traveling in the hold. Over 1/3 of you are suffering from hunger, malnutrition, or both, and 3/4 of you do not have adequate water or shelter. More people died from starvation this year than at any time in the history of our voyage...

The report to the 3.8 billion people aboard Spaceship Earth continues. The captain notes that Americans--but 5.5 % of the population--used 35 % of supplies, produced 1/2 of the global man-made pollution, and had 25 to 50 times as much impact on the spacecraft's life support systems as did passengers in the hold. He notes that some engineers think the ship's resources and recycling systems can support at most 10 to 15 billion people, while others think numbers are already too large for all to live comfortably with freedom and dignity.

The report ends on a note of crisis. But along with warning of dangers ahead, the message conveys hope that someday humans can "learn to live together in co-operation and peace".

From this report and the hypothetical scenarios its author constructs in reaction to it, we glimpse a worldview far more prevalent than Western affluence-based outlooks.

* #24 THE SURVIVAL-ORIENTED WORLDVIEW *

For my family, life is a struggle to provide basic necessities--food, clean water, clothing and shoes, shelter, heat when it's cold--and to maintain fields, animals, tools, roads, and transportation so we can continue to survive. Hot and cold running water, indoor toilet facilities, refrigeration, bright light at night, heat and air conditioning at the turn of a knob, household entertainment from television and radio, a telephone, cooking without first making a wood, charcoal, or dung-based fire--these are luxuries of rich people. We are poor materially, but we are a close family. We have happy moments despite a tiring struggle and often weakened condition. But a cloud, an unsettling feeling hangs over us. There is fear within us. We know that somewhere slow painful death lurks nearby--ready to strike us when we are down. For we have seen it before.

We might imagine that, to supplement his report, the captain submits numerical data pertaining to the Spaceship Earth situation--including what appears in Fig. #20.[2] Of course these numbers tell us nothing of human misery--of what it's like for the 2/3 of mankind who exist on less than 30 cents a day, about the suffering of millions in poor countries who toil under a broiling sun from dawn to dusk for miserable rewards and premature death and never learn why-- but they are of some use.

The per capita income ratio between rich and poor-- obtained by comparing the figures for rich capitalist nations and poorest 1/4 of humanity--i.e. $3893 to $105--is 37 to 1. World military spending--$242 billion/year-- is 2.6 times the total annual GNP of the world's poorest quarter.

Despite the gloomy quantitative and qualitative assess-

```
+--------------------------------------------------------+
|       FIG. #20  1970 SPACESHIP EARTH ECONOMIC SUMMARY   |
|                                                        |
|              POPULATION    GROSS NAT.PROD   GNP/CAPITA  |
|              billions  %  $U.S.trillions  %  $U.S./person |
|                                                        |
|  World total  3.68  100      3.97      100     1079    |
|                                                        |
|  Rich,         .60   16      2.32       58     3893    |
|  Capitalist                                            |
|                                                        |
|  Middle       1.35   37      1.41       36     1044    |
|                                                        |
|  Poor,         .85   23      .158        4      186    |
|  Developing                                            |
|                                                        |
|  Poorest,      .89   24      .093        2      105    |
|  Developing                                            |
|                                                        |
+--------------------------------------------------------+
```

ment of the global scene, there is some reason for optimism.
People in the developed capitalist nations are awakening to
the seriousness of the situation. Just the year before, the
1st Report to the Club of Rome, as part of their Project on
the Predicament of Mankind, has been issued. The report,
prepared by a prestigious team of mostly MIT scientists, has
now reached millions in the form of a best-selling book, The
Limits to Growth.

V. THE MIT / CLUB OF ROME WORLD MODEL

The work at MIT began with the development of a computer
WORLD MODEL, based on systems dynamics theory. This would
be used to assess future values of five main world variables:
population, food per capita, an industrial output index, a
resource index, and a pollution index. Constructing this
model required establishing the interactions between the five
main variables and other variables in terms of causal relationships and feedback loops. Then, using the best data
available, these interactions were written as mathematical
expressions and incorporated into a computer program. The
computer simultaneously tracked all variables over time, and
this, combined with historical data from 1900-1970, was used

to fit WORLD MODEL predictions to past realities.

The first predictions made by the WORLD MODEL were alarming. They indicated that "business as usual" would eventually lead to "overshoot and collapse". This phenomenon is often seen by ecologists studying natural prey/predator, plant/animal relationships. It occurs when the numbers of a certain species--say Species A--exceed the carrying capacity of the environment for a time. Sometimes this happens because another species' numbers--say Species B, which serves as food for Species A--are low. Often, the Species A population will then drastically decline, species B population will grow since its predators aren't as numerous, and eventually Species A will make a comeback. Sometimes, however, if a species' demands on its environment have become too great, the carrying capacity will be permanently reduced and there will be no comeback. This example describes a simple system. Most natural systems and the WORLD MODEL are more complex.

After recovering from the shock of the WORLD MODEL standard run, the MIT team used their model to test various policies being proposed to produce a more desirable world. In numerous trials, they encountered resource depletion, rising pollution, food shortage, and arable land availability problems. The search for a set of policies leading to a sustainable world was a long one.

Finally, a stabilized world emerged from the computer. The thrill of seeing the promised land was tempered by considering what it took--policy and assumption wise--to obtain it. To produce the stabilized world, nine policies had to be introduced in 1975: 1) 100 % effective birth control, 2) desired family size of two children, 3) industrial output per capita kept at 1975 levels, resource consumption per unit of industrial output held to 25 % of 1970 values, 5) economic preferences shifted away from material goods to services, 6) pollution generation per output unit held to 25 % of 1970 level, 7) emphasis given to producing food sufficient for all, 8) efforts to preserve soil fertility, and 9) the average lifetime of industrial capital increases.

The MIT computer indicates that if the introduction of these policies is delayed 25 years until 2000, then the stabilized world is only temporarily achieved--it soon slips away as industrial output and food per capita plunge, leading to catastrophe.

VI. AMERICA CONFRONTS THE CLUB OF ROME

In late 1974, the 2nd Report to the Club of Rome--a book Mankind at the Turning Point --was published. In March, 1975, economist Kenneth Boulding reviewed it in Science.[3] He began by recalling the 1st report:

> ...its main message was that if Nineveh, that is, the
> great city of the developed world, did not repent, it
> would be destroyed...The 1st report was criticized on
> the grounds that it took a far too holistic view of an
> extremely diverse and complex planet, though one could
> perhaps defend this as a very first approximation. The
> 2nd report seems to answer this criticism by breaking
> the world into ten regions...Each of these has a model
> of its own...

Boulding mentions the trade, investments, and economic aid relationships between the regions that the new WORLD MODEL considers, and relates computer scenarios given various population control measures, production activities, and transfers of economic aid from rich to poor regions. He then reports,

> ...the general message of all these scenarios is "the
> earlier the better". If certain basic sets of decisions
> are made very soon the printouts give us some hope, but
> pretty soon it will be too late to avoid major catas-
> trophes..In some ways, for all its modestly optimistic
> tone, this report is even more depressing than the 1st
> report...What the report does not say is how we are to
> be persuaded to repent.

How are we to be persuaded to repent? The Club of Rome's answer would come at the group's highly publicized 1976 meeting in Philadelphia. At its opening session, Aurelio Peccei--at whose home the club was founded in 1968--recalled the spirit, ethics, and morality of the American Declaration of Independence.

The sessions to follow were mostly devoted to making public the findings, prescriptions, and conclusions of various 1975 Club projects--including Ervin Laszlo's Goals for Global Societies. They specified the economic aid transfers and other policies that would reduce the ratio of rich nation to poor nation income by a factor by four. To accomplish this, developing poor countries would need $30 billion in development funds by 1980, technological know-how, fertili-zer, tariff reduction, looser immigration restrictions, and taxes assessed to fund a world treasury.

Eventually the discussion turns to Goals and the how of repenting. Engineering professor Samuel Florman, covering the meeting for Harper's[4], recalls what happened next.

> "What we need," Laszlo said, "is an evolution of a new
> ethical consciousness." The lights dimmed, and a slide
> was projected with the heading, "The Required Trans-
> formation in Contemporary Values and Beliefs." At this
> point my notes become sketchy: "all religions... uni-
> versal compassion...brotherhood...world solidarity."
> ...a sudden hush seemed to descend as Laszlo concluded,
> "We all have a moral obligation," he said, "to spur
> development of a sense of solidarity".

After all the elaborate data gathering, systems theory, sophisticated mathematical models, computer analysis, the Club of Rome had rediscovered brotherhood and wrapped itself in "The Family of Man/Other People Orientation" !

The self-interest based economic forces would respond furiously. Their spokesman--in the person of then U.S. vice president Nelson Rockefeller--addressed the conference. Again, Florman recalls the occasion.

> ...he said that the most meaningful thing America can do
> to solve world problems is to increase its own well
> being, so as to serve as an example for others...he cal-
> led the Club of Rome naive for the second time...He con-
> cluded by berating doomsday prophets and expressing to-
> tal faith in the American people. There was hardly any
> applause. He shook hands with Peccei, who was flushed
> but grinning,trying to pretend he had not been insulted.

VII. THE 1980s--FROM DIFFERENT VIEWPOINTS

Many years pass. Nelson Rockefeller dies. While global modeling becomes more sophisticated[5], The Club of Rome's influence wanes. A "me first" consciousness, the opposite of what Laszlo, Peccei, Meadows and the others hoped would develop, now pervades America.

1984 brings two publications deserving comment. First, the Worldwatch Institute--seeing the need for a captain's "State of the Spaceship" report--produces the first of what is to become the annual State of the World series. Second, Club of Rome president Aurelio Peccei's remarkable book, Before It Is Too Late --a collaboration with Japanese lay

Buddhist Daisaku Ikeda--appears.

Both its authors see the world on the brink of disaster and write,

> We agree that today's major problems are still spiritual
> and ethical and that no amount of scientific or techno-
> logical power or economic means can solve them.

Peccei points the finger at a worldview that dominates western civilization. This conception of the nature of things is an old one--we use the words of Francis Bacon (1561-1626) and Bernardin de St. Pierre (writing in 1784) to describe it.

* #25 ANTHROPOCENTRISM *

"Man...may be regarded as the centre of the world; insomuch that if man were taken away from the world, the rest would seem to be all astray, without aim or purpose,....and leading to nothing." "The Creator has aimed...only at the happiness of man."

Many years earlier, historian Lynn White, Jr. linked environmental destruction to Judeo-Christian anthropocentric teachings. He wrote[6],

> We shall continue to have a worsening ecologic crisis
> until we reject the Christian axiom that nature has no
> reason for existence save to serve man.

Peccei laments what this view is doing to the planet.

> (Humans are) so presumptuous and self-centered that we
> have forsaken communion with nature. (We are) trying to
> reshape the earth as if we alone were to inhabit it,
> whereas the planet is beautiful and generous precisely
> because many other forms of life contribute to making it
> what it is. (Man has become) the insatiable, obtuse
> tyrant of the planet.

The 1980s bring unparalleled environmental destruction and widening of the global rich/poor gap. In many Third World countries per capita incomes decline. One international development leader laments "a lost decade for most of the developing world". Indeed, for many caught up in a "Survival-Oriented Worldview" (theme #24), the 1980s are miserable.

In contrast, Westerners dominated by Economic Man (theme #19) and Expansionist (theme #22) worldviews, thought this decade was splendid. While conceding that some economic activities might have to be redirected to address environmental problems, they nonetheless see a future filled with their increasing prosperity.

There won't be fundamental economic changes-- massive redistribution of wealth or no growth, sustainable society policies--these people confidently say. After all, during the 1980s their corporate media friends have become vastly more powerful. New technologies have greatly aided their quest to surround the Western public with persuasive consuming images --images with their own values imbedded. Corporate mergers enhanced their financial clout. That the America of the future would be a consumerist society seemed to them a foregone conclusion.

As the 1980s ended, after decades of media manipulation, a new worldview theme was becoming a force to be reckoned with inside American heads[7]--shoving aside more old-fashioned notions.

* #26 THE CONSUMERIST MENTALITY *

I'm no longer a citizen--just a consumer. I understand democracy in terms of choices I can make as a consumer. If I like a product's image--whether the product be soda pop or presidential candidate--I embrace it. When I tire of a possession, I discard it for something new. I express who I am through what I buy and how others see me. Someday, perhaps my own image will rise above the clutter and I will be somebody. For now, at least I am not a nobody--someone without money to be a consumer.

During the 1980s the developed world entered "The Information Age". Increasingly, costs for the information content (advertising, market forecasts, legal expenses, etc.) of what consumers bought approached and sometimes exceeded raw materials costs. Economists began focusing more on this information flow--and continued to ignore resource depletion and environmental costs. As the decade dragged on, the integrity of planetary ecosystems and chemical cycles steadily worsened, and ecological disruption mounted, given the behavior of the "tyrant of the planet".

VIII. DISRUPTING WATER, CARBON, OXYGEN CYCLES[8]

Problems with the quantity and quality of water humans obtain from the water cycle appear to be growing. With demand exceeding sustainable supply in many regions, water tables are falling--under 25 % of U.S. irrigated acres, and by one to two meters per year in parts of China's North Plain, and elsewhere. Pollutants threaten groundwater and--more ominously--rainwater. As automobiles, power plants, and industries belch nitrogen and sulfur oxides--which change to nitric and sulfuric acid in the atmosphere--acid precipitation results. Many areas in Europe and North America receive rainfall 30 times as acidic as pristine, natural rain. In southwestern Sweden and southern Norway, 6500 lakes, and in Canada another 4000 lakes, are now without fish due to acid rain.

Human activity--particularly burning fossil fuels and clearing forests--has destabilized the carbon cycle. Total carbon emissions from fossil fuel combustion has increased by 1/3 since 1970--to 5.7 billion metric tons per year. Cutting and burning forests--chiefly in the tropics--adds another 1 to 2 billion additional tons per year to the air. Carbon dioxide levels have risen steadily over the last century. Many meteorologists have concluded that the signs of CO_2 / greenhouse effect-induced warming and climatic change are already visible.

A British team of scientists, after studying global temperature records of the last 135 years, concluded that the six warmest years on record were 1988, 1987, 1983, 1981, 1980, and 1986 in that order. (Preliminary data suggested 1989 was the fifth warmest year on record.) By April 1989, a <u>Scientific American</u> article entitled "Global Climatic Change" begins ominously,

> The world is warming. Climate zones are shifting.
> Glaciers are melting. Sea level is rising. These are not
> hypothetical events from a science fiction movie; these
> changes and others are already taking place...

Besides carbon dioxide, rising atmospheric concentrations of other greenhouse contributing trace gases--particularly chlorofluorocarbons, methane, and nitrous oxide--are also of concern. One team of U.S. meteorologists concluded, "the magnitude of this warming in the future can potentially be as large as the warming due to projected CO_2 increases."

While the mean global temperature has risen about .6°C since 1900, projected increases of 1.5 to 5.5°C by 2030 and beyond could threaten agricultural production, terrestrial ecosystems, and--as sea levels rise-- coastal population centers. As sea water warms, many scientists expect killer hurricanes with top speeds in excess of 230 miles/hour to occur more frequently. Dealing with these changes will be costly. Globally, the cost of adjusting irrigation systems in response to climate change could reach $200 billion. Constructing dikes on the U.S. East Coast--despite all the jokes about "Who needs Florida, or New York City, anyway?"--could require $120 billion. A single killer hurricane--like Hugo in 1989--can cause billions of dollars of damage.

Manmade chlorofluorocarbons are assaulting the oxygen cycle, specifically the planet's ozone layer. The discovery of a seasonal hole in the ozone layer above Antarctica in the fall of 1985 alarmed many.[9] At maximum extent the hole is the size of the United States and ozone depletion peaks at 50 %. Large bands of ozone-depleted air have broken away from this hole and produced 7 % ozone drops over five large cities in Australia, New Zealand, and Tasmania. A similar hole--with lower depletion levels and but 1/3 the size of the Antarctic hole--has been found over Norway. In Switzerland, long-term research has documented a 3 % ozone loss--most of it occurring in the last decade. According to EPA estimates, a global 1 % drop in global ozone could let enough ultraviolet radiation penetrate to cause 20,000/year more U.S. skin cancers.

While upper atmosphere ozone is being depleted, near the ground in some 60 U.S. urban regions, ozone levels exceed EPA standards. This component of photochemical smog--produced when atomic oxygen (freed from nitrogen dioxide when ultraviolet rays from the sun hit it) combines with molecular oxygen--can irritant eyes and damage crops.

IX. PROBLEMS WITH OTHER CYCLES

Parts of the nitrogen cycle have been accelerated by two human efforts to intensify crop and livestock production: the application of large amounts of industrially-fixed fertilizer to soils and the concentration of livestock and their wastes in feedlots, poultry farms, etc. Such practices, combined with soil erosion and runoff in streams, can lead to nitrate pollution of drinking water. Between 5 and 10 % of wells tested in the U.S. and Europe exceed safe nitrate levels.

Both nitrates and phosphates can cause algae blooms, whose intensified biological activity depletes oxygen, endangering fish and other creatures. Large sewage concentrations from industry and urbanization can be similarly disruptive.

Various combustion processes produce the high temperatures needed for atmospheric nitrogen to react with oxygen forming nitric oxide (NO), which slowly reacts with oxygen, forming nitrogen dioxide (NO_2). This reddish-brown, choking gas, and other compounds it spawns through photochemical reactions, are major constituents of urban smog. Fortunately, nitrogen dioxide persists in the atmosphere for only a few weeks. This is not the case for nitrous oxide (N_2O), released from fertilizers, wastes, and combustion. This gas-- like CO_2, a greenhouse gas--can remain for a century.

Sulfur dioxide (SO_2) is a component of industrial smog produced by burning coal, to a lesser extent, oil, and smelting of metallic ores. Largely due to these activities, the human contribution of sulfur to the atmosphere now roughly equals that of natural sulfur cycle sources. The water gets its share of man-made sulfur compounds. In particular, soil bacteria can convert water contaminated with sulfur from coal-mining operations to sulfuric acid (H_2SO_4), the cause of so-called acid mine drainage.

Human activities are accelerating the deposition of phosphates in ocean bottom sediments--where the natural phosphate cycle tends to keep it for so long. Phosphate mining and runoff of phosphate fertilizer from agricultural land are chiefly responsible. Deforestation and other erosion-causing factors aggravate the situation. Because of the natural imperfection in the phosphate cycle, and disruptive human activities, phosphorus may be the first of the six essential elements to be in short supply.

Industrial activities have resulted in heavy metal releases far in excess of what natural sources insert--an estimated 333 times more for lead, 20 times more for cadmium. While the reverse is still true for mercury, human input of mercury into the environment has been increasing. This is largely due to burning coal, which naturally contains mercury in trace amounts. Acid rain may aggravate mercury poisoning problems. In lakes and streams, mud bottom dwelling bacteria can convert elemental mercury and mercury salts to lethal methyl mercury under acidic conditions.

High level nuclear wastes typically exceed low natural background radiation levels (from cosmic rays and traces of radioactive elements in rocks) by 10 trillion times. These wastes will have to be isolated from the biosphere for at least 10,000 years. Reprocessing spent reactor fuel was the step originally envisioned as (partially) completing this nuclear fuel cycle. Because of dangers inherent in this recycling step, only two of 26 countries with nuclear power plants are using it. Instead, burying the waste deep underground in geologically secure formations is planned. Unfortunately, not a single country has developed such a permanent repository and temporary stockpiles are growing.

In the United States, some 12,000 metric tons of commercial high level waste--and a similarly large amount from nuclear weapons production--await ultimate disposal. The waste volume will quadruple by the year 2000. The U.S. Dept. of Energy estimates that cleaning up nuclear weapons related water pollution might cost $64 billion.

X. ASSAULTING ECOSYSTEMS, DEPLETING RESOURCES

Changing environmental chemistry has led to stresses on major planetary ecosystems. Consider forests. In Europe, 35 % of the total forested area--a 50 million hectare forest area (bigger than Califonia in size)--has been injured by air pollutants. Unexpected tree growth declines in the Appalachians and New England suggests a similar problem may soon plague the U.S. China's forests are likewise suffering.

As the global assault on ecosystems and disruption of chemical cycles continues, resources are being depleted. The world's forest land is disappearing at the rate of 18 to 20 million hectares a year (a forest area the size of California disappears every two years). Formerly fertile areas the size of Maine become deserts due to soil erosion every year. Much of this desertification is occurring in the U.S.

Every day, the world loses 70 million tons of top soil. Such losses amount to 7 % every decade and erosion exceeds formation on 35 % of the world's cropland. Africa and the Middle East have experienced massive deterioration of grasslands. In the U.S. cornbelt, three bushels of top soil are lost for every bushel of corn produced.

The resource depletion is not limited to land. Overfishing is now commonplace. Even with growing aquaculture operations included, per capita world fish catch has decreased by 15 % since 1970.

One biologist believes that all of this destruction will result in the eradication of one million species--many of them in tropical rain forests--in a single decade. Another, Harvard's E.O. Wilson, writes,

> The extinctions ongoing worldwide promise to be at least
> as great as the mass extinctions that occurred at the
> end of the age of dinosaurs.

The problem, according to Lester Brown, president of the Worldwatch Institute, is one of "consuming our biocapital, not living within our biological income." He adds, "The price for our short-sighted choice to live beyond our means will be paid by our children and grandchildren." Instead of figuring the loss of biocapital and environmental impacts into the price of food, water, wood, fuel, etc., book-keeping errors continue and prices remain low. Instead of restructuring economies around more environmentally benign solar-based renewable energy and resource recycling, depletion of non-renewable resources continues.

Between 1950 and 1986, while human population doubled, fossil fuel consumption increased by four times. Of the world's energy needs that can be readily gauged, fossil fuels meet 78 % (oil furnishes 33 %, coal 27 %, natural gas 18 %--while renewables (chiefly hydroelectric and biomass) and nuclear supply the rest). Total world energy use amounts to around 338 quads / year (1 quad=10^{15} BTU) or 65 MBTU / person-year. The global energy reliance on fossil fuels will undoubtedly change in the next century.

Despite current low prices, the long-term outlook for oil is not encouraging. The size of the pre-fossil fuel era global oil reserve is estimated at 1600 to 2400 billion barrels. Of this, 575 billion have already been used, and 705 billion barrels of proven reserves have been found. At the 1985 global oil extraction rate of 21 billion barrels per year, all the oil will be gone in 50 to 88 years. Of course, proven oil reserves are not evenly distributed: 56 % of them are in the Middle East. U.S. proven reserves are 36 billion barrels--an eight year supply at current U.S. usage rates.

The outlook for natural gas is a little better. Of the traditional fossil fuels, only coal remains in abundance--a few hundred years worth. Unfortunately, coal is dirty. Increasing its use will aggravate air pollution, acid rain, and CO_2/greenhouse problems.

Many attribute increased biosphere stresses and resource depletion problems to the rapidly growing human population. In 1850, after tens of thousands of years as a separate species, the number of Homo Sapiens finally reached one billion people. In another 80 years the figure topped two billion. By 1960--30 short years later--there were three billion people. It took only 15 years for another billion to be added. The increase from four to five billion took only 11 years from 1975 to 1986.

Startling though they are, these numbers fail to tell another story: of a demographically divided world. Whereas populations of developed countries are increasing very slowly--some have stabilized--populations of nearly all developing, poor countries are rapidly increasing. Fortunately, one important country, China, has made the demographic transition from rapid to slow population growth. Assuming poor countries are not helped in making the transition, population projections are staggering. Most demographers see world population eventually stabilizing at around ten billion people. Much of the growth is expected in Africa, the Indian subcontinent, the Middle East, and Latin America.

XI. COUNTERING GLOOM--AN OPTIMIST'S RESPONSE

In planning for the future, one must avoid two extreme viewpoints: "Naive Technological Optimism" and "Gloom and Doom Pessimism". The previous discussion--while intended to provide a realistic assessment of the planetary situation-- perhaps strikes some as too pessimistic. Consider then how a technological optimist might counter this picture.

AN OPTIMIST'S RESPONSE

In contrast to your pessimism, I can cite a number of positive trends. Since World War II, life expectancy in poor countries has increased by an average 15 years. Despite The Population Bomb author Paul Ehrlich's 1973 prediction that one-quarter of humanity would starve by 1983, between 1965 and 1985 food per capita increased by 10 % in the less developed world. The success of the Green Revolution--new high yield seeds, coupled with more fertilizer, pesticides, and irrigation--shows the ability of humanity to solve problems.

For example, India no longer relies on grain imports and its per capita income between 1980-1986 rose by 14 %. Indonesia, once the world's largest rice importer, now feeds its population and exports rice.

You regard population increases as harbingers of disaster. One can argue--like J.L. Simon in The Ultimate Resource --that more people means more ability to solve problems, improve, and innovate. That benefits the entire society. Larger populations also allow economies of scale. Incorporating human ingenuity and ability to innovate into computer models is nearly impossible. This--and failure to fully recognize that as a resource becomes scarce its price increases, and substitutes are found--were fatal flaws in the Limits to Growth study.

Ecologists' assessments of the future are flawed by their focus on material resources and energy flows. In contrast, economists note that consumers want services. End users don't care whether the cooking pot is made of copper, aluminum, stainless steel or what, as long as it adequately serves their food preparation needs. So economists concern themselves with the flow of information, since this determines the costs of services. Simon argues that the real cost of natural resources--fuel, timber, grains, and metals--has dropped over the last century. In the future, he claims, projects dominated by raw materials costs will be cheaper to implement than today. He argues that human knowledge and information growth leads to technological advances that trigger cost decreases.

Some pollution problems have improved. Air quality in London--once plagued by killer fogs--is better. Between 1970 and 1987, U.S. lead emissions fell by 96 %, particulate emissions by 62 %, and sulfur oxides emissions by 28 %. Water quality in many American rivers has improved.

As for global warming, supposed worldwide temperature increases over the last century can't be documented with U.S. weather data. Some scientists think "urban heat island effects" skew temperature measurements. Others note solar activity / terrestrial weather correlations and doubt humans are to blame for warming. If the global climate is to be warmer, some parts of the world may benefit. Actually, there are technical fixes that can turn unwanted carbon dioxide into a resource. For example, it can be combined with hydrogen to make methanol--potentially a cleaner burning automotive fuel than gasoline.

I have no doubt that if the biosphere is in real danger, world political and business leaders will respond. For example, the alarming 1985 discovery of the ozone hole over Antarctica and growing evidence of ozone depletion triggered the September, 1987 Montreal signing of international agreements to limit chlorofluorocarbon production. In March, 1988, the duPont Company--producer of 1/4 of these ozone-destroying chemicals--announced it would ultimately stop their production. They noted that efforts to develop substitutes were progressing steadily.

XII. EARTH DAY, 1990

Were we to update the Spaceship Earth 1973 report presented earlier in the chapter--perhaps for Earth Day, 1990--
we might imagine the captain reading the following....

On January, 1, 1990, your population stood at 5.28
billion. Sadly, over 1/5 of you--1.225 billion people--live
in absolute poverty. 400 million of you are gripped by
starvation that is devastating your body and mind. About
two billion of you drink and bathe in water full of deadly
parasites and pathogens. A billion people often breathe
unhealthy air--including 60 % of the American population.

I wish I could say that living conditions for those of
you in the spaceship's hold will soon improve. But, alas
there is more bad news. For the first time since such record-
keeping began, global grain consumption has now exceeded
production for three straight years. What reserves there are
(at dangerously low levels) poor countries can not afford--
given the $1.2 trillion Third World debt. As the latest eco-
nomic figures[10] (Fig. #21) show, the per capita income ratio
between those in first class quarters and the poorest
quarter of you (in the hold) has soared to 62 to 1. World
military spending--$ 1 trillion/year--has increased to 2.9
times the total annual GNP of the world's poorest...

```
+------------------------------------------------------------+
|    FIG. #21  1987 SPACESHIP EARTH ECONOMIC SUMMARY         |
|                                                            |
|                POPULATION    GROSS NAT.PROD    GNP/CAPITA   |
|                billions %   $U.S. trillions %  $U.S./person|
|                                                            |
| World total    5.02  100        18       100      3600     |
|                                                            |
| Rich,           .77   15       12.1       67     15700     |
| Capitalist                                                 |
|                                                            |
| Middle         1.54   31        5.1       28      3300     |
|                                                            |
| Poor,          1.37   27         .46       3       340     |
| Developing                                                 |
|                                                            |
| Poorest,       1.34   27         .34       2       250     |
| Developing                                                 |
|                                                            |
+------------------------------------------------------------+
```

As 1990 begins, these numbers, and ones cited earlier documenting the disruption of natural cycles and ecosystems, resource depletion, and population increases, paint a sobering picture of the state of the world.

Shortly after the first Earth Day in 1970 Barbara Ward wrote,

> The door of the future is opening onto a crisis more sudden, more global, more inescapable, more bewildering than any ever encountered by the human species.

Two decades later, the door is open wider and the view is not an encouraging one for those possessing a Sustainable World (theme #23) / Family of Man (theme #16) orientation.

By Earth Day 1990, many are touting the 1990s as a "turnaround" decade. Changes are needed; responsible citizens must elect new leaders, they assert. Debts must be paid; injustices must be righted; undeniable realities must be confronted. A new society founded on environmental ethics must rise from the ashes of the old. It begins with showing and telling people the truth, they emphasize.

The consumerists counter with what has been their advertising ethic for years: the truth is what sells.

Questions & Projects

1. Estimate the number of people whose worldview is significantly shaped by worldview theme #24. Have you seen or talked with any of them? Discuss.
2. Of the nine policies for a stabilized world identified by the MIT team in 1972, have any been achieved? Which will be easiest to implement? most difficult?
3. From what sources has the U.S. obtained its energy in the last 150 years? Report on the changing U.S. energy supply/consumption scene. Contrast U.S. and world energy mixes.
4. What effects do the following have on natural cycles? a) deforestation of the Amazon basin, b) air conditioners and refrigerators, c) electricity from a coal plant, d) electricity from a hydro-electric plant e) fast food hamburgers, f) converting a wooded area to a parking lot.
5. Some commercially-important plants--like soybeans--are particularly sensitive to increased ultraviolet radiation (an ozone depletion concern). Report.
6. Some organizations are anticipating the effects of global warming and planning accordingly. For example, the Nature Conservancy is no longer buying southeastern coastal

wetlands. Provide other examples.

7. Scientists are divided over responding to the global warming threat. Some urge immediate action to mitigate the effects. Others urge studying ways to adapt. Discuss.

8. On a map of the world, identify areas a) of fuelwood shortages, b) threatened by acid rain, c) where tropical rainforests are being destroyed, d) with major petroleum reserves e) with major coal reserves.

9. 1988 estimates indicated that 10 million people fled from environmental degradation. Identify current environmental refugee movements and their cause.

10. The world's birth rate (2.8 %/year) exceeds its death rate (1.0 %/year). The world population grows by roughly 90 million people/year. Calculate how many people would have to die every year in famines before zero population growth was achieved.

11. Imagine a plot of population density (persons/sq. mile) vs. per capita income. Identify places in the world whose data would be plotted at one of the corners of this plot. For locations at each corner, list environmental problems.

12. Contrast the age vs. number of people distributions of affluent and poor countries by drawing rough plots.

13. What specific actions did Japan and China take to make the demographic transition? Investigate and contrast.

14. Defend or refute U. of Maryland economist J.L. Simon's ideas regarding the desirability of population increases. (For an ecologist's lambasting of Simon see the Ehrlichs' Earth.[11] They refer to Simon as "an American specialist in mail ordering marketing"!)

15. Identify differences of opinion between sustainable world advocates and expansionist, technological optimists regarding a) limits to growth, b) resource and energy availability, c) promise of new technologies, d) the perceived threat of future global environmental problems.

16. Distinguish between "consuming our biocapital" and "living within our biological income" with examples.

Notes

1. Miller, G. T. Living in the Environment , Wadsworth, Belmont, CA 1975.

2. based on U.S. Statistical Abstracts , Comparative International Statistics Table. Note these calculations use national figures--thus the poorest quarter of the

world's population is a grouping of those living in nations with the lowest average per capita GNP. If true individual income data was available, the poorest quarter average income would be lower, the rich share higher. Worldwatch Institute researchers estimate this refinement would raise the rich to poorest ratio by a factor of two or more. The figure's data has not been corrected for price differences for basic goods. Prices can vary widely in different countries. Data incorporating this correction provides a better comparison of relative purchasing power. Worldwatch Institute data suggests that making this correction would reduce the rich to poorest ratio (37 to 1 in Fig.#20) to around 12 to 1. See Durning, A. "Ending Poverty", State of the World 1990 for details regarding both these corrections.

3. Boulding, K. "Conditional Optimism about the World Situation", Science , Vol. 187, March 28, 1975.

4. Florman, S. "Another Utopia Gone", Harper's Magazine , vol. 253, August 1976.

5. Meadows, D.H. et al, Groping in the Dark:The First Decade of Global Modeling, Wiley, New York, 1982.

6. White, L. "The Historic Roots of Our Ecologic Crisis", Science , vol. 155 pp.1203-1207.

7. inspired by the PBS / Bill Moyers series The Public Mind

8. much of the information regarding disruption of the Earth's biosphere in the next few sections is from The State of the World series ed. Lester Brown, Norton, New York. Another excellent reference in this regard is the September, 1989 issue of Scientific American--a special issue devoted to "Managing Planet Earth".

9. Stolarski, R. "The Antarctic Ozone Hole", Scientific American , January 1988.

10. rather crude estimates based on U.S. Statistical Abstracts, and The World Bank Atlas. This data is uncorrected for the two factors cited in note 2. above. If price differences for basic goods are factored in, the rich to poorest ratio (62 to 1 in Fig. #21) would become around 15 to 1 (according to A. Durning, Worldwatch Institute). If the true income breakdown for individuals was known, Durning suggests this 15 to 1 would become 30 to 1 or 40 to 1. See note 2. above.

11. Ehrlich, P. and A. Earth , Franklin Watts, NY 1987

PART B :

THE PLAYERS IN THE HUMAN DRAMA

"Societies...evolve in directions that are opened or constrained in part by internal forces such as technological developments or political traditions...Governments generally attempt to engineer social change by means of policies, laws, incentives or coercion. Sometimes these efforts work effectively and actually make it possible to avoid social conflict ...Different peoples have different ideas of how (social) tradeoffs should be made which can result in compromise or in continuing discord. How different interests are served often depends on the relative amounts of resources or power held by individuals or groups."

from <u>Science for All Americans</u> , The American Assoc. for the Advancement of Science, Washington D.C. 1989

While no one can say with certainty what the future will bring, scholars in future studies have proposed five distinct paths down which the future may lead:

1) A return to the idealism and liberal practices of the 1960s,

2) An acceleration of environmental deterioration and widening social conflicts,

3) A strengthening of the corporate state as the goals of industry and government increasingly merge,

4) Employing technological fixes to remedy current problems and overcome seeming limits,

5) Achieving societal stability through a new emphasis on spirituality, attitudinal fixes, and an environmental ethic.

While we can not wander down these paths into the future, we can identify forces that might push both the United States and the world in these directions. Similarly, we can familiarize ourselves with players on the human stage and their power to engender social tradeoffs which reflect their own values and interests.

(note--the above list was adapted from Wenk, E. <u>Tradeoffs</u> , Johns Hopkins University Press, Baltimore, 1986)

LIBERALS

I. LIBERALISM, DEMOCRACY, FREEDOM / RESTRAINT

Liberals--this loaded word has connotations which conjure up images dictionary definitions never hint at. Furthermore, the popular meaning of the word has changed over the last two centuries.

By a liberal, I mean one who embraces liberalism. By liberalism, I mean a rational, tolerant, generous, hopeful orientation that emphasizes individual freedom from restraint.

The 18th century represented the classic era of liberalism. In America it peaked with the revolution, declined shortly thereafter, only to surge with Jeffersonian and then Jacksonian democracy. With the Civil War, liberalism went into eclipse. By 1955, Arthur Ekirch's The Decline of American Liberalism would trace its steady erosion.

Whereas liberalism embraces many pillars of democracy, it conflicts with the democratic ideals of majority rule and equality. Why? Liberals fear majorities will restrict the rights of minorities. Liberals will not support drives for equality that encroach on the privileges of an elite few.

Liberalism is often associated with progressivism--but such an association is not always warranted. Consider progressive (onetime New Republic editor) Herbert Croly's 1909 attack on laissez faire and liberalism:

> The Promise of American Life (the title of his book containing these remarks) is to be fulfilled--not merely by a maximum amount of economic freedom, but by a certain measure of discipline; not merely by the abundant satisfaction of individual desires, but by a large measure of individual subordination and self denial....The automatic fulfillment of the American national promise is to be abandoned...precisely because the traditional American confidence in individual freedom has resulted in a morally and socially undesirable distribution of wealth.

During the 1960s liberalism underwent a mild resurgence. The era's activism targeted concentrations of power and authority that threatened freedom. With their tolerant, generous orientation, 60s activists were able to be compassionate. During those hopeful days, the quest for freedom was everywhere: free speech, hippies freeing themselves from societal

conventions, freedom riders, free love, consciousness raising
to free the mind, etc.

But freedom is not without complications. In the words
of Lynton K. Caldwell[1],

> The freedom and ability of...Americans in particular to
> exercise some rational choice over their futures is
> severely handicapped by a number of mutually reinforcing
> modern myths...The most pervasive and invalid belief of
> all is that "freedom" is free--that it exacts no price,
> that freedom exists when each individual does whatever
> he pleases, wherever he pleases.

One man's freedom can be another man's a) prison, b) night-
mare, c) dream, d) battle, or e) livelihood. This sentence
can be completed in many ways.

Any substantial discussion of a particular freedom un-
avoidably also concerns its opposite: restraint. How individuals in positions of authority--whether as parents, bosses,
elected officials,etc.--strike a balance between freedom and
restraint depends on their worldviews. As an example, consider a March, 1989 analysis of freedom of speech by Donella
Meadows--prompted by the Ayatollah Khomeini's threat against
author Salmon Rushdie for The Satanic Verses.

II. FREEDOM OF SPEECH

Freedom of Speech--Up to a Point, by Donella H. Meadows
Our endless public discussion of the awful Rushdie affair
would be more useful if we'd all admit we have something in
common with the murderous mullahs. Not that we would issue
death sentences against those whose writings anger us. But
most of us can readily identify some person or group we would
silence, if we could, by means more gentle than those the
Ayatollah advocates.

Fundamentalist Muslims want to make the book The Satanic
Verses disappear. Fundamentalist Christians hated the book
The Last Temptation of Christ , but didn't demonstrate in the
streets until it was made into a movie. (They know, as
Khomeini does not, that hardly anyone reads books unless
Ayatollahs happen to denounce them!)

If I could choose the publications the world would be
better off without, I'd start with the Dartmouth Review and
other smug scribblings that imply, subtly or crudely, that
human virtue and political correctness reside only in white,
male, American conservatives. Next I'd eliminate all speeches

*in which members of the military-industrial complex whip up
national fears and hatreds--I can't think of any communications more costly in money and lives than those.*

*I'd ban pornography. I'd shred the supermarket pulp
literature that drugs downcast people with fantasies of
superstars, witchcraft, and sex. I'd happily do in all
advertising, print and broadcast. It makes people feel ugly
and unfulfilled--we'd be better off without it. As long as
I'm on this roll, I might as well eliminate sitcoms too, and
game shows, soaps, and shallow sensationalist network news.*

*If you engage in this exercise, you'll come up with a
list different from mine. The point is not my list or yours.
The point is that we all have one, and that there is some
basis for having one. Much publicly aired speech and writing
is worthless, raunchy, destructive. I'm proud of our
courageous Western defiance of Khomeini's violent edict, but
I also believe that we Westerners have leaned too far in the
direction of freedom of speech and press. Those freedoms have
never been absolute, and they never should be.*

*Yelling fire in the crowded theater is the textbook
example of impermissible speech. There are more common
examples. Governments do not tolerate speech that advocates
their own violent overthrow and often, unfortunately, do not
tolerate speech that merely makes them look bad. We don't
permit people to make unsubstantiated public claims about
medicines. We ban advertisements for most harmful, addictive
substances. We no longer tolerate overt racism in the mouths
of our national leaders.*

*These limitations are well accepted, and to my way of
thinking there should be more of them. The power of words is
too strong to let just any tripe loose in the world. Hateful
words can tear a community apart. Contemptuous words can
crush the spirit of a single person or, if repeated often
enough, of a whole people. Lying words can eat away the trust
that permits society to function.*

*Inversely, uplifting words can help people rediscover
the strengths within them, which are so easily lost in the
modern storm of cynical, crass communication. Some words are
sacred, not because they are demonstrably "true"--they exist
on another plane than that of scientific demonstration--but
because their repetition establishes a meaning for life and a
firm moral foundation for wavering minds and souls.*

Different peoples have different sacred words, and it's

*always been one of humanity's most malicious sports to
ridicule the sacred words of others. It's a sport that
shouldn't be tolerated; in that I agree with the Ayatollah.
Of course the Ayatollah's own contempt for other people's
beliefs and his barbaric calls for terrorism disqualify him
to be the Moral Censor for Humanity.*

*So who should be the censor? It certainly shouldn't be
any single individual. It shouldn't be a government, nor a
church, nor publishers, nor writers' associations, nor any
institutions with a vested interest (which rules out all
institutions).*

*The only entity I'm willing to trust with the critical
judgement of public words is the public as a whole, just as
the First Amendment says. But I'd like to do much more to em-
power all members of that public both to choose what they
hear and to understand their responsibilities when they speak
out.*

*I'd like children to be raised not only hearing about
freedom of expression, but understanding the social consequences of that expression. I'd like them to be awash not
in mindless media outpourings, but in wonderful examples of
precise, considered, socially uplifting words. I wouldn't
prohibit them from encountering any publication, but I would
do everything in my power to encourage them to judge publications and to close pages, turn dials, and eliminate destructive speech by the most powerful means possible--their
own refusal to give it their attention.*

III. HUMAN INTERACTIONS

Let us assess the potential of human beings to exercise
freedom wisely. To do this we return to the 1960s and begin
our analysis there.

In 1966--as America's involvement in the Vietnam War
escalated--Kenneth Boulding wrote an essay, The Economics of
the Coming Spaceship Earth. He identified three value systems for real, face-to-face human interactions: 1) the integrative system, in which transactions are based on love,
sharing, and altruism, 2) the exchange system, the narrow
give and take interactive market world of economics, and 3)
the threat system, based on "Give it to me or I'll kill you"
or "How much will you pay me to stop harming or annoying
you?"

Many interactions involve no face to face meeting--they

are anonymous. In face to face situations--when the participants can empathize with each other, or when they expect to encounter each other again, outcomes 1) and 2) (integrative and exchange systems) predominate. While unrestrained aggressive behavior is a possibility, often self-interest is tempered by self responsibility. Richard Critchfield describes it in his book Villages[2]:

> Almost everywhere, I've found the same pattern over the
> years: youth makes demands, parents resist; after a
> period of rebellion, youth surrenders to tradition. This
> is not always, perhaps, the best thing in terms of
> personal self-interest, but it keeps the villages going.
> The freedom that really seems to matter in villages...is
> the voluntary limitation of individual choice so that
> you can live together with other people in a group. Most
> villagers as they mature, find themselves doing it, one
> might call it the freedom to choose self-responsibility.

In human interactions where the other member of the pair is unknown and impossible to empathize with, aggressive, selfish behavior, i.e. defecting, comes easier. Anonymous, de-humanized interactions characterize the urban metropolis and the corporate state. Often it's not an individual but some multinational corporation--where any one person's responsibility for the behavior has been diluted--doing the defecting. If this can be done by surrogates behind closed doors or in some remote part of the Earth, away from public scrutiny and far from corporate boardrooms, so much the better.

It appears that the mix of all de-humanized interaction outcomes is skewed, not toward outcome 1)'s cooperative / integrative system, as in face to face humanized encounters, but toward the antithesis of that. Sadly, as the world has become a more populated, anonymous, complex place, human interactions have increasingly become either unfair exchanges (corporate cents of values for individual hard-earned dollars), or based on outcome 3)'s defector/threat system.

War, the ultimate recourse in human interactions which have deteriorated into aggressive conflict, will likewise elicit more support if the killing can be done in anonymous fashion. During wartime, nations cultivate the weeds of national identity and pride, rather than the solidarity of the human species. They make "foreign" people seem sub-human, impossible to empathize with, and anonymous. This is done by exploiting differences in skin color, religion, ideology, or culture. Modern technological tools to kill or threaten these "sub-humans" likewise remove face-to-face, possibly humanizing, encounters. Bomb-dropping airplanes or death-delivering missiles are tidy, efficient ways of killing hundreds of thousands of unknown victims. For masters of war, this is preferable to seeing the agonized death of each innocent person.

IV. THE HUMAN POTENTIAL MOVEMENT

Television brought Americans face to face with the dehumanized killing in Southeast Asia. Out of their revulsion grew a movement that eventually forced the withdrawal of U.S. troops from Vietnam.

Few who were part of "the movement" will forget what happened on American college campuses in the 1960s and early 70s. The goal for many was revolution--revolution to create a more humane society. Participants had their worldviews change during these upbeat times of hope, togetherness, and solidarity. These "movement" people were more accepting of themselves and others, less judgemental and competitive, more open to new experience, more honest than "straight" people. "We can make it happen" they thought.

There was a related movement: the human potential movement. Those left psychologically impoverished by the consumer way of life turned to growth centers, encounter or sensory awareness groups, or therapeutic communities for help. Here, the teachings of Carl Rogers, Abraham Maslow and other humanistic psychologists were practically applied. People learned that after their basic needs of security, belongingness, and dignity were met, their growth needs could be addressed. After identifying the desired growth and cultivating it, some blossomed into self-actualized individuals.

Such people would not only be free of psychological problems, but according to Maslow[3], would have achieved, "the full use and exploitation of talent, capacities, potentialities, etc." As might be expected, they are self-confident, but also possess humility that allows them to listen carefully to others and admit their ignorance. They see life more clearly than others partly due to a better understanding of themselves. With this superior perception, they have a clearer notion of right and wrong.

Their values and ideals, which are based on experience
rather than blind acceptance of religious authority, are
nearly identical to those taught by the great religions.
Among their attributes, Maslow included "honesty and
naturalness, the transcendence of selfish and personal
motivations, the giving up of lower desires in favor of
higher ones". Such people feel a strong bond or kinship with
the rest of humanity. They seek important and meaningful work
and are so dedicated to this that the usual distinctions
between work and play are fuzzy. Such a commitment seems in
fact a prerequisite for growth, happiness and fulfillment.

V. THE AMERICAN NEUROSIS; MASLOW VS. FREUD

As the 1970s began, the new humanistic psychology seemed
poised to change many people's lives and society as a whole.
Who would be helped? --perhaps, The Neurotic Personality of
Our Time , itself the title of a 1937 book by psychologist
Karen Horney. There she described a peculiar American neurosis. Supposedly, this was brought on by excessive competition and characterized by three things: 1) aggressiveness
so stimulated that it began to conflict with the tenets of
Christian brotherhood, 2) desire for material goods so
vigorously stimulated that it could never be satisfied, and
3) expectations for untrammeled freedom soaring so high,
people could not square them with the societal limitations
necessary for everyone's welfare.

When this analysis was published, Sigmund Freud's
influence on psychology was everywhere. Unlike Maslow decades
later, Freud studied not the healthiest, most fulfilled
people, but those with mental problems. Influenced by Charles
Darwin, his viewpoint emphasized the lower, instinctual,
animal nature of humans--rather than their highest, most
refined possibilities. Freud felt that all religious
experience was childish delusion. He wrote,

> Culture has to call up every possible reinforcement to
> erect barriers against the aggressive instincts of
> men...hence, too its ideal command to love one's
> neighbor as oneself, which is really justified by the
> fact that nothing is so completely at variance with
> human nature as this.

Psychology professor Paul Wachtel sees Freud's work as,
at the time, providing scientific support for those who
wanted to equate "selfishness and the profit motive with

human nature". Wachtel[4] claims that Freud,

> ...presented a powerful new version of what were in large measure well-rooted myths of original sin and primal, individualistic selfishness, myths even more central to maintaining the status quo than were the myths of conscious and rational choice that he did challenge.

Many psychologists, including Maslow, intellectually grew up with Freudian thought and later turned away from it. Maslow felt that both Freudian and some Christian viewpoints overemphasized the negative in human nature. This, he reasoned, contributed to building an emphasis on controls and negative motivation into society. Maslow felt that natural human tendencies were not always toward pleasure and away from pain. In psychologically healthy individuals they were often toward growth and self-actualization. Growing as an individual requires facing feelings of inadequacy and overcoming fears associated with new and challenging situations. Thus before one enjoys pleasures resulting from growing, developing, and mastering new challenges, much work, self-discipline, and some pain are required.

Maslow also disagreed with Freud on another key point. He wrote[5],

> To accept as intrinsic an antagonism between individual interest and social interests was a terrific begging of the question. Possibly its main excuse was that in a sick society and in the sick individual, it actually tends to be true. Individual and social interests under healthy social conditions are synergic and not antagonistic.

Maslow got the term "synergic society" from Columbia University anthropology professor Ruth Benedict, who studied several cultures. He characterized a high synergy society as one in which virtue paid.

Benedict characterized such societies in slightly different terms[6]:

> Societies where nonaggression is conspicuous, have social orders in which the individual, by the same act and at the same time, serves his own advantage and that of the group...Nonaggression occurs, not because people are unselfish and put social obligations above personal desires, but when societal arrangements make these two identical.

She noted that wealth seemed to be spread around more in high synergy societies than in those with a few rich and many poor. She described these low synergy societies as "where the advantage of one individual becomes a victory over another, and the majority who are not victorious must shift as they can." Maslow felt that, "A healthy society would be one which fulfills the most potentialities of the greatest number of men." He saw "universal self-actualization" as an ultimate goal.

VI. THE DEMISE OF ONCE PROMISING MOVEMENTS

Both the human potential movement and the counter-cultural movement spawned visions of utopian societies, some of which were given names. Maslow was responsible for one of these: Eupsychia. This he defined as "the culture that would be generated by one thousand self-actualizing people on some sheltered island where they would not be interfered with..."

The utopia that captured the imagination of the counterculture was called Ecotopia. It was described in a similarly titled 1975 novel by Ernest Callenbach. This eco-logically based, steady state society supposedly results when Northern California, Oregon, and Washington secede from the U.S., declare independence, and seal their borders.

Of course by 1985, even as states of mind, Eupyschia and Ecotopia were generating little of the excitement they were producing a decade earlier. Many 1960s hippies had become the yuppies of the 1980s, the flower children of Woodstock nation had become the "me generation". The revolution through con-sciousness-raising that Greening of America author Charles Reich envisioned never materialized. While he was right about the color that would transform America, the "greening" was green as in the color of money.

The human potential movement changed also. For many, EST, a thriving big business which has been called "the McDonald's of the human potential movement", became its logi-cal extension. Unfortunately, EST and other human potential growth programs have been plagued by excesses and abuses. They often seem to help people grow in ways Maslow never in-tended: toward selfish preoccupation and neglect of societal responsibilities. Maslow, who died in 1970, was aware of similar early misinterpretations of the term self-actuali-zation. He lamented, "This has turned out to be so in spite of my careful efforts to describe the empirical fact that self-actualizing people are altruistic, dedicated, self-transcending, social, etc." Paul Wachtel worried that distortion of Maslow's ideas was breeding "an extreme individualism that might make even Ayn Rand blush."

Why has countercultural and human potential movement rhetoric sometimes been used to justify selfish pursuits, rather than finding that "circle of affection in which all men join hands" as originally envisioned ? Both Reich's and Maslow's formulations share a common flaw: they are self-oriented. The first commandment of Reich's new consciousness is "thou shalt not do violence to thyself". In response, Paul Wachtel asks, "Where does meaningfully endured sacrifice end and 'violence to the self' begin ? " It is an important question that Reich doesn't consider.

VII. SCIENCE AND CO-OPERATION VS. COMPETITION

Despite the demise of these once promising movements toward a more humane society, recent scientific findings may provide motivation for those working for a world based on brotherhood, empathy, and co-operation. New research somewhat negates Freud's dark view of human nature and Darwin's evolutionary focus on competition.

Psychologists studying emotion in children at the Laboratory of Developmental Psychology at the National Institute of Mental Health have uncovered evidence of complex empathic behavior in children as young as 15 months. Martin Hoffman, a University of Michigan psychologist, after studying crying patterns in hospital nursery newborn infants, believes empathy is innate--a possibility other researchers are beginning to take seriously. More than just triggering a sympathetic response, Hoffman says,

> The data strongly suggest that empathy is part of the developmental foundation for the child's future system of moral behavior, as well as for social behaviors such as altruism and sharing.

Speculation that empathy is innate human behavior and that is why people help each other, is a viewpoint opposed to Freud's innate animalistic savagery, aggression, and selfishness. For those seeking a society built on positive motivation and loosening of negative controls / social restraint laws--among them many liberals--such findings are welcome. In recent years biologists have likewise questioned the Freudian/Darwinian view of competitive interaction within the human species.

Years ago ecologist Evelyn Hutchinson found something wrong with the conventional interpretation of evolutionary mechanisms--in particular with the mathematics one would expect from the "survival of the fittest". Studying complex natural communities out in the field, she simply never observed a "winner take all" situation where one superior species dominated all the others. On the contrary, she saw stable ecosystems with hundreds of species maintaining a dynamic balance. Biologist Lewis Thomas and others have been influenced by Hutchinson's findings and now view evolution, in terms of cooperation, not competition.

Thomas feels that symbiotic relationships, co-operative behaviors in the extreme, are more common than generally believed. He writes[7],

> I am convinced that the driving force in nature, on this kind of planet with this sort of biosphere is co-operation. In the competition for survival and success in evolution, natural selection tends, in the long run, to pick as real winners the individuals, and then the species, whose genes provide the most inventive and effective ways of getting along.

VIII. COMPUTERS & THE EVOLUTION OF CO-OPERATION

Thomas admits being inspired by results from computer science. Actually, it was University of Michigan political science and public policy professor, Robert Axelrod, who organized a computer tournament in which 14 contestants-- psychologists, political scientists, mathematicians, econo-mists, and sociologists--played a game in which they were all authorities: Prisoner's Dilemma. The game is named for an imagined interaction of two accused criminals who are given a once only chance of squealing on each other (defecting) in exchange for a more lenient sentence. If both squeal they each get longer sentences than if they had kept quiet (co-operating). Over the past 30 years, many variations of the game have resulted. All are based on the co-operate / defect choice.

These are so-called non-zero sum games. In zero sum games, getting ahead means taking something from your oppo-nent, for his loss is your gain and vice versa. In Prisoner's Dilemma and other non-zero sum games, both players can some-times together benefit.

In Axelrod's tournament, contestants entered their own C (for co-operate) or D (for defect) generating programs, which took on similar software opponents. The game was played over and over--altogether about 200 times. (Scoring is summarized in Fig.#22). In the tournament, all 14 programs played each other, as well as a duplicate of themselves and a program that randomly generated C's or D's. The program which won-- not only the initial tournament, but also a second much larger one--was authored by Anatol Rapoport of the University of Toronto. It's called TIT FOR TAT and contains only four lines. It starts by co-operating and then does whatever its opponent did on the previous move.

```
+-----------------------------------------------------------+
|        FIG. #22  TWO-PLAYER PRISONER'S DILEMMA SCORING     |
|                                                           |
|      Case    If Program 1      If Program 2    then score  |
|              Chooses     and   Chooses,        as follows  |
|                                                           |
|       #1         C                 C        both get 3 pts.|
|                                                           |
|       #2         D                 D        both get 1 pt. |
|                                                           |
|       #3         C                 D       program 1 gets 0|
|                                            program 2 gets 5|
|                                                           |
|       #4         D                 C       program 1 gets 5|
|                                            program 2 gets 0|
|                                                           |
+-----------------------------------------------------------+
```

Axelrod and others think the TIT FOR TAT strategy has real life applications wherever a non-zero sum interaction type situation exists. In his book, The Evolution of Co-operation, he cites the arms race, nuclear proliferation, crisis bargaining and military escalation as important examples in international relations. Apparently the results of another tournament Axelrod arranged, one in which the programs mimicked competing plants or animals in a closed system environment, impressed Lewis Thomas. He wrote, "The computer game persuades us that TIT FOR TAT is the kind of biological logic that one might expect to emerge by natural selection in the course of evolution."

A logic similar to TIT FOR TAT may have also been important during human cultural evolution. Primitive people possessed an outstanding ability to recall human faces--for this provided critical information about the results of past interactions with individuals. This ability fostered discrimination between past conflicts and past beneficial encounters, and with cultivation allowed for a rich set of co-operative relationships to develop. Bound together in a village community, out of necessity people learned to nurture co-operation and weed out behavior not in the interest of the village as a whole.

Lacking much ability for abstract reasoning, when human interactions resulted in complex problems, these people relied on special wisdom for help. Some of the teachings of great leaders had been distilled into "simple programs" for behavior. These eventually became internalized inside people's heads.

One such program--universal to many cultures--was based on the Golden Rule: do unto others as you would have them do unto you. This co-operating strategy became the approach to try first. Another such behavior program, one also well-known to those of Judeo-Christian heritage, was "an eye for an eye, a tooth for a tooth" reciprocity. Here individuals are instructed to treat another person the way that recipient first treated them.

Summarizing these two programs common to many religions into one practical moral behavior prescription yields, "You should co-operate first. If others co-operate, continue to do so. If someone defects on you, you should defect on them in similar fashion. But if they start co-operating again, you co-operate and so on..." This prescription is essentially the TIT FOR TAT strategy !

IX. LESSONS FROM PRISONER'S DILEMMA GAMES

How might the lessons from Prisoner's Dilemma games be used in understanding non-zero sum situations in today's world? Consider two problem areas: 1) getting people to co-operate initially, and 2) once established, what forces might destroy co-operation?

The lone practice of co-operation in a hostile world of defectors is difficult if not impossible to sustain for any appreciable length of time. However, in a world of many co-operators, such a lifestyle is natural and richly rewarding.

How can such a world emerge? Axelrod writes[8],

> Co-operation can emerge from small clusters of
> discriminating individuals as long as these individuals
> have even a small proportion of their interactions with
> each other. So there must be some clustering of
> individuals who use strategies with two properties: the
> strategies will be first to co-operate, and they will
> discriminate between those who respond to the co-
> operation and those who do not.

As to forces capable of destroying co-operation, Axelrod identified two. He notes that of all the principles for fostering co-operation, not being envious is the toughest for people to grasp. In his classes he sometimes has students play Prisoner's Dilemma for several dozen moves. He describes it as follows:

> I tell them the object is to score well for themselves
> and it shouldn't matter whether they do better or worse
> than the other player. But the instructions don't work.
> They inevitably compare their score to their partner's.
> And this leads to envy, which leads to defections, and
> both partners wind up with lower scores than they would
> have had if they co-operated in the first place. A
> better standard for comparison is to ask, 'How well am I
> doing compared to someone else in my shoes ?'

Besides envy, the other force that can undo co-operation occurs at the end of a Prisoner's Dilemma game. One can always win by defecting on the last move. In tournaments no one knows how long the game is to last ahead of time. Unless the "shadow of the future" is known to be very small, there is no advantage to being the first to defect. (A summary of Axelrod's findings appear in Fig. #23)

Several conclusions emerge from Prisoner's Dilemma games and social psychologists' exploration of co-operate/defect choices. We summarize these and provide examples which relate them to real life situations as follows:

1) Co-operation is more likely if human interactions are face to face and repeat interactions are likely. This maximizes the shadow of the future--that is fear of the consequences of reciprocity. One-time only or anonymous interactions minimize it. For example, a study of auto repair shops showed that "ripoffs" decreased with the shop's distance from an interstate highway. Shops near such highways --typically servicing cars of tourists they'd never see again

```
+-------------------------------------------------------------+
|        FIG. #23  CO-OPERATION THEORY PER R. AXELROD         |
|                                                             |
|   Conclusions                                               |
|   1) Co-operation can get started by a small cluster        |
|      of individuals who reciprocate co-operation in a       |
|      world of defectors.                                    |
|   2) Co-operators can successfully protect themselves       |
|      from attack by uncooperative strategies.               |
|                                                             |
|   Pre-Requisites Needed                                     |
|   1) Co-operation must be based on reciprocity.             |
|   2) The shadow of the future must be large enough to       |
|      make this reciprocity stable.                          |
|                                                             |
|   Not-Needed                                                |
|   1) Rational Individuals                                   |
|   2) Words, exchange of messages or commitments             |
|   3) Trust                                                   |
|   4) Altruism                                               |
|   5) Central policing authority                             |
|                                                             |
+-------------------------------------------------------------+
```

--were most guilty of ripoffs. Similarly, when researchers[9] purposely abandoned cars (stripping license plates and raising the hood) in dissimilar neighborhoods both an equal distance from major universities, what happened was strikingly different. In the neighborhood where people moved in virtual anonymity, the vehicle was vandalized by several (middle class) adults first, then children. In contrast, the car left in a close knit neighborhood was untouched (with the exception of someone closing its hood during a rain).

  2) If individuals perceive widespread co-operation, they are more likely to co-operate. Similarly if they perceive widespread defection they will be more likely to defect. These observations are supported by the well-known peer pressure that young people are specially subject to. Often children cite "Everyone else was doing it, so I went ahead and did it" as a reason for their transgression. Adults are not immune to this pressure. If everyone is driving past the speed limit or engaging in stock market insider trading, isn't one more likely to do so as well?

3) Societal forces that attempt to influence behavior by appealing to envy hinder co-operation. For example, pushers of the conspicuous consumption lifestyle interfere with co-operation in resource sharing matters.

4) If individuals perceive chaos, societal breakdown or "the end of the game", they are more likely to incorporate defection behaviors into their lifestyles. Thus looting often follows natural disasters. Not only food but guns get stockpiled in nuclear war fallout shelters.

5) Co-operation is enhanced if individuals can discriminate potential co-operators from non-co-operators. During the 1960s, countercultural members could readily identify each other because their alternative lifestyle had outwardly visible signs. Potential co-operators were long-haired, bearded males, braless females, and anyone wearing personally-decorated clothing, driving a similarly colorful old vehicle or using marijuana. Those to avoid would be found in businessman suits, fur coats, or driving Corvettes or Mercedes. In general, around small clusters of co-operators, large communities based on co-operation can be built.

X. THE TRAGEDY OF THE COMMONS

Imagine a resource allocation situation. Through co-operation, all can emerge victorious. Suppose co-operation involves using only one's fair share of the resource; defection amounts to selfishly exploiting the resource.

University of California Biology professor Garrett Hardin has used the following argument[10] to fault co-operative sharing of resources schemes and attack those with a "Spaceship Earth" sense of justice.

The fundamental error of spaceship ethics, and the sharing it requires, is that it leads to what I call "the tragedy of the commons". Under a system of private property, the men who own property recognize their responsibility to care for it, for if they don't they will eventually suffer. A farmer, for instance, will allow no more cattle in a pasture than its carrying capacity justifies. If he overloads it, erosion sets in, weeds take over, and he loses the use of the pasture. If a pasture becomes a commons open to all, the right of each to use it may not be matched by a corresponding responsibility to protect it. Asking everyone to use it with discretion will hardly do, for the consider-

ate herdsman who refrains from overloading the commons
suffers more than a selfish one who says his needs are
greater. If everyone would restrain himself, all would
be well; but it takes only one less than everyone to
ruin a system of voluntary restraint. In a crowded world
of less than perfect human beings, mutual ruin is inevitable if there are no controls. This is the tragedy of
the commons...

In 1974, Hardin wrote a controversial article entitled
"Lifeboat Ethics: The Case Against Helping the Poor". There
he metaphorically imagines the

rich nation can be seen as a lifeboat full of
comparatively rich people. In the ocean outside each
lifeboat swim the poor of the world, who would like to
get in, or at least share some of the wealth. What
should the lifeboat passengers do ?

After some analysis, he sees a "tragedy of the commons"
developing because some peoples will not be able to rein in
the rate at which they are reproducing. Such exploitation of
the commons leads to an intolerable situation in which Americans are ultimately sharing resources with huge numbers of
non-Americans, by Hardin's reckoning. He decides that no more
should be admitted to the lifeboat and that a constant vigil
should be maintained to guard against possible boarding
parties. To those aboard who are morally abhorred by this
policy and feel guilty, he advises, "Get out and yield your
place to others".

One alternative would be to appeal to individual con-
sciences. Hardin sees a problem with asking a man who is
exploiting the commons to desist in the name of conscience.
He writes[11],

Sooner or later, consciously or subconsciously, he
senses that he has received two communications, and that
they are contradictory: (i) (intended communication) "If
you don't do as we ask, we will openly condemn you for
not acting like a responsible citizen", (ii) (the
unintended communication) "If you do behave as we ask,
we will secretly condemn you for a simpleton who can be
shamed into standing aside while the rest of us exploit
the commons."

One way out of this "double bind" for the affected
individual, or for anyone in a freedom of the commons
situation, would be to employ the TIT FOR TAT strategy. That

is start by co-operating-- i.e. respecting the rights of
others and taking only one's fair share from the commons--
and continuing as long as others do.

However, the reputation of this strategy was established
in two - player Prisoner's Dilemma games--not a complicated
interaction between large numbers of players, call that number N. Using the results of a much more complicated computer
tournament based on an N - player Prisoner's Dilemma game
would be a more valid approach. While the N - player version
has been well-studied--Garrett Hardin being one of the inves-
tigators--such a tournament has never been held. There are
three qualitative ways in which the N -player case would differ from the simpler pair interaction:
1) the harm of defection is not focused on one person but
spread out over many people, 2) in N - player games behavior
may be anonymous, and 3) since payoffs are determined by what
different players are doing, each player does not have total
reinforcement control over all the others. Given these differences, one must be careful in applying results obtained
from two - player Prisoner's Dilemma games to more complex
real life situations.

Humans have always faced overexploitation of the commons
problems--whether the commons was a forest for gathering food
or firewood, a pasture for grazing animals, a marine coastal
area for catching fish, a place to dump wastes, or a breeding
ground. Solutions to these tragedies have involved:
1) Moving to where exploiting the same resource is possible.
This move can be done physically or temporally--the later
involving dependence on a stored form of the resource until
use of the commons is again feasible.
2) Closing the commons. Thus we have private property, fenced
pastures, restricted hunting and fishing areas, forbidding
disposal of certain wastes in the commons, and population
control efforts.
3) Restraint of individuals in their use of the commons. This
is accomplished by voluntary means: people opt for the
freedom to choose responsibility (achieved by attitudinal
fixes)--or by coercion (achieved by appropriate social
restraint fixes).

Forced coercion represents anathema to liberals. As
Hardin writes[12],

> Coercion is a dirty word to most liberals....The only
> kind of coercion I recommend is mutual coercion,

mutually agreed upon by a majority of the people
affected.

He suggests coercion only because the other two possible
solutions are not workable when the commons being exploited
involves the air we breathe or the health of the planet's
biosphere as human impacts increase. (Note his "lifeboat
ethics" is a closing the commons strategy for a different
problem.)

How will this coercion be implemented? Hardin contends
that a "criterion of justice" and a "system of weighting" can
be devised so that "incommensurables" can be assessed, and
this used as the basis of an administrative and policing system to protect the commons. He realizes however, that without
a world government and with the opposition of some liberals,
carrying out such a plan would be difficult.

XI. LIBERALISM AND THE FUTURE

Our discussion of classic liberalism has focused on its
political and economic dimensions. As a philosophy, liberalism is based on reason. It is rooted in beliefs of the
essential good (but imperfect) nature of man and his continuing progress toward a society based on "liberty and
justice for all" through education.

Liberals have traditionally feared those who irrationally base actions on instinctual desires and feelings
(often identified with lower classes or with worldview theme
#18). Yet, beginning with 19th century Victorian intellec-
tuals, liberals have wrestled with the dilemma posed by rational self-interest vs. aroused-feeling-inspired altruistic
concerns. Growing populations, crowding, and dwindling resources have forced another dilemma on Western liberals.
Both society's 1980s swing from altruism toward selfishness
and increasing corporate state mastery over individuals have
discouraged many of them.

What is the future of liberalism? In addressing this,
MIT history professor Bruce Mazlish writes[13],

> Liberalism seems lost today, groping for some solid
> footing either in a social science...or a reformer's
> faith in the moral educability of mankind, now seen as a
> more instinctual rather than rational creature. No
> solutions can be forthcoming to these dilemmas of
> liberal belief until all parts of the problem are
> addressed: the nature of humans, the nature of the

social sciences, and the morality involved in social existence.

Human survival, whether in protecting people from the law of the jungle or from each other, has always required co-operation. As population and biosphere stresses increase, so may use of social restraint laws. Continued survival will require rethinking not only human political and economic systems, but also value systems pertaining to freedom and relations among people. No one knows whether or not future human society will be to the liking of liberals.

Questions & Problems

1. Certainly a classical liberal (as the word is defined and used here) differs from today's American style liberal. Distinguish Reagan Republicans' classical liberal tendencies from their conservative ones.
2. While classical liberals and libertarians (see LAW) can be distinguished using the words "generous" and "selfish", they clearly share common beliefs. Discuss.
3. Following Donella Meadows' example, compose your own list of persons, groups, publications, advertisers, etc. you'd like to silence. Give a reason why each is on your list.
4. In his 1962 book Capitalism and Freedom , Milton Friedman suggests there are two sets of values a liberal will emphasize: those 1) "relevant to relations among people" and 2) "relevant to the individual in the exercise of his freedom". Distinguish between these.
5. Make up your own double-edged statements about freedom. Use the format of the following example: One person's freedom of the seas, is another person's depleted fishing grounds.
6. V.C. Ferkiss, in an essay "Toward the Creation of Technological Man", argues that for individuals "freedom does not exist apart from society." Discuss.
7. Relate Boulding's three value systems to Heilbroner's three systems of social organization (see LAW).
8. Summarize the key differences between Freud's and Maslow's worldviews. Which do you better relate to?
9. Write a BASIC computer program to keep score for two-person Prisoner Dilemma C/D games. Provide it with an optional TIT for TAT program.
10. Defend or refute "lifeboat ethics".
11. Give an example of a social restraint law. Distinguish

such laws from technical and attitudinal fixes. Provide an example of a social restraint law that could be eliminated by a technical fix. Might failed attempts at attitudinal fixes lead to social restraint laws? Discuss.

12. Provide examples which support the viewpoint that steady erosion of individual freedoms necessarily accompanies population growth.

Notes

1. Caldwell, L.K. Environment:A Challenge to Modern Society , Anchor/Doubleday, New York, 1970.
2. Critchfield, R. Villages , Anchor/Doubleday, New York 1981
3. Maslow, A. Toward a Psychology of Being , Van Nostrand, New York, 1962.
4. Wachtel, P. The Poverty of Affluence , MacMillan, New York 1983.
5. Maslow, A. Motivation and Personality , Harper & Row, New York, 1954.
6. Maslow, A. "Synergy in the Society and in the Individual", Journal of Individual Psychology , 20, 1964.
7. Thomas, L. "An Argument for Co-operation", Discover , August, 1984.
8. Axelrod, R. The Evolution of Co-operation , Basic Books, New York, 1984.
9. Zimbardo, P. and Ruch, F., Psychology and Life , Scott, Foresman, and Co., Glenview, IL 1975.
10. Hardin, G. "Lifeboat Ethics:The Case Against Helping the Poor", Psychology Today , 8 (4), September 1974.
11. Hardin, G. "The Tragedy of the Commons", Science , vol. 62, pp. 1243-1248, 1968.
12. ibid.
13. Mazlish, B. "Psychohistory and Classical Liberalism", Society , Nov./Dec. 1988 pp.55-60.

KINGS & LAMENTATIONS

I. NUMERICAL WEALTH / POVERTY COMPARISONS

Numbers can be used to make some striking wealth/poverty comparisons. Consider super wealthy individuals--billion- aires--keeping in mind that $1 billion might typically re- present one year's total GNP for a poor country. In its 1989 listing of the world's billionaires, Forbes magazine counted 205 individuals (including 66 Americans). The combined as- sets of these people total over $ 1/2 trillion. This exceeds the total annual GNP of the nations containing the poorest fourth of the world's population (>1.25 billion people)!

The wealthy have a special relationship with banks. Some have used banking/financing ventures to build their fortunes; all use banks to secure and manage them. There are 1.25 million Americans who have $2.5 million or more in banks. Collectively, this group holds about the same share of wealth as the world's poorest half (>2.5 billion people) -- owning roughly 2000 times as much as each poor person!

Consider two quite different banks. In catering to the wealthy, New York's Citibank maintains a list of "Global Elite"--including over 5,000 people with net worths exceeding $100 million. In Bangladesh, the Grameen Rural Bank has pio- neered in extending credit to the world's poorest. It has made loans of from $1 to $200 (average loan $60) to over 300,000 families. The bank has one rule: borrowers use the money to generate income. Its policies have worked: 98 % of the loans have been repaid and bank branches now serve 6,000 villages.

The left-leaning weekly The Nation involved one finan- cier--junkbond peddler Michael Milken-- in a rich / poor comparison. Its April 24, 1989 issue compared Milken's 1987 earnings--$550 million-- to the annual wages of someone la- boring 40 hours/week at the U.S. minimum wage--then $3.35 /hour. It concluded, "Milken's 1987 salary equals the yearly income of almost 79,000 people on the minimum wage. Or to earn what Milken made, one person on the minimum wage would have to work for 79,000 years."

Hundreds of millions of people worldwide would feel rich if they had a regular job paying $3.35/hour. Consider the Philippines--where 70 % of the 56 million people live on less than $1/day ($300/year).

Early 1980s Manila showcased a shocking contrast:

"Smokey Mountain" as the city dump is called and the palace of Ferdinand and Imelda Marcos. The dump is home to 3,000 families--including 6,000 children. Meanwhile, by plundering the national treasury, the Marcos family amassed a personal fortune estimated at $10 billion. So in her Manila palace, Imelda had--along with 500 black brassieres--4600 pairs of shoes.

We could continue these rich / poor numerical comparisons. Yet, somehow numbers alone fail to adequately contrast the daily lives and concerns of the KINGS and those much less fortunate. For numbers themselves can not convey injustice, pain, suffering, and LAMENTATIONS.

II. CHILDREN IN BEVERLY HILLS AND BRAZIL
The children's clothing store on Rodeo Drive in Beverly Hills has just sold its fortieth and last $250 kid's cashmere sweater--so the mother's store-wide hunt is in vain. She instead buys her daughter a tiny Valentino cashmere coat for $425. Another girl and mommy decide on a $495 black velvet dress with taffeta sleeves. Nearby at a children's boutique called "This Little Piggy", a four year old boy is outfitted in a $200 leather jacket and $180 pants. The store's co-owner remarks[1], "My feeling is that by the time these children are 16, they will have exquisite taste levels and will demand quality and expert fashion."

It is 1985 and the children's fashion business is poised for another sales extravaganza. Soon "Dynasty" infant and children's clothes--a fashion line based on the tastes of television's fictional millionaire Carrington family--will be in the stores. Already men can buy their wives Dynasty perfume called "Forever Krystle" for $150 an ounce, or Dynasty fur coats for a tidy $200,000 each. Given the TV show's popularity, some are expecting a "Cabbage Patch Doll" style run on the clothing. The demand for these high-priced dolls produced lengthy waiting lists, near riots at some stores, and peak $600 million wholesale annual sales. In Beverly Hills, designer doll clothes are available for Cabbage Patch Dolls for a nifty $10,000.

Meanwhile, children in the favellas surrounding Brazilian cities are not as fortunate as their Beverly Hills counterparts. Consider[2] the situation in the slums of Goiania. Dozens of shacks line each side of a gray-green, slime-covered culvert. The people wear dirty rags. Many look sick.

There is no sanitation and the culvert reeks abominably in rainy weather.

A family with four children--a ten year old girl and her three younger brothers--live in one of these tiny hutches. It is built of sticks, matting, rags, cardboard, and rusty, discarded pieces of corrugated iron. Its floor is made of boxwood and an old door. Its ceiling is so low one can barely stand. Its furniture is boxes and the beds are piles of old clothes.

The children's father is trying to earn money by selling sweets from a tray he carries through the nearby streets of Goiania. Their mother is sick "somewhere" with malaria--so the girl must watch her brothers. Insects have bitten the three year old so his skin is covered with purple blotches the size of his hands. Both he and his brothers have round pot bellies indicative of malnutrition.

The girl has made a garden. It is but two feet square and flowers and onion stalks poke up from it. When strangers arrive, this pale, fair-haired, light-skinned girl stays close to her garden. She is shy and has no mother or dolls to cling to.

Elsewhere in Brazil--in front of a hut sinking in mud near the bridge over the River Guaibe in Port Alegre--an eight year old girl is not so shy when a social worker visits her home.[3] Even though her parents are away foraging in garbage heaps, she confides in the woman when asked whether she has eaten recently.

"Yes, miss, yesterday Mummy made little cakes from wet newspapers."

"What? Little cakes from what?" asks the woman.

"Mummy takes a sheet of newspaper, makes it into a ball and soaks it in water. When it is nice and soft, she kneads it into little cakes. We eat them, drink some water and feel nice and full inside."

III. LAMENTATIONS IN ETHIOPIA

In the poor African country of Ethiopia in mid-December of 1984, things are even worse. Berhan Nuguissie sits cradling her two children. Only 25 years old, she has the worn and weary look of an old woman. Eight days ago she sold the family's belongings--two goats and a cooking pot--and began the long walk out of the starving village--which had run completely out of grain. Berhan is now sitting outside a feeding center run by a Christian humanitarian organization. She is crying--her tears mixed with a fine dust. "We got here last night," she says, "but I'm afraid the little one is dying."

Ared Kadre and her emaciated four-month old twins are also nearby.. After leaving their mud homes, they journeyed from Mehoni village--walking 35 miles over parched earth and past corpses.

These are two families in a gaunt, withered crowd of 800 people who form an orderly, seated line in front of a medical compound. Both mothers have helplessly watched as their starving children's bodies started converting first fat, and then muscles into energy. Now, having burned the very enzymes they need for digestion, these dull, listless children's desire for food has abated.

At 7 A.M. a Dutch doctor arrives with an interpreter. His daily work begins with a walk through the rag-wrapped, barefoot crowd--a walk in which he decides whom the limited supplies and personnel can save and whom they can not. "Walking down this line I have the feeling I'm playing God, and I don't like that," he says.

He checks body fat and weighs the children to determine their state of malnutrition. "Ok, boy, you get a feeding ticket " he says to Berhan's youngest son. He moves on. "Sorry, boy, not for you," he says to another. The youngster's withered mother tugs at the doctor's trousers as if to say, "Wait, you've made a mistake!", but he moves on.

Also in the crowd is a Western newsman. Something he heard that morning before the doctor arrived has made quite an impression. He will write about it later.[4]

> In the last moments of the icy, windy night, when all valley is as still as death and the foreboding darkness seems eternal, the wailing begins, softly at first, like the distant chant of ghosts. It is a high-pitched, eerie howl that slices through the night, gathering strength until it lingers and echoes over the mile high valley-- thousands of voices united in prayerful pleas for mercy and forgiveness, voices that mourn the dead and beg the privilege of living another wretched day.

Perhaps 200,000 have died in Ethiopia in the last nine months and another seven million are threatened with starvation. In the African countries of Mauritania, Mali, Chad,

and Mozambique, the food shortages are nearly as critical.
The UN Food and Agriculture Organization estimates that tens
of millions of Africans in at least 20 countries are either
starving or facing malnutrition. In Mali, where one million
people are in dire need of food, Red Cross feeding centers
have been overwhelmed. At one center, about 100 hungry children who won't get anything stand behind a rope--watching
others eat. Fari Mata, a severely malnourished girl too weak
to walk, is carried to one center by her mother. She hopes
her daughter can get another bowl of rice mixed with milk.
The four year old weighs just 10 pounds.

The next day back in Ethiopia, the first of Aread
Kadre's twins dies at 3 P.M. The wasted four-month old boy
weighs just two pounds. The tiny body of Mustafa Kadre, a
Muslim, is laid next to the cloth-wrapped body of an old
Christian woman in the same grave. Both are covered with a
spray of mint before the grave is sealed.

The 1983-85 drought and famine in Ethiopia, where the
GNP per capita is $110/year, seems almost a re-run of one a
decade earlier which claimed one million lives. Then, 81 year
old Ethiopian ruler Haile Selassie was overthrown after dis-
gruntled army officers distributed photos of him throwing
fresh meat scraps to two Great Dane dogs.

IV. AFFLUENT AMERICA'S PAMPERED PETS

The impeccably clean, colorfully-decorated gourmet
restaurant is in a fashionable mid-Manhattan neighborhood.
The menu features a fine assortment of meals including boeuf
a la bourguignon, shrimp cocktail, chicken chowmein, braised
fish fillet, and Swedish meatballs. It serves 300 meals a
week and can furnish a nice setting for special occasions
like birthdays. For these, it will provide invitations, set
up attractive centerpiece, bake birthday cake, and handle
party favors.

Nearby in Mahwah, New Jersey is a related establishment
--a rather special motel which grosses $350,000/year.
Selecting the deluxe suite and opting for the all-inclusive
Personal Services Plan, gets one a nicely carpeted room with
a fireplace, cathedral, sky-lighted ceiling, a bed with
special mattress, exclusive use of a one-acre fenced area,
and catered, home-cooking style meals. Given the $33.50 to
$46.50 per day single occupancy rates, the 50 room motel is
very popular. Rooms are booked 18 months in advance and

clients come from Europe, South America, Canada, and the Far East.

In upstate New York is a third, related operation: Camp Lindo. This summer camp sits on a picturesque farm a quarter mile off a winding mountain road. There are 75 acres of field and forest with a crystal-clear mountain stream and a nearby waterfall. The daily schedule includes various training lessons, an exercise and play period with group activities, and swimming in a pond. Special activities include treasure hunts and a Sunday hotdog and hamburger barbecue. Given these happenings, the campers need plenty of sleep, so nightly bed check is at 8:30 P.M. All this fun costs camper's parents $20 per weekend, $40 per week, or $150 per month. On a recent Labor Day there were 70 campers in attendance.

These commercial operations have been described as they were in the mid-1970s. Then each was rather unique. Today such establishments are more widespread. Besides being profitable, the three operations are related in that they all provided services for <u>DOGS.</u>

Affluent America's animals, especially its pets, often receive better food, housing, and medical care than do hundreds of millions of poor people throughout the world. Of the $7.9 billion Americans spent on household pets in 1988, nearly $6 billion went for pet food. Once pets ate table scraps. Now the U.S. pet food market is four times the size of the baby food market. Why the dramatic increase? One investigator concluded[5]

> ...a great deal of the huge increase in the sale of pet food appears to be attributable to the strenuous promotional efforts of the pet food manufacturers, whose television ads, with their shots of dogs, puppies, cats and kittens in adorable action, not only have helped persuade pet owners to buy their products but may even have influenced many people to go out and buy pets so that they could dish out for them the pet food being advertised.

Many pets receive high-priced meals. Birds get Waldorf salad--dehydrated fruits, vegetables and nuts at $10 a bottle, cats dine on microwaveable gourmet cat food, and dogs feast on Frosty Paws--an ice cream-like treat. Sales of pet non-food accessories are growing at a hefty 14 % annual rate. Many cats eat out of $20 crystal feeding dishes. Fancy dog collars are a hot item. Alongside competing $30 14 karat gold necklaces and $22.50 reptile skin collars, Pooch, Inc.'s $12.95 14 karat gold collar chains are a real bargain. The firm projects 1989 sales of this item at $1.2 million.

V. THE AFFLUENT WASTE, AFRICANS STARVE

With the proliferation of American pets eating corporate food, what's happening to table scraps they once were eating? Often, they are thrown out. One General Accounting Office report concluded that American households throw out some 10 % of all food purchases. The report--citing a University of Arizona anthropologist's study of people's trash--noted

> The middle-income neighborhoods waste almost 25 %. Over half of the food thrown out over a three-year period was not table scraps; it was straight waste--half a loaf of bread, untouched fruits, half a bag of vegetables, and, in some cases, unopened packages of food...

At the grocery store, one step before the dinner table, even more food is wasted. In Las Vegas, Nevada, free food markets for hungry people, stocked entirely by "old" food donated by co-operating supermarkets, have been organized. Such food, which is cosmetically flawed or has been on the shelves for too long, is routinely thrown away. According to the Las Vegas woman who organized the markets, such throw away food could feed 49 million Americans.

In Africa--in the capital city of the 10 million person Ivory Coast nation--extravagance of a different sort is occurring. The country's aging president is spending $200 million building the biggest church in Christendom. At 525 feet tall, the opulently adorned church is taller than St. Peter's Basilica in Rome. This massive, air-conditioned structure incorporates nine acres of French stained glass and Italian marble. Despite this commitment, Catholics compose but 10 % of the population in this nation of $650/yr income.

The massive church was completed in late 1989. About the same time, a rich American positively portrayed on a 1985 TV news program--which also featured a segment on the Ivory Coast's neighbor Mali--was going to jail...

The January 27, 1985 edition of CBS' '60 Minutes' begins in the drought-stricken nation of Mali. There--along the Niger River delta--the hungry comb anthills in search of pieces of grain. Farmers who have long since eaten the seed they bought for planting, have turned to salting, cooking, and eating leaves pulled from trees. Diane Sawyer interviews a boy, who in broken English tells an American prime time audience how he sleeps in the dirt, is hungry all the time, and has seen many children die. The camera films a little girl with dysentery who is crouching in the dirt waiting to die.

Ms. Sawyer talks to a farmer who cultivates his fields with the same simple hand tools used for centuries. He waters his garden with a gourd and dreams of someday owning an ox--nevermind that he doesn't have a plow. His wife weaves straw mats which she sells in order to buy corn--which she grinds into cornmeal. The most "high tech" thing the family owns is a pair of sunglasses.

Foreign aid to Mali has mostly been a disaster, Ms. Sawyer reports. Often it has gone for large "status" projects--such as a $30 million hydroelectric plant which produces far more electricity than the country needs--or comes without technical advisors. One exception has been the small cash grants for individual families program.

The next story on '60 Minutes' presents quite a contrast: it is the portrait of a super affluent elderly couple, Harry and Leona Helmsley. 75 year old Harry owns 200 New York City buildings--including the Empire State Building. His wife--known as "The Queen of the Palace"--manages their chain of 27 hotels.

Together, they accompany Mike Wallace in touring two of their homes. One is in Connecticut, where they keep a 28 room mansion on 26 acres for just the two of them. No one else lives there. The other is their penthouse on the 47th floor of the Park Lane Hotel. They chat with Mike while he inspects their $1 million Connecticut indoor swimming pool, their 47th floor New York pool, their ballroom dance floor, etc.

Shortly after the flattering CBS piece, Harry purchased another 80 buildings. By early 1988, the Helmsleys again received national attention--but the picture that emerged was quite different. Federal and state indictments charged them with illegally claiming as business expenses millions of dollars spent on luxuries for their Connecticut home in avoiding income taxes. Leona was also accused of extortion and conspiracy. Along with a top aide, she was depicted as receiving kickbacks after threatening suppliers with a cutoff of Helmsley business and employees with loss of jobs.

After following the starvation in Mali episode with a

look at the Helmsleys, the CBS team could have made a
monetary comparison. Estimates of the Helmsley's wealth range
from $1.4 billion to $5 billion. The GNP of the entire 7.5
million person nation of Mali is but $1.1 billion.

VI. MEDICAL CARE--GHANA AND AMERICA

In Accra, Ghana--where Felicia shares a tiny back-room
apartment with her mother--many are barefoot. She is a nurse
at a clinic that receives patients for the country's main
hospital. Conditions there are very poor.

"We have no drugs," Felicia says in a late 1984
interview.[6]

> No bed sheets. No paper to write down the case
> histories of the patients. The doctors are disgusted.
> There is no pain killer, no aspirin. The lights go off
> and on all day. We leave a box out for donations from
> the patients, but we don't get much. The rats are
> invading us. We have no stretchers. Dead bodies are
> left for 24 hours or more. The mortuary man says he has
> no instructions to carry people to the mortuary. We
> have no needles for giving injections, but we have no
> drugs so it doesn't matter. If we get disposable
> syringes, we boil them and use them again. When you go
> to the hospital, if you have to go, you take along your
> own sheets and pillows and a bucket--just to bathe.
> There is no hot water, no dressing for wounds.

Meantime, back in the U.S., the news media focuses on a
Louisville, Kentucky hospital owned by Humana, Inc. There,
52 year old William Schroeder is recuperating from surgery.
During a seven hour operation, doctors removed his diseased
heart and inserted a 10 ounce plastic artificial heart.

In a country that spends 12 % of its GNP on health
costs, Humana, Inc. operates one of the largest hospital
chains. In the year before the William Schroeder operation
brought it national attention, its 90 hospitals quietly
brought in revenues of $2.6 billion and showed a $193 million
profit.

Some think there is big money to be made in the artificial heart business. A Stanford University study touts
this potentially $15 billion/year industry--foreseeing 50,000
Americans annually getting these plastic pumps at roughly
$250,000 each. Such reports bring grumbling. Critics claim
that money put into preventive health programs, i.e.

campaigns to stop smoking, improved pre-natal care, or preventive heart medicine, would be a better investment.

By the end of William Schroeder's first post-operative week, his condition has stabilized. He kisses his wife, takes a few steps, drinks a beer, and hopes to go home soon. Elsewhere in the U.S., an estimated 200 to 300 pets--mostly dogs, but a handful of cats--have already recovered from their cardiac surgery. Now, with artificial electronic pacemakers implanted, they have returned to normal life.[7]

Back in Ghana it's 2 P.M. and Felicia--who works six hours a day six days a week at the hospital clinic--has finished and is leaving. Today's work has earned her 25 cedis-- about 64 cents, barely 10 cents per hour. The next morning she is up at 5 A.M. Yesterday she was able to get some cooking oil and flour. Now, with her mother's help, she begins preparing doughnuts which they will sell to more affluent Ghanans. At around $900/year GNP per capita income, her country is well-off by African standards. At 8 A.M. Felicia departs for the clinic, so her mother takes over doughnut sales. At about the same time--a third of the way around the world--another man is beginning work in a Burbank, California TV studio...

VII. MARRIAGES--IN HOLLYWOOD AND INDONESIA

...And now here's Johnny! Johnny Carson is reportedly the second wealthiest comedian in show business, after Bob Hope. As you might expect he is not eager to make his extensive property holdings public. His salary for each hour-long "Tonight Show" is likewise not available. Supposedly, singer Wayne Newton, at $45,000 per Las Vegas show and $17 million/year, ranks at the top of the entertainment earnings world. Carson, making an estimated $15 million/year, isn't far behind.

Our portrait of "The King of the Night" begins in late 1984.[8] Johnny's estranged wife Joanna has made news with her alimony demands. Simply to meet her own needs, Joanna wants $2.6 million/year in temporary support (Fig. #24). Carson is not overly concerned with these demands. During one Tonight Show monologue he quips "I heard from my cat's lawyer today. My cat wants $12,000 a week for Tender Vittles."

By 1985, Johnny is dividing his time between a Beverly Hills pied-a-terre and a 12,000 square foot beach home on 2 1/2 acres near Malibu--recently purchased for $8.6 million.

```
+-------------------------------------------------------------+
|                                                             |
|       FIG. #24   JOANNA'S MONTHLY EXPENSE NEEDS             |
|                                                             |
|                                                             |
|    A. Total Household Expenses,            $ 21,625         |
|       including:                                            |
|             servants                         4,945         |
|             maintenance & security          3,185         |
|             groceries                        1,400         |
|             telephone bills                    800         |
|                                                             |
|    B. Jewelry & Furs                        37,065         |
|    C. Clothing & Department Store Purchases  5,000         |
|    D. Travel                                 2,700         |
|    E. Two New York Apartments               10,000         |
|    F. Gifts to Friends & Relatives          12,000         |
|    G. Other                                128,277         |
|                           Monthly Total  $ 216,667         |
|                                                             |
|                     x 12 = $2.6 million per year           |
+-------------------------------------------------------------+
```

It features

a sumptuously furnished living room, a mirror-walled
gym, a refrigerated cellar that can store 10,000 bottles
of wine, garages for six cars, five built-in stereo
systems, three spiral staircases, an elevator, a sauna,
a sun deck, several gardens, a guest house, of course,
and every convenience money can buy.

Johnny's lifestyle didn't change much after the mid-1985 divorce settlement. Joanna received four of the couple's 12 residences, $240,000/year for ten years, and valuable paintings. Shortly thereafter, Johnny married for a fourth time.

Halfway around the world in the slums of Jakarta, Indonesia, Karlina is happily married to a printer.[9] She lives in a two-cubicle bamboo shed. Her family shares an open well and a pit privy with 40 people. She considers herself fortunate as her husband's earnings rank in the upper third of Jakarta incomes. She can afford to buy cans of drinking water from a neighbor's city water tap. Still, her home has the salty, sour stench of poverty. The oldest of her five children is patiently pulling lice from the baby's hair.

Karlina is planning to give a gift. She anticipates scrapping together the $2 admission and 60 cent monthly

charges so that one of her children can go to school. She
plans to send her daughter--although her sons are older.
Why? She's worried that her daughter, to escape from a neighborhood so poor that men work for 20 cents a day combing the
streets for used cigarette butts, will turn to prostitution.
Prostitutes can earn $10 a day. It's Karlina's greatest fear,
so she hopes to give her daughter a gift that matters.

VIII. A GIFT THAT MATTERS

Back in affluent Southern California, many are browsing
the Robinson's Christmas "Believe in Magic" catalogue, and
contemplating gifts they could give. Inside are complete descriptions, prices, and ordering instructions for 412 conse-
cutively numbered, high-priced gifts.

"I invite you to join these joyful celebrations of tradition and to share in the fantasies and spirit of our children" says a message in the front from Robinson's chief executive officer. You turn the page to a magical picture of Gift
#1...

> It was Christmas morning. You became the baron. Home was
> now a castle in Scotland with a 700 year old legacy of
> glamour, chivalry and magic...the ghosts of Christmases
> past welcome you to Castle Lee...

A modernized medieval mansion with tennis court, wine cellar,
stable, kennel, helipad, etc. is described. The price is
$5,750,000--availability subject to prior sale.

Turning pages brings you to Gift #6: a two week cruise
for you and 1200 friends you select aboard the Royal
Princess. The ship--which recalls TV's "Love Boat"-- is
described as

> ...the world's most majestic seagoing resort, where
> picture windows replace portholes in every stateroom,
> champagne and fine wines always flow...Two acres of open
> deck, freshwater spas, four pools and a joggers track on
> the promenade...Massage rooms, beauty salons and a
> complete casino deal only in superlatives. Sevruga
> caviar, a perpetually open bar, cuisine of master
> European chefs await. And night after night, gala
> revues rival those at each port of call. Make the Royal
> Princess your Kingdom on the Sea...

The price is $5,856,200.

Ports of call in Mexico are favorite destinations for
such Pacific luxury cruises. Although the Robinson's cata-

logue doesn't mention the possibility, perhaps one of the more adventurous cruise goers will encounter Nita on an inland excursion. Nita is a pretty, dark-eyed little three-year old girl. Unfortunately, Nita's mother can't earn enough money selling the straw mats she makes to support Nita and her two brothers. So Nita spends her days in the village marketplace around the corner from her mother, with a tin cup in hand, begging.

Upon turning the page in the Robinson Christmas gift catalogue, the headline reads "Wish for Diamonds...Precious Color and Gold". Gift #9 is a 15.63 ct TW diamond necklace for $29,900. The ad urges, "Give a gift that matters".

IX. CROSSING INTERNATIONAL BORDERS

While the affluent are taking luxury cruises, paying $4,876/person for a Concorde flight from New York to Paris, or touring Europe in $205,500 Rolls Royce Corniche convertibles, people like Enrique and Rosita are also traveling. While 1989 Congressional legislation permits up to 4800 wealthy foreigners to pay $1 million each and legally settle in the U.S., this teenage brother and sister must sneak into America. Their story is told in the award-winning movie El Norte.

Rich land grabbers, aided by the Guatemalan army, have brutally killed their father, who was part of a resistance effort, and abducted their mother. Minutes before his death, the father tells his son, "For rich people, poor peasants like us are just a pair of arms to do their work...They treat their animals better than us!" Fleeing their village on foot through the mountains, Enrique and his sister journey to the Pan-American Highway. They find a friendly Mexican truck driver and then a bus to carry them north to Tijuana. At the U.S.-Mexico border, Enrique and Rosita face the high-tech equipped U.S. border patrol on one side, and robbers and desperadoes on the other.

Their first attempted crossing is unsuccessful. They narrowly escape a knife-wielding thief and are captured by U.S. immigration authorities. They try again a few days later, crawling for miles through a stench-filled old sewer pipe. Near the end of this tunnel, they are attacked by dozens of rats. After incurring many painful bites, an exhausted Enrique and Rosita fend off the rodents. Before they can exit and link up with their "coyote" who's waiting, they must avoid the spotlight of a circling helicopter...

Illegal immigration has swelled the percentage of Hispanics in Los Angeles to 24 %. Given Mexico's per capita income--less than 1/10 of the U.S. value--many bridge the gap between rich and poor with their feet.

Another such person is Aurelio. He prefers life in Huecorio--but has been forced to work in Southern California more than once in recent years. Huecorio is a small mountain village which spreads out from the shores of Lake Patzcuaro up the slopes of an extinct volcano. In spring, these slopes are a golden patchwork of wheat fields. In summer they're green with corn and beans.

Aurelio often helps his grandparents with their wheat crop. To get to the wheat field, high on the volcano's slopes, he must climb for an hour. While wheat has replaced corn as the major Mexican cash crop, Huecorio families don't get rich from their average 13 acre holdings (often badly eroded). Field laborers with no land of their own can make no more than $800/year.

Given Mexico's debt crisis, the poor's real income has fallen as imports and domestic spending have been slashed to meet interest payments. Yet a few well-placed Mexicans have benefitted from massive foreign bank loans and prospered. In March, 1986, a Mexico City newspaper named 575 citizens, each having at least $1 million in foreign banks. Markedly absent from the list were names of two Mexican presidents.

After leaving office in 1984, Lopez Portillo moved to Rome taking a reported $1 billion with him. Succeeding him, Miguel de la Madrid promised to seek a "moral renovation". But U.S. intelligence reports soon documented de la Madrid's substantial deposits in a Swiss bank account: $162 million during 1983 alone. Thus, while Mexico's poor must leave in search of work and money in the U.S., its wealthy send their money out of the country. By late 1987, $250 billion of capital had left Latin America. Thus Venezuelans' overseas deposits totaled $58 billion, its foreign debt $37 billion.

X. THE INFORMATION AGE--HERE & THERE

In the last two decades, America moved from an industrial to an information dominated era. Microchips, fiber optics, lasers, and a score of new technologies have transformed the communications, information, and entertainment landscape. Portable computers connect to public telephones and send information thousands of miles. Cellular car telephones enable commuters to conduct business discussions. Large screen or projection TVs, TV signal-receiving satellite dishes, VCRs, microcomputers, personal copiers, and FAX machines have increasingly found their way into millions of American homes.

During these same years, there has been progress in Third World village communications, but often extreme poverty necessitates a "make-do" approach. In his 1972 book, Design for the Real World , Victor Papanek describes his one transistor radio that was used in Indonesian villages.

The radio's housing is a readily available tin can. This holds the heating fuel needed to produce a feeble amount of electricity via thermocouple. Wax, wood, paper, and dried cow dung can all serve as fuel. In the can's upper third are its electrical components: ear-plug speaker, hand-woven copper radial antenna, a ground wire incorporating a nail, thermocouple, and tunnel diode. That the radio is unidirectional is a small concern--most developing countries support only one broadcast channel. The cost of the entire radio is nine cents. (Today, a small solar cell could replace the thermocouple/fuel without raising the price much.)

Over a decade later, Indian engineer Shiv Prasad Kosta began teaching poor villagers to use coconut, mango, eucalyptus, date palm and other large leaf trees as antennas for pulling in weak signals from the distant transmitters of the country's one TV network. "I have demonstrated the experiments with trees in rural areas," says Kosta, "and when people see the picture on my small Sony, they get excited." His enthusiasm is fueled by an ancient belief that God and man can use trees to communicate.

Although religious beliefs play an important part in Indian life, the country's increasingly affluent urban middle class has developed a taste for Western consumer goods and lifestyles. They are targeted by commercials--which one of India's two government-owned TV channels allows.

70 % of the Indian countryside is now within range of these TV signals, thanks to INSAT--a communications satellite launched in 1983. Since then, hundreds of village satellite receiving stations have been established and television has come to rural India.[10] While there are but tens of thousands of TV sets in the countryside--and only a small percentage of Indian villages even have electricity--the educational and

problem-solving needs are great.

400 million Indians are illiterate. 2/3 of India's schools have no buildings and 1/3 are unstaffed. Many of those schools fortunate enough to have buildings or teachers, lack blackboards, drinking water, etc. Mandikonda, a village of 1500 people, is fortunate to have a satellite receiver and a school building--which also houses the community TV set...

Tonight a crowd of 500 has gathered around the television. Typical of these people is a 45 year old thin man. His family of five earns 60 cents a day by rolling crude cigarettes which are sold by someone else. Not really enough to get by on, he says. Although he is a frequent viewer, TV is still a novelty and he sees much he does not understand.

10 % of the programs are from the West. Many programs are directed to India's middle class who want entertainment not education, and there are commercials. Some are already grumbling about Indian television. One is political opposition leader George Fernandes. He doesn't like what the programs and commercials are doing to India's villagers. He says they "cater to the rich but in so doing they tantalize the poor...The poor are told that some things are very necessary for them, but these are beyond their reach...They shake confidence in their own values and give them nothing in return. ...they're destroying them..." A noble effort to include rural India in "the global village" is disturbing the have-nots, as their eyes are opened to how the affluent live.

XI. CROWDED AMERICAN CLOSETS

Wealthy Sharon McCutchin of Dallas has a problem, one she shares with other American women. "If you polled every woman in the U.S. you would not find one who has enough closet space," she says. When one faces a common problem, surveying others' solutions is wise.[11]

The Robbins were desperate. As Harold, a well-known novelist recalls, "None of our cooks would stay. My wife's clothes filled up all their closets too!" Then wife Grace went away for a two week vacation on their yacht Gracara, and Harold met the problem head on. He hired an engineer who designed an automated clothes conveyor. Now, $3500 plus labor expenses later, Grace can push a button and the revolving carrousel displays the desired portion of her wardrobe. However, while the new arrangement is an improvement, it only accommodates 700 garments. So just the evening dresses, resort wear and luncheon clothes live in new carrousel. Overflow still ends up in the servant's closets.

Dani Needham, wife of film director Hal Needham, employs another "high tech" approach to closet management. Since she travels lots, she carries with her a list of every garment by number and description. This approach, she explains, has simplified life. "If I'm in Paris and I find a purple suit that I want to buy, then I need a lavender blouse. So I look in my book to see if I have one. If I do, I call the housekeeper and have her send blouse No. 43."

Other women solve the closet problem by employing more space. Comedienne Phyllis Diller has converted a 23 ft. by 14 ft. bedroom into a closet by employing moveable racks. This room abounds with her clothes, movie costumes, 44 furs, and four nose warmers. However, this one room solution would hardly work for Carolyn Farb, ex-wife of a Houston real estate tycoon. She devotes six rooms to storing and caring for her $ 3/4 million wardrobe.

Back in Dallas, Jerry and Sharon McCutchin have decided to incorporate many of these ideas in the building of their two room supercloset. It will have skylights, marble floors, a fireplace, an alterations room, and a rotating conveyor rack for 400 garments. As Sharon describes it, "There are shoe and bag rooms with enough space for 300 pairs of shoes and 400 handbags. The part where my hanging clothes will be is as big as some one-bedroom apartments." Appropriately, before moving clothes in, the McCutchins plan to throw a "coming out of the closet" party for 100 friends--to be held in this apartment-sized closet.

Elsewhere in urban America, many families would feel fortunate to live in an apartment the size of the McCutchin's closet. Consider the situation in Los Angeles, as described in a 1989 article, "A Tale of Two Cities".[12] According to UCLA urban planner, Edward Soja,

> The polarization of rich and poor is producing a permanent underclass that is expanding at extraordinary rates. Los Angeles County has as many as 65,000 homeless people, 200,000 people living in garages, and perhaps 100,000 downwardly mobile families who have become trapped in cheap, run-down hotels and motels, unable to pay the two months' advance rent necessary for an apartment...There are close to half-a-million people in

the county living in conditions that resemble Third
World urban settlements.

XII. AMERICA'S HOMELESS AND ITS KING

For homeless Americans, dignity is something you lose
after you lose your job and home, but before you lose your
health or your life. Losing one's dignity is like giving up
hope--sort of a breakdown. One man is humiliated when his
hungry little girl tells a Sears Roebuck Santa Claus that all
she really wants for Christmas is a job for Daddy. Another
family of four is severely tested by a few nights sleeping in
their old, cramped Chevy Vega. With a towel taped over the
windshield for privacy, the father slumps behind the steering
wheel--the mother next to him in the passenger seat and the
children in the back. Elsewhere, perhaps off the interstate,
a fully-loaded station wagon's engine has just blown. The
family--with no money for repairs--must abandon it.

Harking back to the 1930s, out of work people are on the
road searching for a better life. Many have their hard-luck
stories to tell....In February, in Atlanta, alcohol-intoxi-
cated Roosevelt Richardson climbs into an abandoned car late
one night. Shivering in the winter cold, but falling asleep
anyway, he wakes in the morning with frostbite. This soon
turns to gangrene. "I didn't have a blanket. I guess that's
why I lost my feet," he says. Having lost a Texas welding
job, Ronald Thompson journeyed to Seattle with his wife and
two small boys. He hoped to find shipbuilding work. Work was
not to be found--so the Thompsons moved into an apartment
provided by local charity. "I always thought I could give my
family a home. Now, well, it just feels hopeless!" he says.

In winter, in the nation's capitol, the steam grates are
peopled with the homeless trying to keep warm. In Lafayette
Square--across from the White House--sits Tom Pittson, a 30
year old former Kentucky coal miner. "After my benefits
played out back home, I come to Manassas, Va. looking for
work, then here," he recalls. "Bad mistake. For awhile, I had
a big cardboard box to sleep in beneath a bridge. Another
guy, he took it, along with my coat. Can't get work now
because I'm sick a lot. My job now is to get by. It's a sorry
way to live. After two years on the street, I'm near giving
up, " he says.

As the 1990s begin, there are as many homeless in
America--two to three million--as there are millionaires. In

the White House while the spectacle of homelessness burst onto the American scene--was Ronald Reagan. Reagan is the hero of the millionaire class, the leader of the selfish, super affluent few. As the 1980s end, the ex-President, as if to underscore his own values, goes to Japan for a speaking tour. Sponsored by a large Japanese corporation, he returns $7 million richer. One reporter calculates he receives $50,000 per minute for his services.

During the Reagan years, a "Me, First" ethic pervades the country. Reagan gets the country "feeling good about greed in Gomorrah" in the words of one dissident reporter.[13] Poverty is long out of fashion.

In response to the plight of the poor and homelessness, the Reagan administration,
1) in the person of Edwin Meese comments that people choose to eat at soup kitchens because "it's easier than paying",
2) slashes subsidized housing for low income families from $32 billion expenditures in 1980, to $6 billion in 1987.

But Reagan gets the country moving again and to many Republicans is a great president. Democrats think otherwise. Retired House Speaker Tip O'Neill writes, "It was sinful that Ronald Reagan ever became president". Despite his denunciations of the Reagan presidency, O'Neill writes, "Let me give him his due: He would have made a hell of a King."

Questions & Problems

1. This chapter's most striking contrasts are between people dominated by worldview theme # ? and those dominated by theme # ? Discuss.
2. Walt Disney chief executive Michael Eisner earned $40 million in salary and bonuses during 1988. Was he worth it? Discuss according to the points of view taken by people embracing worldview themes a) #19, b) #24 / #16
3. News of a utility company president's $4 million bonus prompts a disgruntled customer to write, "No wonder our gas bills have gone through the roof." Discuss the relative merits of the utility's 200,000 customers each getting $20 rebates vs. giving the bonus.
4. How does the 1990 U.S. budget shortfall--around $200 billion--compare with the GNPs of the world's nations?
5. "Real needs of ghetto dwellers and of developing nations are sacrificed to the pseudo-needs of the upper classes." Discuss.

6. George Gilder, author of <u>Wealth</u> <u>and</u> <u>Poverty,</u> writes, "Since their wealth is mostly invested, the American rich, in general, can not revel in it." Defend or refute.

7. A Smith-Barney commercial ends, "They make money the old-fashioned way: they earn it." Discuss the inherent irony.

8. Report on Marcos (Philippines), Mobutu (Zaire), Duvalier (Haiti), the Sultan of Brunei, Ceausescu (Romania) or other past or current national rulers who accumulate fortunes while their countrymen starve.

9. Several vet hospitals now have oncology departments where cancer-stricken dogs and cats can get CAT scans and chemotherapy. Should pampered pets have such treatment, when medical needs of the world's poor go unmet? Discuss.

10. Arrange to help out at a soup kitchen or shelter for the homeless. Report.

11. According to Richard Lamm, 700,000 Americans who receive social security benefits earn over $50,000 a year in other retirement income. 1/4 of all such benefits go to people with incomes over $25,000 a year. Is this taking from the poor and giving to the rich? Discuss.

Notes

1. Goodwin, B. "Cradle to Label: Luxury Wear for the Child with the Silver Spoon" <u>L.A.</u> <u>Times</u> , 1/11/85

2. based on account in Hopcraft, A. <u>Born</u> <u>to</u> <u>Hunger</u> , Houghton Mifflin, Boston 1968.

3. based on 1989 account in <u>The</u> <u>Information</u> <u>Newsletter</u> <u>of</u> <u>the</u> <u>Brazilian</u> <u>Evangelical</u> <u>Lutheran</u> <u>Church.</u>

4. Lamb, D. "Famine in Ethiopia:Suffering and Grace", <u>L.A.</u> <u>Times</u> , December 30-31, 1984.

5. Whiteside, T. "Din, Din", <u>New</u> <u>Yorker</u> , November, 1976.

6. Powers, C. "Africa--Omens of Advancing Disaster", <u>L.A.</u> <u>Times</u> , December 19, 1984.

7. "Pacemakers Going to the Dogs", <u>Science</u> <u>85</u> , March 1985.

8. information regarding Johnny Carson and his divorce based on <u>Newsweek</u> October 31, 1983, <u>People</u> <u>Weekly</u> February 27, 1984, and <u>Parade</u> January 20, 1985.

9. Critchfield, op cit.

10. based on PBS / Nova program "Global Village".

11. "The Challenge of Inner Space", <u>Time</u> March 5, 1984

12. Wolpert, S. "A Tale of Two Cities", <u>UCLA</u> <u>Magazine</u> , Spring, 1989.

13. Blumenthal, op cit.

GRABBERS

"Grabbers"--it's not the usual chapter title you'd expect in a book that purports to present an even-handed approach to controversy. Neither are "Pushers & Prisoners" and "Masters"--titles to the subsequent two chapters. "Aha!" you say. "What I suspected in the last chapter now seems established: the author has abandoned an objective approach in favor of preaching and propaganda promoting a particular point of view!" Since there is some truth in this assertion, allow me to defend my inclusion of this material.

University of San Diego philosophy professor Dennis Rohatyn notes that "propaganda plays an indispensable role in determining the outcome as conflicting worldviews square off against each other." Anyone growing up with U.S. public schools, television and newspapers has been subjected to a barrage of propaganda promoting self-interest / capitalism, economic growth, and consumerism. Most never question the essential message of this assault--thus themes #19, #22, and #26 dominate the American mentality.

Sadly, most Americans have adopted values and structured their worldviews without ever seeing fundamentally "conflicting worldviews square off against each other". As Gore Vidal notes, "The corporate grip on opinion in the United States is one of the wonders of the Western World. No First World country has ever managed to eliminate so entirely from its media all objectivity--much less dissent."

This book attempts to restore objectivity by voicing concerns and making connections the corporate media ignores. The central portion of Part B (which you're beginning) amounts to a frontal assault on the values and ethics behind the American corporate / consumerist mentality. Part C depicts an other-oriented / fair play alternative and debates this orientation's merits with those of selfishness.

I. GOD-BASED VS. MONEY-BASED RELIGIONS

Since the 1948 publication of George Orwell's novel <u>1984</u>, futuristic police states, where people might be forced to worship a Big Brother-like master, have been feared. However, when that dreaded year finally dawned, many people in affluent Western society were even more fervently worshipping the same master that their grandparents had worshipped 50 years earlier. He was the one Orwell described in his 1935 novel <u>Keep</u> <u>the</u> <u>Aspidistra</u> <u>Flying</u> .

> Money worship has been elevated into a religion. Perhaps it is the only real religion--the only really felt religion--that is left to us. Money is what God used to be. Good and evil have no meaning any longer except failure and success.

Orwell went on to suggest that but two rules to live by have replaced the Biblical Ten Commandments, "Thou shalt make money" and "Thou shalt not lose thy job".

As the 1990s begin, many Westerners are worshipping the money lord, the almighty Grab, instead of God. These people are the Grabbers.

One can draw parallels between the two religions, an ancient one based on God, a modern one based on Grab. What sharing is to one, grabbing is to the other. Brotherhood is replaced by a single word, "me", in the modern religion. The role of temples and churches in one, is played by financial institutions in the other. Bill Moyers described the ever-present, product-pushing TV commercial as "the communion wafer of the marketplace". Gambling--something Americans spend a staggering $250 billion/year on--has been called a "way to sing hymns to wealth". Buying a lottery ticket has been likened to a prayer. Attaining wealth is like going to heaven.

Seldom do sharing and grabbing mentalities present themselves for side by side comparison--except at Christmas. This is a time of fierce competition between Grabbers and Christians, i.e. those spreading the good tidings of Jesus Christ, the celebration of whose birth Christmas is supposedly all about. Often during this season, either the message or the symbols of both religions appear together.

Consider three examples, which appeared in <u>The</u> <u>Los</u> <u>Angeles</u> <u>Times</u> during one week in December 1984: 1) On December 13th, side by side ads appear. One suggests you take your spouse to a "Gala New Year's Holiday" for five days and four nights, and spend $798. The other asks that you (instead?) use your money to "provide free meals for homeless and destitute men and women." In fact, $798 would buy Christmas dinners for 618 Skid Row people, information in the ad enables you to calculate. 2) On December 17th, a feature article declares, "Christmas may now be as much an economic necessity to all of America as it is a spiritual necessity to Christian America". With expected sales of $25 billion jingle belling around in their cash registers, no one needs to tell Grabbers that Christmas "tis the season to be ... profitable". 3) On December 18th, an ad (Fig.#25) placed by the Episcopal Church most unusually pictures Jesus and Santa Claus, a Grabber patron saint, next to each other.

FIG. #25   CHRISTMAS...WHOSE BIRTHDAY?

To find an Episcopal Church near you
consult the yellow pages or call 213/482-2040

II. CHARACTERIZING GRABBERS

University of Maine economist Mark Lutz has attempted[1] to identify fundamentally what makes people Grabbers.

> Let us posit that there exists some powerful, alien Force that seems so often to effectively frustrate the realization of well-intended ideas and social ideals.
> ...We believe the source of this Force is the quest for individual self-gratification. It is satisfied by either political power...or economic power. The Force is latent in everybody. It actualizes...as soon as we seek to use others or our environment for our own purposes.

Lutz laments

> Social legitimization of this Force is generously pro-
> vided by economic science acting like a church preaching
> the worldly gospel of how individual self-regarding ac-
> tion ends up producing the common good.

While economists invoke Adam Smith's "invisible hand"
to rationalize grabbing, modern corporate media pushers in-
cessantly promote it. They give Grabbers numerous and repeated instructions daily as to appropriate behavior. Can
their messages be distilled into a few commandments for the
money-based religion--a task Orwell began?

The results of one such effort appear in Fig. #26. This
list starts with Orwell's two commandments, then, apparently
inspired by titles of best-selling books, adds a third and
fourth. The fifth commandment positions Grabbers at the top
of the food chain. The sixth provides a fundamental borrowing orientation for Grabbers. The last four commandments
apparently are general principles for Grabber businessmen to
follow. The metaphorical language they employ --drawn from
the bathroom, a popular bumpersticker, and the barnyard--was
chosen to aid in remembering them.

Still, the authoritarian tone of these commandments
seems strangely out of place, given the loose, "anything
goes", permissiveness of Grabber society. Maybe a comforting
counterpart to the 23rd Psalm (Fig. #27) would be more
appropriate...

III. THOU SHALT MAKE MONEY

Let us consider each of these commandments, beginning
with commandment #1. In KINGS & LAMENTATIONS, we
contrasted the lifestyles of the successful few, with the
numerous unfortunate. Sadly, for every American who is
outraged by such lavish lifestyles, many more are envious.
To these people who long for such financial rewards, high
earnings and luxuries are evidence of "making good".

In that previous chapter, among those with enough money
to indulge their every whim, were bankers, corporate executives, real estate magnates, utility company presidents,
talk show hosts, comedians, film directors, best-selling
authors, ex-U.S. presidents, Third World despots, Beverly
Hills affluent, the jet set, ocean luxury cruise goers, and
those with pampered pets. Recently, those in another occupation have unexpectedly joined the high-salaried elite:

television evangelists.

```
+----------------------------------------------------------+
|            FIG. #26   THE GRABBER TEN COMMANDMENTS       |
|                                                          |
|   #1 Thou shalt make money.                              |
|                                                          |
|   #2 Thou shalt not lose thy job.                        |
|                                                          |
|   #3 Thou shalt win the battle with thy money hangups.   |
|                                                          |
|   #4 Thou shalt look out for Number One.                 |
|                                                          |
|   #5 Thou shalt eat high on the hog.                     |
|                                                          |
|   #6 Thou shalt not be afraid to borrow from tomorrow    |
|      to pay for today.                                   |
|                                                          |
|   #7 Thou shalt flush thy wastes whenever thou can get   |
|      away with it.                                       |
|                                                          |
|   #8 Thou shalt preach a free market not a free lunch.   |
|                                                          |
|   #9 Thou shalt not be afraid to use the revolving       |
|      door or let the fox guard the chicken coop.         |
|                                                          |
|   #10 Thou shalt not be afraid to buy a politician       |
|       or rent a scientist.                               |
|                                                          |
+----------------------------------------------------------+
```

Given Jesus' "Go sell all you have and give the money to the poor and you will have riches in heaven" advice to the rich young man, one hardly expects to see Christian preachers building personal fortunes and conspicuously consuming. So while reports of corporate executives' seven figure salaries raised few eyebrows, the story of TV superstar minister Jim Bakker's and his wife Tammy's grabbing excesses was viewed with revulsion.

Even the Reverend Jerry Falwell was disturbed. Of the Bakkers he remarked, "I see the greed, I see the self-centeredness". Personally, he got buy on a mere $100,000/year salary, he explained. ("What about the million dollar advance he received for a book? " many wondered.)

```
+----------------------------------------------------------------+
|        FIG. #27   23RD PSALM--GRABBER CORRUPTION OF            |
|                                                                |
|   The lord Grab is my shepherd, I shall want. He makes        |
|   me work 8 to 5 daily for green money, then leads me         |
|   to the corporate media waters and conditions my soul.       |
|   He sends me down the hard path of growth, production,       |
|   meat-eating, and conspicuous consumption--for his           |
|   name's sake. Even though our toxic dumping is done in       |
|   a valley in the shadow of death, I fear no evil. Thy        |
|   foxes entering through the revolving door to guard          |
|   the chicken coop, thy paid politicians, thy rent-a-         |
|   scientists, they comfort me. Thou preparest a free          |
|   market before me in the presence of my free lunch           |
|   enemies. Thou anointest my head with materialism, my        |
|   trash overflows. Surely Pushers and unpaid bills shall      |
|   follow me all the days of my life, and I shall dwell        |
|   in my mortgaged house until nuclear winter.                 |
+----------------------------------------------------------------+
```

Except for a "We're sorry, Snuggles" remark made on national television and directed to their dog, who lost an air-conditioned dog house as PTL auctioned off luxuries to pay bills, the Bakkers offered no apologies. Not to the faithful from whom they ripped off millions of dollars. Nor for the lifestyle that featured six homes, 14 furs, gold-plated bathroom fixtures, expensive antique automobiles, a $265,000 payment to keep Jim's 1980 sexual indiscretion hushed up, and, for Tammy, breast-enlargement surgery (paid for by the PTL executive health plan). In her book, Christian Wives , Tammy, whose lust for shopping has been compared to Imelda Marcos', confided, "There's times I just have to quit thinking, and the only way I can quit thinking is by shopping."

Jim Bakker's preaching sometimes combines God and materialism. "If you pray for a camper, be sure to tell God what color" , he once instructed. Apparently, Jim sometimes confuses God and the almighty Grab. But there can be little doubt of his devotion to Grabber commandment #1: "Thou shalt make money".

IV. KEEP YOUR JOB; AVOID MONEY-BASED GUILT

The second and third Grabber commandments are related to maintaining John Calvin's "unceasing activity in the service

of God", i.e. the Puritan work ethic. In the modern work
ethic formulation, however, God is absent. This void leads to
people keeping busy just to make more money. Sometimes that
realization produces guilt. According to money hang-up expert Bob Weinstein[2], money stirs powerful emotions. Some
suffer from, "I want it, but feel guilty about wanting it."
These people are bothered by commandment #3. Weinstein says
such people are not likely to make a lot of money.

Weinstein has interviewed people who have an internalized value system built around money, as their remarks reflect: "Money...is the national yardstick by which ability is
measured...Having a great deal of money means you're respected." Unfortunately, many judge not only others, but also
themselves by such standards. So sadly, when one is not making money, i.e. unemployed, severe mental health problems can
follow. One study found a 3 to 4 % increase in first admissions to mental hospitals and 318 additional suicides associated with each percentage point rise in the unemployment
rate. Similarly, it noted 5 to 6 % increases in imprison-
ments and homicides.[3] Research by UCLA sociologists on Los
Angeles' homeless, pinpointed recent job loss as the triggering factor in the demise of these lives.

Anyone who has been in down and out unemployed straits
will strive doubly hard to obey the "Thou shalt not lose thy
job" commandment in the future. The person will think twice
before complaining about health or safety work hazards, or
low pay, and never consider joining a union. Such scared and
docile creatures are ideal workers from many corporations'
viewpoint. By keeping jobs hard to come by, Corporate America can maintain a supply of such workers.

Christmas is a difficult time for those affected by
failure to follow either of these commandments. "The Hard-
Luck Christmas of 1982" brought much suffering to the 12
million unemployed and perhaps two million homeless. Undoubtedly many parents felt almost taunted as Santa Claus helped
their children voice their wants--wants which the parents
knew would go unmet. Similarly, the commandment #3 guilt-
ridden affluent are troubled at Christmas. Why is the celebration of Christ's birth marked by a repulsive national orgy
of money changing hands--most often to buy things people do
not really need--they wonder?

V. LOOK OUT FOR YOURSELF; EAT HIGH ON THE HOG

Robert Ringer opens his best-selling book[4] with the assertion, "Looking out for Number One is the conscious, rational effort to spend as much time as possible doing those things which bring you the greatest amount of pleasure and less time on those which cause pain." He questions the motives of the other-oriented. Ringer preaches self-interest as if some natural law makes anything but selfishness impossible. His book, like Weinstein's, urges on those who might otherwise retreat from full-time self interest.

Weinstein asks, "Would you rather eat hamburger or filet mignon, spam or ham, pork ends or center cut pork chops...?" Then he concludes, "If you relate to money openly it won't upset you to devote a large portion of your time to working for it." He devotes as much discussion to the notion that there are better ways to spend time than making money as he does to objections over eating a wasteful, unhealthy, meat-based diet, contingent on enslaving and slaughtering animals: none!

Weinstein's assumption that everyone wants to "eat high on the hog" brings us to commandment #5. In eating high on the food chain, Grabbers ignore that 1) 17 lbs. of grain fed to feedlot cattle make but one lb. of meat, 2) 1.3 billion people could be fed by the grain and soybeans eaten by U.S. livestock, 3) 1/3 of <u>all</u> raw materials used in the U.S. go for meat, dairy, and egg production (10 tons of water is needed to produce one lb. of meat!), 4) a typical top of the food chain diet consumes 20 times more raw materials than a grain / fruit-based diet, and 5) 95 to 99 % of toxic chemical residues in the U.S. diet come from meat, dairy products, eggs, and fish.

One person who decided he could not overlook these facts is <u>Diet</u> <u>for</u> <u>a</u> <u>New</u> <u>America</u> author John Robbins. Son of the founder of the Baskin-Robbins ice cream company, John gave up a $20 million inheritance to crusade against the dairy industry. "I made the choice for conscience and integrity and walked away from wealth and power", he recalls. He views meat addiction as "perhaps the single most powerful driving force behind the devastation of the biosphere".

VI. BORROW FROM TOMORROW; FLUSH YOUR WASTES

Borrowing to buy things you don't have the money for and waiting until tomorrow to pay for them--commandment #6 behavior--has become an American pastime. One survey[5] revealed 7 of every 10 American adults in debt--owing an average $30,900--and that half would have trouble paying an unexpected bill for $1000. Reportedly[6], the average student graduating from college owes $8,000, while some are in debt $60,000 to $70,000.

Nationally, the story is similar. As 1986 began, debt in all sectors of the U.S. economy had soared to $8.2 trillion--up 78% from 1980 levels, the increase being twice the corresponding rise in GNP. Later that year America surpassed Brazil and Mexico and became the world's top debtor nation--a swift turnaround from its world's leading creditor nation status of a few years before. As 1990 began, the U.S. net debt to other countries had soared to $663.7 billion!

During 1990, the U.S. government's national debt passed $3 trillion --$12,000 /person and growing by $330 billion/yr. (If the $100 billion/yr social security /trust fund coverup and $63 billion S & L bailout payments are restored, the real deficit has grown despite laws mandating its reduction!) Merely to cover interest payments (around $190 billion/yr) on this huge debt requires 18 % of annual government revenue. Even the U.S. corporate sector, after a decade of merger mania, was debt ridden. As the new decade began, a full 1/4 of its cash flow went for debt service.

Few Americans realize that earlier in this century "buying on the installment plan" was viewed as going into <u>debt</u>--thought to be both dangerous and wrong. Today, people obtain <u>credit</u>. Who was responsible for this change in perception? The Pushers. The change represented an important Grabber victory over an older God-based morality. The massive shift to a debt-based American economy had two unfortunate repercussions. First, it limited freedom by tying people to working their way out of debt. Second, the mentality it fostered of "borrowing from tomorrow to pay for today" is perilous from an ecological and personal health viewpoint.

Many Americans sacrifice long-term health for short-term pleasures in leading unhealthy lives. Heart and artery disease annually kill over one million Americans and cost $65 billion. Its chief causes are diets high in animal fats, cholesterol, and highly-refined, sugary foods, along with stressful, sedentary lifestyles. Likewise, cancer, the second leading killer claiming 450,000 lives out of the 855,000 Americans stricken with it each year and costing $30 billion, is another "social disease". Perhaps 70 to 90 % of human cancers are caused by man-made environmental factors and unhealthy lifestyle habits. Much heart disease and cancer could be prevented if people considered their own long-term health important, and quit borrowing from tomorrow to pay for today.

Besides leaving a huge monetary debt for the next gen- eration, Americans have borrowed from the environmental health of tomorrow to pay for today's conveniences. While 21st century children may face greenhouse-induced hot sum- mers, increased skin cancer risk due to ozone depletion, and lakes/forests killed by acid rain, infants already are denied something that 200,000 previous generations have thrived on : safe, wholesome mother's milk. Today, this once optimum infant food is so tainted with pesticides, PCBs, and other toxic residue, that, were it a commercial product, FDA regu- lations would prohibit its sale. According to the Environ- mental Defense Fund, the average nursing infant receives 100 times more PCBs/bodyweight than does an adult--an amount 10 times the allowable limit.

While some worry that Americans are faced with the grim possibility of trying to survive in a medium of their own waste, many don't worry. Instead, they obey the seventh commandment and flush waste as readily as they flush their toilet. This "flush syndrome" is in the spirit of "looking out for Number One"--one doesn't worry about the people downstream even if the waste is toxic.

Industry produces about 600 lbs./year of toxic waste for every American. Early in the 1980s, the EPA estimated that 90 % of this was dumped improperly or illegally--sometimes after midnight in the nearest river or sewer. For profes- sional dumpers, money is the motivation. For the corporate producers who employ them, similar motivations dictate that they seek out the lowest bidder and ask no questions regard- ing the waste's fate.

EPA estimates there are 50,000 U.S. hazardous dumps-- with 1,200 to 2,000 posing "significant risks to human health or the environment". In 1989, the Congressional Office of Technology Assessment estimated that 50 years and $500 billion would be needed to clean them up. Dr. David Rall, then Director of the National Institute of Environmental Health, told Congress, "75% of the waste dumps are either over aquifers or wet areas...the greatest risk to large populations may be through contamination of drinking water." These toxic chemicals, many of which cause cancer, birth defects, genetic damage, and nervous or immune system damage, potentially endanger millions of Americans.

Not all poisons are flushed to the ground: the air gets its share too. In 1987, according to Chemical Manufacturer Association / EPA estimates, American industries routinely released five billion pounds of toxic chemicals into the atmosphere. Air pollution jeopardizes the health of 35 million Americans. A 1986 Brookhaven National Lab estimate put the annual number of American deaths due to acid rain/fog at 50,000. Unlike polluted drinking water--for which bottled water is a substitute--one can not easily stop breathing air pollutants.

VII. PROFIT FROM FREE MARKETS AND FREE LUNCHES

Many proponents of the "free market" economy do not like some of the U.S. government's domestic policies. Social programs are giveaways to lazy people, business regulation stifles the economy, and government subsidies should end, they have been arguing for the last few decades. However, many corporate executives also realize that government "interference" can work to their advantage, and accordingly they are more selective in their denunciations.

During the early 1980s these people would: 1) applaud when $1 billion was cut from school lunch programs, forcing more than 2,000 schools and three million children to drop out of it--but say nothing about the tax deductible three-martini lunch for business people, which amounted to a $3.2 billion handout ;[7] 2) bemoan that rent and housing subsidies for 1.2 million public housing units annually cost the U.S. treasury $1.2 billion. They called for an end to this program--despite two million homeless Americans, another two million living in substandard quarters, and hundreds of thousands on public housing waiting lists, facing typical waits of 20 years in Miami and 12 years in New York. However, they would say nothing about ending the home mortgage tax deduction--which applied even to summer homes and represented a $42.8 billion/year handout;[8] and 3) urge an end to the $1 billion annual subsidy the U.S. government gave the renewable energy industry (solar, wind, wood, hydro, etc.)--but say nothing about ending the $5 to $10 billion/year nuclear energy industry subsidy. (To compound this disparity, by 1985

renewables were supplying 10 % of the country's energy vs.
but 4.3 % for nuclear.)

Usually such one-sided remarks calling for an end to
government programs they couldn't profit from were punctuated
with an occasional, "Let's give the free enterprise system a
chance to work!"

VIII. GREED, HEALTH CARE AND INSURANCE

Before continuing our discussion of commandment #8, we
pause to examine the American health care system. This system
is based on an unfortunate reality: doctors, hospitals, drug
companies, etc. will make more money if people are sick ,
than if they stay well. Thus there is a marked preference
for medical care which treats symptoms of illnesses, rather
than prevents their occurrence. (In four years of medical
training, the average U.S. physician receives but 2.5 hours
instruction in nutrition!) Could it be that health maintenance is not emphasized because it is not profitable for the
"health care" industry?

Certainly Americans are paying more for health services.
In 1989 each American paid an average $2450 to health profes-
sionals--up from $29.65 per person in 1940. Why have medical
costs--and likewise health insurance costs--exploded?
Consider Donella Meadows' response ...

Disintegration of Insurance System , by Donella H. Meadows

*"Dear Member Insured:" said the letter from my health
insurance company. "A year ago we wrote that rising medical
costs and Plan usage meant serious rate increases. Unfortunately, the picture has not changed."*

*"Yet you, along with the majority of our insureds, have
kept your health care expenses to a minimum. Therefore, we
have been able to keep your rate increase within the 20 - 30
% national average of the increased costs of medical care."
Enclosed was my bill, 25 % higher than the previous one.*

*So I am considering dropping my insurance and throwing
myself onto the harsh mercies of the great American public
health system--as 30 % of the population has already done.
I'm self-employed and self-insured. I've shopped around for
the cheapest coverage, and still I can barely afford $1000
deductible. Health care now takes one out of every 12 dollars I earn--all of which goes to insurance, not one penny to
actual health care. With house insurance and car insurance,
I am spending 1/5 of my disposable income on protection*

against disaster. The insurance itself is beginning to be
disaster enough.

Something is terribly wrong with a health insurance
system that ordinary working people can't afford. Something
is wildly out of control when one sector of the economy has
25 % cost increases while general inflation is less than 5 %.
But when you try to figure out what has suddenly happened to
an insurance system that worked fine for decades, you find
that everyone has a different theory.

Many people blame the greedy doctors. If doctors didn't
make ten times as much as the average patient, the average
patient might be able to afford their services. If doctors
didn't pad bills, order unnecessary tests, and perform other
overexpensive procedures, insurance would cost at least 10 %
less, say the insurance companies. (The equivalent in the car
insurance system is the mechanic who can turn a bent fender
into an $800 repair bill.)

Doctors tell me the problem is greedy patients, greedy
lawyers, and indulgent juries, who collaborate on outrageous
malpractice suits--generous income for the pain, suffering,
and lost income of the litigant's wife, children, dog, and
second cousins. When the doctors show me their malpractice
insurance bills, I can see they've got a point. They're
caught up in the insurance mess as much as I am.

Surely, then, the problem is the greedy insurance companies. That's the reasoning behind California's Proposition
103, in which angry voters decided to cut their own automobile insurance rates. The result, say the insurance
companies as they pull out of California, is that they lose
money. Whoever is profiting from the enormous increase in
insurance costs, they assure us, it isn't them.

There seems to be some truth to that claim too. Settlements in all branches of insurance are rising 20-25 % /year.

A friend who is a consultant to the business tells me,
however, that the companies have some responsibility for
those rising claims. Insurance is attracting new players,
people more interested in managing great money pools than in
providing insurance. The average claims adjuster is a kid
just out of college with low pay and low status, who will
stay in the job 2-3 years. If there were more professionalism
in the insurance part of the business, claims could go down
by 10 - 40 %, the consultant tells me, and the customers
would still feel (and be) better treated.

That theory sounds plausible to me, too. And there are other theories. The problem is the people who eat too much, exercise too little, smoke, won't wear seat belts, contract AIDS, and charge the rest of us for their foolishness. The problem is the entry of the government with its layers of well-paid, inefficient paper-pushers. The problem is folks like me, healthy people who drop out of the system, leaving the less healthy behind.

Maybe the fundamental problem underneath all the others is the general culture of greed that has been so cheerfully encouraged in our nation in the past decade. Greed has a tendency to feed upon itself. A few thirsty lawyers and clients go for big damages, which sets the legal precedent for others to do so. A few doctors abuse the system, make out like the bandits they are, and tempt others to get in on the game. A few companies learn they can make more on the stock market than on selling policies, and the business attracts gamblers rather than insurers.

No insurance system can work without a high level of integrity in its customers and its practitioners. The opposite of integrity is, I guess, disintegration.

My insurance company ended its letter with masterful understatement, "Our present system of private health insurance, independent practitioners, hospitals, and HMOs, is probably not the most efficient and equitable model for delivering health care."

Let's say that more loudly and clearly. It's a lousy system. It deprives people of decent health care. It's destroying itself. It will not be fixed by blaming it on one set of scapegoats, or by the reform of one set of actors, or by shifting it all to the public or private sector, or by voters setting the rates. The insurance crisis calls for major restructuring and for high-level, clear-thinking leadership--leadership that above all insists upon and sets an example of steadfast integrity.

IX. HEALTH-RELATED RIPOFFS

Despite annual $600 billion health expenditures, the U.S. ranks only 20th among nations in male life expectancy, and 22nd in infant mortality. The infant death rate in the nation's capitol is higher than in the developing countries of Barbados, Jamaica, Costa Rica, and Cuba. Speaking of the rest of the world, American per capita health care costs are over 3/4 of the world average per capita income!

Unfortunately, a significant part of this money goes, not toward fostering health, but into the pockets of the greedy. Columnist Carl Rowan, after lamenting that 10 million American children still have no source of medical care despite the tremendous growth of federal Medicaid and Medicare expenses (from $4.8 billion in 1967, to $57.2 billion in 1980, to $81.75 billion in 1983), charges, "We lead the world primarily in providing good health money to a disgusting array of ripoff artists."

Consider the heart pacemaker scandal--headline news in mid 1983.[9] A federal investigation found that over 200,000 people (mostly senior citizens) had pacemakers implanted that weren't needed. Doctors had accepted bribes and kickbacks from pacemaker manufacturers. Hospitals had charged patients (and Medicare) inflated prices. Reportedly, 1500 doctors who performed pacemaker operations were pursued by over 400 well-paid salesmen--some earning $1 million/year! Sen. J. Heinz claimed $1 billion/year was wasted or stolen on pacemakers.

Consider the cataract surgery scandal--headline news in July, 1985. A government report charged that $2 billion/year was wasted on eye operations for the elderly. It estimated that 23 to 36 % of the surgery was unnecessary and documented eye lens manufacturer kickbacks to doctors and other incentives. Reportedly, some $525 million was wasted on operations for people with <u>perfect</u> <u>vision</u> ! Who paid for it all? Medicare.

Not surprisingly, in May, 1989, former Health, Education, and Welfare secretary Joseph Califano charged that $150 billion/year-- 25 % of the nation's health care bill --is wasted on unneeded operations and medical tests.

In contrast to Medicare - financed ripoffs, between 1977 and 1987, 800,000 women and children were cut off Medicaid-- which went from covering 65 % of the nation's poor to just 39 %. By 1987, 37 million Americans had no health insurance --up by 10 million from 1977. Sadly, hospitals are continually confronted with sick or injured people unable to pay. Many are turned away.

Consider what happened to Sharon Ford. While in active labor, she was "dumped" by two community hospitals. Her baby was born dead. "I thought maybe a person's life came first before, you know, money or anything" she remarked.[10]

Consider what happened to 22 year old Kitty Connell

Harrington. Born with transposed arteries, two hospitals told her she needed $150,000 before they'd let her in the door for a heart transplant operation. She could raise only $5,000 and died. As her brother puts it, "The expense cost my sister her life..."

With their "Thou shalt make money" orientation, Grabbers profit from those "free lunch" federal programs and the American public is shortchanged.

X. COMMANDMENTS #9 & #10

Commandment #9 implores Grabbers to seek government positions--not to serve the public--but for personal gain and to help business escape regulation.

Government regulation puts the public at ease and lulls them into thinking someone is looking out for their interests. In reality, the corporate sector often manages to get the fox assigned to watch the chicken coop.

Consider a not uncommon scenario. A corporate executive accepts a government position (in the revolving door) working for the very agency that regulates his former company (uh oh--the fox is loose in the chicken coop). He pretends to have undergone a conversion and acts out his role as defender of the public interest (Ouch! -- you slapped my wrist! Gimme that chicken.) In truth, he is careful to 1) avoid making corporate sector enemies, and 2) increase his own marketability as to potential jobs thwarting regulation. Finally, the day he has prepared for arrives. He leaves the public sector (out the revolving door) for a cushy private sector job at two to 20 times his government salary.

Government regulator/corporate coziness has long existed--mostly hidden from public scrutiny. But during the Reagan administration it was hard to overlook.

At the Environmental Protection Agency (EPA), it started with the appointment of Ann Gorsuch, a Denver attorney with a pro-industry, anti-regulation background, as chief. "To name Gorsuch to this post is like sending the grand dragon of the Ku Klux Klan to stand guard over a meeting of the NAACP," Carl Rowan commented. The foxes Gorsuch proceeded to appoint to key positions in the EPA chicken house are listed in Fig. #28.[11] How other EPA officials exited through the revolving door later in the decade is charted in Fig. #29.[12,13]

```
+-----------------------------------------------------------+
|              FIG. #28  IN THE REVOLVING DOOR              |
|           THE FOXES APPOINTED TO EPA IN 1981             |
|                                                           |
|   Appointee        Position at EPA     Background         |
|                                                           |
| 1) Kathleen    Asst. Administrator for  as paper company  |
|    Bennett     Air Pollution Control    lobbyist, fought  |
|                                         Clean Air Act     |
| 2) Nolan E.    in charge of policy &    his lawfirm helped|
|    Clark       resource management      Dow Chemical battle|
|                                         EPA over herbicides|
| 3) John E.     Anne Gorsuch's           lawyer & lobbyist |
|    Daniel      Chief of Staff           for Johns-Manville,|
|                                         asbestos manufacturer|
| 4) Rita M.     Asst. Administrator      PR exec. for Aerojet-|
|    LaVelle     for Superfund, toxic    General Corp., a big|
|                waste cleanup            polluter/illegal dumper|
|                                                           |
| 5) Robert M.   General Counsel          lawyer for Exxon, |
|    Perry                                the huge oil company|
|                                                           |
| 6) Frank A.    in charge of     General Motors'lawyer,chief|
|    Shepherd    law enforcement    Clean Air Act opponent  |
|                                                           |
| 7) William     Deputy in charge of  lawyer for steel mills|
|    Sullivan    law enforcement      who fought environ-   |
|                                     mental controls       |
| 8) John        Asst. Administrator   opposed pesticide    |
|    Todhunter   for Pesticides &      regulation for       |
|                Toxic Substances      industry clients     |
|                                                           |
+-----------------------------------------------------------+
```

There were similar Reagan administration appointments in other regulatory agencies, budget cuts, layoffs, and ripoffs. Many environmental, occupational health and safety, and consumer protection laws went unenforced. Other public needs were neglected--such as low income housing.

Over at Reagan's Dept. of Housing and Urban Development (HUD), shoddy accounting hid scandals in which Grabbers stole around $7 billion from government housing programs. How was this done? Real estate brokers entrusted with handling sales

```
+----------------------------------------------------------+
|              FIG. #29  OUT THE REVOLVING DOOR            |
|        EPA OFFICIALS' SOFT LANDINGS IN THE PRIVATE SECTOR |
|                                                          |
|   1) William Ruckelshaus--twice head of EPA, left his    |
|      $72,600/yr job in 1984. Now heads waste disposal    |
|      giant Browning Ferris (where multi-million fines    |
|      are routine operating costs). Makes $1 million/yr   |
|      salary plus incentives, stock options.              |
|                                                          |
|   2) Phillip Angell--top aide to Ruckelshaus at EPA,     |
|      in 1987-1989 led (along with Ruckelshaus) a         |
|      coalition of Fortune 500 companies seeking to       |
|      weaken Superfund law; now Browning Ferris lobbyist  |
|                                                          |
|   3) Walter Barber--acting EPA head before Anne Gorsuch, |
|      now vice president at Chemical Waste Management,     |
|      subsidiary of major polluter. 1988 salary:base      |
|      $191,300, bonus $67,300.                            |
|                                                          |
|   4) Joan Bernstein--former General Counsel (Carter      |
|      Adm.), now General Counsel at Chemical Waste        |
|      Management. 1988 salary:base $170,400, bonus $59,900|
|                                                          |
|   5) Gene Lucero--supervised enforcement of Superfund and|
|      hazardous-waste laws for six years,salary $75,000/yr|
|      Now represents companies involved in Superfund      |
|      lawsuits at around $190,000/yr salary.              |
|                                                          |
|   6) Steven Leifer, Burton Gray, and many one-time EPA   |
|      attorneys now make far more money representing       |
|      polluters. During 1988, EPA's hazardous waste       |
|      enforcement division lost 1/3 of its attorneys.     |
|                                                          |
|   7) Douglas Costle--EPA head in Carter Adm. In 1981     |
|      founded Environmental Testing and Certification     |
|      Corp. with three other senior EPA officials. By 1986|
|      his stock in the company was worth $3.5 million.    |
|                                                          |
+----------------------------------------------------------+
```

of HUD's foreclosed homes (in exchange for a small fee) often simply kept all the money from the sale. Republican insiders profited handsomely from HUD rehabilitation projects. Former Interior Secretary James Watt collected $400,000 in consulting fees for but a few phone calls with HUD secretary Samuel Pierce.

Reagan's deregulation "successes" gave Grabbers a chance to assault savings & loans. Now U.S. taxpayers have begun financing a $500 billion bailout of that industry. Many S & L chief executives drew $250,000 to $7 million annual salaries up until their institutions were finally closed down. In Florida, despite $100 million losses the previous quarter, one S & L president continued to receive his $4.7 million/year salary. An audit also found the S & L had paid for the $30 million art collection in his home.

Finally, we consider commandment #10, focusing on Grabber use of politicians and scientists. We begin with the former.

Given the legislative reaction to Watergate era scandals, as the 1970s ended many Americans sensed a return of integrity to public service. They were wrong. A decade later, after over 100 Reagan appointees, Democratic House Speaker and Majority Whip left government under ethical clouds, Americans better understood the "buy-a-politician" aspect of their government. Perhaps they were stuck with institutions like The Best Congress Money Can Buy --as the title of Phillip Stern's 1988 book suggested.

Whereas "buy-a-politician" methods are well documented, Grabber "rent-a-scientist" strategies have not been well publicized. This approach is based on four observations: 1) Scientists are human, 2) They won't bite the hand that feeds, 3) Surprisingly often, scientists can be rented to bolster any unpopular viewpoint--from "smoking cigarettes is not harmful" to "a little radiation never hurt anyone", and 4) Winning a dispute isn't necessary if the waters can be clouded to obscure the need for action to halt Grabber plans.

Consider how Grabbers in America's chemical and drug companies used IBT Labs' scientists to test the safety of their products.[14] According to mid 1983 testimony, IBT Labs' scientists exhibited, "a disturbing pattern of scientific ethics giving way to business greed." Employees conducted feeding studies in cramped and dirty facilities while many rodent deaths went undocumented. Summary tables were filled with phony numbers.

From a 1953 beginning, IBT grew to become a $10 million

/year business because, as one Justice Dept. investigator put it, "Companies knew this was the place to get the results they wanted." More than 10,000 IBT studies were used by FDA and EPA to register hundreds of products including insect-icides, herbicides, pharmaceuticals, and food additives. Many of these would not have been registered without IBT testing results. With evidence of scientific fraud mounting, Amer-ican and Canadian scientists reexamined IBT studies of 325 insecticides and herbicides. The vast majority were found "invalid".

Are scientific results often fabricated by "rent-a-scientists" or by those eager to secure grant money or pro-motion? How much integrity do scientists have? Opinions vary. Science editor D.E. Koshland claims 99.9999 % of published scientific reports are accurate. However, FDA studies of clinical trials of experimental drugs found evi-dence of significant misconduct in 11 % of 1758 random audits.[15]

XI. GRABBERS AND PUSHERS

As the 1980s drew to a close, some media commentators proclaimed the "Age of Greed" over. Despite such pronounce-ments, few were surprised by securities firm Drexel Burnham Lambert's actions in January, 1990. With the junk bond market having collapsed, Drexel faced filing for bankruptcy. How-ever, before actually filing, the company made sure few as-sets were left for creditors to fight over. It issued over $260 million in bonuses to its executives. Some got $10 million each.

As the new decade began, evidence for an American corpo-rate capitalists' "invisible hand" working for the social good was hard to come by. America had long since ceased being "one nation under God". If there was a dominant ethi-cal code it was something like the Grabber's Ten Command-ments. America was better described as "one nation under Grab". Having avoided domination by Orwell's Big Brother, Americans were caught up worshipping his Money God. How did the philosophy of these Grabbers of Gomorrah come to para-sitize the brains and permeate the nervous systems of so many? That has been the work of the Pushers.

Questions & Projects

1. Futurist Hazel Henderson claims that American society

"over-rewards greed, selfishness, pride, and aggressive, irresponsible behavior". Discuss.

2. Discuss the question section IV. ends with. Then describe the best Christmas present you ever got--keeping the true meaning of Christmas in mind.

3. A Ray Stevens song asks the question, "Would Jesus wear a Rolex?" Discuss the meaning of the question as well as substantiating your answer.

4. Many felt Jim Bakker's sentence--40 years in jail, with no chance of parole for 10 years--was too harsh. After all, they argued, preachers have conned people out of money for centuries--promising rewards in heaven for offering-plate contributions now. Discuss.

5. Contrast today's sometimes greedy saving & loan executives with S & L chief George Bailey (Jimmy Stewart) in the 1940s movie It's a Wonderful Life. Discuss the movie in terms of Grabber vs. other-oriented conflict.

6. By 1990, the average U.S. home cost $90,000. Assume a family pays 5 % down, and finances the balance at an 11 % fixed rate over 30 years. Compute monthly payments and calculate total interest paid out over the loan lifetime.

7. Unlike Alexander Hamilton, Thomas Jefferson held that a nation's accruing debt unjustly imposed a burden on future generations--something it had no right to do. Discuss.

8. What if, asks a health industry critic, the March of Dimes had thrown all its resources into iron lungs--instead of helping to develop polio vaccine? Are parallels to this happening today? Discuss.

9. Why do you suppose America pays $50 billion/yr health care costs for people in the last six months of life, while closing pediatric clinics?[16] Is this sensible? Discuss.

10. "During the Reagan years, instead of HUD helping those with housing needs, it served greed." Discuss.

11. Consider two opposite viewpoints regarding revolving door realities. PRO: Revolving door shifting between public and private sectors leads to higher quality management in both. CON: If such arrangements are tolerated, the government-corporate marriage will be consummated. Without a check and balance arrangement, the public interest will be compromised. Discuss.

12. "Before the 1980s no one could convincingly argue that the nation's dominant ethical code resembled the Grabber Ten Commandments. By the decade's end, one could make a

good case for this indeed being true." Discuss.

13. In the 1987 movie <u>Wall Street</u>, corporate raider Gordon Gekko says, "Greed...is good. Greed...cuts through to the very essence of what we're doing." That same year, Bernard Baruch College economics and finance professor, Jack Francis, noted, "Greed is a great religion". Discuss.

14. Music lyrics can be used to contrast the 1960s and 1980s. While the Beatles noted that money couldn't buy love, for "material girl" Madonna, Mr. Right was always the boy with the cold hard cash. Provide similar examples.

Notes

1. Lutz, M. "A Meditation on Economy and Society", <u>Bull. Sci. Tech. Soc.</u> Vol. 7 pp.655-57, 1987.
2. Weinstein, B. <u>Winning the Battle With Your Money Hangups</u> , Wiley, New York, 1982.
3. Rogers & Cohen, <u>On Democracy</u> , Penguin Books, New York, 1983.
4. Ringer, R. <u>Looking Out for Number One</u> , Funk & Wagnalls, New York, 1977.
5. based on a nation-wide poll of 2,465 adults conducted by <u>Money Magazine</u> in conjunction with Lieberman Research, October, 1984.
6. transcript of <u>MacNeil-Lehrer Report</u> , April 10, 1986.
7. "The Myth of the Safety Net", <u>Common Cause</u> , Vol. 9, #3, May/June 1983.
8. <u>U.S. News and World Report,</u> January 2, 1984.
9. <u>Reader's Digest</u> , October, 1983.
10. WNET / PBS TV documentary <u>Who Lives, Who Dies?</u>
11. Regenstein, L. <u>America the Poisoned</u> , Acropolis Books, Washington, D.C., 1982.
12. Sibbison, J. "Revolving Door at E.P.A.", <u>The Nation</u> , November 6, 1989.
13. Waldman, S. "The Revolving Door", <u>Newsweek</u> , February 6, 1989.
14. Schneider, K. "IBT Labs Trial Reveals Faked Data", <u>In These Times,</u> May 11-17, 1983.
15. "Truth or Consequences?" <u>Scientific American</u> , August, 1988, p.24.
16. see note 10.

PUSHERS & PRISONERS

I. PRISONERS OF THE PUSHERS--THEN AND NOW

Princeton University professor Julian Jaynes (see EXODUS) claims that ancient people heard inner voices and hallucinated images. Instructions these voices and images gave, thought to be commands of gods, were especially sought out when decisions needed to be made. Lacking the ability to self reflect and rationally decide, the people were prisoners of these messages which helped push them into action.

Science fiction or not, these prisoners of the god-pushers eventually suppressed the voices and images by not paying attention to them. A cultural bias arose and by 1000 B.C. hearing or seeing them was no longer fashionable. 3000 years later, another culture is again paying attention to inner messages. Of the situation, one of their better known poets writes[1], "We're in science fiction now...whoever controls the language, the images, controls the race."

Who is controlling these people, these American consumerists? Can they possibly be prisoners in the so-called "land of the free"? A scholar[2] who long studied the voices and images invoked a great thinker from antiquity in offering his answer:

> Archimedes once said, "Give me a place to stand and I
> will move the world." Today he would have pointed to our
> electric media and said, "I will stand on your eyes,
> your nerves, and your brain, and the world will move in
> any tempo or pattern I choose." We have leased these
> 'places to stand' to private corporations.

Corporate America's Pushers--Grabbers acting for greedy selfish gain--are responsible for this sensory carefully-planned assault. In the words of one reporter[3], the voices and images have been scientifically designed

> ...to grab the public's attention...That's the big
> challenge facing the promoters who hawk products...Never
> before have so many been bombarded by so much informa-
> tion that often means so little. Yet that is the fate
> of American consumers in the "age of hype".

So Americans are walking around "hype-notized" by the Pushers'... why all the fuss, you ask? Can't people turn off television or radio, not read newspapers or magazines, and they're free, right? No--escaping the Pushers is not that easy. They're everywhere. Even if you suddenly became blind,

deaf, and dumb, the Pushers would still be with you--inside
your head, those sounds and reflections of the consumerist
lifestyle. Think you can get away? Consider four arguments
why you can't escape the Pushers.

II. WHY YOU CAN'T ESCAPE THE PUSHERS

1--The Magnitude and Pervasiveness of their Message

Pushers are spending big money to hook you. 1990 U.S.
advertising expenditures are projected to total $133 billion
--up 6.2 % from 1989 figures. That's $530 annually spent on
every American in efforts to put messages inside heads.
Robert Heilbroner[4] thinks you can't escape them.

> We cannot be immune to the cacophony that intrudes into
> our lives--a kind of commercial white noise audible
> every time we read a newspaper or magazine, switch
> on the radio or TV, open a book of matches, or look up
> at billboards on the sides of buildings. Now even some
> taxis in New York subject their hapless passengers to a
> continuous sequence of messages running tickertape
> fashion before their eyes. One would have to be blind or
> deaf not to feel beset in such an environment.

Their advertising pitches reach you through the mail, by
telephone, and are piped into shopping malls. Ads are
blazoned on vehicles, tee shirts, plastic cups and even on
the walls of toilet stalls at airports. Commercial message
carrying airplanes and blimps fly over events with large
outdoor crowds. One aggressive company--already reaching
millions of captive schoolchildren with TV commercials--is
now targeting patients waiting to see doctors; another is
similarly aimming at those in supermarket checkout lines.

2--Their Influence

"Advertising has placed a 'burning brand' on the crest
of our civilization" says Harvard's Daniel Bell[5] in seemingly
conceding that the Pushers have snared most Americans. Their
brand, he writes, "is the mark of material goods, the exem-
plar of new styles of life, the herald of new values." How do
the all-pervading voices and images--and the strong cultural
bias to heed them--shape our lifestyles and values?

Consider television. Americans spend more time involved
with it than any other activity except sleeping. The average
household watches seven hours/day. The average person sees
32,000 TV commercials/year. What is television's message?
According to former Federal Communications Commissioner

Nicholas Johnson[6], it

> ...educates us away from life and away from our
> individuality. It drives us to line up at the counters
> of drugstores and supermarkets, shaping our needs and
> wants, and ultimately ourselves into the molds that are
> the products. Not only do the programs and commercials
> explicitly preach materialism, conspicuous consumption,
> status consciousness, sexploitation and the fantasy
> worlds of quick shallow solutions, but even the settings
> and subliminal messages are commercials for the
> consumption style of life.

Television acts as a cheering section for the side that
has already won, to paraphrase PBS news anchorman Robert
MacNeil. The West has become a consumer, rather than Christian,
socialist, or ecologically-sound society. Trying to
live apart from consumerism can be dangerous to your psychological
health--unless you enjoy being ostracized.

3--Carrying The Voices With You

Heard above the cacophony of the estimated 1600 commercial
messages thrown at the average household daily, are
approximately 80 which are noted. Of these, an estimated 12
provoke a reaction. The most compelling one or two voices or
images enter the brain's long-term memory.[7] Each day the
sensory assault continues.

What the brain stores it can also retrieve. People in
their forties still hear those TV commercials they listened
to as children. Those are the winners in the Pushers' 1950s
effort to design messages for the "survival of the fittest"
competition inside your head. Today's Pusher efforts are more
psychologically refined since the competition is fiercer. If
some advertising professional can haunt your head with the
message he's designed, then he's succeeded. If he can't, he
may be out of a job. In advising those creating ads, one
professional urges, "You have to break through the clutter."

4--Subliminal Suggestions

You can be consciously ready to ward off the Pushers--
but they can still get you. How?--By programming and conditioning
your subconscious mind. Consider this example,
something you might find in a psychology textbook.

The tachistoscope, a high speed film projector which can
flash messages lasting but 1/3000th of a second, was used to
superimpose "Hungry? Eat Popcorn" and "Drink Coca Cola" over
motion pictures shown in a theatre. Apparently the movie

goers' unconscious minds picked up the consciously invisible
messages. In a six week test involving 46,000 patrons,
popcorn sales jumped 58 % and Coke sales 18 %.

Wilson Bryan Key argues that sophisticated techniques
for inducing subliminal stimuli and massaging the unconscious
mind are manipulating millions of Americans each day. His
books, Subliminal Seduction, Media Sexploitation, and others,
document how TV commercials, printed ads, and department
store background music use devices conscious minds can't detect to arouse sexual drives and sell products.

While Pushers deny Key's specific charges, they generally acknowledge what they're up to. "We believe people
make choices on a basic primitive level. We...probe to get
down to the unconscious" says the research director of
Saatchi and Saatchi, the world's largest advertising agency.
The conglomerate operates in 80 countries, buys 20 % of all
broadcast commercials, and has annual billings of roughly $20
billion. It employs a team of anthropologists and psychologists to target primal drives and subconscious minds.

Can this be resisted? N.F. Dixon, author of Subliminal
Perception, thinks not. He writes, "It may be impossible to
resist instructions which are not consciously experienced."
Both he and Key think subliminal stimuli and post hypnotic
suggestion have much in common, including, as Key puts it,
"a unique trusting relationship between subject and hypnotist
or audience and media". While acknowledging many unknowns, he
concludes, "The hypnosis model may provide insight into the
individual or social influences of subliminal media control."

So today, even when Americans are not actually seeing or
hearing the Pushers' media hype, they are nonetheless prisoners of inner voices and trances which foster irrational
behavior.

III. FAST FOOD PUSHERS

You're lounging around the house when suddenly you feel
some rumblings in your stomach. Immediately a voice fills
your head, an echo of some long ago TV commercial...."It's
the oldest question in the world, what to have for dinner?"
You see the images...someone taking a frozen dinner out of a
package...pulling it out of the oven...Hey, that looks
good...Then another voice, some female country music star
singing, "I've got a taste for some real food!" Then another
voice and an image: some smiling young lady in a cute outfit

is dangling car keys in front of you....inside your head that
is. She's saying something--actually singing it. Your right
brain with its penchant for music picks it up. You hear it
again..."Aren't you hungry for Burger King now? ...What are
you waiting for?" Did I imagine that last question, or did
the young lady say that too? You can't decide, it doesn't
matter anyway...there's more help on the way...more singing..."It's a good time for the great taste of McDonald's!"
You dimly perceive more smiling and some golden arches...but
wait! The skeptical left brain of yours intercedes and
something else comes to mind...no more, naive, pretty young
girls, but a hard-nosed, wrinkled old grandmother saying,
"Where's the beef?" I'll go to Wendy's and get a real hamburger you decide, grabbing the car keys...

The U.S. restaurant and fast food industry spends over
$1 billion/year on television advertising alone. Given this
influence, Americans now eat 35 % of their meals away from
home. More important than where, however, is _what_ they eat.
A recent study found that most U.S. children had one or more
meals a day from fast food sources. It also found their diet
to be high in processed and convenience foods--and in fat.
Typically, the fat content of their meals was 50 %--higher
than the 40 % dietary fat content of the average U.S. diet.

Not surprisingly, American children are getting fatter.
"Childhood obesity is epidemic in the United States," says
Dr. William H. Dietz Jr. of New England Medical Center.
According to research done by Dietz and Dr. Steven L. Gort-
maker of the Harvard School of Public Health, for children
aged 6 to 11 years there was a 54 % increase in the prevalence of obesity between the years 1963 and 1980. For children aged 12 to 17 years, the increase was 39 %. As for
American adults, a 1989 Prevention magazine / Louis Harris
study found 64 % of them overweight. Despite $33 billion/year
American expenditures on dieting (1990 Congressional subcommittee estimate), "We have managed to maintain our status
as the fattest nation on Earth" the magazine concludes.

The report of a 13 member National Institutes of Health
panel, recommends limiting dietary fat content to 30 % and
reducing cholesterol intake. They recommend trading high fat
foods, including meat, for low-fat diets of fish, grains,
vegetables, and fruits. "We think that all Americans are at
an unnecessarily high risk of coronary heart disease because
of the diet we eat," says D. Steinberg, the panel chairman.

Pushers only tell one side of the story. Those hawking hamburgers don't mention nutritional and health studies. In urging you to eat at the top of the food chain, they overlook the enormous resource waste and inefficient use of grain behind feedlot beef production. Burger King would rather you didn't connect it with the conversion of tropical rain forest to cattle grazing land. McDonald's doesn't advertise that its original Ronald McDonald--actor Jeff Juliano--is now a vegetarian. The Meat Board won't be having actor James "Real Food for Real People" Garner discuss his April, 1988 quintuple coronary artery bypass surgery.

Given their role in wasting, the meat pushers don't want you to heed the hunger cries of the Third World's children or the death cries of millions of cattle who are slaughtered each year. Of course, someone lacking the financial clout of the fast food industry would not have a prayer of getting anti-meat, pro-health messages on the corporate airwaves. You'll never see a rational, psychologically well-designed commercial message that counters the meat propaganda.

IV. SODA POP PUSHERS

By 1986, advertisers were onto another gimmick to get their messages to live in your head: using hit songs in their commercials. Despite the surviving Beatles' lawsuit, Nike used John Lennon's "Revolution" to hustle shoes. The Byrds' "Turn, Turn, Turn" helped sell Time magazine, Buddy Holly's "It's So Easy" was selling Toyotas, "Lean on Me" was used for both pickup trucks and jeans, and so it went. Advertisers targeted particular segments of the population through use of specific songs and music videos.

Not all musicians would sell out to Pushers. Despite a $12 million offer, Bruce Springsteen refused to let Chrysler use his "Born in the U.S.A.". John Fogerty--once famous as head of Credence Clearwater Revival--sarcastically poked fun at music marketing in his 1987 song "Soda Pop".

> There's a generation out there waiting to be tapped
> If we play our cards right, we'll be sitting fat
> Play a little rock n' roll music, tease 'em with a tune
> Show a coupla old time pictures from the baby boom

Few heard these lyrics in comparison to the millions who watched rock superstars David Bowie and Tina Turner peddle Pepsis to the beat of "Modern Love".

Excluding water, over half of what a typical American

drinks is soft drink or alcohol beverage. Whereas in 1960, Americans drank three times more milk than soft drinks, two decades later 45 % more soft drinks than milk were consumed.

Half of the soft drinks consumed are either Coke or Pepsi. Coca Cola is the world's best selling product, with consumers annually shelling out $25 billion for it. Given that lofty position, you'd expect Coke to offer both health benefits and good taste, right? The truth is sobering.

Chemically, Coke is 99.8 % water and sugar. Coca Cola buys 10 % of all sugar sold in the U.S. It also contains caffeine, a 12 ounce can having 60 % as much as a cup of coffee. Sugar and caffeine hardly offer health--unless you're a dentist's wallet or someone fighting to stay awake while driving. The taste is pleasing to some, unsatisfying to others. An Italian newspaper once described it as "halfway between the sweetish taste of coconut and the taste of a damp rag for cleaning floors"--certainly nothing extraordinary!

So why is Coke the world's top product?--in a word, Pushers. The company's market researchers investigate why people drink what they do. Advertising personnel use these findings in designing their messages. Sales promotion and support personnel help bottlers and retailers increase sales. How the company introduced Diet Coke in 1982 provided a lesson in hype.

They rented New York's Radio City Music Hall and invited 4,000 people to an extravagant party--complete with celebrity entertainment and a 14 foot high mockup of Diet Coke. Elsewhere in the city, a July 4th atmosphere with fireworks, free food and Diet Coke entertained guests. Coca Cola repeated these events in other cities with a $100 million advertising / promotion effort. Even five years before Diet Coke's debut, one writer described the company's marketing efforts as "the most incredible mobilization of human energy for trivial purposes since the construction of the pyramids."

Unfortunately, sometimes these efforts have less than trivial consequences. While some have only to carry soft drink commercials around in their heads, others have no choice but to let the product itself accompany them. One such prisoner of addiction is Playboy magazine founder Hugh Hefner.[8]

> Draining his Pepsi bottle, Hefner was immediately on his feet, rummaging behind the bar for another. He is addicted to Pepsi, he lamented. He drinks around

two dozen a day. "It's an energy source," he sighed,
"but I've paid a fortune to dentists." Then, the man who
is perhaps the world's most famous flamboyant, carefully
packaged playboy, opened his mouth to display his dental
damage. Ugly stains, lots of caps, Pepsi Cola breath.

Children especially gear up for the fidgety, adrenaline
joyride that sweets provide. They acquire a metabolic need
for sugar and the soft drink vehicle that brings it to them.

V. WHEN SOCIETY BECOMES AN ADDICT

When most Americans think of pushers and addicts, they
think of big city pushers hooking the young and unwary on the
cheap thrills provided by drugs like cocaine and heroin. They
think of crimes committed to pay for addicts' expensive drug
habits. They think of the enormous profits in the $110 bil-
lion/year trade in illegal drugs. Their outrage has lead to a
war on drugs and a national drug frenzy.

Yet most Americans fail to recognize, in the words of
Barbara Ehrenreich,[9] "the biggest pusher of all--the
thoroughly legal and entirely capitalist consumer culture".
As she describes it

No street corner crack dealer ever had a better line
than the one Madison Avenue delivers at every commercial
break: Buy now! Quick thrills! You deserve it!

She describes our love-hate relationship with these pushers.
We resent the "incessant, hard sell seduction" and are uneasy
with our "moral surrender" to their "message of unrestrained
hedonism", she claims. Rather than directly challenge "the
consumer culture to which we are all so eagerly addicted",
Ehrenreich asserts, we direct our rage toward illegal drugs.
"So we feed our legal addictions and vent our helplessness in
a fury at drugs" she concludes.

"In a consumer society," Ivan Illich says[10], "there are
inevitably two kinds of slaves: the prisoners of addiction
and the prisoners of envy". Most Americans don't see themselves as junkies hooked on consumerism. So while they right-
fully declared war on those peddling drugs on elementary
school playgrounds, few objected to a 1989 corporate pusher
attempt to hook children inside the classroom. Hiding behind
concerns over student lack of exposure to current events,
Time-Warner, Inc. controlled Whittle Communications gave
$50,000 worth of TV equipment to schools who subscribed to

their daily, 12 minute long "Channel One" newscast. The
program is interrupted by two minutes of commercial messages
peddling Levis, acne medicine, soft drinks, etc.

Given the Pushers' tenacity, one can now argue that all
Americans are addicted to something. In her 1987 book, When
Society Becomes An Addict , Anne Wilson Schaef describes
various American societal addictions: to money, work,
religion, sex, chemicals, military power, food, nicotine,
drugs, and other substances. To this list, Donella Meadows
adds another item: the news-jazz-hype electronic media
onslaught itself.

> Some people are so addicted to this onslaught that they
> carry electronic noise with them everywhere, to be sure
> they never spend a moment alone with their increasingly
> empty minds and souls.

She thinks this last addiction is serious--and laments "the
degradation of a nation". She fears, "We are losing our ability to separate the important from the trivial".

VI. PEDDLING ALCOHOL AND TOBACCO

In 1987, American deaths from legal addiction to alcohol
or tobacco exceeded illegal drug deaths by over 100 times.
While annually 105,000 deaths and hundreds of thousands of
injuries can be directly blamed on alcohol, and smoking
claims 390,000 victims/year, just 2,000 die each year from
cocaine use. Despite this disparity, we allow Pushers to
encourage people to smoke and drink, and have declared war on
illegal drugs.

An estimated 10.5 million Americans exhibit symptoms of
alcoholism, while another 7.2 million abuse alcohol but show
no signs of dependence. According to the U.S. Health and
Human Services Dept., alcohol will cost the nation $136.3
billion during 1990 in lost productivity, disability and
death. One fourth of all hospital patients have alcohol-
related problems, and nearly half of all auto accident deaths
can be traced to its use. While alcoholics receive more
attention, around 100 million other Americans consume alcohol. In some amount this beverage is probably harmless. In
greater quantities it has been linked to heart disease, birth
defects leading to mental retardation, and cancer.

While a majority accepts alcohol's legitimate, moderate
use, its abuse is unquestionably America's #1 dangerous drug
problem. It often creates a living hell for the one out of

every three American families it affects. Yet the country continues to tolerate the over $1.5 billion annually spent on advertising alcohol. In their attempts to increase consumption, Pushers continue to "bring out their best" commercials and distract us with silly "less filling" vs. "tastes great" disputes. Meanwhile their product is breaking up families, and claiming innocent victims on highways.

Each year smoking-related disorders cost the U.S. $52 billion (chiefly in medical costs). Assessing the anguish, misery, and waste that tobacco products inflict on people is not so straight-forward. Deaths from lung cancer or emphysema are prolonged miserable suffering--yet tobacco pushers anually spend $2.6 billion attempting to hook more Americans on their deadly offerings. Indeed, it is nearly impossible to pick up a newspaper or mass audience magazine without encountering cigarette ads...

Its called Discover --and subtitled "The News Magazine of Science". Yet typically 10 % of its pages are devoted to encouraging totally irrational behavior: cigarette smoking. Here reason has been abandoned. Only a picture, a fleeting image one's brain might file away for later, a feeling, and perhaps a simple message are important....

* * * * * * * * * *

A pack of cigarettes lying on the padded interior, under the stick shift of an expensive car. Sterling ...it's only a cigarette like Porsche is only a car...

* * * * * * * * * *

Two affluent young men are discussing details of a movie they're filming. One is very naturally holding a cigarette. Vantage ...the taste of success...

* * * * * * * * * *

The fun at a crowded, glamorous party is spontaneously captured in a scene of a dozen young, affluent, sexy-looking men and women loosely holding their cigarettes and interacting with laughter. Players go places...Easy-going taste.

* * * * * * * * * *

While the rest of the magazine is about the application of the scientific method, these pages appeal to something else: "The Collective Cognitive Imperative". They build a belief system, a culturally-agreed on expectancy of what being happy, successful and respected is--then define the roles to be acted out, narrowing your consciousness. Although each ad has the Surgeon General's Warning--you don't really see it.

For an instant you're in a trance, no longer an outsider viewing through a window--but suddenly transported
there. You can feel the Porsche respond as you shift gears
....Imagine getting up out of the director's chair...See
yourself leaving the party with that special someone...Then
the fantasy fades and is gone. But before you turn the page
you perceive that something made your pleasant daydreaming
possible...a cigarette.

* * * * * * * * * *

Cigarettes are like women: the best ones are thin and rich.
Silva Thins are thin and rich.

* * * * * * * * * *

Encouraging prisoners of envy to also become prisoners
of addiction is a frequent Pusher tactic. The cigarette ad,
which shows a wealthy, attractive woman holding a cigarette,
demanding other people envy her, is a tragic reminder of what
cigarettes have done to women's health. The American Cancer
Society says that the lung cancer rate in women has increased
over 300 % since 1950 and now kills more women than breast
cancer. Women who smoke are not to be envied.

How have two women's magazines helped alert their readers to the cigarette smoking reality? The answer is a lesson
in self-interest economics. Consider the following, as reported in a September 1984 Reader's Digest article,
"Cigarette Makers are Getting Away with Murder".

> The American Council on Science and Health has compared
> the amount of coverage magazines give to smoking and
> health issues with their dependence on cigarette ads for
> revenue. The Council's 1982 survey, for instance, re-
> vealed that, between 1972 and 1981, Redbook , where 16 %
> of ad revenues came from cigarette ads, and Ms. , where
> the figure was about 14 %, didn't publish a single arti-
> cle on the hazards of smoking. Nor have they in the
> years since 1981. This is striking when one considers
> the dramatic increase in lung cancer among women.

Sadly, under the pushing and prodding of the $60 billion/year
tobacco industry, one can say, "You've come the wrong way,
baby" to women who smoke.

Besides magazines, advertising agencies also pay homage
to tobacco industry money. In 1988, a Saatchi and Saatchi
subsidiary created a Northwest Airlines TV commercial in
which passengers applaud the airline's no smoking policy.

Food and tobacco giant RJR Nabisco promptly found another company to handle its vast advertising expenditures. Saatchi quickly learned its lesson. When it acquired the Campbell-Mithun Company, it immediately dropped one client--the Minnesota Dept. of Health--so as not to jeopardize remaining cigarette accounts. Campbell-Mithun had been creating public service anti-smoking ads for this state agency.

The National Cancer Institute estimates that unless smoking patterns change, 37 million Americans alive today will die prematurely from smoking-related illness. Will patterns change?--not if the tobacco pushers can help it.

Actually, in the Third World, there is a new pattern. Cigarette consumption is rising by 2 % / year. In Asia--where the tobacco pushers (lead by the U.S. Cigarette Export Association) and their "buy-a-politician" friends have successfully pressured governments to import cigarettes--the increase is 5.5 % / year.. How did this happen?[11]

Under section 301 of the revised 1974 Trade Act, the U.S. government can impose economic sanctions against countries which discriminate or are unfair to U.S. exporters. Such threats--and lobbying by Republican heavyweights Michael Deaver, Richard Allen, Alexander Haig, and Jeese Helms--successfully opened Japan (1986), Taiwan (1987), and South Korea (1988) to the tobacco pushers. In Japan, American cigarette market share went from zero to 13 % in an initial 14 month marketing campaign. After 26 months of such activity, ads for cigarettes on Japanese television--which previously occupied 40th place amongst products vying for commercial time--had jumped into 2nd place.

By 1989, the tobacco pushers were ready to invade Thailand--whose cabinet had approved a ban on cigarette consumption in 1987. In September, 1989, the Office of U.S. Trade Representative considered the tobacco companies' petition to force Thailand to import their products under section 301. Finally one Republican--Surgeon General Dr. C. Everett Koop--had had enough. His decision to testify at the hearing--against the wishes of the Bush administration--was undoubtedly influenced by his impending resignation.

> Our trade policy is to push addicting substances into
> foreign markets, disregarding the sentiment of the
> foreign government and the future health of its
> population...it is scandalous...at a time when we are
> pleading with foreign governments to stop the

> export of cocaine, it is the height of hypocrisy for the
> United States to export tobacco.

Before you conclude that government policies only promote tobacco in foreign countries, note that U.S. tobacco growers receive $279 million/year in government price supports.

VII. DRUGS--LEGAL AND ILLEGAL
"Pop, pop, fizz, fizz, oh what a relief it is!"
* * * * * * * * * * *

For six years, a Senate subcommittee--chaired by Senator Gaylord Nelson--investigated the role TV commercials were playing in making America the world's most drug-pervaded country.[12] After receiving many letters like this one,

> My six year old daughter and eight year old son have on
> several occasions got me out of bed and told me they
> couldn't sleep and nagged me for pills. Neither my hus-
> band nor I take prescription or over-the-counter sleep-
> ing pills, and my children have admitted to me that the
> idea that they should take pills comes from television
> commercials.

the Senator became convinced that millions of American children and adults started taking pills in response to the estimated 1000 TV drug commercials they saw every year.

Although he was concerned about these "electronic hypochondriacs", letters like this one,

> TV advertisers are teaching our children to use drugs.
> ...That they arrive at heroin is not surprising. I
> know of no drug except heroin or morphine which will
> produce the dramatic relief from all worldly cares TV
> vividly pictures.

concerned him even more. He ultimately became worried that TV "magic chemical" ads were unintentionally steering millions toward dangerous illegal drug use.

Drug companies push prescription drugs with the same intensity as over-the-counter ones. According to FDA 1987 data, they annually spend almost $9000 on every American doctor in efforts to get the physicians to prescribe their drugs (over $4 billion/year).

U.S. drug expenditures--both legal and illegal--have reached staggering proportions. Using a 1989 White House estimate of $110 billion/year spent on illegal drug outlays, altogether American drug expenditures total roughly $245 billion/year--including $30 billion on over-the-counter and

prescription drugs, $35 billion for tobacco, and $70
billion on alcohol--around $1000/person/year.

Happy, healthy, satisfied people have no use for drugs.
Drugs are for those who are sick, in pain, or dissatisfied
with the reality their ordinary sensory perception provides.
The dissatisfaction may spring from boredom, or grow out of
feelings of frustration and hopelessness produced by intolerable social conditions. Whatever the cause, a large percentage of Americans often rely, not on their body's own natural
healing mechanisms, not on the everyday satisfactions of
unintoxicated natural living, but instead on drugs. This
would not be the case in a healthy, synergistic society.

VIII. CREATING DISSATISFACTION, NEGATIVE IMPACTS

Many Americans are dissatisfied with their appearance
and will go to expensive extremes to change it. Many adorn
themselves with expensive superficialities that have little
or no functional advantages--some may have functional disadvantages. Others utilize deception or unnecessary surgery.

Most are ashamed of their natural body odors and hide
them with deodorants. Many cover their bodies with uncomfortable, impractical clothing, shoes, or jewelry--spending
around $20 billion/year on the latter. Men try to hide hair
loss; women change the color of theirs. While some women
employ padded bras and lipstick, others use surgical implants
to enlarge breasts and create luscious--looking lips. Those
seeking a smaller looking mid-section employ girdles. Young
men take steroids to build up the appearance of their physi-
que. Most women use cosmetics ($10 billion/year expendi-
tures) to paint new faces or eyelashes on themselves. Older
affluent women often turn to plastic surgery and liposuction
procedures for a new face or fatty tissue removal. Younger
ones will nearly starve themselves to death to be thinner
than they were meant to be.

Why can't Americans accept themselves as they are--
instead of trying to look like someone else? Pushers are
partly to blame. They make people identify with their conspi-
cuous-consumption oriented, beautiful TV show characters--and
want to be like them and look like them. To look like these
TV people takes continually spending money unnecessarily on
corporate products and services.

It is human nature to go along with the crowd--few will
chart their own course alone. Unfortunately, the crowd por-

trayed on television is not a representative sampling of
humanity. It is a crowd of the most beautiful, most affluent
humans--ones who happen to be super consumers. And American
consumerists go along with the crowd.

Unfortunately, the Pushers' soft and hard sell does more
than just clothe Americans with that steel cage of material
possessions. First, it grabs what's inside the cage and
squeezes. The founder of America's second largest cosmetics
company, Charles Revson, used to do a similar thing with
advertising agencies--once going through seven in three
years. "Creative people are like a wet towel. You wring them
out and pick up another one," he said.

Pushers have long had Americans in the emotional wring-
er: they are masters at breeding dissatisfaction. Nicholas
Johnson used the words "vicious" and "predatory" in describing TV's "stalking of the poor". He recalled "the disappearance of the early 1950s dramatists from television was
due to advertisers' revulsion at the message that happiness
could be found by ordinary people in lower-class setting,"
and then wrote,[13]

> The affluent have nothing to lose but their money and
> control over their own lives and personalities. The poor
> are not so lucky. They must sit there, without even the
> liberating knowledge that money can't buy happiness, and
> constantly be told that their lack of material posses-
> sions is a badge of social ostracism in a nation that
> puts higher stress on monetary than moral values.

Besides the pusher-inflicted emotional trauma, there are
negative biosphere impacts. For every unneeded, unhealthy
product for which a market is created, there are resource
depletion and environmental health costs to pay. There are
also human costs. Pathetically, conventional economics is so
flawed that many negative side-effects show up as increases
in the country's GNP. Paradoxically, as more garbage is
created, as environmental messes require cleanup, as shoddy
products wear out and need replacing, as more people get
sick, economists chart growth and "health" of the economy.
Meanwhile, living in America becomes increasingly unhealthy.

Associated with consumerism is a type of negative syner-
gism. Consider one simplified example of how a negative rip-
ple effect sustains the economy.

Decades of Pusher activity have addicted Americans to

sugary soft drinks. Besides causing other health problems, sugar rots teeth. This has enabled dentistry to be a more lucrative profession than it otherwise would have been. One writer laid the blame for ten billion plus tooth cavities on the soft drink industry. Many of those cavities were filled with mercury-containing amalgam--leading to environmental health and waste disposal concerns. Unfortunately, the poor can't afford dentists and others simply neglect their teeth. Sadly, by the time they reach age 55, half of all Americans have false teeth. That's the bad news.

The good news is that millions of people now wear dentures. So along with the false teeth industry, there is a market for denture cleaners. This explains why, stored inside millions of brains is the recollection of a commercial voice saying, "And now, denture wearers, here's Martha Rae... Take it from a big mouth...gets your mouth super clean!"

IX. A CONSERVATIVE'S CRITIQUE / ANOTHER VIEWPOINT

Other people see what plagues the nation's media and the role of advertising differently. Consider the following viewpoint.

* A CONSERVATIVE'S CRITIQUE *

The major television networks are dominated by liberals and atheists. Thus network offerings incorporate an anti-business, anti-family, anti-God bias.

Anti-business themes--from industrial accidents/chemical pollution to negative corporate executive characterizations abound. Dallas' tycoon J.R. Ewing is portrayed as greedy, malevolent, and corrupt. Offerings seldom reinforce family values. Consider how women are portrayed. Heroines are typically not traditional housewife/homemaker types--but rather aggressive, career-oriented feminists.

As for God, CNN, TBS, and TNT network heavyweight Ted Turner's remarks--"(Christianity) is a religion of losers ...(Christ should not have died on the cross) I don't want anybody to die for me....I've had a few drinks and a few girlfriends, and if that's gonna put me in hell, then so be it..." --are representative of network values.

As regards advertising, most people find TV advertising messages entertaining and informative. Everyone should remember that these provide the revenue that makes commercial television possible. Certainly advertising can not force people to buy things they don't want to. A recent study[14] questions whether subliminal messages can affect behavior.

Many of your criticisms ignore human nature. For example, consider your blaming people's need to change their appearance on advertising. Anthropologists have documented other primates' use of deception to get what they want. Richard Alexander, University of Michigan biologist, theorizes that human manipulation and deception of each other provided an important evolutionary driving force for intelligence. He doubts that the human mind would have developed in an environment where everyone told the truth and where appearances and realities didn't sometimes diverge.

* * * * * * * * * *

* A REBUTTAL *

In the words of Christopher Lasch,[15]

> To see anti-capitalist propaganda in a program like "Dallas"...requires a suspension not merely of critical judgement but of ordinary faculties of observation. Images of luxury, romance, and excitement dominate such programs the same way they dominate TV commercials. "Dallas", like almost everything else on television, is itself an advertisement for the good life conceived as endless novelty and excitement, as the titillation of the senses by every available stimulant, as unlimited possibility.

Also, people who purchase advertised products pay for commercial television by paying higher prices than they otherwise would.

* * * * * * * * * *

In the last two chapters of this book we have taken a hard, unflattering look at the reality of American society. Many will object to the picture we've painted. Instead of an increasingly tarnished land in which people pursue money and quest for gratification as directed by media pushers, they see something else. Winslow Homer and Norman Rockwell captured this America of yesteryear in paintings: beautiful countrysides, bountiful harvests, family farms, simple tradition, simple pleasures, innocence, clean friendly neighborhoods, the warmth of family together--eating, laughing, caring, giving thanks, worshipping. The Americans in this world are hard-working, frugal, upright, and play by the rules.

Critics will point out that this America is vanishing and increasingly is only to be found in the fantasy world of advertising.

X. PUSHERS AND VALUES

Shortly after a 1988 presidential campaign--in which George Bush is repeatedly televised saying "I share your values"--Nicols Fox focused on "What are Our Real Values?" in an essay with that title.[16] Her initial answer was, "They would appear to be the same fantasies we use to sell soft drinks, phone services, and color film--and they have proved equally adaptable to selling presidents." But, realizing that, "a healthy future will be based on reality, not on ad copy", she probed deeper.

She considered "who our heroes are" and noted,

> They aren't the people who volunteer in the soup kitchens; they aren't struggling writers and artists; they aren't the librarians or the nurses or the social workers. Mainly they are the rich and the famous and the successful and the beautiful, the film and sports stars, the Wall Street barons...Perhaps the best indicator of what we really are is what we spend our money on.

Here we pause and recall expenditures noted in the last two chapters--for gambling, interest payments on the national debt, dieting, health-care ripoffs and waste, advertising, drugs, jewelry, and cosmetics. Annually, they total over ONE TRILLION DOLLARS (over 1/5 of the GNP)-- $4,000 per person.

American values are not what we would like them to be. Other than urging us to focus on reality, Fox offers no solutions. She laments, "It's not a question of hoeing at the weeds of society, but of a real root job." After this remark, she puzzles over "Who makes the rules these days?" She laments, "Simply saying, 'Because God says so' doesn't work very well anymore."

Indeed, in America where the almighty Grab has supplanted God, perhaps there are no hard and fast ethical rules. Yet, someone at the top instructs the Pushers and dominates nearly all of us--who? The Masters.

Questions & Projects

1. Where may Pushers' quest for our eyes and ears ultimately lead? To space and orbiting advertisements. "Can you imagine a night sky filled with...luminous Golden Arches advertising McDonald's?" asks astronomer Sidney Van den Bergh.[17] "That day may be closer than you think" he warns. Would you be visually thrilled or horrified? Discuss.
2. Think back on your last major purchase. To what extent

were you influenced by advertising? Were you responding to a real or artificially-created need?

3. Select an unwittingly classmate or friend and explore the subconscious contents of his or her mind using a free association technique. Analyze the responses--how many were inspired by media pushers?

4. Imagine you're directing an advertising campaign for a whole industry (perhaps the dairy industry or beef producers). Provide examples showing how you would gear your messages to the worldview of the intended audience.

5. Pick an ad that presents a rosy, one-sided view of a potentially controversial issue. Parody the ad by presenting the opposing viewpoint in similar fashion.

6. Relate "clutter" to images, pushers, big city life, and the Consumerist Mentality (theme #26). How might "a simple life" overcome clutter?

7. Wall Street media analysts predict that six huge media conglomerates (recently merged Time-Life and Warner Communications being one of them) will control most of the Western media by the mid-1990s. Relate the increasing media monopolization trend to public access to a diversity of viewpoints, censorship, fostering mass illusion, and Big Brother concerns.

8. Consider three representations of truth: 1) truth is something real out there waiting to be found, 2) truth is continually created by humans, 3) truth is that which sells. Discuss and relate to question 7.

9. Advertising can be seen as a specific type of propaganda. In general, propaganda encourages people to conform and to take actions without thinking. While deploring propagandists' intentions and misinformation, leaders who value democracy nonetheless often face a catch 22 type dilemma when it comes to taking action against them. Explain.

10. To what are you addicted? Would you need help and a supportive environment to overcome the addiction? Is the addiction compromising your health? Will people with the biggest problems be able to answer truthfully? Discuss.

11. At age 15, suppose one twin starts smoking a pack /day. Suppose the other twin invests the $1.50 per pack saved at 8.75 % interest. Compare the two twins at age 65. (Assume the cost of cigarettes stays constant.)

12. In "The Ultimate Slavery" episode of the PBS series, A Planet for the Taking , modern Americans are likened to

domesticated animals--whose behavior has been shaped by technology producing listless cogs in a machine. Relate this characterization to the "prisoners" of this chapter.

13. Compare the > \$1 trillion/yr American expenditures (for gambling, debt interest, dieting, health care ripoffs, advertising, drugs, jewelry, and cosmetics) with the total income of the world's poorest 1/4 (>1.25 billion people).

14. Describe the following in terms of negative synergistic effects rippling through the U.S. economy. a) FAX machines in Southern California cars, B) sales of carbon filters, reverse osmosis membranes, germicidal lamps, and bottled water (the latter totaling \$2 billion/year) are booming.

15. Consider two popular Southern California bumperstickers: a) "Shop Until You Drop" and b) "I'm Spending My Children's Inheritance". Speculate on the worldviews of people who would display these messages.

Notes

1. Allen Ginsberg
2. McLuhan, M. Understanding Media , McGraw Hill, NY 1964.
3. U.S. News & World Report, December 5, 1983.
4. Heilbroner, R. "Advertising as Agitprop", Harper's , January, 1985 p.71.
5. Bell, D. The Cultural Contradictions of Capitalism , Basic Books, NY, 1976 p.68.
6. Johnson, N. Test Patterns for Living, Bantam, NY 1972.
7. Fox, S. The Mirror Makers, Morrow, NY 1984.
8. Stumbo, B. "Hugh Hefner at 57--He Wants Respect", L.A. Times , December 26, 1984.
9. Ehrenreich, B. "Drug Frenzy: Why the War on Drugs Misses the Real Target", Ms. November, 1988.
10. Illich, I. Tools for Conviviality, Harper & Row, NY, 1973
11. Cockburn, A. "American Drug Lords", The Nation ,10/30/89
12. Brewin, R. and Hughes, R., The Tranquilizing of America , Warner Books, 1980.
13. Johnson, N. op cit.
14. Beatty, S. and Hawkins, D. "Subliminal Stimulation: Some New Data and Interpretation", Journal of Advertising , Vol. 18, #3, 1989, pp. 4-8.
15. Lasch, C. "What's Wrong with the Right and the Left", Utne Reader , #19, January/February 1987.
16. Fox, N. "What are Our Real Values?", Newsweek, 2/13/89
17. see Sky & Telescope , July 1987.

MASTERS

I. MASTERS, MINORITIES, AND MONEY

Masters, i.e. those having authority over others, is a word with many connotations. To black Americans, the word recalls the "mastah" of the pre-Civil War South and the horrors of the peculiar institution of slavery. To feminists, the word smacks of male domination. Others who ponder "master" eventually link it with "money".

As the 1990s began, the total net wealth of the richest 1 % of Americans--two and one half million people--exceeded that possessed by the bottom 90 % --225 million people. At the very bottom, the poorest 50 % of American families owned but 4 % of the nation's net wealth. 35 million Americans live below the official poverty line--half of them children.

During the 1980s, representation of both minorities and women among America's poor increased. While one of eight white Americans is poor, one of every three blacks, and one of every four Native Americans and Hispanics are. Near the end of the decade, black worker income stood at but 56 % of white worker income--dropping by 5 % during the decade. For comparable work, women received only 60 to 70 % of the pay men got. A woman with a college degree commanded the same salary as a man with an eighth grade education. The 1980s was a time of "the feminization of poverty". Although fewer than one in five American households was headed by a woman, these families made up 61 % of those living in poverty.

II. WOMEN AND MALE MASTERY

Equality--supposedly it's an idea woven into the fabric of American life, part of what America is all about. Certainly it's the key word for the American feminist movement. Yet some women worked to defeat a law guaranteeing women equal rights. After the defeat of the Equal Rights Amendment, Andrea Dworkin, in her book Right Wing Women, wondered, "Why aren't all women feminists?" She concluded that many women prefer traditional promises of Christian marriage, i.e. that wives and mothers will be respected and cared for, and men will behave, to what the feminist movement offers.

Around 1900, many women became disillusioned with traditional marriage, and particularly with husbands who abused both alcohol and them. The anxiety these women felt over feeling vulnerable, their frustration with irresponsible,

domineering males, eventually became burning anger which
ignited a mass movement. Historian Barbara Epstein claims
the resulting crusade for temperance and prohibition had
roots in feminist equality concerns. It focused on alcohol
only out of necessity.

Today the American family is seldom what the New Right
wants it to be. Only 12 % of American families are composed
of a job-holding father and a full-time housewife mother.
When marriages fail, usually mothers take main financial
responsibility for the children. Typically, only 35 % of
these women receive any child support payments from their
estranged husband. Those are often paltry. When marriages
stay intact, domestic harmony doesn't always prevail. A 1984
Family Violence Research Center report estimated that 65 % of
all couples engage in some type of physical abuse during
their marriages and that 25 % of these are serious beatings.

With many women living in real or imagined fear of their
husbands, Dworkin argues that threat of male violence keeps
many women tied to traditionalist values. Some women break
under the fear; for others the fear turns to wrath. Where
this wrath is directed, Dworkin argues, is misplaced in right
wing women who reject feminism. Instead of venting anger on
the men who oppress them, Dworkin maintains that the New
Right manipulates women's fears and redirects their anger
toward homosexuals, Blacks, and Jews.

While some feminists may fault Epstein's psychohistory
or Dworkin's analysis, for many the focus on anger seems
appropriate. Anger is difficult for women to cope with, given
conditioning they've experienced growing up in male-dominated
society. Taught to be "selfless, sweet, passive, and dependent" so that "our princes will find us and we'll live happily ever after" , many women suppress qualities labeled male
by society. This leads to inner conflict and anger. Until
they identify the male mastery and oppression of their own
lives, women can't channel anger toward constructive change.

III. THE BLACK QUEST FOR EQUALITY

Blacks and other minorities realize they must con-
structively channel anger. With their Eyes on the Prize --
the name of a book and PBS documentary about the civil rights
movement--blacks worked patiently to gain freedoms supposedly
guaranteed them by law. Before the black activists, preachers, lawyers, and masses of people working in solidarity

brought the prize within reach, a handful of black athletes of the late 1940s-1950s era broke down important barriers.

Bill Russell, who joined basketball's Boston Celtics in 1956 as the team's only black, was one of those athletes. He lead his team to the greatest success of any professional sports team in history--winning the NBA championship 11 of the 13 years he played. Was he beloved in Boston? Hardly.

In 1966 Russell co-authored an autobiography, Go Up for Glory. This was dedicated "to our children...in the hope that they will grow up as we could not...equal...and understanding." In 1969 he retired and moved to the West Coast.

In a mid-1987 article[1], one of those children, daughter and Harvard Law School graduate Karen Russell described her "growing up a black child of privilege". Her first memory in Boston, when she was three or four, involves a white man walking past her family. He looked at her and said, "You little nigger." Even as the little girl smiled back at him he added, "They should send all you black baboons back to Africa." She recalls continual vandalism of their home during Celtics' road trips and one burglary:

> Our house was in a shambles, and 'NIGGA' was spray-painted on the walls....They had broken into my father's trophy case and smashed most of the trophies. I was petrified and shocked at the mess... The police came and, after a while, they left. It was then that my parents pulled back their bedcovers to discover that the burglars had defecated in their bed.

The black quest for equality continues under the leadership of a new generation. Despite progress, all is not well. In a late 1986 article[2], Eyes on the Prize author Juan Williams described Washington D.C.'s prevailing benign racism. Reportedly, a black person seeking to rent an apartment or house there has a 50 % chance of being turned away solely because of race. Blacks are more likely to be imprisoned than are whites. A 1990 government study reported that a shocking one quarter of all black men aged 20-29 are either in prison or on probation--versus but one in every 16 of a similar white group. Karen Russell fears, "The old racism seems, these days, ever ready to surface with a vengeance". As the 1990s began, a disturbing number of racial prejudice incidents had unsettled college campuses.

IV. THE U.S. CORPORATE STATE; CORPORATE CRIME

At the very top of the U.S. economic pyramid are the power elite. Besides grabbing immense wealth for themselves, these economic masters wield awesome power over the lives of others through their control of multinational corporations.

The American corporate state functions like an extended family. The gap that seemingly separates government and business is bridged by foxes guarding the chicken coop, lobbyists, paid politicians, and corporate heavies feeding at the public trough. The bridge is actually a revolving door through which corporate and government officials move back and forth into different rooms of the same house. Sometimes quarrels upset this cozy arrangement. Then, if the dispute wasn't manufactured to begin with, a solution is usually found which preserves the health of the relationship.

It wasn't always so. In the early 1900s, after passage of the Sherman Anti-Trust Act, the government actively sought to break up large monopolistic corporations. This culminated with the 1911 breakup of The Standard Oil Company of New Jersey. During the 1920s and 30s interest in trust-busting waned, rekindled in the 1960s and 70s (culminating with the AT & T breakup), and faded during the Reagan years.

The separate and highly competitive nature of American business is partly illusion. Not only does _Time_ own _Life_ (and now Warner Communications!), all large corporations own and control each other to some degree. This happens through mutually advantageous business relationships, individuals common to several corporate board of directors, shared stock, and shared values. Some companies remain outside this corporate fold and insist on old-fashioned competition. Multinationals will tolerate some of this: they realize maintaining the illusion of competition is important. However, should maverick companies become financially attractive, they risk being gobbled up by some conglomerate.

Corporations worried Thomas Jefferson. He wrote, "I hope we shall crush in its birth the aristocracy of our moneyed corporations, which dare to challenge our government to a trial of strength and bid defiance to the laws of our country." Unfortunately corporate contempt for U.S. laws (i.e corporate crime) was to grow dramatically.

In 1980 the U.S. Justice Dept. finally did a study[3] on corporate crime--after hundreds of studies on ordinary crime. Some of its key findings included: 1) During the 1960s a sin-

gle corporate crime, the antitrust conspiracy in the electric
industry, cost the public $2 billion--twice what the three
million annual burglaries cost. 2) In the early 1970s, the
Senate Judiciary Subcommittee on Antitrust and Monopoly estimated that monopolies, shoddy goods, and similar violations
annually cost the public between $174 and $231 billion. These
amounts are only slightly less than the total federal budget

```
+-----------------------------------------------------------------+
|                                                                 |
|        FIG. #30    A SAMPLING OF CORPORATE CRIME                |
|                                                                 |
|                                                                 |
|     A.H. Robbins Co. --Dalkon Shield                           |
|     Allied Chemical Co. --Kepone dumped in James River         |
|     banks --not reporting transactions/money laundering        |
|     Chrysler Corp. --odometer rollback                         |
|     coal-burning ultilites--acid rain killing NE lakes         |
|     defense contractors--massive cost over-runs⁴, fraud⁵        |
|     Dow Chemical Co.--napalm; Agent Orange; Rocky Flats        |
|     E.F. Hutton --defrauding 400 banks of $8 million           |
|     Eli Lilly --Oraflex                                         |
|     Exxon --massive Valdez oil spill                           |
|     Firestone --Firestone 500 belted radial tires             |
|     Ford Motor Co. --slipping transmissions;Pinto gas tank    |
|     garment industry --Tris(children's pajamas);Brown Lung    |
|     General Motors --killing urban mass transit systems       |
|     Hooker Chemical --Love Canal                               |
|     Kerr McGee --sloppy with plutonium/Karen Silkwood death   |
|     Manville-Johns --asbestos                                  |
|     Monsanto --PCBs                                            |
|     Nestle and other companies --infant formula scandal       |
|     oil companies --conspiring to fix fuel prices             |
|     Pittson Corp. --W. Va coal mine waste "dam" disaster      |
|     savings and loan executives --fraud, $ billions stolen    |
|     tobacco companies--massive promotion of deadly products   |
|     Union Carbide--Bhopal, India accident                      |
|                                                                 |
|                                                                 |
+-----------------------------------------------------------------+
```

FIG. #30   A SAMPLING OF CORPORATE CRIME

A.H. Robbins Co. --Dalkon Shield
Allied Chemical Co. --Kepone dumped in James River
banks --not reporting transactions/money laundering
Chrysler Corp. --odometer rollback
coal-burning ultilites--acid rain killing NE lakes
defense contractors--massive cost over-runs[4], fraud[5]
Dow Chemical Co.--napalm; Agent Orange; Rocky Flats
E.F. Hutton --defrauding 400 banks of $8 million
Eli Lilly --Oraflex
Exxon --massive Valdez oil spill
Firestone --Firestone 500 belted radial tires
Ford Motor Co. --slipping transmissions;Pinto gas tank
garment industry --Tris(children's pajamas);Brown Lung
General Motors --killing urban mass transit systems
Hooker Chemical --Love Canal
Kerr McGee --sloppy with plutonium/Karen Silkwood death
Manville-Johns --asbestos
Monsanto --PCBs
Nestle and other companies --infant formula scandal
oil companies --conspiring to fix fuel prices
Pittson Corp. --W. Va coal mine waste "dam" disaster
savings and loan executives --fraud, $ billions stolen
tobacco companies--massive promotion of deadly products
Union Carbide--Bhopal, India accident

during that era. 3) Corporate violations of federal regulations annually cost U.S. taxpayers between $10 and $20 billion. Upon the report's release, Ralph Nader claimed that,
besides monetary losses, corporate crime was injuring and
killing more people than street crime and criminal homicides.

As the 1980s progressed the corporate crime problem
worsened. In 1985, one writer suggested that <u>Fortune</u> maga-

zine publish a "500 Most Wanted" list! While this proposal was a frivolous one, Harvard sociologist Amitai Etzioni, studied Fortune 500 corporation 1975-1985 behavior. He concluded that 2/3 of these companies were convicted of serious crimes.

In his 1988 book <u>Corporate</u> <u>Crime</u> <u>and</u> <u>Violence</u> ,Russell Mokhiber, detailed 36 infamous deeds of corporate law-breaking. Fig.#30 lists many of these and other significant incidents where corporate misbehavior led to death, environmental destruction, or irresponsible waste of taxpayer monies. While many of these crimes are discussed elsewhere in the text, the next section details two of them.

V. INFANT FORMULA SCANDAL; BHOPAL DISASTER

In the late 1960s, with birth rates in the developed world declining, corporations like Ross Laboratories, a subsidiary of Abbot Labs, Bristol-Meyers, American Home Products' Wyeth Division, and Nestle sought new markets for their products. Gradually, the best strategy for marketing their mother's milk substitute emerged. It was aimed at developing countries. There, they would give out free samples, pamphlets, posters, contribute equipment to hospitals, and provide "educational services" to doctors and nurses. Often special "milk nurses" would canvass the countryside visiting new mothers. They would urge them to abandon "old-fashioned" breast feeding in favor of their modern substitute. Free samples and other gifts were provided.

What happened was predictable. Wanting the best for their babies, the Third World women began using the free (or very cheap) infant formula. The supply of this lasted just long enough for their own breast milk to dry up. Then, having become dependent on the milk substitute, they got a rude awakening. They did not have enough money to buy all the (no longer free or cheap) formula their babies needed. The women tried rationing what they had by diluting it. In reconstituting the powdered milk--without clean water, suitable pots for sterilization, enough fuel to boil their one bottle and nipple several times a day, and refrigeration--they introduced other health risks.

Consider one doctor's account[6] of his examination of a sick infant on the Phillipines island of Luzon.

> The baby was less than ten days old. He was burning with
> fever, dehydrated and suffering from severe diar-

> rhea. I asked the mother how she had been feeding the
> baby and she replied that she was using Enfamil. She
> told me that this had been given to her on discharge
> from the hospital in Cabanatuan where she had delivered
> the child. The milk was given to her by a nurse who told
> her that her milk was "inappropriate" ....

Enfamil is a product of the Bristol-Meyers Corp. By the late 1970s, providing the Third World with infant formula was a $1 billion/year business. Sadly, scenarios like the above happened repeatedly, many with tragic endings. Luckily for the multinationals, few women associated the infant formula with their baby's demise. Reportedly in Zambia,[7]

> Mothers put empty Nestle's Lactogen cans and feeding
> bottles on their dead babies' graves, for they believe
> ... that powdered milk and feeding bottles were the most
> valuable possessions their babies once had.

Despite the ignorance of some, public health officials blamed infant formula for one million deaths in one year alone.

Our second corporate crime, the worst chemical disaster in history, struck Bhopal, India in late 1984. A leak of the pesticide methyl isocyanate from the nearby Union Carbide plant killed 2 to 5,000 people and injured another 200,000 (30 to 40,000 permanently disabled), as 25 tons of pesticide contaminated the surrounding 25 square miles. In the words of one reporter,[8]

> Bhopal became a hell. Seventy funeral pyres, stacked 25
> bodies high, all burning at once. Mass graves near
> overflowing. Babies gasping for breath in hospitals
> that reported a death a minute. Streets strewn with
> carcasses of animals. Swarms of flies. Skies with
> circling vultures.

When Union Carbide chairman Warren Anderson flew to India to assess the damage, he was arrested for "negligence and corporate liability", then later released. Besides saying it was sorry, Union Carbide sent $1 million in relief funds (amounting to $5 per victim) and one shipment of medicine to treat 300 or 400 people. The U.S. news media speculated on just how much compensation the corporate giant (with $9 billion total assets) would ultimately have to pay victims. When Indian officials demanded full U.S. compensation rates, corporate officials balked, noting that Indian per capita income was but 1/58 of the U.S. figure.

VI. CORPORATE INVESTMENTS IN PEST CONTROL

How corporations make money, the effects of their operations on workers and the public, whether products or services
they provide are needed or desirable--all of these are often
secondary to the bottomline profit itself. Unneeded or dangerous products can be profitable given the right promotion.

Consider chemical pesticides. Given safe, effective alternative integrated pest management (IPM) techniques, pesticide use could be cut dramatically. Many question pesticide
effectiveness. In 1948, U.S. farmers used 15 million lbs. of
insecticides with 7 % crop loss to pests. By 1989, insecti-
cide use had increased eight-fold with 14 % crop loss. And
pesticides are dangerous--as an estimated 400,000 to two
million cases of pesticide poisoning and 10 to 40,000 deaths
worldwide every year, pesticide residues in food and water,
and Bhopal attest. One begins to suspect that pesticides are
heavily promoted and alternatives are not.

Pesticides have been aggressively marketed in Central
America for over three decades. Until the Sandinistas ended
it, Nicaraguan pesticide imports were a $20 million/year
business--in a country with but a $90 million/year total
operating budget. In Costa Rica, Chevron Chemical Company--a
subsidiary of Standard Oil of California--has sold seven
carcinogenic pesticides (including DDT) whose use has been
banned or severely restricted in the U.S.

Yet, when a 1970s Latin American mealybug infestation
threatened a major African food crop--cassava--corporate
enthusiasm for pest combat was lacking. They saw subsistence
farmers in roadless areas needing insecticides, and decided
the corporation would not profit by supplying them.

The director of the Africa-wide Biological Control
Project of the Cassava Pest (ABCP) later lamented[9],

> If there's a fruit fly problem in the California citrus
> crop, nobody objects to spending $100 million to fight
> it--but here we have 200 million people at risk in Af-
> rica and it has been a struggle to beg for $15 million.

By the late 1980s, the ABCP succeeded in controlling the
mealybug by finding and mass producing its natural predator,
a parasitic wasp. Such biological control projects--which are
expensive to initially implement and don't depend on a product to sell every year--seldom attract corporate investment.
Yet for every dollar spent on the cassava pest control pro-

ject (the U.N. provided initial funding), African farmers benefitted $149 in heightened food productivity according to a U.S. economist's figures.

VII. CORPORATE DOMINATION OF RURAL AMERICA

The grip of these corporate masters extends wherever there are resources to exploit and money to be made. In Maine, a rural reform-minded man is frustrated.[10]

> Aroostook County, Maine where I am from, has lost almost 2/3 of its small, family farmers since 1950. If you look at the way corporations are moving into agriculture, and at the subsidies they are getting through tax breaks, we've really created an inequitable situation...over 2/3 of the state is owned by out-of-state interests (corporations and individuals). Nearly 50 % of the state is owned by 12 corporations. That has a lot of implications. For example, many efforts at community-based economic development have been sabotaged by paper companies because...they don't want to see people getting a sense of mastery over their own lives.

In Missouri, 61 year old Herbert Jones is likewise frustrated. For 39 years he managed a 762 acre hilly farm, using ponds, terraces, windbreaks, and well-placed pastures to control soil erosion. But in 1985 the Mutual Benefit Life Insurance Company foreclosed on his mortgage. Since then, the tenants hired by the corporation have bulldozed the land into one, big rolling field. They pushed over 150 year old walnut trees, leveled terraces, and filled ponds with wire fence and brush in the process. They did this to attract investors hoping to profit from a soybean crop. Three years later[11], when Jones walks over his old place, he sees disaster everywhere: lots of erosion, deep gullies, dead trees, ugly brush piles.

According to the Land Stewardship Project in Minnesota, 14 major insurance companies now own over 4.1 million acres of U.S. farmland worth $2.3 billion. In addition, these same companies hold some 53,333 farm mortgages worth $10.6 billion. Besides American corporations, large foreign investors are also buying foreclosed farms.

As land ownership becomes concentrated, rural areas change from family-farm based communities to places where a few hired hands work for absentee corporate landlords. How can things be righted? According to Mark Van Doren[12],

The necessity is not to produce a handful of masters, it
is to produce as many masters as possible, even though
this be millions.

VIII. WORKPLACE HAZARDS, CORPORATE PLOTTING

The stark realities of corporate domination are not
just encountered in rural land or resource grabbing situations. Indeed, the traditional capitalist's prerogative of
taking their money and jobs elsewhere if they have labor difficulties is an effective weapon anywhere. Thousands of
Youngstown, Ohio former steel workers can vouch for that; so
can millions of other Americans traumatized by commercial
plant closings and relocation in low wage, non-union areas in
the South or Third World countries.

Often, where the docile sheep flock, the corporate shep-
herds know there is danger lurking. There are 5 million industrial accidents/year in the United States. These permanently disable 80,000 and kill about 13,000 Americans every
year. Job-related illnesses, many due to the 13,000 toxic
chemicals used in the workplace, annually strike another
400,000 U.S. workers and kill 100,000.

There are regulations, guidelines, and worker compensation to minimize workplace-caused suffering. Often corporate strategies render these of little help to the worker. 97
% of workplace toxic chemicals lack exposure standards. Occupational Safety and Health Administration (OSHA) inspections
are infrequent (typically years elapse between them), and
often management knows when to expect a visit. While such
fox guarding the chicken coop arrangements are usually subtle, sometimes they are not. In 1981, after Thorne G. Auchter
took charge, OSHA destroyed tens of thousands of government
pamphlets on the brown lung disease--a potential hazard to
the 1/2 million textile workers who breathe cotton dust. Why
did these--and many other films, slide programs, and publications on worker health and safety issues--never reach their
intended audience? Auchter felt they were "anti-business".

As for compensation, only 5 % of those severely disabled
from workplace hazards receive any. Even when lawsuits and
public opinion go against them in compensation cases, and
corporations are faced with paying victims, many will still
not give up. In mid 1982, Manville Corp. filed for bankruptcy
to thwart claims of thousands of asbestos workers and their
descendents. At the time Manville reported $1 billion assets.

Asbestos-related cancers will kill 8 to 10,000 previously exposed workers/year for the next 25 years. Do corporate executives know that sometimes they provide "jobs that kill"? For asbestos hazards, the answer seems to be yes. Back in 1935, the Raybestos-Manhattan Corp. president told the general attorney for the Johns-Manville Corp.,[13]"I think the less said about asbestos, the better off we are." The attorney concurred, "I quite agree with you that our interests are best served by having asbestosis receive the minimum of publicity."

Seldom is it easy to identify corporate machinations as such. Corporate organization dilutes any one individual's responsibility, and makes passing the "accepting responsibility " buck easier. Sometimes corporations argue that their errors were errors of omission rather than of commission. They plead ignorance of potential health and safety dangers. Or they shift the blame to government regulatory agencies, government policies, labor organizations, or consumers. Many employ muddying the waters and standoffish tactics which involve their legal-men, regulatory foxes, paid politicians, media pusher friends, and rent-a-scientists.

IX. MULTINATIONALS AND U.S. FOREIGN POLICY

In foreign policy matters, multinational corporate interests and government policies are often nearly indistinguishable. Instead of working for economic freedom, justice, and better lives for impoverished people worldwide, U.S. foreign policies protect the investments of U.S. based multinational companies and aid their Third World resource-grabbing, exploiting cheap labor pools, and creating new markets. Before examining U.S. foreign policy, consider how corporate agribusinessmen and their rich grower allies exploit Latin Americans.

In Columbia, thousands of peasants have been driven from their farms to urban slums or marginal lands to make way for corporate producers of export crops like flowers. In Central America, the most fertile 50 % of all agricultural land is used to grow cash crops for export--despite child malnutrition rates approaching 70 %. On Guatemala's Pacific coast, vast cotton plantations yield enormous profits. There, some 1/2 million Guatemalans earn 10 cents/hour picking cotton.

Often peasants organize and fight those who oppress them. In 1976 a guerrilla group called the Guatemalan Army of

the Poor, protesting countless pesticide poisonings, destroyed 22 pesticide spray planes. The corporate owners quickly
replaced them and spraying continued. This skirmish occurred
about the time tests were revealing high pesticide level
residues in the blood of Guatemalans (and Nicaraguans). DDT
averaged 30 times American levels.

In El Salvador's San Vincente volcanic region during the
late 1980s, the guerrilla insurgency organized coffee bean
pickers. By threatening reprisals against growers who balked,
they secured a wage hike. Workers formerly paid two and a
half cents/lb. of beans picked, now make four cents/lb.

In Brazil, where 1 % of the landowners control 48 % of
the arable land (half of which is non-producing held only for
speculation), landless peasants settle cut and burned Amazon
rain forest. Over the last two decades, multinational corporations have helped decimate this vast region. Companies
like Anderson Clayton, Goodyear, Volkswagen, Nestle, Liqui-
gas, Borden, Barclay's Bank, Mitisubishi, and multibillion-
airie Daniel Ludwig's Universe Tank Ship Co., have obtained
huge government subsidies to turn the Amazon into cattle
grazing land and a source of beef for affluent Westerners.

Little timber has been produced as land is cleared by
burning. In Brazil, lost commercial timber revenues are put
at $2.5 billion/year. Erosion has reduced cattle ranch meat
output to but 9 % of orginal projections. Sadly, non-timber
forest resources--including game animals, herbal medicines,
fibers and much else--have vanished where forests are cut.
One study showed revenues/hectare from gathering Brazil nuts
and wild rubber to be four times those of cattle ranching.[14]

U.S. based multinationals are supported by American
military power, which has been flexed repeatedly to insure
favorable overseas business climates. To illustrate a long
U.S. tradition of militarily intervening in other countries'
affairs, consider U.S. meddling in Latin America. Between
1896 and 1933, U.S. armed forces intervened 33 times in
Central America and the Caribbean, beginning and ending with
excursions in Nicaragua. In 1954, the CIA helped overthrow
the democratically-elected Guatemala government of Jacobo
Abrenz in supporting the interests of The United Fruit
Corporation. (Since then, a string of military dictatorships
are to blame for 150,000 deaths and 40,000 people missing).

In the late 1950s, the Cubans revolted against the bru-
tal Batista regime, which had subservient ties to American

corporate interests. After taking power, Fidel Castro turned to the United States for help during a 1959 trip. He was snubbed by President Eisenhower, who was concerned about possible nationalization of U.S. based telephone, electric, and sugar companies. Eisenhower soon cut off all oil and gasoline shipments to Cuba, and Castro was forced to seek help from the Soviet Union. In 1961, the U.S. backed the unsuccessful Bay of Pigs invasion of the island. Since then, the American government has admitted to eight unsuccessful assassination attempts on Fidel Castro's life.

In 1964, the U.S. sponsored a coup in which generals toppled the Brazilian government. (Talk of land reform preceded their takeover.) In 1965, 23,000 U.S. marines landed in the Dominican Republic to save the military dictatorship of Reid Cabral from the followers of Juan Bosch. Bosch had gotten 60 % of that island's vote in the 1962 election, the first free election there in decades. He had then been overthrown by the Cabral forces, after he had angered American business interests with desires for economic independence. In 1973, the democratically elected Chilean government of socialist Salvadore Allende was overthrown and its leader murdered--after CIA plotting in collaboration with the International Telephone and Telegraph Corp.

Allende policies challenged U.S. based multinational copper mining companies--who had previously been the real masters of the Chilean economy. A few months before his death, Allende told the U.N. General Assembly about the costs to Chile of this corporate exploitation.

> These enterprises exploited Chile's copper for many years; in the last 42 years alone taking out more than $4,000 million in profits although their initial investments were no more than $30 million. In contrast, let me give one simple and painful example of what this means to Chile. In my country there are 600,000 children who will never be able to enjoy life in a normal, human way because during the first eight months of life they did not receive the minimum amount of protein. $4,000 million would completely transform Chile. A small part of that sum would ensure protein for all time for all children of my country.

U.S. foreign policy has hardly been one of "making the world safe for democracy". Instead, it's been designed to safeguard the overseas money-making activities of American

multinational corporations. U.S. tagging of foreign regimes
as "Marxist" or "communist" really means that the country
will not allow its people to be dominated by the U.S. corporate masters. Since the U.S. government won't grant a country this independence, often it ends up supporting authoritarian regimes that will allow "business as usual".

The American public largely seems to accept how the U.S.
uses its military power. They seem unable to imagine a
foreign power invading to overthrow their government--and
this clouds their ethical judgement. During the 1980s, Americans tolerated not-so-covert U.S. efforts to topple the
Sandinista regime in Nicaragua. They applauded the 1983
invasion of Grenada and the 25,000 U.S. troops which overran
Panama as 1989 ended.

X. TELEVISION, WAR TOYS, AND CHILDREN'S NEEDS

Given the Reagan administration's characterization of
the Soviet Union as "the evil empire", its combative rhetoric, and military buildup, the 1980s brought a flood of
anti-Soviet and/or pro-war media themes--including Amerika,
Rambo, and children's cartoons like GI Joe. These ventures
were profitable, although corporate executives were perturbed
by protests from two dissimilar groups: Soviet officials and
American mothers.

In late 1985, the National Coalition on Television Violence noted a 600 % increase in children's war toy sales
since 1982. They estimated that the average American child
annually watches 800 commercials promoting war toys and 250
war cartoon episodes produced to sell those toys. They found
GI Joe the most violent--averaging 84 acts of violence/hour.
1988 sales of GI Joe toys totaled $200 million.

In April, 1990, the 39,000 member American Academy of
Pediatrics' policy statement tied long-term television viewing to violent or aggressive behavior in children. (Academy
members also linked TV watching with childhood obesity--blam-
ing both the activity's sedentary aspect and "nutritional
messages on television are so terrible".) The statement urged
parents to screen their children's TV viewing and limit it to
one or two hours daily.

Corporate economic ambitions exploit millions of American children who watch television. American mothers must

realize that letting media corporations serve as surrogate babysitters may be dangerous to their children's psychological health. A <u>Mothering</u> magazine article[15] entitled "War Toys and Children's Needs" observed,

> The message of much of our media is that violence is
> wedded with power, and that power over others will
> demonstrate control over our own lives. The
> psychological potency of visual images that depict power
> over chaos is what sells the war toys and teaches the
> use of violence or threat to resolve conflicts. The
> barrage of messages about power are very confusing:
> parents tell their children to use words and not fists,
> and the media tells them to kill for peace.

American children are acutely aware of their lack of control over their lives and their relative powerlessness. Most of their parents experience similar frustrations. Indeed, throughout the world, millions are frustrated by the authority and dominance of the corporate masters and the powers that be.

XI. ANOTHER VIEWPOINT: CORPORATE GOOD GUYS

Of the five paths we identified society might head down in the future (p. 124), most analysts find the corporate state path--where corporation and government goals and possibly organizations merge--the most probable. Using recent history and the current state of society as guides, one can argue that such a move will simultaneously pull the world down a parallel path of environmental destruction, social injustice, and conflict. The previous three chapters of this book, as well as the current one, have advanced this belief.

Many will challenge this negative characterization of multinational corporations. (see Fig. #31[16]) Even critic Anthony Sampson acknowledged these companies' positive contributions in <u>The</u> <u>Sovereign</u> <u>State</u> of <u>ITT</u>.

> The most ardent supporters of multinationals portray
> them, both economically and politically, as benign
> forces for peace, leading us into a new world society,
> and breaking down the bigotry and narrowness of local
> rules...There is some truth in this portrayal. The
> multinational companies have progressed further than
> anyone toward a global organization. Their own managers,
> united in their common purpose, inhabit a world in which
> differences of nationality seem...hardly recogniz-

able...the multinationals have played some part in the
process of intermeshing the nations of Europe...

```
+-------------------------------------------------------------+
|        FIG. #31   A SAMPLING OF CORPORATE DO-GOODISM         |
|                                                             |
|   Philanthrophy -- Corporate giving has increased           |
|   substantially during the past two decades. 1987           |
|   charitable giving was $4.6 billion, representing           |
|   1.64 % of pre-tax earnings.                               |
|                                                             |
|   Environmental Concern -- Largely because of the           |
|   generosity of the corporate sector, the non-profit        |
|   Nature Conservancy has become the nation's leader in      |
|   saving land from development and creating wilderness      |
|   areas / natural preserves. Union Carbide is striving      |
|   for "environmental excellence" and promises, "We will     |
|   ultimately eliminate releases of known and suspected      |
|   carcinogens to the environment". Exxon reportedly         |
|   spent $2 billion responding to the Valdez spill.          |
|   Since 1970, GM has cut CO, NOX, & hydrocarbon emis-       |
|   sions by 76 to 96 %/car, upped fuel economy by 130 %,     |
|   reduced electricity use by 44 % per vehicle built,        |
|   and has developed the highest performing electric car.    |
|                                                             |
|   Concern for Minorities--IBM has a network of 60 job       |
|   training centers for disadvantaged youth--from which      |
|   over 11,000 have been placed in jobs. GE spends           |
|   $50,000/year working with gifted children at a public     |
|   school in Harlem. During the 1986-1988 era, over 170      |
|   corporations, sold their holdings in  South Africa.       |
|                                                             |
+-------------------------------------------------------------+
```

Granted the human future doesn't necessarily have to be
so gloomy. There are progressives in the corporate world
working to make it otherwise. Consider the following example
offered by Donella Meadows.

A Power Plant That Makes A Difference by Donella H. Meadows
*Applied Energy Services (AES) of Arlington, Va. has come
up with a way to do something that everyone thought was impossible. It is building a coal-burning electric plant that
will not add carbon dioxide to the atmosphere--which means it
will not worsen the greenhouse effect and hasten global climate change.*

The plant will also be energy efficient. Its air pollution emissions will be low. Indirectly, it will help combat soil erosion and alleviate poverty. Sounds too good to be true, but it's all true.

The founder and president of AES, Roger Sant, was head of energy conservation for the Federal Energy Administration (before there was a Department of Energy) under President Ford. When Sant left government, he set out to help industry save energy. One way to do that is with co-generation.

Co-generation means using "waste heat" from an electric power plant for a purpose more productive than warming up a river--heating a building, for example, or providing steam for an industrial project. The plant AES is constructing in Uncasville, Conn., will sell electricity to Connecticut Power and Light and steam to the Stone Container Corporation.

It is a "clean coal" plant, using a technique called fluidized bed combustion. Instead of a scrubber in the stack to take out the sulfur dioxide that causes acid rain, limestone is mixed with the coal right in the furnace. The sulfur dioxide is absorbed before it even gets to the stack. The furnace also burns at a low enough temperature to reduce formation of nitrogen oxides, another cause of acid rain.

The main gas coming out of the AES smokestack is carbon dioxide, the inevitable product of burning the carbon in coal, and until recently not considered a pollutant. But Roger Sant knew that carbon dioxide is a greenhouse gas. He kept going to meetings about the greenhouse effect. He'd come back to his company and say, "This greenhouse thing is really bad. We have to do something."

He assigned his strategic planning team, headed by Sheryl Sturges, to figure out what to do. They came up with several options: 1) Go into some other business. 2) Capture the carbon dioxide and inject it into oil wells, where it could enhance the recovery of oil and stay underground where it won't cause greenhouse warming. 3) Capture the carbon dioxide and sell it to soft drink companies to make bubbles. 4) Plant trees, which will fix carbon dioxide into wood.

"How many trees?" asked Sant.

"For the Uncasville plant about 52 million," said Sturges.

Enter Paul Faeth of the International Institute for Environment and Development, who is an expert, not on power plants, but on trees. AES selected him to select (through an

open bidding process) some agency, anywhere in the world,
that could assure the planting and maintenance of lots and
lots of trees.

The winning bid came from a coalition of CARE, the
Guatemalan government, the Peace Corps, and USAID. They had
an ongoing tree-planting program involving 40,000 small scale
farmers. For $2 million from AES, they could extend the pro-
gram by 194,000 acres--52 million trees.

Half of Guatemala's forests have disappeared over the
past 35 years. The result is disastrous erosion and flooding.
The CARE program helps farmers plant trees at the edges of
fields and on eroded hillsides. The trees are used for fruit
crops, lumber, fuelwood, living fences, building poles, and,
very importantly, holding soil and water. The program is
wildly popular--farmers are demanding five times more seedlings than the tree nurseries can supply.

AES staff who have visited Guatemala talk not so much
about fixing carbon from the coal plant as about the need for
trees. Dave McMillen, the no-nonsense manager of the Uncasville plant, admits he thought it was crazy that his budget
and oversight responsibility should include forests thousands
of miles away. But when he went to Guatemala, he became, as
his colleagues say, "Mr. Tree". He could hardly believe the
poverty of the people, the farmers hanging from ropes to hoe
their steep garden plots, the denuded land, the silt running
off the hills and filling up the reservoirs behind the hydro-
power dams--and the good that trees can do for the people and
land of Guatemala.

Paul Faeth says, "The carbon fixation is nice, but the
social benefits are even greater. There will be fuelwood,
better soil, higher crop yields, jobs. If I never do anything
else in my career, I feel I've helped do a little something
good here."

For its next power plant, AES is looking for a way to
plant 100 million trees.

Has AES hit upon a scheme to go on burning all the coal
we'd like while avoiding the greenhouse effect? No, says
Roger Sant, it's only a way to buy time. "We're going to have
to stop burning fossil fuels someday. We have to figure out
how to invest $250 million, not in a power plant, but in
energy conservation. That's the next step I'd like to take."

XII. CAN CORPORATIONS RESPOND TO HUMAN NEEDS?

Consider the ray of hope inherent in the dedication to Ohio State University business professor Frederick Sturdivant's The Corporate Social Challenge , used as a text in various business schools.

> To Kaira, Lisha, and Brian and the other young people who have a chance to make a difference. May they not forget those who are not blessed with the same freedom of opportunity.

Can corporate masters grant economic freedoms? Can corporations respond to human needs and demonstrated frustrations of the oppressed? Sturdivant suggests it's in a company's best interests to do so.

> It is essential that social responsiveness be an integral part of a company's strategic plan and organizational design. A major test of managerial success is the degree to which a company is compatible with its environment.

Short of transforming themselves into community-based, worker-owned co-operatives, there are steps toward social responsiveness that corporations can take. These include, periodic issuing of social balance sheets, appointing ombudsmen in charge of social/environmental concerns and providing public interest groups with seats on corporate boards.

Recently, some executives have become interested in company responsiveness not only to stockholders, but to "stakeholders" as well. This group includes all those who have a stake in the company: workers, customers, suppliers, communities where plants are located, and anyone affected by corporate operations. In mid-1988, NCR Corp. sponsored a symposium on the stakeholder concept at which questions like, 1) "Can Marxist claims about the 'internal contradictions of capitalism' be countered with a stakeholder approach to management?" and 2) "Is stakeholder goodwill a fundamental component of success?", were addressed.

Can "success" be planned for in non-monetary terms and gauged without reference to the bottom-line profit? Can objectives insure that company operations not adversely affect the health and diversity of the biosphere? Can purpose include providing many people with a healthy livelihood, fostering social justice, and letting the Golden Rule guide decision-making? These questions also need to be addressed.

Many have urged governmental action to weave social

responsiveness into corporate structure. What is the proper relationship between business and government? Since both crave stability, business and government need each other. Yet an outright corporate state marriage, in which a power-wielding government aids corporate domination over people's lives and resource/monetary grabbing, is a frightening prospect. Unless corporate goals can be fundamentally changed, a governmental role actively counterbalancing corporate excesses seems more appropriate.

Increasingly the business of America and developed nations has been technology. Increasingly business and government have been partners in technological endeavors. Perhaps human society's hopes will be realized down the road of "technological fixes" ?

Questions and Projects

1. To help you empathize with victims of racism or sexism, compose a "Minority / Persecuted Worldview" theme.
2. In many Third World countries, it is "taboo" for men to perform "women's work". Thus women frequently do more than 50 % of the agricultural labor--including all the seeding, weeding, and harvesting. Investigate and report.
3. Research and report on a corporate crime listed in Fig.#30
4. Prepare lists of both the worst corporate crimes of the year and examples of corporate do-goodism. Compare real costs (fines, penalties, gifts) with corporate profits.
5. Find slick magazine ads promoting products and services of corporations engaged in unethical, sleazy or criminal behavior. Contrast ad claims with realities.
6. A decade after the Third World infant formula scandal, many of the same companies began a controversial marketing campaign on U.S. TV that doctors opposed.[17] Report.
7. Write letters to large corporations, a) announcing your boycott of an offensive product, or b) praising a responsible action. Include reasons for your feelings.
8. Labor unions can provide workers with clout to challenge corporate mastery. Report on a) recent U.S. labor / corporate management clashes, b) organizing workers at multi-nationals' Third World manufacturing plants.
9. Review the 26 worldview themes as to whether holders of each would tend to favor a) oligarchic (few masters) or b) democratic (many equals) types of societies.
10. How might critics respond to Anthony Sampson's phrase

(see text) "managers, united in common purpose"?

11. Write a letter to a large corporation inquiring to as steps being taken to minimize environmental impacts and be socially responsive to "stakeholder's" concerns. While awaiting a reply, investigate their operations.

12. The 1970s film <u>Heaven Can Wait</u> includes a corporate board meeting scene in which the spirit of football player Joe Pendleton in the body of tycoon industrialist Leo Farnsworth announces drastic policy changes. Discuss this scene and the worldview the movie reflects.

13. "Your life is shaped more by corporate policies and products than by elected public officials." Discuss.

14. "Business might be the last best hope for humanity". Discuss.

Notes

1. Russell, K. "Growing Up a Black Child of Privilege", <u>New York Times Magazine</u> , June 1987.

2. Williams, J. "Racism Revisited", <u>The New Republic</u> , November 10, 1986.

3. Willard, T. <u>In These Times</u> , April 16-22, 1980.

4. In the 1970s cost overruns on 25 major weapons systems totaled $234 billion.

5. In one example, instead of paying a $1 total for a 25 cent compressor cap, a 9 cent battery, a 60 cent lamp, and a hardware store variety washer, a defense contractor charged the government $1112 for the four items!

6. Garson,B."The Baby Bottle Scandal", <u>Mother Jones</u>, Dec 1977

7. ibid

8. <u>U.S. News & World Report,</u> December 17, 1984

9. Woge, J. "So Much Hangs in the Balance: Biological Control and Cassava", <u>Journal of Pesticide Reform</u>, Vol.8, #4 1989

10. Yerka, B. <u>Aero Sun-Times</u> Vol. 11 #5,6, Nov. / Dec. 1984.

11. Moberg, D. "The Rise of Corporate Farms Hinders Sustainable Agriculture", <u>In These Times,</u> August 5, 1987.

12. Van Doren, op cit.

13. Rogers and Cohen, op cit.

14. Repetto, R. "Deforestation in the Tropics", <u>Scientific American</u> April 1990

15. Logan, T. "War Toys and Children's Needs", <u>Mothering,</u> No. 43, Spring, 1987.

16. partly based on "Ethical Business" section in <u>Utne Reader</u> #31, Jan. / Feb. 1989.

17. see <u>The Nation</u> , December 4, 1989.

TECHNOLOGISTS

I. SCIENCE & TECHNOLOGY--PROMISE AND BACKLASH

Technology is the sum total of special knowledge and the means employed by people to provide goods and services for human sustenance and comfort. Whereas science involves understanding nature, technology involves controlling it.

Technology is as old as the human species itself. For all but the last three centuries however, technical advances were made via trial and error. Only recently has science-- which provides knowledge enabling predicting consequences-- begun to guide this hit or miss search for techniques that work. This ability to predict results without making trials narrowed the experimentation and increased the efficiency of the old method. Perhaps the last great "trial and error" technological innovator was Thomas Edison (1847-1931).

The impetus for the industrial revolution was partially provided by science. Man began exploiting fossil fuels and learned to harness concentrated energy. The coal-powered steam engine drove the industrial revolution and the petroleum fueled internal combustion engine powered the 20th century. With concentration of energy, the scale of technological endeavors grew. This necessitated greater concentrations of capital and the industrial corporation arose.

In contrast to an individual's often haphazard approaches to making money and solving problems, corporations proceeded methodically. Their management and organization was aimed at efficient operation. Besides employing scientists to solve practical problems, they recognized that new knowledge leads to technological innovation. Thus, in 1900, The General Electric Company set up the first industrial laboratory for carrying on fundamental scientific research. Other such corporate labs were established--particularly after 1940. Today many scientists and engineers work in industrial labs.

In the century since Edison's heyday, science and technology have had a tremendous impact on society. One can recount the first 3/4 of that century in terms of dramatic advances in food production, health, transportation, communications, and entertainment. Indeed, during the 1940s and 50s Americans associated science and technology with "the good life", having seen their own material well being and leisure increase because of it. In dreaming about future technological miracles, their attitude was a guardedly positive "Can we do it?"

By the 1960s however, technology began raising questions and creating controversy. Increasingly, those of a new generation were wondering, "Should we do it?" when considering a proposed technological venture. Some felt that technology was getting out of control. Rachel Carson's 1962 book, Silent Spring--in which pesticides like DDT were blamed for decreasing bird populations--was the first in what would become a flood of books pointing a finger at technology.

Over the next two decades, air pollution would be blamed on automobiles and industries, water pollution on toxic chemicals, noise pollution on jet aircraft, violence, social upheaval, and student apathy on television, sexual promiscuity on birth control pills, the destruction of the family farm on herbicides and large machinery, privacy intrusions on computers, and rising medical costs on sophisticated medical equipment. In general the deterioration of the environment--both physical and social--was blamed on technology. In venting their anger, many tied technology and American business together. As the 1960s ended, Senator Vance Harte of Indiana spoke for many when he said,

> A runaway technology, whose only law is profit, has for years poisoned our air, ravaged our soil, stripped our forests bare, and corrupted our water resources.

Anti-technology feelings turned many against science as well.

Some linked science with warfare. During the 1950s, the government and the physics community pushed an "atoms for peace" effort--as if guilty for the evil atomic potential they'd unleashed as World War II ended. Promises of atomic power so cheap it wouldn't have to be metered helped restore science's tarnished image. But during the Vietnam War era, after a new generation's revulsion with napalm, chemical defoliants like Agent Orange, and imaging devices to kill in the dark, science again became associated with death.

These feelings persisted long after Vietnam. As one science educator recently described[1],

> ...the image of science amongst young people was a regrettable one. In their idealism, they were turning away from science as though it were associated with most of the evils in the world. For them, physics was the bomb, chemistry was pollution, biology was genetic engineering (assumed to be evil)...

He recalls an Italian colleague who claims that in his

country "the word 'chemical' has come to be synonymous with 'harmful, noxious, dangerous'." He comments that the public image of the scientist "does not suggest that science has much to do with people or the welfare of society".

II. TECHNOLOGISTS COUNTERATTACK

As anti-science and technology sentiments grew, scientists and engineers began to defend their work and their professions. Those who blamed DDT for thinning the eggshells of certain birds, were reminded how prevalent malaria once was and told that DDT probably has saved more human lives than all antibiotics combined. Those who faulted western medicine and public health practices were reminded that, 1) life expectancy in developing countries has jumped by 30 % in the last 35 years due to antibiotics and improved hygiene; 2) mortality from once dreaded diseases like smallpox, tuberculosis, meningitis, polio, and pneumonia has been cut dramatically; 3) people with what once might have been life-threatening afflictions or handicaps were rescued by eyeglasses, dental fixtures, corrective surgery, artificial limbs, wheel chairs, insulin, Beta-blocker drugs, etc.

Those who lamented the family farm's demise and the dependence of modern agribusiness on massive energy and petrochemical inputs were reminded that 1) 1 1/2 billion additional people worldwide are fed with food production increases attributable to chemical fertilizers; 2) whereas a single American farmer could feed five people in 1900, today every such farmer's labor feeds over 80 people.

Women who attacked technology were told that contraceptives, household appliances and other technological conveniences made the feminist movement possible. Artists and musicians were reminded that a whole range of artistic pursuits--from music-making and recording, painting, sculpting, photography, and film-making, depended on modern technology. Athletes and recreation enthusiasts were likewise reminded.

Those who referred to science and technology as dehumanizing were met with a long list of freedoms from pain, drudgery or unnecessary restriction that have been overcome by these pursuits: freedom from carrying or pumping water, chopping wood, toiling in fields or in kitchens producing or preserving food, limiting activities after sunset brought darkness, making trips to an outhouse, and geographical / cultural isolation due to immobility. Those who suggested that byproducts of technology--weapons and pollutants--were destroying the planet, were reminded that swift transportation, massive international trade, instantaneous communication networks and viewing Earth from space, had transcended national boundaries and brought closer the day of a single unified, human community. Everyone concerned about poverty was reminded how much wealth science and technology created.

When metropolitan concrete engineering works were ridiculed and engineer's motives were questioned, Samuel Florman responded with The Existential Pleasures of Engineering. After noting "engineering is fun", and likening "mighty works of concrete, steel, or stone" to medieval cathedrals, he concluded,

> Enough then of the civil engineer and his wrestling with
> the elements, his love affair with nature, his yearning
> for immensity, his raising toward heaven the crystal
> symbol of a new faith.

The Army Corps of Engineers, when attacked by environmentalists, responded--not quite as eloquently--by wearing a "THE CORPS CARES" button on their uniforms.

Scientists also tried to acquaint the public with what they did and dispel stereotypes. Their message began like this: Scientists are people--a diverse lot who happen to be involved in a rather special occupation. Lewis Thomas, in The Lives of a Cell , added his own flavor in continuing.

> I don't know of any other occupation...in which the
> people engaged in it are so caught up, so totally pre-
> occupied, so driven beyond their strength and resources
> ....It sometimes looks like a lonely activity, but it is
> as much the opposite of lonely as human behavior can be.
> There is nothing so social, so communal, so inter-
> dependent.

Others stress the universal, supranational, transcending of national boundaries aspect of science. One Indian scientist commented[2]

> ...science is a binding force in the world. In fact to
> me, science has provided a world fraternity. I have
> never felt like a stranger in any part of the world
> mainly because I know that there are scientists around.

He contrasts this with the situation in technology.

> While science is universal, technology is not.
> Technology as practised tends to be more national.

It is not possible to say that technology is the birthright of mankind. Developers of technology claim the rights of ownership--and most developers of technologies are in advanced countries.

III. NEW LAWS: NEPA AND TECHNOLOGY ASSESSMENT

In controversies over energy and resource use, and economy vs. ecology tradeoffs, not all scientists allied themselves with the corporate technologists. Many led the attack on technology gone amuck. In his 1971 book, The Closing Circle, biology professor and environmentalist Barry Commoner wrote,

The chief reason for the environmental crisis that has engulfed the United States in recent years is the sweeping transformation of productive technology since World War II....Productive technologies with intense impacts on the environment have displaced less destructive ones.

After Silent Spring, Americans became sensitized to the growing environmental deterioration around them. Led by various environmental groups, by 1969 they demanded and got action from Congress which reflected their concerns. The result was landmark legislation: The National Environmental Policy Act (NEPA). Its enactment reflected the "Can we do it?" to "Should we do it?" shift in the public attitude toward technology,

NEPA stipulated that, before proceeding with federal projects or legislation, environmental impact statements (EIS) must be filed. Here planners were to outline project objectives and identify various alternate ways of accomplishing them. They were to address "What might happen if...?" type scenarios in evaluating each alternative. Probable social, economic, and environmental consequences-- both short-term and long-term--were to be assessed. Premature commitment to a particular alternative could not be made without examining impacts and costs/benefits of all alternatives. In preparing EISs, public input was required. Public hearings would also provide those impacted by a proposal an opportunity to air their concerns. No longer could federal planners and legislators secretly make decisions and dictatorially carry them out. If the NEPA outlined process was not followed in project planning, technologists could be challenged in court. The result: implementation of many controversial projects was slowed--some halted--as forces battled over EISs and ecology vs. economy tradeoffs.

In 1972 Congress created additional means for maintaining a "look before you leap" orientation in technology-related decision-making. Legislation established The Office of Technology Assessment (OTA). Its job was to provide Congress with "the means for securing competent, unbiased information concerning the physical, biological, economic, social, and political effects of the potential impact of technological applications."

Technology assessment identifies tradeoffs. It typically involves nine steps--instructions which were included in the law setting up the OTA:

1) Define the technology in terms of purpose and hardware content or means of carrying out the purpose,

2) Define the social, economic, political, and ecological context into which the hardware is introduced, institutions involved and assumptions behind the behavior of system participants,

3) Establish a data base and investigate uncertainties,

4) Forecast what is likely to happen using models that account for changing hardware design, shifting public attitudes and the interaction of organizations,

5) Formulate alternatives--including doing nothing,

6) Identify impacted parties, including future generations,

7) For each alternative, identify positive and negative impacts, and tradeoffs, by considering "What might happen if...?" type scenarios,

8) Design a plan for implementing the project that best meets the objectives with the least undesirable effects, and

9) Monitor performance.

Ideally, such assessments should be performed by independent organizations with no stake in a particular project. Otherwise, steps should be taken to counter inherent biases of those performing the analysis.

During the 1970s and 80s, technology assessment helped decide the fate of several controversial proposals: the supersonic transport (SST), the Alaskan pipeline, nuclear power plant construction, extracting oil from Rocky Mountain shales, herbicide spraying on public lands, etc. There was no reason to see future debates as any less spirited or issues at stake any less important.

Many corporate managers view technology assessment as

leading to technology arrestment. Environmentalists feel
differently. When projects they oppose go forward anyway,
often efforts are considered worthwhile if delays improve
hardware and add safeguards. Technology assessments can also
be useful in conflict resolution. In his 1986 book <u>Tradeoffs</u>,
Edward Wenk wrote[3],

> All too often the resolution of differences is blocked
> by an emotionally charged atmosphere, an attempt to
> search for villains and fix blame, perhaps a siege
> mentality and adversarial mood. With impact analysis we
> may clarify how different parties feel and guess <u>why</u>
> they perceive their situation differently. By consid-
> ering different options, we can separate out partiality
> and bias, even if we can't eliminate them, and rank
> remedial steps that may quench a firestorm.

Evaluating tradeoffs involved and making hard choices is
central to technology assessment. Wenk has identified tradeoffs common to many technology-based disputes (Fig.#32), and

```
+--------------------------------------------------------------+
|                                                              |
|          FIG. #32   A SUMMARY OF TRADEOFFS                   |
|                                                              |
|                                                              |
|   free commercial enterprise vs.  government control        |
|                                                              |
|                                                              |
|   short-term, self-interest  vs.  longer term, global       |
|                                        orientation          |
|                                                              |
|   voluntary risk             vs.  involuntary, perhaps      |
|                                        unavoidable risk     |
|                                                              |
|   low risk capital venture   vs.  high risk of capital,     |
|   (low return possible)           (high return possible)    |
|                                                              |
|   husbanding resources       vs.  immediate exploitation    |
|                                                              |
|                                                              |
|   who enjoys benefits        vs.  who suffers adverse       |
|                                        effects              |
|                                                              |
|   conventional, tried        vs.  innovative, new           |
|                                        possibilites         |
|                                                              |
|   public techno-delivery     vs.  private techno-delivery   |
|                                                              |
+--------------------------------------------------------------+
```

noted that, in resolving conflicts, "stress is inevitable".
As he puts it, "since we behaved like children in wanting it
all" we can expect "some temper tantrums" before a "realization of limits sinks in".

There are many reasons why depending on technologists to
resolve value-ridden technology-based problems has its shortcomings. Sometimes complexities are such that a clear solution does not emerge after critical scrutiny. Often highly
specialized scientists find themselves working on interdisci-
plinary problems as part of a team. Given the limited areas
of expertise of each specialist, solutions to problems with
far-reaching societal impacts must be found by consensus.
Scientists with different value systems often find themselves
in legitimate disagreement over the best course of action.

Consider three such examples: debates among scientists
over 1) nuclear power, 2) genetic engineering, and 3) cancer
risks posed by man-made chemicals and dietary choices.

IV. NUCLEAR POWER: PRO AND CON
* PRO NUCLEAR POWER ARGUMENT *

560 nuclear power plants generate 15 % of the world's
electricity. Radiation releases from the normal operation of
these facilities produce radiation levels 100 times less than
natural background levels (due to cosmic rays and trace
amounts of radioactive elements in rocks). Radioactive waste
generated by all the reactors in the U.S. amounts to only two
ounces per person per year. If reprocessing was allowed much
of this waste could be utilized as a resource. Encasing it
in inert, impervious borosilicate glass, and burying it deep
underground in geologically stable rock formations, offers a
long-term solution to radioactive waste disposal.

This waste's toxicity is over-rated. Consider one of
its most feared components: Plutonium. On a gram for gram
basis, plutonium is no more of an ingestion hazard than substances like caffeine or nicotine. And while a small amount
can theoretically cause millions of cancer deaths, distri-
buting it in a way to accomplish this would be difficult.
Plutonium is insoluble in water and tends to settle quickly
if airborne.

Despite the well-publicized accidents at Three Mile
Island and Chernobyl, nuclear power's safety record has been
outstanding, considering the cumulative history of over 5,000
reactor years of operation. No one died at Three Mile Island

and only 31 at Chernobyl. All technologies carry some amount of risk. Your chances of dying from the operation of a nuclear power plant are approximately 10,000 to 100,000 times less than chances of dying in an automobile accident. The practical, electricity-generating alternatives to nuclear power carry greater public health risks.

Coal mining accidents and respiratory damage related to coal burning have killed untold thousands. In comparison to coal's mining and smokestack massive environmental impact, nuclear power is relatively benign. To release the amount of energy available from one gram of uranium, 2 1/2 tons of coal must be dug up and burned. Without nuclear, metropolitan air pollution and global acid rain / carbon dioxide caused greenhouse effect problems would be even worse.

Continued use of oil carries an even greater risk. A world dependent on oil is a world threatened with nuclear war should one of the superpowers grow desperate and seize the Middle East oil fields. Use of abundant uranium supplies conserves dwindling oil and natural gas resources and reduces American dependence on imported oil. Uranium fuel also saves U.S. electricity consumers money on their utility bills. Utilities strive to run nuclear plants to meet demand, since fuel for alternative coal or oil/natural gas-fired plants is more expensive.

* ANTI-NUCLEAR POWER ARGUMENT *

Nuclear power meets but 4 % of the world's energy needs. The United States led the world into the nuclear age, it now appears to be leading it out. No new nuclear plants have been ordered in the U.S. since 1974. In most European countries, more than 2/3 of the population opposes nuclear power. Public concern about safety, waste and rising costs has killed it.

The pro-business <u>Forbes</u> magazine has called nuclear energy "the largest managerial disaster in business history". Industry figures now place nuclear generating costs at $.12/KWH in comparison to $.06/KWH for coal. These figures omit plant decommissioning costs--which some feel may amount to as much as the original construction. Instead of picking the lesser of two evils--coal or nuclear--the U.S. needs increased energy efficiency and more renewable energy.

Between 1973 and 1988, U.S. energy efficiency improvements saved the equivalent of 13 million barrels of oil per day--saving $150 billion/year.[4] Nuclear saved just over one million barrels/day in comparison. Utilities in one state--

California--have turned away from nuclear and to wind, small hydroelectric, geothermal, and solar--all renewable sources-- for electricity. As 1988 began[5], the California-centered U.S. wind electric industry had installed some 16,769 wind turbines generating 1463 megawatts. (A large nuclear plant may produce 1000 megawatts.) Close to 200 megawatts (MW) of solar thermal installations produce electricity by concentrating sunshine on an oil-filled tube and then conveying the heat to a turbine and generator. One such California desert 80 MW plant--completed in 1989-- converts sunlight to electricity at 22 % efficiency and produces electricity for $.08/KWH -- 1/3 cheaper than recently completed nuclear plants.

Radiation releases from routine nuclear plant operations are not an issue--accidental releases are. Estimates of eventual cancer deaths from Chernobyl range from a few hundred to 100,000. (In late 1989, the Soviets announced that deaths from this accident had topped 250.) Parts of Europe recorded their highest radiation levels ever, and perhaps 100 million people altered their diets to avoid contaminated food. The consequences (looking ahead to the year 2000) of this accident will cost $320 billion according to a 1990 Soviet estimate. Yet the meltdown did not occur near a major population center, and favorable winds steered radiation away from Kiev, a city of 2.4 million. U.S. government reports place the cost of a similar accident in a major U.S. metropolitan area at $150 billion and 140,000 immediate deaths are possible if winds are unfavorable. (Three Mile Island cost $2 billion.)

Uranium-235, the isotope used by today's burner reactors, is not abundant. If nuclear is to be a viable long-term energy alternative, a breeder reactor is needed to utilize Uranium-238. Breeder reactors are difficult to control. Most designs propose using liquid sodium as the coolant. Sodium reacts explosively on contact with water and is highly flammable. Breeders also require lots of dangerous plutonium be handled.

Plutonium is 100,000 times more dangerous an <u>inhalation</u> hazard than an ingestion one. The 1/2 lb. of it found lying on the ground outside the Rocky Flats nuclear weapons fabrication plant after a 1969 fire theoretically could have caused 10 billion lung cancers. Dr. John Gofman claims that even if the 440 million lbs. of plutonium a full breeder reactor-based economy would require could be contained so that 99.99 % was prevented from getting airborne, 500,000 more lung cancer deaths per year in the U.S. would result.

Disposal of radioactive waste is plagued by two realities: 1) geologists' concerns that underground disposal will eventually have serious public health consequences--given the 10,000 years that long-lived isotopes need before they decay to safer levels, and 2) the "not in my backyard" syndrome that characterizes public opposition to specific disposal sites. Despite two decades of efforts, not a single country has developed a permanent repository for high level waste disposal. As 1990 began, Dept. of Energy head James Watkins announced that a U.S. repository could not open before 2010.

V. GENETIC ENGINEERING: PRO AND CON

While the battle over nuclear power has raged for three decades, skirmishes over another controversial technology-- genetic engineering--are more recent. Two aspects of this technology can be distinguished: 1) genetic screening--identifying particular genetic traits in a person or organism and 2) genetic manipulation to a) rectify defects found in screening or b) optimize the organism's genetic component with respect to a desired outcome. Until recently, genetic manipulation has been limited to plant or animal breeding.

Since the development of amniocentesis in the 1960s, a primitive sort of (pre-natal) genetic screening has existed. Only recently has human DNA been analyzed to identify genetic defects and attempts made to correct them. In 1980, UCLA hematologist Martin Cline attempted to transplant bioengineered genes into patients whose genes failed to produce essential blood proteins. While Cline's unsuccessful experiment was unauthorized and he was severely reprimanded, by the year 2000, doctors may routinely use this technique to treat any of 3000 diseases resulting from genetic defects-- including leukemia, muscular dystrophy, hemophilia, sickle cell anemia, and severe immune system deficiencies.

Besides gene transplantation therapy, genetic engineering can be used to battle cancer, AIDS, hunger, and to develop vaccines or treatments to combat specific diseases. Pre-natal screening early in pregnancy can inform a mother she is carrying a fetus with Down's syndrome, cystic fibrosis, Huntington's disease, etc. Genetic screening can also aid legal and forensic efforts in establishing paternity and identifying criminals.

In 1973 Stanford's Stanley Cohen and Berkeley's Herbert

Boyer stitched together the DNA from two unrelated organisms, and a new life form resulted. Just seven years after this success, the Supreme Court ruled that such life could be bought and sold. In 1980, they held that a General Electric researcher could patent the microbe he'd engineered to degrade oil. Shortly thereafter, the world's first genetically engineered product--human insulin--was developed by Genetech, Inc. to help diabetics. By mid-1989, 11 such products had secured FDA approval. The last was Epogen--expected to overcome kidney dialysis patients' life-threatening anemia problems.

Yet while supporters hail these and other possibilities as great advances, detractors file lawsuits to halt experimentation and advocate a "go slow" approach. Consider the arguments of both sides.

* ANTI-GENETIC ENGINEERING ARGUMENT *

Creating a world in which all living things have been genetically-engineered to serve man is the goal of biotechnologists seeking complete mastery over nature. Manipulating human genetic makeup represents an invasion of "the inner sanctum of what it means to be human". Tinkering with creation in both of these ways is unethical. Putting such awesome power in the hands of profit-minded technologists is dangerous.

As genetic screening and manipulation capabilities develop, ethical concerns will multiply.[6] Might applicants for jobs or life/health insurance be denied because of poor future health prospects? Might insurance companies claim genetic defects are pre-existing conditions and demand termination of pregnancy or refuse to pay associated costs? Might industrial corporations require workers be genetically engineered for resistance to hazardous workplace chemicals? In the quest for perfect human beings, who decides what are good and bad genotypes? In such a world might societal discrimination against the disabled increase?

Consider events of the past decade's biotech company scramble for wealth. These companies have lured research scientists from government labs and dangled dollars to entice university scientists to co-operate with them. At Harvard, some 60 scientists have ties to 65 biotech companies. One such former association, between Harvard medical researcher Scheffer Tseng and Spectra Pharmaceuticals--in which Tseng held 530,000 shares--led to scandal. October, 1988 revelations showed that Tseng had falsified data to enhance the profitability of a drug he was testing for Spectra.

Such biotech business concerns have led scientists to withhold data so that competitors won't benefit. Business pressures can produce hasty, substandard, or even fraudulent research. Given corporate pre-occupation with making money, some genetic engineering potential for meeting human needs may go unrealized.

Consider the effort to produce a vaccine for malaria. According to Barry Commoner, the World Health Organization approached Genetech, Inc. attempting to interest the firm in producing sporozite vaccine. When WHO refused to grant Genetech exclusive rights (i.e. monopoly) in marketing malaria vaccine, the firm ended the discussion. As a Genetech vice-president explained,[7]

> We are forced at this stage in our corporate development to compare vaccines with other opportunities.... Thus it seems apparent that the development of a malaria vaccine would not be compatible with Genetech business strategy.

Commoner claims that Genetech produced human insulin to insure a monopoly for its partner, Eli Lilly, Inc. This product wasn't needed, he says, as pig insulin is effective and available.

Genetic engineering scares people. Many fear it will lessen respect for life. Health activists worry that patients' interests will be overlooked in the scramble for gene therapy profits. Environmentalists worry about the potential risks from new organisms that industry creates. Those who have watched the petrochemical companies thwart environmental regulation fear the growth of a similarly powerful industry. Civil libertarians fear widespread genetic screening for identification purposes.

* PRO GENETIC ENGINEERING ARGUMENT *

Universal prenatal screening for a multitude of genetic conditions will insure that fully functioning humans populate the world of the future. By preventing the birth of defective individuals, expenditure of untold billions of dollars and man-hours that otherwise would be needed for treatment and care will be avoided. Similarly, parental satisfaction with the children they choose to have will be increased.

Gene therapy will trigger a redesign in health care. By offering treatment for thousands of previously untreatable diseases, millions of people will avoid misery and pre-mature death. Many gene therapy critics fail to realize that such procedures would not tamper with genes that are passed on in sperm and eggs. Treatments would differ little from current administering of drugs in fighting illness. Patient rights would be safeguarded by informed consent laws.

Genetic engineering can help battle problems brought on by overpopulation, resource depletion, and global climate change. High yielding crops resistant to frost, drought, and heat are only a beginning. In his book, Future Man, British writer Brian Stableford considers 1) artificial leaves--where human ingenuity has improved the efficiency of photosynthesis 2) factories where lamb chops are grown on production lines, "with red meat and fat attached to an ever-elongating spine of bone", and 3) humans engineered to digest cellulose-- supposedly possible after "minor modification".

Current arrangements between federal research labs, universities, and private companies will speed up the development of genetic engineering techniques. Financial incentives are similarly important. Of those who have stalled this development one can ask, "Is it ethical for a few people to hold up a technology which promises to alleviate untold suffering and produce a more comfortable, healthier world?"

VI. CANCER RISKS--TWO PERSPECTIVES

Cancer is characterized by rapid uncontrolled cell division leading to the growth of malignant tumors. Unless action is taken, such tumors can spread to other parts of the body through metastasis and lead to death. Cancer is not one but perhaps 100 different diseases--one for each major cell type of the body. For example, leukemia is cancer associated with blood cells.

Cancer originates from mutations in genetic nucleotide sequences--mutations due to radiation (including ultraviolet light) or chemical carcinogens. During the typical 15 to 40 year latency period between the cancer's initiation and the onset of symptoms, non-mutagenic chemicals called cancer promoters encourage tumor growth.

While 10 to 30 % of cancers may result from genetic inheritance, the remainder probably have an environmental basis. Scientists agree that specific environmental lifestyle factors cause cancer: cigarette smoking, high level ionizing radiation, viruses (like Epstein-Barr), and chemicals--

asbestos, benzene, vinyl chloride, etc. Yet the risk posed by many potential or known carcinogens is hotly debated. The significance of dietary factors--particularly pesticide residues on food--in causing cancer is especially controversial. While many see improper diet as the second leading cause of cancer--behind inhaled tobacco smoke--others attribute no more than 10 % of all cancers to it. Consider two divergent viewpoints on what causes cancer--one presented by scientists with ties to industry, the other by scientists working for a national environmental organization.

* CANCER--PRO-INDUSTRY PERSPECTIVE *

The massive cancer epidemic that supposedly would result as industrial pollutant initiated cancers finally manifested has not developed. Indeed, for non-cigarette smoking related cancer, no overall increase in cancer deaths has occurred (Fig.#33). Most likely, no more than 2 % of cancers have an <u>involuntary</u> exposure to <u>man-made</u> environmental factor cause.

Regarding pesticide food residue induced cancer, Dr. Bruce Ames, University of California at Berkeley biochemist and originator of the well-known Ames test for identifying potential carcinogens, doubts that pesticide residues cause any cancer deaths at all. He asserts that natural carcinogens are 10,000 times more plentiful in food than man-made carcinogens. While he maintains that eating vegetables like spinach, cabbage, and broccoli is healthful, he notes they contain natural carcinogens.

Many supposed chemical carcinogens have been identified on the basis of animal feeding studies. The results of such tests are ill-suited for assessing potential human cancer risks for two reasons. First, the rodents used typically suffer genetic impairment due to inbreeding. High incidence of spontaneous tumors makes their use inappropriate for such testing. Second, risk is based on the most cancer-sensitive animal species fed high doses of a suspected carcinogen and linear extrapolations to assess the effects of low doses in humans. This ignores any human cell damage repair mechanisms and differences in cell chemistry between animals and humans.

For example,[8] consider why unleaded gasoline is called carcinogenic. Hydrocarbons in it impair the male rat's ability to excrete a certain low molecular weight protein. Female rats, mice, and humans don't have this problem--so they don't develop kidney cancer from such exposures. Investigating chemical carcinogen mechanisms, instead of

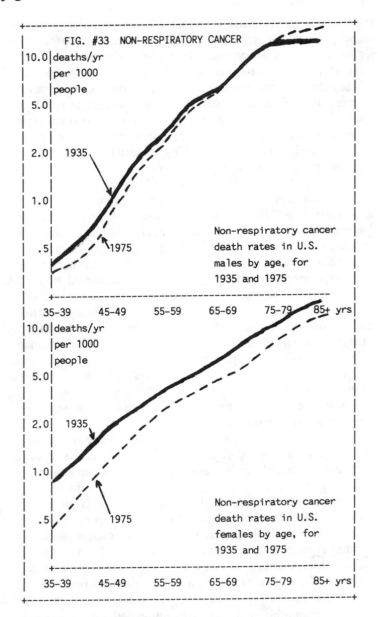

FIG. #33   NON-RESPIRATORY CANCER

Non-respiratory cancer death rates in U.S. males by age, for 1935 and 1975

Non-respiratory cancer death rates in U.S. females by age, for 1935 and 1975

relying on inappropriate animal testing, is needed.

No one has demonstrated that an individual's dietary changes inhibited a cancer's development or kept it from spreading. Calling for changes in societal dietary habits is premature. In light of increasing disease caused by food microbes and the role of pesticides in reducing bacterial mold, fungal, and insect excrement components in food, restricting their use would be unwise. No one has clearly shown that a routine pesticide exposure caused cancer.

* CANCER--CAUTIOUS, PRO-HEALTH, PERSPECTIVE *

Around 1/4 of all U.S. deaths are due to cancer. Nearly as many are stricken with cancer but recover after (sometimes painful, expensive) treatment. Cigarette smoking causes no more than 40 % of cancer deaths--what causes the rest? Other than genetics or the few carcinogens noted, corporate scientists have no answers. This area of ignorance is magnified by another sobering fact: of 48,500 chemicals inventoried by the EPA, fewer than 10 % have been tested for chronic or cancer causing effects, according to U.S. National Research Council (NRC) estimates. Given today's unacceptable cancer impact and scientific ignorance, compassionate, health-minded people-- hoping to spare themselves and their children from future misery--will choose caution over recklessness.

Particularly reckless--and not surprising given his libertarian, anti-government regulation orientation and cozy relationship with chemical industry groups--are Bruce Ames' statements trivializing cancer risks. Says National Cancer Institute (NCI) epidemiologist Ken Cantor, "If you accept Ames' worldview, you'll stop trying to control cancer hazards." Dr. Sidney Wolfe, director of Ralph Nader-founded Public Citizen Health Research Group, faults Ames for calling a food carcinogenic based on one ingredient. That substance may be rendered harmless by another component of the same food, Wolfe asserts. Caution should guide dietary choices and pesticide residues entering the human body minimized.

Fairly strong evidence[9] links dietary fat to breast cancer (Fig. #34) and colon cancer. Similarly, stomach cancer is tied to consumption of salted, pickled, or smoked food. One can also link (not so strongly) dietary fat to pancreatic, ovarian, and prostate cancers, simple carbohydrates to colon and breast cancers, low fiber intake to colon cancer, and vitamin A deficiency to cancer of the esophagus. Until more information is available, heeding NRC dietary guidelines intended to reduce cancer risk--lowering fat intake to less than 30 % of total calories, eating more fiber, fruit and vegetables, trading simple carbohydrates (refined sugar) for complex ones (starch in grains and potatoes), and eating less salted, pickled, or smoked food--seems wise.

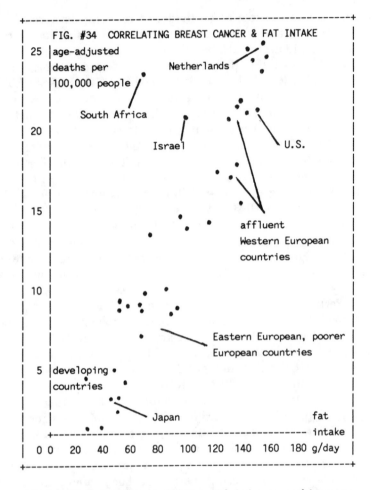

FIG. #34   CORRELATING BREAST CANCER & FAT INTAKE

EPA notes that 55 pesticides which leave residues on food are suspected carcinogens--over 2/3 of all herbicides applied (by weight) also fall into this category. 1986 and 1987 NCI sponsored studies found six-fold and seven-fold increased risk factors (when compared to control groups) in farmers exposed to herbicides and children living in homes where household and garden pesticides were used, respectively. Commenting on the 1986 study involving Kansas farmers--some now stricken with lymphatic system cancer--Charles Benbrook, Executive Director of the Board of Agriculture at the National Academy of Sciences, said,

> For the first time there is clear and rather unequivocal
> evidence that environmental exposure to pesticides

causes cancer in man.

Even ignoring pesticide residues entering the body through two routes--via water pollution and on imported foods--a 1987 NRC worst case scenario figured that pesticides could cause 1.4 million additional cancer cases over the lifetime of the current U.S. population. A 1989 National Resources Defense Council-sponsored study singles out one group for particular concern, as the title of its report suggests, "Intolerable Risk: Pesticides in Our Children's Food".

VII. ARRANGING THE WORLD TO HIDE REALITY

Technology can be looked at in a quite different way. The frontspiece to Pulitzer Prize winning historian Daniel Boorstin's 1961 book, The Image: A Guide to Pseudo-Events in America , contained the following definition of technology: "the knack of so arranging the world that we don't have to experience it." The book documents how Americans have used technology to "create a thicket of unreality" through a rampant substitution of the artificial for the real and through a flood of pseudo events. According to Boorstin, Americans suffer from "extravagant expectations" which have fostered a "national self hypnosis". Many have trouble distinguishing illusions and images of reality from reality itself. Three decades later, Boorstin's analysis is as relevant as ever. Consider the following.

Two happenings are occurring during the same week in early 1988, both of potential interest to those in the nation's capitol and thus vying for media attention. In downtown Washington D.C., The National Geographic Society is celebrating its 100th anniversary with a week long symposium focusing on the planet's biosphere. There, some of the nation's most distinguished scientists are painting "the big picture" and contemplating real, pressing problems.

Harvard's E.O. Wilson is talking about mass extinction of species as tropical rain forests are cut down. Stanford's Paul Ehrlich discusses industrial activity and population growth stresses on global life support systems. Professor Mohamed Kassas notes that human mismanagement over the last 50 years has resulted in desert wastelands totaling half the size of all acreage currently cultivated. Among hundreds in attendance are a few reporters.

In contrast, in San Diego a week before Super Bowl Sunday, reporters are everywhere. All week long, evening news broadcasts in the nation's capitol are full of pre-game coverage--anticipating the game between the Washington Redskins and the Denver Broncos. Television provides rock-video montages of cheerleaders, players, and fans, scenes of lavish pre-game parties, reports of the $675,000/minute that Super Bowl TV advertisers will pay, and endless interviews. There are interviews with 1) all the players, even the reserves, 2) a Gypsy fortune teller, who gazes into a crystal ball and predicts the 'Skins will win but the score will be close, and 3) even the killer whales at Sea World in San Diego!

Each day Donella Meadows has attended the Geographic Symposium and then returned to her Washington D.C. hotel room and watched the evening news. Now she is frustrated. Given their attention to making the pseudo-event "Super", the media has neglected coverage of a significant discussion of the world's real problems. Meadows describes her experience in a mildly sarcastic newspaper article carrying the headline, "Week in Nation's Capitol--Who Won?" The article concludes in this fashion.

> Reporters clustered around the two quarterbacks in San Diego like honeybees around their queens. "How are you feeling, John? Are you ready, Doug? Who do you think will win?"...There were no reporters present when Dr. Peterson, (Chairman of the Geographic Symposium) said that we face four truly great battles--against nuclear weapons, population growth, poverty, and ecological degradation. "If we can win out over them, our great-grandchildren will create monuments to us." How are you feeling, folks? Are you ready? Who do you think will win? I think the score will be close.

After contemplating the upcoming battles pitting humanity against these modern-day four horsemen of Armageddon, the concerned person on the street might react with some questions. "How can scientists and engineers save us? Take nuclear weapons--they got us into that mess, how are they going to get us out?"

VIII. SCIENTISTS' EFFORTS TO AVOID NUCLEAR WAR

One metagon is roughly the amount of explosive energy expended during all of World War II. By 1980 the United States possessed over 9,000 strategic nuclear warheads with a total equivalent of 4,000 megatons. It also had another 15,000 tactical nuclear warheads yielding another 3,000 or so megatons. A debate had been raging for years as to how many nuclear warheads were enough--enough to deter the Soviet Union from attempting a nuclear first strike. The previous year Henry Kendall of the Union of Concerned Scientists showed that even in the worst imaginable scenario--a highly unlikely strike in which 93 % of all U.S. ICBMs, all its bombers and submarines were destroyed--the surviving 100 megatons of ICBMs could still destroy the 22 largest Soviet cities and kill 22 million people. More probably, surviving U.S. bombers and submarines would deliver 1900 to 3000 megatons in a 2nd strike.

By 1984, nearly $1 trillion of U.S. military spending later, nuclear war scenario discussions began to contain a new phrase. The December 23, 1983 issue of <u>Science</u> contained reports entitled "Nuclear Winter: Global Consequences of Multiple Nuclear Explosions" and "Long-Term Biological Conse- quences of Nuclear War". The authors were some 20 scientists including Carl Sagan, Paul Ehrlich, and Stephen J. Gould.

Based on computer model simulation studies of various nuclear wars ranging from 100 to 10,000 total megatons expended, the reports described what would follow a nuclear war. A sun-blocking cloud of smoke would restrict sunlight by 99 % and everywhere drop temperatures to sub-freezing levels for months, i.e. a nuclear winter. The researchers predicted that even the relatively feeble delivery of 100 megatons, if targeted on cities, might trigger a nuclear winter.

Scientists had given those contemplating a 1st strike something to think about. A nuclear attack of sufficient magnitude to trigger a nuclear winter could prove suicidal for the aggressor nation, even if there was no retaliation! The researchers also reopened the old debate over whether the world would end in fire or ice. Their answer seemed to be both: first fire and then ice.

A 1985 SCOPE-ENUWAR project involving 200 scientists from 30 countries seemingly confirmed and added details to this study. Yet, by the decade's end, some scientists--most notably Stephen Schneider and Stanley Thompson, both of the National Center for Atmospheric Research--questioned these findings. Using their refined atmospheric / climate predic- tion computer models, Schneider and Thompson report that the "initial nuclear winter hypothesis can now be relegated to a vanishingly low level of probability".

Many scientists work for peace. A prestigious organization founded in the late 1940s by atomic scientists who helped create the first nuclear weapons, has led these efforts. However, getting scientists and engineers to unite behind arms control and sanity may be difficult. Worldwide, over half of them work for the military. From this group comes a supposed "technological fix" to the nuclear weapons problem: "Star Wars".

The Strategic Defense Initiative (SDI) project, as envisioned by Ronald Reagan would free the world from nuclear terror by rendering nuclear weapons impotent. But most scientists agree that such a space-based laser and particle beam weapons system to destroy missiles in flight, would hardly provide real security. Bombers, low-flying cruise missiles, and portable nuclear weapons could easily thwart it. Sheer numbers of ICBMs--each loaded with many indistinguishable real and fake warheads--could overwhelm it. Even if 99 % of incoming Soviet nuclear warheads could be destroyed, the remaining 1 % could wreak havoc.

While some critics focused on SDI's technical shortcomings, others struck at its core. Donella Meadows referred to it as

> ...the technical fix that makes it unnecessary for us to make peace in the world, even when our enemies want to make peace--and that keeps the billions flowing to the military contractors.

The projected fully implemented cost to U.S. taxpayers was estimated at $500 billion to $1 trillion. As the 1990s began, many expected the project to eventually die--despite $24 billion expenditures since 1984. While SDI work proceeded, Mikhail Gorbachev's leadership brought dramatic changes to the Soviet Union and Eastern Europe. Prospects for an American-Soviet "attitudinal fix" to end the arms race grew.

IX. CONTROLLING POPULATION / THE CONTROVERSY

How were scientists and technologists battling the other three horsemen of Armageddon? In aiding efforts to curb the growing human population, medical researchers sought "the perfect birth control pill".

In December, 1986, a group at the Roussell-UCLAF Company in Paris lead by biochemist Etienne-Emile Baulieu announced the synthesis of a drug called RU 486. This pill inhibits progesterone--a hormone that maintains the uterine lining during pregnancy. Clinical trials showed RU 486 to be 85 %

effective at inducing abortions in the earliest stages of pregnancy. By 1989, 25,000 French women had used it in this fashion. As a contraceptive, RU 486 can be taken (once a month) late in the menstrual cycle to prevent a fertilized egg's implantation on the uterine wall.

Proponents tout RU 486 as a much safer alternative to surgical abortion, and hail its contraceptive use as potentially offering fewer side effects than "the pill". Opponents raise moral dilemmas and call RU 486 "the death pill". Unfortunately, RU 486 occasionally results in incomplete abortions. When this happens, women need professional health care--something often unavailable in Third World countries where the need for "perfect birth control" is greatest.

Proponents of abortion often ask, "Doesn't a woman have a right to freely choose whether to carry a baby to term or abort early in pregnancy--rather than be forced by the government to have an unwanted baby?" This "small picture" focus, while emphasizing an important issue, nonetheless narrows the debate. Consider the "big picture" look at population control provided by Donella Meadows in a 1987 article.

Thinning of Turnips or Right to Life? by Donella Meadows

"Twenty-fifth of July, plant turnips wet or dry," the old-time gardeners say. So on that day I always plant the fall turnip crop. It's a big planting. I can't get anybody in the house to eat turnips, but I store them in the root cellar and feed them to the sheep all winter long.

The twenty-fifth of July was dry and hot this year. I was afraid the seeds wouldn't germinate in the heat, so I sowed them extra thick and watered them down with the hose.

Every last seed came up. I could swear that more came up than I planted. I had a big job getting those turnips thinned down.

Thinning is the only garden chore I dislike. Those thriving baby plants, green and promising, are all trying to fulfill their genetic potential, and I must pull up three-fourths of them and leave them to die in the August sun. I have to grab hold of some hard thing inside myself before I can grab hold of the young turnips. I feel like an imposter god, arbitrarily dealing out life and death.

As I worked down the row this year, I thought of the protests of the right-to-life people against the children's TV program Sesame Street some time ago. Sesame Street had done a segment about thinning marigolds, explaining carefully that plants can't grow cramped. To grow properly they need nutrients and water, light and space, "just like children".

"Why thin the marigolds and throw them away?" fumed the Pro-Lifers, reading much more into the message than kids were likely to do. "Why not transplant them?"

I smiled at that as I yanked out turnips. If I transplanted all these seedlings, they'd cover my whole farm. It would take months to do the transplanting, and who could use so many turnips?

Of course the protesters were talking about human beings, not marigolds or turnips, and about birth control and abortion, not thinning. They say that practical calculations are fine for turnips, but not for human beings, who are special and precious, to be treasured and nurtured, every last one of them.

That is the position of the Reagan Administration, which has worked for seven years to undo government programs in family planning, both domestic and foreign, and to convince all hearers that population growth can never be a problem. It has been steadily resisted by environmentalists, by aid organizations, and, for the most part, by Congress. The battle is emotional and far from over.

I sympathize with both sides of this controversy. I also think that each side, untempered by the other, is dangerous.

The Pro-Lifers seem to think of life as a scarce commodity that needs to be protected. But on this planet life is in exuberant abundance. Especially in abundance are seed and young. I don't have to lift my eyes far beyond the turnip row to contemplate the crabgrass seedlings, the potato bug larvae, the fat lambs in my pasture. They are all capable of taking over the farm and ruining its harmony and productivity, if permitted to reproduce without restraint.

The multiplicative potential of every species, including homo sapiens, is an immense force. Yet one of the great principles of nature is enough. Only so many turnips can fit in the row and still be healthy, fulfilled turnips. Only so many sheep can graze on the pasture. Whenever I have failed because of softheartedness or busyness to thin the turnips or cull the sheep herd, the result has been spindly turnips, sickly lambs, and eroded pastures.

Human beings are subject to the physical laws of the planet. We can overpopulate and destroy our resource base. Our current numbers are without precedent and still growing rapidly. But I get uneasy when my environmentalist friends compare population growth to a locust plague or an uncontrolled cancer spreading over the face of the earth. I understand their point, but cringe at their analogies.

The reduction of humanity to statistics, the equation of populations with plagues, can lead well-meaning people to suggest solutions to the population problem that come uncomfortably close to thinning. The environmentalists I know are such softies that, like me, they have trouble pulling up a baby turnip, but when they get worked up, they can exude an appalling lack of respect for human beings.

There's an old saying that the opposite of a great truth is another great truth. Therefore it could be simultaneously true that human beings are both part of nature and something special in nature. We are the only species that can feel love for each other and for all the other species of earth. We are also the only species with the intellect to control our numbers voluntarily in a way that respects both the preciousness of each individual and the limits of the planet. We haven't yet figured out how to do that. But we have a chance to pull it off as long as both the idea of Enough and the idea of sanctity of life are vigorously represented in our society. Neither should be permitted to overpower or silence the other.

X. BATTLING ECOLOGICAL DEGRADATION AND POVERTY

Many scientists are battling to reverse ecological degradation due to growing human impacts on the global environment. To ascertain causes and extent of the damage and globally co-ordinate responses, in 1984 the international scientific community proposed the Global Change program. In 1986 The International Council of Scientific Unions established The International Geosphere-Biosphere Programme: A Study of Global Change (IGBP). This program represents, in the words of two of its founders[10],

> ...a herculean effort by scientists worldwide to give humanity the knowledge base to fashion policies that will reverse the global environmental decline.

By 1990, IGBP efforts were being co-ordinated with various foreign space agencies involved in "mission to planet Earth". This theme was being used to characterize both the 1992 International Space Year (ISY), and NASA's 1998 projected launch of the space-based components of its Earth Observing

Station.

Other scientists are occupied with more down to earth pursuits. Keeping the world's poorest from going hungry is a constant challenge. Largely due to the technology-wrought "Green Revolution", between 1965 and 1985 world food production grew at a 2.4 % annual rate--exceeding population growth rates. Many look to exotic genetic engineering-based techniques to meet long-term food production challenges.

More immediately, planners at Resources for the Future[11] are considering three types of technologies: 1) those which lessen environmental impacts of fertilizers and pesticides, 2) those which lessen the need for irrigation water, and 3) those that improve food production/acre. Since nitrogen is a major fertilizer component, genetically engineering (non-legume) crops like corn to fix nitrogen would fall in the first category, as would IPM (see MASTERS). Shaping land contours to save water and trickle irrigation systems are examples of category two technologies. Finally, multiple cropping--crop rotation and simultaneously growing two complementary crops in the same field, may help meet the third need.

Poverty can be effectively combatted with a familiar weapon: money. Unfortunately, the world spends most of its loose change on something else: weapons and armed forces. As the 1990s began, total world military spending stood at a staggering $1 trillion/ year!

In the last decade, one nation--China--has made substantial economic progress and raised its standard of living by cutting military expenditures. Another--the Soviet Union--has similarly begun shifting resources from its military sector and also indicated a willingness to provide monetary / humanitarian assistance to poor nations. Given this, researchers at the Worldwatch Institute outlined a program[12] to combat Third World poverty as well as the population growth and ecological deterioration that typically accompanies it.

The plan is built around a redefinition of global security, not in military terms, but in sustainable development terms. Like the Club of Rome in the early 1970s, the Worldwatch Institute is looking for a path the world might take to reach a healthy, stable state. The plan specifies world military spending cuts leading to a 1/6 reduction in five years. Freed-up capital would be used to fund projects in six areas: 1) protecting topsoil 2) reforesting the Earth, 3) slowing population growth, 4) raising energy efficiency, 5) developing renewable energy, and 6) retiring Third World debt.

Implementation of this or a similar program for a sustainable world will involve more than "technological fixes" It will require compassion and the type of attitude and commitment that helped rebuild Europe after World War II. It will demand that nations co-operate and together build a better, more secure future for all.

XI. BEYOND TECHNOLOGICAL FIXES

In returning to the question, "How will scientists and engineers save us?", we can respond, "They can't provide any simple solution." While there are areas in which "technological fixes" look promising, it seems evident that technologists alone can not solve the world's problems.

Before he died, Martin Luther King, Jr. acknowledged the technologists' contribution to the quest for a unified humanity, and indicated what was still needed:

> Through our scientific and technological genius we have made this world a neighborhood. Now through our moral and spiritual genius we must make it a brotherhood.

To find ways to foster brotherhood--and intangibles like compassion, empathy, humility, and trust that it is built on--we must look elsewhere.

Questions and Projects

1. Do you see technology as a friend or a foe? Explain.
2. Attribute the following statements to pro or anti-technologists. a) "Technology transforms everything it touches into a machine", b) "Technology exacts a high price: the loss of independence of thought, autonomy", c) "There are no problems--only solutions." d) "Technological man will be man at home with science and technology...the question of who is in charge will never arise".
3. According to Chellis Glendinning[13], 19th century Luddites--often portrayed as machine smashers, can be understood in terms of a "clash between two worldviews". They fought capitalism hoping to preserve "the interconnectedness of work, community, and family through craft guilds, village networks..." Investigate the Luddite movement and discuss.
4. Moyers: God is everywhere... including the computer. Campbell: It's a miracle, what happens on that screen.

Have you ever looked inside one of those things?
Moyers: No, and I don't intend to.
Relate this to 2d. above and The Two Cultures (GENESIS).

5. "Technology can only be appropriate if it considers the full spectrum of human needs." Discuss.

6. Many people associate "chemical" with "toxic" and "natural" with "safe". Accept this and explain the following. a) A Rotenone spill kills 40,000 fish. b) Nicotine is as addictive as heroin. c) Aflatoxin's toxicity is comparable to dioxin's. Is your logic correct? Give other examples.

7. Obtain an environmental impact statement for a proposed project of local interest. Summarize the project, the alternatives, the impacted parties and their concerns.

8. Technology assessment critics say it stifles innovation, creates time delays, gives foreign competitors advantages, and poorly protects societal interests. Discuss.

9. In What is Science?, Norman Campbell wrote, "Science is the study of those judgements concerning which universal agreement can be obtained." Discuss.

10. List controversial issues requiring scientific, technological, or ethical assessment not mentioned in this book.

11. Compose pro and con responses to a) Nuclear power can be made safe, b) Solar electricity is cheaper than nuclear. c) Glass is preferable to plastic for beverage containers

12. Repeat 11. for a) Abortion is safer than childbirth. b) Human life begins at conception. c) Making abortion illegal would make millions of women murderesses.

13. The creation of new life forms through genetic engineering has been termed "the second Big Bang". Discuss.

14. Which of the issues raised in the "Anti-Genetic Engineering Argument" concerns you most? Discuss.

15. What does an epidemiologist do? How does this work differ from conducting feeding studies to identify carcinogens?

16. Suppose a parent gives this advice to a son or daughter: "Don't confuse reality with images of reality." Discuss in relation to "pseudo-events" and worldview theme #26.

17. Controversial population control measures are viewed differently by individuals possessing different worldviews. Review the list of worldview themes and provide examples of this for a) abortion, b) forced sterilization, c) laws allowing but one child per family.

18. Distribution of RU 486 outside France has been blocked by the West German company that owns Roussel-UCLAF. The

parent company fears anti-abortionists. To the pill's creator the decision is "terrifying and immoral". Discuss.

19. Fact: Every time a loaf of bread is baked, 150,000,000 yeasts are killed. Imagine--this happened at an American Society of Human Genetics meeting--a flier appears displaying the above fact. It notes the slogan of groups called "Bakers for Social Responsibility" and "The Anaerobe Liberation Front": "Defend all life, from greatest to least, from human to yeast!" Using an electron microscope the groups have made a film, "The Very Small and Quiet Screams", which depicts yeasts being baked. Relate the flier to abortion and animal testing issues.

20. Which of the modern-day four horsemen of Armageddon (see text) most concerns you? Discuss.

21. Discuss the extent that attitudinal and technological barriers impede progress in the following areas. a) the battle vs. lung cancer, b) the battle vs. AIDS, c) space travel to the moon or Mars, d) birth control, e) eugenics.

Notes

1. Lewis, J.L. in Science, Technology Education and Future Human Needs (ed. Lewis & Kelly) Pergamon, Oxford, 1987.
2. Rao, C.N.R. in Ethics and Social Responsibility in Science Education (ed. Frazer & Kornhauser)Pergamon, Oxford, 1986.
3. Wenk, E. Tradeoffs , Johns Hopkins U. , Baltimore, 1986
4. Rosenfield, A. and Hafemeister, D. "Energy Efficient Buildings", Scientific American , April, 1988.
5. Shea, C.P. "Shifting to Renewable Energy", State of the World 1988 , Norton, New York, 1988.
6. Baum, R. "Genetic Screening: Medical Promise Amid Legal and Ethical Questions", C & E News , August 7, 1989.
7. Commoner, B. "High Risk, High Tech: Who Decides How It Is Used?", Science for the People , March / April 1987.
8. Abelson, P. "Cancer Phobia", Science , Vol. 237, 7/31/87
9. Cohen, L. "Diet and Cancer", Scientific American, Nov '87
10. Malone, T. and Correll, R. "Mission to Planet Earth, Revisited" Environment, April, 1989.
11. Crosson, P. and Rosenberg, N. "Strategies for Agriculture", Scientific American, September, 1989.
12. Brown, L. and Wolf, E. "Reclaiming the Future", State of the World, Norton, New York, 1988.
13. Glendinning, C. "Notes toward a Neo-Luddite Manifesto", Utne Reader , March / April 1990.

CHILDREN, TEACHERS, & PREACHERS

I. THE WORLD'S CHILDREN--TODAY AND TOMORROW

With respect to the human future, we have examined aspects of four themes that might dominate the human drama: Liberalism, environmental and social decay, heightened corporate state, and the world of technological fixes. Before looking at a fifth possible theme--religion and "attitudinal fixes"--consider another way to assess the future. We can get an indication of what the future 30 or 40 years from now holds by examining the part of it that exists right now. In this regard we turn our attention to children--who will become tomorrow's adult leaders- and consider the forces that will act on them as they grow into adults.

In general, the predicament of the world's children reflects that of human society. Throughout the world increasing numbers of children are growing up in an atmosphere of crisis.

Poverty threatens the lives of many children. 280,000 of the world's children die <u>every</u> <u>week</u> due to under-nutrition and infection.[1] In the developing world, an estimated 500 million children suffer diarrhea infection three or four times a year. Consider the fate of 100 randomly chosen newborn children in poor countries.[2] 40 will be dead before they reach age 6. Of the 60 remaining, 40 will suffer nutritional deficiencies so severe that irreversible physical or mental damage can not be ruled out. Only 12 will finish elementary school, only 3 complete high school. At least 20 of the survivors will not be able to find work and will barely eke out a living.

In many places, children grow up with soldiers and killing--leaving memories of fear and flight. From refugee camps in Mexico and Honduras have come children's pictures of what they've experienced in war-torn Guatemala and El Salvador. As the samples in Fig. #35 illustrate, it is a "coloring book of catastrophe".[3]

In the United States, increasing social environmental decay threatens children. Many kids' physical and psychological health is jeopardized as they grow up in broken homes and with violence lurking around them. Between 1960 and 1985, the U.S. divorce rate doubled. Six million children suffer from beatings and neglect. There are more than one million teen-age pregnancies every year. By the time they are 18,

FIG. #35 A COLORING BOOK OF CATASTROPHE

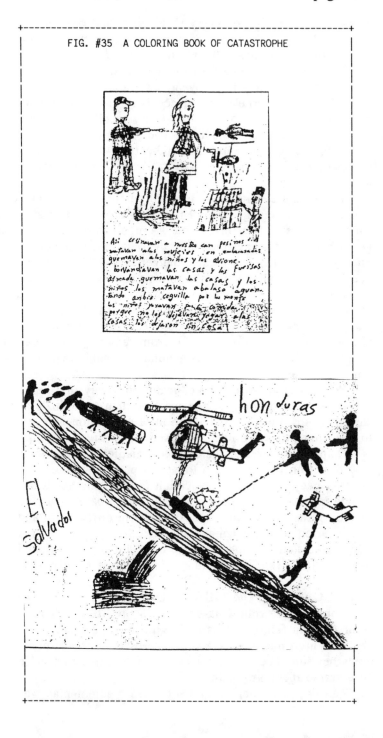

an estimated one out of every three girls, and one out of every eight boys have been victims of sexual molestation. There are an estimated 600,000 teen-aged female prostitutes and 300,000 young male prostitutes (average age 15). Their street life expectancy is one year. 80 % of the deaths of those 15 to 24 are the result of accident, suicides or homicides. 400,000 American teen-agers try to kill themselves every year and about 10,000 succeed. The average American child watches an estimated 200,000 acts of violence on television by age 16, and by age 18 has heard 100,000 beer commercials.

The Chinese, with their fascination for the yin and the yang, have a language symbol for crisis composed of symbols for two words: danger and hope. As much as humanity is endangered by poverty, environmental degradation, violence, and nuclear war, perhaps a greater danger is that children who could one day help rectify the human condition will not be prepared to do so. This could happen if--sensing the "end of the game" was near--they were to adopt a selfish, hedonistic, "get it while you can" attitude toward life. It could also happen if they turned away from reason. These are great dangers because without compassionate, capable people, what hope does humanity have?

Perhaps children can be educated in a way that helps them see "the big picture" and teaches them to both think and care. Perhaps, out of this education, a generation will arise to lead humanity to a healthy, sustainable future. If this is to happen tomorrow, society needs dedicated teachers and a new direction for education today. In particular, human educational needs include: 1) education to meet the needs of people in developing, poor countries, 2) global education, including instruction in responsible world citizenship, and 3) education which enhances scientific literacy and builds ethical decision-making skills (to cope with issues raised by new technologies). We consider each of these in turn.

II. EDUCATION FOR THIRD WORLD / GLOBAL EDUCATION

Consider the following episode[4] in the life of a poor, rural African family... It is midnight. Inside a small, crowded mud hut--lit by a single kerosene lamp--a mother holds her son. The boy has a badly infected ear and suffers an extreme throbbing pain.

Ten days ago the village's supposed medicineman went

through an elaborate ritual to help the boy. Believing the boy's troubles were caused by his deceased grandfather's spirit, the boy was seated--facing north--on the dead man's grave. There, the remains of a black sheep were offered along with various incantations. To placate the spirit, the boy's name was changed to honor the grandfather. Now the boy's mother realizes the futility of these actions.

At dawn, mother and son begin the long journey--by foot and animal-drawn cart--to the village medical clinic. That afternoon a doctor examines the pus-filled ear and prescribes penicillin, aspirin, and eardrops. Fortunately these drugs are in stock at the pharmacy--often they are not. That night the boy is back home and already feeling better.

The benefits of modern science and technology are dramatically evident to Africans who have had experiences similar to this--yet such modern tools are not widely available in Africa. P.B. Vitta of the Science and Technology Unit, Economic Commission for Africa sees several obstacles to be overcome before the fruits of science and technology can be enjoyed by all Africans. Internal obstacles include 1) rigid social traditions, 2) wasted human resources, 3) natural resource deficiencies / unreliable weather, and 4) logistic problems. As external obstacles he cites 1) economic difficulties stemming from trade with the developed world, 2) transfer of technology, and 3) high technology is not always suited to people's needs. Besides help from the developed world, Vitta looks to education to overcome these obstacles.

Past educational assistance provided by Westerners has often been inappropriate to meet the real needs of the people. At the 1985 Bangalore Conference on Science and Technology Education and Future Human Needs, R. Chambers[5] argued that biases point professionals who want to help in the wrong direction. He contrasts their preferences--usually put first--with the needs of the rural poor. Instead of rewards for "first" advances in Western eyes--huge dams, agricultural research catering to plantation export cash crops of rich farmers, medical technology to meet "the effects of overeating by the rich: heart disease and obeisity"--he urges the opposite. He suggests

> promotion and prestige for those who work on "last" subjects like subsistence food crops, smallstock, women's unpaid drudgery, children's diarrhea, village water supplies, community health; for those who

work in "last" locations--villages, homesteads, fields,
in remoter areas and poorer regions...

He thinks Western students and scientists should learn first
hand from the rural poor about their situation and real
needs. He calls for integrating traditional rural technology
and culture with modern (and appropriate) technology and
assistance.

Kenya's E.B. Rugumayo[6] similarly urges the use of
integrative themes in African science education. He urges
such education be "related to concrete real-life problems,
thus correcting the image of science from the esoteric and
obscure to the useful and real". In this way science education can be brought down to earth. He recalls an African
proverb, "Anything that flies can be trapped on ground; the
eagle doesn't feed on clouds."

While the world's rural poor need education to acquire
technical know-how and build problem-solving skills, affluent Westerners similarly need education that will enhance
their survival prospects. For them, making the transformation
to a sustainable society is the concern. Before one can be
hopeful about long-term human prospects, education must be
restructured. Children must be taught new rules to live by,
and ultimately a new type of individual must emerge.

Abraham Maslow took a scientific approach to find rules
to live by. As he described it,[7]

> What I am doing is to explore the theory that you can
> find the values by which mankind must live, and for
> which man has always sought, by digging into the best
> people in depth. I believe, in other words, that I can
> find the ultimate values which are right for mankind by
> observing the best of mankind.

Yet something more than Maslow's self-actualized man (see
LIBERALS) is required. This self-actualized individual in
whom hope for the future resides must have a spatially and
temporally broader outlook than most people. He or she must
be able to empathize not just with family and friends, but
with humanity living in distant lands and in the future.
Global education (as envisioned by many with objectives
similar to those of Fig. #2 in LETTERS) ultimately aims to
produce such individuals.

III. VALUE JUDGEMENTS / ETHICAL POSITIONS

An important part of global education involves the study

of human values. By a value, I mean a rational statement
expressing a preference for a certain course of action.
Behind values are strong feelings and an educational/cultural
heritage that provides some idea of what is "good" or
"right". Getting from a "what is" situation to a "what ought
to be" one, requires making a value judgement. Ultimately,
such judgements may be expressed as actions, i.e. in the
"doing" realm. Making these judgements involves "thinking"
and "feeling" realms, guided by feedback from doing.

Often, judgements can be made in more than one way and
values can conflict. Ethical issues typically involve many
such conflicts. Resolving such issues requires careful
weighing of these values.

Before you can responsibly participate in ethical
decision-making, you must articulate your own values. While
you may initially limit this to values relevant to the issue
at stake, in general you should examine your values and their
origin. It is not enough to state your preferences, you must
look for reasons behind them. Sometimes there will be no
rational basis for a preference--only feelings.

Before values can be articulated, a description of your
worldview in terms of general themes is useful. (These can
come from this book--Fig. #1 in LETTERS--or you can create
them yourself.) Once you understand the components of your
worldview, look to these components for reasons behind your
preferences.

After you've articulated values, two other considerations are important. First, check your values for consistency. If a few values seem inconsistent with many others,
they need re-examining (or perhaps weeding). This may result
in additions or modifications to your worldview framework.
Consistency implies that your worldview is well-defined, you
possess sound reasoning skills and are honest. If seemingly
inconsistent values uncover perceived moral ambiguities,
don't despair if rectification is impossible. Worldviews can
contain opposing, but complementary beliefs. Which belief to
act on will be situation dependent.

Second, have you had a global education? Ideally, you
have formulated your worldview after exploring diverse cultural traditions, viewpoints, and beliefs. Such an education
aids not only developing a healthy worldview, but understanding others as they articulate their values. You may
not agree with those values, but your background enables you

to check them for consistency and empathize with the person expressing them.

To illustrate the worldview dependent nature of value judgements, consider the following example. Imagine a large crowd in an early 18th century European courtroom is watching the trial of a woman accused of witchcraft. If convicted, she will burn at the stake. (Between years 1450 and 1550 this happened to around 100,000 women in Germany alone.) Pertinent laws are marginally applicable and rather subjective. In the crowd are various people with narrow worldviews.

A humanist (theme #10) values human dignity in a way that includes respect for women. He is tolerantly willing to forgive the ignorance that led her to embrace irrational, supernaturalism. A scientist with a Newtonian mechanistic outlook (theme #5)--besides lamenting the subjective nature of the laws--feels similarly. An other-oriented (theme #16) Quaker compassionately imagines switching roles with the accused. She doesn't feel good about convicting the woman-- she wouldn't want to be treated that way. To a Gypsy woman, the trial is religious persecution. She sees God everywhere (theme #7) throughout nature and recalls ancient wisdom that God is a woman. A very poor woman (theme #24) learns the accused is a mid-wife. She recalls a journey and a stranger who provided pain-killing herbal concoctions and made the birth of her son easier. Perceiving this bond with the woman, she is for acquittal.

Others feel differently. A profit-minded (Economic Man theme #19) doctor hopes the trial's outcome puts fear into other mid-wives who take business away from him. The doctor's wife recalls the affair he had with a "loose woman". Feeling vengeful (theme #17) the wife decides the accused is a "loose woman". A fundamentalist Christian (theme #9) whose God is the Old Testament's vengeful God recalls Exodus XXII, 18: "Thou shalt not suffer a witch to live" in deciding the woman's fate. Another fundamentalist whose God is the forgiving New Testament God remembers, "Thou shalt not kill" and is confused. An old man recalls the frenzied burning of a witch long ago. He had felt sympathy for the woman, until the authority of the crowd chanting "Burn, burn, burn..." got hold of him (theme #15).

Today, there are many difficult choices we face as individuals and a society. Many of these choices have been forced on us by two disturbing trends: 1) an exploding human population that is rapidly outgrowing its planetary home, and 2) a technology that increasingly is putting "the power to play God" in human hands. Only those whose scientific literacy enables understanding issues involved can responsibly participate in this "brave new world" decision-making. Such decisions will be reached only after careful deliberation and heated debate.

For example, consider two ways in which humans might actively direct their own evolution, by 1) replacing defective or inferior genes with superior ones, or 2) producing genetically "xerox" copies of superior individuals by cloning. While some see such developments as steps leading down an evolutionary path to a more perfect world, others see immoral experimentation, ultimate de-humanization, and a "brave new world" of subhumans and tyrants. Perhaps society will allow one of these but not the other, both, or neither.

While issues raised in the above example are such that society (either wholly or in part) will decide them, increasingly individuals themselves are faced with choices involving ethical considerations. Learning to distinguish right from wrong is no easy task. Young children can trust in what their parents and teachers tell them in matters related to their own safety. Adults know that issues can be raised which go far beyond individual self-interest--many involve no less than planetary well being.

In evaluating ethical positions, general guidelines--based on moral and philosophical wisdom--can be employed. After identifying those affected by a specific course of action, individuals can consider the following:
1) "If I were in the shoes of someone affected and facing similar circumstances, could I live with this action?" (The Principle of Fraternal Charity) If the answer is yes, the action is consistent with your own values. If not, you should ask, "Why does this action bother me?"
2) "What would be the results if everyone acted in this manner?" (The Principle of Universality)
3) In evaluating the answer to the above question one can look for a course of action that maximizes "the general good" and minimizes evil (The Greatest General Good Principle).

IV. RESPONSIBLE LEADERSHIP
Having introduced ethical decision-making and provided some general guidelines, I turn to leadership. First, I

quote Robin Lovin[8] who recalls German sociologist Max Weber.

> Weber, in his essay "Politics as a Vocation", contrasts
> the politician's "ethics of responsibility"...with the
> "ethics of conviction"...of a true believer, who is
> prepared to go to irresponsible extremes to realize
> values in public life....Responsible leadership treats
> all values as essentially equal and attempts to arrange
> compromises between them that will allow persons to live
> together...

Second, I let Donella Meadows provide another perspective and more specifics in the following mid-1987 article.

Moral Leadership Questioned by Donella Meadows

"Assaulted by sleaze, scandals, and hypocrisy, America searches for its moral bearings," the cover of the May 25 Time magazine says. The essay inside describes how the Reagan administration has failed in moral leadership--or, more precisely, how it has succeeded in promoting, "mindless materialism" and "values vacuum".

Given the national confusion on ethical issues from Baby M to the defense of the Persian Gulf, we could use some moral leadership. But if I'm typical example, I'm afraid we are likely to look for it in the wrong place.

My all-American public school education was not exactly heavy on ethical analysis. In fact, since I took mostly science courses, my moral confidence was systematically eroded. Every day I absorbed strong messages--values have no place in the laboratory; observe what is happening outside you, not inside you; your feelings have no validity.

My scientific training taught me to determine rightness and wrongness from outside, from measurable criteria such as economic profitability, not from the promptings of an invisible, unquantifiable conscience. And my elders provided me with hundreds of examples of how to rationalize glibly just about any act I might want to commit.

Then I was asked by my university to teach a course on ethics. I didn't know how to begin. How could I lead students through the thickets of moral controversy about population growth, nuclear power, acid rain? And yet what could be more important than to provide them with some ethical grounding?

To prepare for the course, I sat in on philosophy and religion classes. I read books on ethics. I talked to pastors, priests, and gurus from many religions. I looked outside myself for moral leadership.

What I discovered was that I had known right from wrong all along.

Religions and ethical theories all have lists of moral rules. The rules generally all boil down to the ones we learned at our mother's knees. Don't hurt people, don't steal, don't lie. Help each other out.

The rules are not the primary authority, say the ethicists. They derive from something we all have within us, a clear sense of rightness, a sense that is given many names. We can get in touch with it whenever we want to. Prayer and meditation are ways--not the only ways--of getting in touch, of listening for moral guidance.

What that guidance says is consistent and simple. You are precious and special. So is everyone else, absolutely everyone. Act accordingly.

Don't do to someone else what you wouldn't want done to you. Don't do what would cause society to fall apart if everyone did it. Try to do what you would want done if you were someone else--a homeless person in New York, a child in Ethiopia, a Nicaraguan peasant, a Polish dockworker.

You don't want your spouse to commit adultery, so don't do it yourself. You don't want to raise a family on a minimum wage, so pay your workers decent incomes. You don't want to live near a hazardous waste dump, so don't create one. If everyone cheats on income tax or insider trading laws, the government and the stock market wouldn't function. So don't cheat.

It's really not hard to see what's right. What's hard is to admit how much of what we do is wrong.

Moral confusion is greatest not at the individual level, but at the level of nations. We forget that nations involve people too, people who are all as unique and precious as we are. The rules still apply. We don't want Libyan jets sweeping down in the night to bomb Washington--therefore it is wrong to bomb Tripoli. We don't want Nicaragua to finance hoodlums to shoot our people and destabilize our government-- so it's wrong for us to do that. Creating weapons that can destroy not only enemy nations but also our own is so irrational it defies ethical theory. To think ethically you have to be at least sane enough to recognize an evil when it threatens YOU.

The usual excuse for state-sponsored immorality is that

it opposes the evil of others. When the Soviet Union invades Afghanistan, when white Afrikaners oppose blacks, when Qaddafi harbors terrorists, when Chile tortures political dissenters, they are acting immorally. Don't we have an obligation to do something about it?

That's the hardest part of moral theory for me--what to do about the evil of others. I found Gandhi to be a wise guide here. Do oppose evil, he says, with all your might. Use every form of resistance and non-co-operation. But don't use violence, which sucks you down into evil yourself. Even a person doing wrong is a person, whose soul you must respect, though you do not respect his actions.

The base assumption of our foreign policy--assumptions not invented by the Reagan administration but greatly strengthened by it--are clearly immoral. Americans are more worthy than other human beings. Our nation ought to have its way at the expense of other nations. The existence of evil elsewhere justifies committing evil ourselves. Not one of those statements is morally defensible.

New moral leadership does not mean someone to tell us what to do. It means someone to help us discover that we already know what to do. Someone who can recognize the smoke-screens we all throw into ethical discussions to make us feel good about what we know we should feel bad about. Someone to keep reminding us that we are special and precious--all of us, every one of us.

V. FUTURIST PREACHERS

Children's values and attitudes are shaped not only by parents, teachers, and friends, but by national institutions and mass media. These latter forces ground children in national (rather than world) citizenship and a short-term self-interest orientation. What forces traditionally have guided people toward a more long-term, other-oriented, universal worldview? Preachers.

We shall broaden who we call a preacher by concurring with Thomas Thompson and including in this category those seemingly in a different occupation.[9]

> All the futurists I know are more like preachers than pure scientists. They resemble biblical prophets in that they tell us their scary tales of the future in order to bring us back to virtue and sense. Or they are like evangelical ministers in that they paint a

picture of future fire and brimstone only in order to
hold forth a gospel of salvation.

The gospel of salvation varies with the futurist you're
talking to. The MIT / Club of Rome computer world models
suggested that--given an "Expansionist Worldview"-- technological fixes will eventually encounter limits that human
ingenuity can't overcome. A sermon from these folks might
urge "control yourselves". In his <u>An Inquiry Into The Human
Prospect</u> , Robert Heilbroner discounted the role of liberalism in the future--claiming that human short-term selfishness is so ingrained that freedom will have to be traded for
survival. He saw the need for stoic endurance, writing, "If,
within us, the spirit of Atlas falters, there perishes the
determination to preserve humanity..." Garrett Hardin's
lifeboat ethics held out little hope for a healthy, just
world for all.

Thompson wonders,

> If a 20th century futurist preacher calls upon me to
> sacrifice my short-term good to forfend the suffering of
> others who may live in some far-off future, why should I
> change my ways?...If God is not there to instruct me, or
> punish me, why should I regard those faceless, potential
> beings as my 'neighbors'?

He concludes that we owe nothing to future generations.

While some futurists feel that traditional religions are
no longer viable for moving society in the needed direction,
others disagree. E.H. Schumacher[10], an economist equally at
home in London or in poor villages in Burma or India, spoke
of one reward--finding wisdom--to be gained by adopting a
"Family of Man / Other People Orientation".

> ...To be able to find it, one has first to liberate
> oneself from such masters as greed and envy. The still-
> ness following liberation--even if only momentary--
> produces the insights of wisdom which are obtainable in
> no other way.

Peccei and Ikeda looked to "spiritual and ethical solutions",
others to "a values revolution" and an environmental ethic.

Having recalled the messages of futurist preachers, let
us search the realm of religion for "attitudinal fixes" to
human problems. We look to, in turn, 1) the traditional
forces for God, goodwill and brotherhood, 2) fundamentalist
preachers, and 3) new religious movements.

VI. CATHOLIC BISHOPS' PASTORAL LETTERS

During the same week in early May, 1983 two important events were happening in Chicago. The trial of the notorious "Rent-a-Scientist" firm IBT Labs' top executives was beginning. Nearby, in the Palmer House Hotel, 247 U.S. Catholic Bishops were voting to approve the final draft of their pastoral letter, "The Challenge of Peace: God's Promise and Our Response". By a 238 to 9 vote, the Bishops approved a document that opposed the defense policies of their government.

The press immediately began speculating how the Reagan administration, which did not want a confrontation with the nation's 51 million Catholics, would react. Also reported was the Bishops' continuing work on a pastoral letter critiquing capitalism. There were suggestions that American Catholicism was being transformed into a "peace and poor church".

On November 11, 1984 the first draft of their pastoral letter "Catholic Social Teaching and the U.S. Economy" was released.[11] It begins, "Every perspective on economic life that is human, moral, and Christian must be shaped by two questions: What does the economy do for people? What does it do to people?" Their discussion soon focuses on the world's poor. It suggests that all people "must measure their actions and choices by what they do for and to the poor." "To turn aside from those on the margins of society, the needy and the powerless, is to turn away from Jesus, who identifies himself with them...This split between the faith which many profess and their daily lives deserves to be counted among the more serious errors of our age," it adds.

After lauding the American "experiment in the protection of civil and political rights" the letter continues. "We believe that the level of inequality in income and wealth in our society and even more the inequality on the world scale today must be judged morally unacceptable...Unless combatted by social and political action, the influence of the new industrial and technological order favors the concentration of wealth, power and decision-making in the hands of a small public or private controlling group." Later they add, "To resist this danger we believe that America needs a new experiment in co-operation and collaboration. Such an experiment has a moral and cultural aspect: the renewal and enhancement of the sense of solidarity...It will also...broaden the sharing of responsibility in economic society."

The bishops recognize that such a transformation will

not be easy to accomplish. They note one obstacle: "How the corporations' pursuit of profit can be reconciled with the common good...is one of the most persistent and vexing moral problems we face" and another danger, "Excessive consumption threatens the well being of future generations and violates the obligations of stewardship."

The second part of the bishop's letter is devoted to policy applications. They assert, "A job with adequate pay should be available to all who seek one", and recommend, "Income for families should also be sufficient to enable one of the parents to spend time at home devoted to the education of small children, without prejudice to the equal rights of men and women in family and society." Relations between workers and management should be marked by a "spirit of co-operation" the bishops say. They urge "co-operative ownership and worker participation in ownership and decision-making" arrangements be developed.

As for those who claim to be religious, in their conclusion the bishops recommend, "Simplicity of lifestyle and identification with the struggle of the poor should characterize their lives." Here the letter echoes Pope John Paul II who has advocated a break with "the frenzy of consumerism" and said, "We must find a simple way of living." Such words make one recall a sentence from the bishop's 1980 pastoral letter on Marxist Communism, "A sober and responsible lifestyle (by Americans) would be more effective than anti-communist propaganda in dissauding the uncommitted from joining the Marxist camp."

The U.S. representatives of the traditional forces for brotherhood and goodwill had spoken. Did the poor have new hope for economic justice?--Not if the reaction of the U.S. corporate state leaders was any indication. Business leaders dismissed the bishop's views as "lacking economic realism" and "socialism". President Reagan ignored them. About the same time he also ignored the World Court meeting in The Hague, which condemned the United States for its subversive activities against the Nicaruguan government.

Soon Christmas Day, 1984 arrived and Americans were busy grabbing the largesse left by Santa Claus. Elsewhere on the planet, from the balcony of St. Peter's Basilica in Rome, the Pope, before a crowd of 100,000, declared his solidarity "with the peoples of Ethiopia, Mozambique and other regions of Africa, decimated by the scourge of famine and drought."

He also identified with "all those who in other parts of the world, too, are dying of hunger." To those in the affluent world weary from the onslaught of conspicuous consumption pusher activity, he pledged, "We affirm our solidarity with the families that are suffering from the moral upheaval introduced into them by the cynical society of consumerism."

VII. RELIGIOUS RIGHT VS. HUMANIST AGENDA

Of the traditional mainstream religions in the U.S., only the Catholic Church (16 % increase) has not experienced a membership decrease during the 1970s and 80s. Since 1965, five mainline Protestant churches have lost 5.2 million members (typical 27 % decrease) despite a 47 million person growth in U.S. population. In contrast, membership in conservative, evangelical churches has soared.

As to the latter, should one feel hopeful based on good works they undertake, or see dangers in their right wing political activity? These forces are often in conflict with those possessing science-based worldviews. Clearly, many fundamentalist Christians desire a future for their children based on something other than thinking and reason. With their attempts to write into science books a "theory" of creationism--which claims God created the universe a mere 6,000 years ago and that evolution does not exist--fundamentalists confront science head on. Not just scientific insights and methods are under attack, so is the whole rational orientation of modern society. TV superstar preacher and one-time presidential candidate Pat Robertson has claimed that logic and reason are tools of the Devil.

Besides the Biblical creation vs. evolution controversy, fundamentalist Christians have attacked other aspects of public school education. Confrontations have occurred over the use of values clarification. Some Christian parents feel threatened because children are encouraged to question not only what their values are, but where they come from. Parents used to inculcating their own values in their children won't tolerate this.

Since the 1970s, many right-wing Christian groups have been actively involved in the political process. They have attacked a so-called "humanist agenda for a world without God". In Oklahoma, their fight against values clarification was successful. There, in 1981, legislators passed the Parents Rights Bill, which among other things, prohibits the

teaching of values clarification. This action brought protests from civil libertarians and educators. Many echoed the
humanistic authors of the 1972 book Values Clarification, who
wrote,[12]

> Young people brought up by moralizing adults are not
> prepared to make their own responsible choices. They
> have not learned a process for selecting the best and
> rejecting the worst elements contained in the various
> value systems which others have been urging them to
> follow. Thus, too often the important choices in life
> are made on the basis of peer pressure, unthinking
> submission to authority, or to the power of propaganda.

While many fundamentalists attacked humanism for producing self-oriented people, and themselves claimed to worship Jesus and be other-oriented, most saw no conflict with
that religious perspective and a self-interest economic orientation, i.e. a "Gospel of their own wealth". In formulating
the Values Clarification strategy, the book's authors warned
of something like that.

> Another problem with the direct inculcation of values
> is that often it results in a dichotomy between theory
> and practice; lip service is paid to the values of
> authority, while behavior contradicts these values. Thus
> we have religious people who love their neighbors on the
> Sabbath and spend the rest of the week competing with
> them.

These religious zealots also attacked global education.
A 1986 right wing, fundamentalist paper, "Blowing the Whistle
on Global Education"[13] charged that the content of such an
educational approach,
1) overemphasized the redistribution of world resources,
2) promoted One World over national sovereignty,
3) overemphasized co-operation, downplayed competition,
4) implied a moral equivalence between the U.S. and USSR, and
5) rejected Biblical creation and the rights of the unborn by
   omission.[14]

VIII. THE POWER OF THE RELIGIOUS RIGHT
The electronic media is as important to this Christian
fundamentalist "revolution" as the new printing press was to
the Protestant Reformation. In late 1985, the A.C. Nielsen
Company estimated the monthly audience for television evan-

gelists at 34 million households--rivaling top-ranked network shows. Annual earnings for this "electronic church"--mostly from appeals for offerings and the sale of religious merchandise--had passed $500 million. Shortly thereafter, University of Virginia sociologist Jeffrey Hadden, author of <u>Prime</u> <u>Time</u> <u>Preachers</u> , asserted that such preachers "have greater unrestricted access to media than any other interest group in America. The Christian right," he added, "is destined to become the major social movement in America."

By 1989, Sara Diamond, in her book <u>Spiritual</u> <u>Warfare:</u> <u>The</u> <u>Politics</u> <u>of</u> <u>the</u> <u>Christian</u> <u>Right</u> , noted that 10 % of radio station and 14 % of television station U.S. licenses belonged to the Christian right. Her data showed that this network of 1,000 radio stations and 200 TV stations was still expanding.

The Christian right media message includes a denunciation[15] of humanism as "a secular religion which now rises like a tidal wave to put God away and establish the predominance of man within every sphere of life." They attack the character and integrity of those who disagree with them. On one TV broadcast an electronic superstar minister said[16]

> Let me tell you something else about the character of God. If necessary, God would raise up a tyrant--a man who might not have the best ethics--to protect the freedom and interests of the ethical and the godly.

Such statements reinforce fears that a right wing fundamentalist drive for political power might ultimately end with the fascist authority of a despot replacing American democracy and civil liberties. There are reasons to believe that a society built on unquestioning faith rather than humanistic free inquiry may be more susceptible to dictatorial rule (contrast worldview theme #10 "Humanism" with theme #15 "The Collective Cognitive Imperative").

Political activities of the religious right warrant concern. In 1982, those seeking to impose their values on others filed lawsuits in Indiana, Washington and other states trying to repeal laws making a husband's physical abuse of his wife or child a crime. Their argument was that government should not interfere with a "husband's divine right to discipline" his own family. The same forces often pressured libraries to remove books with liberal dogma or humanistic themes. Every so often TV news broadcasts actually showed them burning books.

IX. TURNING AWAY FROM BOOKS AND REASON

While a few religious extremists are burning books, many Americans are having trouble learning from them. Still others are turning away from reason itself.

American reading disabilities and illiteracy have become increasingly serious problems--despite massive state and federal expenditures to combat them. Consider the following[17]
1) An estimated 20 to 40 % of all American school children have reading disabilities that require special attention.
2) The U.S. Army issues comic books as instruction manuals to its many nearly illiterate recruits.
3) 60 million American adults or 35 % of its citizens cannot read. The U.S. ranks only 29th of 158 nations in literacy level, according to U.N. data.
Given this evidence, it seems that American interest and involvement with reading is declining.

Meanwhile American interest in pseudoscience seems to be growing. Some feel that belief in the irrational, occult, and the supernatural has permeated society to nearly the extent it did during the Middle Ages. There are an estimated 2/3 million active practitioners of the occult, and millions of less fanatical followers. These pseudoscientific phenomena have also become big business. Bookstores and bestseller lists contain far more volumes on pseudoscience than on science. Millions of dollars are spent on books, movies, magazines, cassettes and even computer programs with these "far out" themes.

Ancient arts of witchcraft, palmistry, faith healing, fortune telling, and astrology have widespread following. 30 million Americans regularly consult newspaper horoscopes and some 10,000 make their living as astrologers--including one influential with President and Mrs. Reagan. With somewhat more modern roots are beliefs in contact with extra-terrestrials and UFOs, plants that have feelings, biorhythms, Kirlian photography, the Bermuda triangle, Bigfoot or other monsters, pyramid power, etc.

Growing up alongside this dramatic resurgence in pseudoscience is the renewal of American Christianity. Complementing this movement's more orthodox evangelicals are Charismatics. In the words of one investigator, they number "millions upon millions". He notes[18]

> (Their) belief in supernatural gifts of faith healing,
> speaking in tongues, and prophecy represents a monu-
> mental assault on the Modern Age itself. For Charis-
> matics these supernatural powers are beginning to
> replace science, technique and reason as the critical
> reference points for interpreting one's day to day
> existence.

Those practicing a New Age brand of religion were likewise involved in what many would call pseudoscientific silliness. Their efforts to promote peace have included events in which lots of people meditate and send "good vibes" to world leaders. Transcendental meditation practitioners claim that when 1 % of the population meditates they create a physical influence of coherence that has measurable effects: reduced war deaths, crimes, hospital admissions, and social violence, and increased stock market performance.

Among their latest TM techniques is yogic flying. Such "flyers" sit in a cross-legged position, and after medita-tion, they are able to bounce off the ground startlingly high and far. After initial gyration, supposedly liftoff occurs at a moment of "intense peak brain wave coherence". Citing de-scriptions in ancient Vedic texts, many flyers are confident that their "hopping" will eventually lead to hovering and then directed flight! TM guru Maharishi Mahesh Yogi hopes to one day co-ordinate 10,000 flyers to enliven peace tendencies in the collective consciousness and neutralize negative tendencies.

X. NEW RELIGIONS / TWO APPROACHES TO BUDDHISM

In counseling those attracted to new religious move-ments, historian William Irwin Thompson writes,[19]

> ...if a group generates hate or fear, violence,
> suspicion...or negative...emotions, then suspect it. If
> it generates love and trust, commitment and loyalty and
> faith and all those other qualities of joyous human
> sharing, then you can begin to relax. And if it can
> tolerate criticism and if the forms of leadership are
> open to dialogue, then you can relax even more.

Many either intentionally or unwittingly trade a rational perspective for "The Collective Cognitive Imperative" and get caught up in such movements. Consider how one of America's fast growing religions--the Nichiren Shokhu Soka Gakkai of America (NSA), a Buddhist sect--operates.

To be a member in good standing, a devotee must recruit others to join this faith through a process called shakubuku ("to break and subdue"). In Southern California such people-- typically well-dressed and smooth-talking--conduct their aggressive campaigns on street corners. Their pitch, as one who was approached recounts, might be as follows.[20]

> Have you ever heard of nam-myoho-renge-kyo? Have you heard about Buddhism? Want a better job? A new car? Perfect health? Whatever you want, you can have just by chanting nam-myoho-renge-kyo. I'm not fooling, it's the mystical sound of the universe.

After this opening, potential members are asked to sus- pend judgement and come to a meeting. Such meetings typically involve many people seated on a floor facing a Gohonzon (a parchment with Japanese characters) and chanting in precise, rapid unison. After an exhorting "Shakubuku, Shakubuku, all the way. Attack!" cheer, stories of how this "true" Buddhism changed lives and healed the sick are exchanged.

One mid-1986 NSA estimate claimed 500,000 U.S. members in all 50 states, and worldwide membership of 20 million. Members typically end up buying a $15 Gohonzon, an altar for it, a bell, incense, and are urged to subscribe to NSA news- papers and magazines (altogether amounting to $72). The group dissociates itself from other Buddhist organizations and members see themselves as "the only true Buddhists".

Traditionally, Buddhism is associated with renouncing worldly possessions. Buddha also taught, "We are members one of another". More in keeping with this (and related Chris- tian) tradition, a much smaller religious group has wrapped itself in "The Family of Man/Other People Orientation".

"If you're going to say we're all One, let's give up competition at that level of food and life and death and housing and things like that", writes their spiritual leader Stephen Gaskin. Beginning at Monday night standing room only lectures given by Gaskin in late 1960s San Francisco, the movement relocated to rural Tennessee and "The Farm". By 1980 its population numbered 1350 people. Since 1974, The Farm has operated Plenty, an international assistance effort that has sent volunteers to help the rural poor in 12 countries. The group's name and mission comes

from the realization that all people are members of the
human family, and that, if we wisely use and share the
abundance of the earth, there is plenty for everyone.
The recognition that we are one family inspires kindness
and generosity in response to suffering, courage and
moral outrage in response to injustice.

XI. LOOKING FOR A MESSIAH

Where should those weary of Western materialism and
technology, and looking for a spiritual path go to find it?
"Go to a village," writes Richard Critchfield in his 1981
book Villages , "and you can't be too far wrong if you assume
everybody is just like you. For in the largest sense and in
those human qualities that really count, on this rather small
planet there is only one big us."

Critchfield likes the low stress, natural life villages
offer and enjoys getting away from cities and "those electronic voices coming at you". His book recalls close friend-
ships with villagers around the world. He appreciates the
special things village worlds have to offer and will challenge those who don't.

Critchfield notes that out of villages and thatched huts
have come all of the world's great religions. In the midst of
some comments on great religions, he speculates as to what
humble villages may someday offer the world.

These religions were all formed as little village
traditions in revolt against existing city traditions
which had somehow failed millions of villagers...
They all emerged in civilizations which, like ours, were
in extremis. Prophets come from villages...Perhaps, if
we wish to speculate about what kind of new spiritual
challenge to the West could arise from villages, it is
to Jesus we should look...The words and deeds of this
simple man...exemplifies the kind of prophet we might
expect to arise in our spiritually similar times. Doubt-
less his life, at the time it happened, would be equally
obscure.

Elsewhere on the planet, fundamentalist Christians
eagerly await the second coming of Jesus. Some of them scorn
the "all is one, one is all" belief of other religions. Con-
stance Cumbey has written books attacking this notion and the
New Age movement. In her first book, Cumbey worried that
esoteric groups would create a spiritual bridge to the Devil

and usher in an "age of barbarism". In her latest book, <u>A Planned Deception</u> , she claims that New Agers are planning to stage the "coming of a planetary Messiah".

Questions & Projects

1. Contrast the fates of 100 children in poor countries with fates of such children where you live (use local data).
2. Investigate the clock on the cover of <u>The Bulletin of the Atomic Scientists</u> as to how its setting is determined and what the setting has been. Focus on changes in each.
3. Suppose astrophysicists announced they had conclusive proof that the star Betelgeuse would undergo a supernova outburst in 100 years. Suppose the deadly radiation flux would end life on Earth and there was no way of averting the catastrophe. How might people react? Discuss.
4. Using a format similar to the "accused witch" example in the text, present your own example illustrating the dependence of values on worldviews.
5. Debate: Can a good politician also be a good person?
6. Holders of which of the 26 worldview themes would tend to favor attitudinal over technological fixes? or vice versa?
7. Pick a topic you recall studying as a student. Contrast treatment it received with a global education approach.
8. Consider two approaches to global education. #1: Bound by "Americanism", material is covered from a global viewpoint to promote better understanding, Approach #2: Goal is same as above; but students taught to think and feel like world citizens. Which might foster attitudes contrary to patriotism and national loyalty? Would advantages in effectiveness warrant risking controversy? Discuss.
9. Cultural differences--in customs, history, beliefs--make it difficult for someone from one culture to make value judgements about another culture's practices. Such judgements can also cause controversy. Some educators-- seeking to promote understanding, tolerance, and respect for cultural differences--nonetheless shy away from comparing values. Some may claim "all values are equal"; others that "it is impossible to make moral judgements across cultures". Such teachers have been criticized for disserving their goals. Why? Suggest a better approach.
10. Internal conflict has plagued the Catholic Church in recent years. Research and report.
11. In a 1936 novel, <u>It Can't Happen Here</u> , Sinclair Lewis

imagined fascism coming to America. Christian revivialism supposedly merges with conservative business interests to manipulate mass psychology. Could it happen now? Discuss.

12. New Age critics charge, "If God is everything, then anything goes." Discuss.

Notes

1. UNICEF, The State of the World's Children 1990 , Oxford University Press, New York, 1990

2. Vitta, P.B. in Science and Technology Education and Future Human Needs (ed. Lewis & Kelly), Pergamon, Oxford, 1987.

3. Japenga, A. "A Coloring Book of Catastrophe", L.A. Times , December 24, 1986.

4. Vitta, op cit.

5. Chambers,R. in Science and Technology Education and Future Human Needs (see note 2.)

6. Rugumayo, E.B. in Science and Technology Education and Future Human Needs (see note 2.)

7. Maslow, A. quoted in Goble, F. The Third Force , Pocket Books, New York, 1971.

8. Lovin, R., op cit.

9. Thompson, T.H., "Are We Obligated to Future Others?", Alternative Futures , Vol. 1, #1, Spring, 1978.

10. Schumacher, op cit.

11. "Catholic Social Teaching and the U.S. Economy", Origins, Vol. 14, no. 22/23, November 15, 1984.

12. Simon, Howe, and Kirschenbaum, Values Clarification, Hart Publishing Co., New York, 1972.

13. Cunningham, G. "Blowing the Whistle on Global Education" circulated by T.G. Tancredo, U.S. Dept.of Education,Denver

14. for a look at this controversy, "Global Education: In Bounds or Out?", Social Education, April / May 1987.

15. Rowe, Edward H., Church League of America.

16. according to People for the American Way, a group formed to counter the religious right.

17. Kozol,J. Illiterate America, New American Library, NY 1986

18. Rifkin, J. and Howard, T. The Emerging Order , G.P. Putnam's Sons, New York, 1979.

19. Thompson, W.I. "The Elimination of Religion", The Sun , May, 1986.

20. Badiner, A. "The Fastest Growing Religion in the West", L.A. Weekly, May 16-22, 1986.

PART C :

IN SEARCH OF TRUTH AND
AN ETHICAL WAY OF LIFE

This growing awareness that we are part of a global system--a global village...--is a tremendously revolutionary concept....Its implications are vast; it provides a basic understanding and a simple set of ethical principles capable of remaking our entire planet.

We...recognize that the world is urgently in need of a simple lifestyle...We are one world and the resources of the earth are limited. What I consume relates directly to what is available for others; if I consume more than my fair share, I am literally taking food from the mouths of others, clothes from their bodies. Therefore if I am...to take Christ's teachings seriously, I must restrain my consumption of the world's resources.

Adam Daniel Finnerty
No More Plastic Jesus

The Supreme Critic...is that great nature in which we rest... that Unity, that Over-Soul, within which every man's particular being is contained and made one with all other; that common heart, of which all sincere conversation is the worship, to which all right action is submission...We live in succession, in division, in parts, in particles. Meantime within man is the soul of the whole; the wise silence; the universal beauty to which every part and particle is equally related; the eternal ONE...Only itself can inspire whom it will and behold! their speech shall be lyrical, and sweet, and universal as the rising of the wind.

Ralph Waldo Emerson
"The Over-Soul"

INSPIRATION

I. NEEDED: A PRACTICAL RELIGION?
October, 1984

I spent the day in The Reality Marketplace. Late in the afternoon I returned to the bench where I had eaten lunch. Under the orange-leafed maple trees, I sat thinking. I was about to depart, when the older man I'd talked with at lunchtime (see GENESIS) returned and sat down. He asked me what I'd learned that afternoon and I gave him a summary. I awaited his comments--but he seemed lost in thought.

So I began again, telling him that he looked like a university professor and asking him the same question he'd asked me at lunchtime. He'd been a professor of theology, he admitted, and he too sought Truth and the right way to live. "What have you been doing the last three hours?" I wondered. He said he'd been across the street making inquiries about opening a "Practical Religions" shop. I expressed surprise and asked, "Don't you think people want a religion with answers to shield them from the frightening unknown of death and hope when they suffer?"

"Perhaps you are right," he said, "but there is a void in religion today." He went on to relate a story about centuries of religion in ancient China.[1]

> ...the Buddhist influence upon the people of China is not as great as the influence of Confucianism. The chief reason why the Chinese people accepted Buddhism was that it explained to them things they wanted to know about death and about heaven. But people do not spend all their time thinking of what happens to their souls after death....If we could put side by side the time the Chinese spend in thinking of God and worrying about what becomes of their souls after death, and the time they spend doing all the other things, it would look very much like a small red cherry placed near a big, big pumpkin.
>
> And if Confucious did not tell his people anything about the cherry, he did tell them much about the pumpkin. Though he told them nothing about God and Heaven, he did tell them what to do in order to make out of the pumpkin very delicious pumpkin pie. Confucious told his people how to live and how to do things that would make them happy and good.

"How do you propose to make everyone happy?", I asked.

"You said 'everyone'," he noted. "The type of education children need considers everyone and everything: it looks at the big picture. Such a global education will help people build worldviews solidly grounded in planetary realities. Too many Americans have narrow worldviews. Our population has always had a religious fanatic and true believer component. But today, when modern technology could make the world a global village, most Americans see only the small picture and worship the Money God. I'm afraid that Grabbers are now dominating human affairs to such an extent that planetary well being is jeopardized.

"People with global vision tolerantly integrate many worldview themes into a broader structure and live--not just in one room--but in the whole house. Consider how such a person relates to economics and money. From a scientific viewpoint, minimizing waste of resources, energy, and their seeming equivalent--money--is important. Traditional religious wisdom calls for an equitable distribution amongst all people of the means to obtain a livelihood. From a oneness with nature orientation, insuring planetary life support systems remain healthy is the chief concern."

We talked for another half-hour about cultivating world-views for planetary well being. I felt something unusual about him: a type of hypnotic magnetism that is hard to explain. As we parted, I promised to visit him in his "Practical Religions" reality shop someday. He was pleased.

II. UNCHARACTERISTIC DREAMING OF A PERSONAL GOD

That night I had a lucid dream. I was listening to a conversation. Initially, I had trouble pinning down the identities of the two participants and their relationship. I believed them to be a father / son or supervisor / trusted employee pair. But then I saw the elder figure resembled the wise old physicist Einstein had trusted and the younger man was my ex-theology professor friend. Finally I understood: I was hearing a conversation between a manifestation of God and some assistant who helps get things done.

God: What is it?

Asst: Earth, those damned Americans again! Now the President is talking about Armageddon prophecies!

God: I thought he got rid of that Interior Secretary?[2]

Asst: Apparently, he's been listening to the religious

right's electronic ministers. He brought up Armageddon
on national television during an election campaign.

God: What!? This is serious! Don't they know about self-
fulfilling prophecies? They still can save themselves
from their nuclear arsenals and toxic pollutants--but if
everyone adopts "end of the game" strategies the species
is doomed. Long ago we outlined the brotherhood, Golden
Rule, sharing solution--why can't they save themselves?

Asst: That's part of the problem! Those who aren't just
using this Armageddon theology as a smokescreen to
plunder what belongs to future generations and take
more than their fair share, are trying to save people.
Unfortunately, many don't care about suffering, poverty, education, environmental quality, long-lived
toxic wastes, or budget deficits, just saving souls .

God: Why do these fanatics have such narrow worldviews?

Asst: I think that holy book we helped the Hebrews with so
long ago may be partly responsible.

God: It's ironic. The Hebrews religion was so practical for
them in those days--same thing with Confucious and the
Chinese. But a lot has happened in the last 2000 years!
Maybe what these affluent humans need is a new practical
religion? Perhaps you can inspire someone to write a
new holy book. I don't especially like this religion
business though.

Asst: You have mentioned that before! Of course I would be
glad to help--what did you have in mind?

God: ... I'm thinking...We haven't exactly been ignoring
the human crisis. We did commission the U.S. Catholic
Archbishops to write those pastoral letters on peace and
the economy--and they're good--but we need something
more specific. We inspired the Pope to allude to a
"simple way of living"--now someone must elaborate with
details, guidelines, and real world scenarios. And that
someone needs to have an integrated mentality--not a
narrow religious perspective.

Asst: This conversation reminds me of one we had long ago.
What were those guys' names?...Emerson and Whitman.
Remember, you gave the go ahead?

God: That's right--we had such high hopes for Americans in
those days. And look at what has happened! I have spent
billions of years designing their biosphere and the
last few million years on their gene pool. Now they are

threatening my work. I am not just talking Armageddon--
they will ruin it if they continue business as usual!
Asst: So what do we do?
God: What we always have. You screen a group of candidates
with the usual qualifications--plus one more. Given the
current situation, we need someone with much insight who
can also be fair and even-handed--perhaps a scientist?
Asst: A scientist? Now that may be impossible! Today's
scientists are analytical specialists--you will not
find one with those other qualifications. I doubt I
could get inside one of their heads even if I tried!
God: Well, give it a try.

* * * * * * * * * * *

This dream disturbed me--not so much its specific content, but what it implied about my mentality. Apparently,
part of my psyche was capable of imagining a personal God who
moralized, judged human actions, and was not above intervening in human affairs when the situation dictated. Given my
background, I would not have suspected this. But the dream
got me thinking--as had the professor. I returned to The
Reality Marketplace often during the weeks that followed.

III. DISILLUSIONED
As I walked through the streets of The Reality Marketplace, I was upset. I'd spent weeks wandering in and out of
its shops, trying to pull it all together--to see "the big
picture". I thought back to where I'd been.
I had been disturbed by growing poverty and environmental destruction throughout the world. If only people in
rich countries cared, something could be done... But most of
those people were captives of consumerism. Their leaders were
busy enriching themselves and steering corporate steamrollers
to wherever there was a profit.
I went looking for those who didn't like being imprisoned or taken for a ride. Were there powerful forces or
enough whistleblowers to halt the Grabber machinery and alter
the dangerous course? Could anyone offer people promises
more appealing than the Pushers'? Who hadn't been co-opted by
the Money God and saw the human predicament as it really was?
What solutions were they offering? I had hoped to find out.
Once, I felt good inside "The Science is Our Salvation
Shop". Then I learned that scientists often disagree, how

emotionally charged technology assessment can become, and
about "attitudinal fixes". I had been comfortable in "Today's Liberalism: Freedom for All"--then made a discovery.
Looking out this shop's rear entrance, I noticed a sign
across the street: "The World of Suffering and Lamentations".
After I uncovered this blunder in the layout and design of
The Reality Marketplace I went back and forth between those
two shops. Life was no longer the same after seeing the
shocking contrast. I forgot all about freedom.

I had warmed up to the priest/salesman inside "The
Catholic Church". Then I stopped to talk with two of the many
demonstrators outside this building. Their picket signs read,
"Women demand, put your own house in order!" and "Practice
what you preach: Divest!". The lady recalled recent church
history in terms of its continuing discrimination toward
women. The man told me that if the Church really wanted to
help the poor it would part with some of its own riches--
including $300 billion of monetary assets, gold deposits and
land holdings exceeding those of many governments.[3] Another
complained about Church sabotage of family planning efforts.

I was discouraged. Hope of finding what I was looking
for in The Reality Marketplace was fading--after all, where
else was there to look? I sat down on a bench, still lost in
thought. I noticed signs with arrows pointing to malls in
opposite directions. Suddenly I recalled eating lunch here
and talking with "the professor". I hadn't seen him again--
but I thought about him often. I glanced across the street--
there still wasn't any "Practical Religions" shop over there.
I wondered if his plans had changed.

IV. FOLLOWED AND CHECKED UP ON

Suddenly a familiar voice said, "Hello, care if I join
you?" It was the ex-theology professor! I told him I had
just been thinking of him and expressed my amazement at his
presence. I started talking about coincidence, synchroncity,
and singularities in the explicate realm. He said little more
than, "It's strange how things sometimes work out." He asked
about my search for Truth and the meaningful, right way to
live. I shared my growing disillusionment. I concluded by
throwing the ball back to him and expressing my sadness there
was no "Practical Religions" shop to browse in.

He apologized and said he was still working on it. We
talked about his religion based on reason, fair play, bro-

therhood, the Golden Rule, minimizing suffering, limiting guilt, and preserving the integrity of the biosphere. I told him it all sounded pretty good but that I needed more details. "When do you anticipate opening your shop in The Reality Marketplace?" I asked.

"Stephen," he said, looking me in the eyes and catching me off guard--I was sure I'd never told him my name. "I've wanted to make it happen, but it seems I can't do it alone. I need help. Since we last talked, I've had trouble selling people my religion. Many tell me I make it seem too theoretical, and damn it, I'm beginning to think they're right! I'm worried that, all these years, I've spent too much time sequestered in ivory towers, in specialized niches, and with my head in books and in the clouds, and not enough time in The School of Hard Knocks.

"Now, I'm losing what every salesman must hold onto or perish: confidence. Oh, I could work some magic and snare a few sales. But I'm not after the 'con' in confidence--there's too much of that going on. I'm after legitimately winning people's trust. But how can I win that when this doubt keeps creeping in: I haven't really practiced what I preach--at least not in the real world of common people. Perhaps I have no business trying to sell it to others. I can tell them Confucious' story about the cherry and the pumpkin--but they want a modern hero to worship. I mention the freedom to choose responsibility and the need to cultivate worldviews for planetary well being--but many want a Messiah to follow."

"Why are you telling me all this?" I gently demanded. He sighed and said, "Ok, I'll be straight with you. Without your knowing it, I've been following you around The Reality Marketplace as part of an assignment I'm on. After you went from "The Implicate Order" to "The Big Bang Shop", I knew I had to talk with you."

"Since our first meeting, I've learned a great deal about you. You're 33 years old and in the affluent West where you live you're an anomaly. In a world built on arrogant, macho pride, your favorite word is 'humble'. But unlike most Americans, you refuse to be a pawn of the corporate masters and their electronic voices. You scorn the Money God everyone else worships, and live far below the U.S. poverty line. Yet you feel your family of four is extraordinarily wealthy, both materially and spiritually. And you're not a specialist like me--you've divided your time wisely between The Reality

Marketplace and The School of Hard Knocks."

V. RECRUITED AS A MESSIAH?

I was utterly amazed by his account, and could only mutter, "So you want me to help you set up and operate a 'Practical Religions' shop?" He nodded and I continued. "Before we carry this further, you need to understand two things. First, I am not satisfied with any of the existing frameworks for making sense out of life that I've seen in The Reality Marketplace. Second, the only framework I'll ever spend my reality cash on, or try to get others to purchase, is one I've either created or pieced together myself. I can't guarantee I'd accept your version of a practical religion. Just as you can't sell a lifestyle you haven't lived, I can't sell something I don't believe in."

"That won't be a problem," he assured me, "I'm authorized and fully prepared to go with whatever you come up with...." I looked at him incredulously and didn't pay much attention to what he said next. I was recalling my strange dream after first meeting him. When I pulled my thoughts together, he was still talking.

"It's important to use precedents that have worked in the past--so our holy book must be structured in a certain way. It'll be a big project, but I'll help you get started. Since I'm still in the dark about your early years and how you ended up in the Ozarks, I'd like to interview you this afternoon. Then you can start on the book, alright?"

"Sure," I chimed in--still not fully appreciating what he was saying. He went on, "Call those early days BEGINNINGS and your later years CHRONICLES. And turn that diary of your shopping in The Reality Marketplace into a consumer's guide for the perplexed. We'll use it for the book's first half."

We ate lunch together and afterwards he listened as I reminisced about growing up and leaving California. It was late afternoon when we finished. As I was leaving to meet my little boy getting off the school bus, the professor said we'd be talking again in a few months. "We'll need to work out some philosophical details and discuss how to end the book." he said. I nodded. After I'd begun walking away from him, he appeared to have some second thoughts. "Wait a minute!", he yelled, hustling toward me. "You're up to it, aren't you, putting your whole being into writing this book?"

"I hope so!" I told him, "but I'm still not sure how I

fit into your practical religion?"

He looked a little surprised, but answered slowly and carefully. "It could be that the only real hope humanity has for avoiding colossal suffering and finding happiness depends on the lessons we can teach and the faith we can inspire. And when the time comes and the flock is on its way to greener pastures, perhaps you'll be recognized as a Messiah."

Questions & Projects

1. Report on former Interior Secretary James Watt's religious beliefs and why his worldview wasn't appropriate for someone in his position.
2. Armageddon theology or the Christian belief in millennialism has shaped the worldviews of adherents in ways that encourage "passivity" says University of Wisconsin professor Paul Boyer. Discuss. Relate to 1. above.
3. Whitman's poems "Song of Myself" and "Prayer of Columbus", and Emerson's essay "The Over-Soul" reveal the intensity of their peak experiences and moments of "cosmic consciousness". Read these works and discuss.
4. Ted Turner thinks the Ten Commandments need updating. He notes, "When Moses went up on the mountain, there were no nuclear weapons. There was no problem with the ozone layer..." Ted Koppel responds, "Truth is not a polite tap on the shoulder; it is a howling reproach. What Moses brought down from Mount Sinai were not the Ten Suggestions ...they are Commandments. ARE, not were." Do differences in worldview here preclude reconciliation? Discuss.
5. Many people don't believe in a personal God, but do believe in God. Discuss.
6. Philosopher Richard Smullyan argues[4],"That (God) should have been conceived in the role of a moralist is one of the great tragedies of the human race." Discuss.

Notes

1. Gaer, J. How the Great Religions Began , New American Library, New York, 1935.
2. refers to James Watt. He once told a Congressional committee, "I do not know how many future generations we can count on before the Lord returns."
3. Martin, M. Rich Church, Poor Church , Putnam's, NY 1984
4. Smullyan, R. "Is God a Taoist?", in The Tao is Silent , Harper & Row, New York, 1977.

BEGINNINGS

I. NEW STAR

> When a child is born, the entire Universe has to shift
> and make room. Another entity capable of free will, and
> therefore capable of becoming God, has been born. In
> that way, every child's birth is exactly like the birth
> of Jesus. The Christ child is born every time a child is
> born, and every child is a living Buddha. Some of them
> only get to be a living Buddha for a moment, because
> nobody believes it.
>
> Stephen Gaskin[1]
The Farm

I left the warm waters of my mother's womb one afternoon
in the spring of 1951. It took her uterine muscles five
seconds to push my eight pound body into the world. Elsewhere
during those seconds, nine other new human beings similarly
joined the existing 2.6 billion others. Of these ten additions, I was the only one born in the U.S.A. I grew up, the
second in a family of three children and the only boy, in a
suburban Burbank, California neighborhood. My childhood was a
happy one filled with love, toys, and playmates.

Yet my early days were not all carefree: I grew up fearing nuclear bombs. Fall, 1962 brought anxiety. During the
Cuban missile crisis, friends and I half expected to die in a
nuclear war. At its height, we interrupted our usual lunch
recess basketball game to pray for peace. Even "hard guys"--
who normally would have mocked such activity--joined in.

During my first 12 years, I learned to get along well
with others and feel that I belonged to something bigger than
myself. My parents were especially proud of my 5th and 6th
grade teachers' comments on my report card. One had written,
"Stephen's ability to be friends with everyone and at the
same time maintain high standards for himself is an attribute
to be admired." The next year the other noted, "All of the
boys and girls respect his fairness on the playground." However, while this considerate, fair play treatment of others
would characterize me throughout my life, the feeling of
belonging would not. Increasingly over the next 12 years I
would feel like an outsider.

As I got older, I began to think more about my future.
My parents urged me to pursue whatever I was best at and felt

happiest doing. I had talent in math and science. I enjoyed being outside at night looking at the stars with my telescope. Indeed, the night sky with its familiar coterie of stars was there for me when the more worldly "circle of affection" was lacking. As this association developed, I began to read more about astronomy and astronomers. Soon my career choice became obvious.

During my high school years, two significant events related to my amateur astronomy pursuits occurred. The first almost made me famous. In early July, 1967--while conducting my regular program of recording the brightness of numerous variable stars--I nearly discovered a nova or new star. The object, Nova Delphini, became one of the brightest and best-studied novae of the previous 25 years. I glimpsed it and suspected its real nature two days before its official discovery--but failed to follow up my hunch.

The passing years have helped me realize that it didn't matter that the world wasn't properly notified about the real discovery of Nova Delphini. To me it would always be "my" star. It celestially presided over a time when I was born as an adult human being with potentially unlimited power.

The power could be used selfishly, in "me first" fashion, or responsibly in other-oriented activities. The power could be used for pain, misery, destruction, and death, or for happiness, fulfillment, creation, and life. About the time Nova Delphini began its climb to brilliance, I crossed that coming of age threshold that millions of American teenagers dream about: I got my auto driver's license. My life of assuming full responsibility for my actions had begun.

18 months later, a second event effectively ended stargazing from the observatory I'd built in the backyard of my parents' house: the city of Burbank lined the street with mercury vapor lamps. Night no longer came to my observatory. I could do nothing about it. Years later, I would trace my alienation with "the system" to this traumatic experience.

II. UNDERGRADUATE

I left home and went off to college in the fall of 1969. While my formal undergraduate education in astronomy at UCLA was largely one of studying increasingly specialized topics whose description required ever growing mathematical complexities, otherwise my worldview broadened considerably. Politically, my attitudes changed from a May, 1970 analysis of the U.S. invasion of Cambodia, "I think Nixon's doing the right thing", to a June, 1972 chanting of "Ho, Ho, Ho Chi Minh, the NLF's gonna win!" during a protest march down Westwood Blvd. to the Federal building.

To some extent I had undergone a "conversion". To Yale professor Charles Reich these were an "increasingly common" and striking aspect of contemporary life in the late 1960s / early 1970s. As Reich described it,[2]

> The clean-cut, hard-working, model young man who
> despises radicals and hippies can become one himself
> with breathtaking suddenness...

There was at least one difference between Reich's idealized conversion and my actual one. Reich's "consciousness III" type youth were rejecting linear and analytical thought; my left brain was studying to be an astrophysicist, although right hemisphere non-linear tendencies in me otherwise benefitted.

My "conversion" had been prompted by a mid-1971 breakup of a long-time romance with a high school sweetheart. The resulting emotional turmoil led me to re-examine my attitudes and values. I began a search for meaning in life. I started doing things I'd never done--reading Eastern philosophy, writing poetry, and spending hours alone in naturally beautiful areas. While my right brain began to assert itself, my left brain was able to turn its attention away from astrophysics long enough to begin investigating the U.S. corporate state.

After reading The Limits to Growth , I began to see uncontrolled growth as dangerous. Whereas on the first Earth Day in April, 1970, I had little interest in the day's activities, two years later I considered myself an environmentalist. By then I'd identified what destroyed my backyard stargazing as the corporate steamroller which seemed to be squashing the finer things in life wherever it ventured.

My four undergraduate years were busy. Time not in school or studying was often spent working to cover expenses my four-year scholarship didn't provide for. My summer job as a corporate mailroom worker largely engaged my left brain, while my weekend and evening job at the Griffith Park Planetarium gave my right brain some exercise. What memories of these jobs linger? At the former, I punched a time clock four times a day. The latter job triggers images of the red glow fading in the planetarium sky and the soft sunset music playing while the stars came out.

In the spring of 1973, during the same week that a UCLA astronomer's "Light Pollution" article appeared in <u>Science</u>, a phone call informed me that I would be leaving Los Angeles. The caller was offering a position with research assistant- ship in the Department of Astronomy and Astrophysics graduate school at the University of California, Santa Cruz.

III. INNER TURMOIL AT GRADUATE SCHOOL

My right brain loved the UC Santa Cruz campus with its redwood forest setting, its parties and liberated counter- cultural lifestyle. But while my right brain was enjoying walks on the nearby beach, sunsets over the Pacific, and hikes in the mountains behind the campus, my left brain was having trouble. The academic competition was stiff; the sub- ject matter challenging. I would later tell people that my stellar atmospheres text <u>Radiative</u> <u>Transfer</u> was so complex that I was sure not more than a couple hundred people in the whole world really understood all of it.

But neither the competition nor the complexity was the problem. The problem was this: faced with the obvious need for rigorous self-discipline in pursuing these highly-spe- cialized studies, my right brain wouldn't let my left brain do all the linear thinking the situation called for. I wasn't aware of the left brain / right brain battle raging inside my head, but as summer turned to fall I got steadily more depressed, "bummed out", and full of internal conflict.

It was as if one voice inside my head was saying, "You're too much of a thinker, you need to be more of a doer and sometimes you need to just "be". This Ph.d in astro- physics trip is gonna take five, six, seven years of grind- ing it out, keeping in line, and then what? More of the same. How much open-air looking for those star patterns, and studying star maps--what you really love--are you gonna get to do? It's more likely that some photomultiplier or spec- trograph will interact with the starlight, not you. You'll spend your time hassling getting equipment to work, with some random computer or plate-measuring machine, or with your nose in some scientific paper of nothing but equations. I mean, look at how it's been these last four years? Now you've done a little moving in the right direction--remember reading <u>The</u> <u>Electric</u> <u>Kool-Aid</u> <u>Acid</u> <u>Test</u>[3]? Someone, maybe Kesey, said 'Life is a circle and so it's the going, not the getting

there, that counts. Live in the moment...Go with the flow!"
That's where you need to be headed, back to the natural flow,
not on some arrogant, status trip!"

And then, elsewhere in my head, a retort was building
..."Well, look who's talking, the fool on the hill, old
muddled head. I can eat those equations alive if you'll let
me get down to business, get organized, and be efficient.
I'm not scared of the astronomical instrumentation and you
know I love playing with computers and reducing data. And
what do you suggest we do? Go live in the woods with some
Lucy-in-the-Sky-with-Diamonds type, screw around a lot, eat
berries and freeze? We gotta make a living, don't we?"

The other voice would answer, "Hey, that doesn't sound
so bad, but we wouldn't freeze--you're 'the fool who plays it
cool by making his world a little colder'! How much real
warmth do you feel from these narrow, specialist types, not
much right? Hey man, the world's teetering on the brink and
you want to use your talents for something that will never
really help people put it right again. We need to see the
troubled big picture clearly, you can analyze it, and do your
part to help. It's not fair otherwise, it's amoral. You want
to become what McLuhan or somebody warned against, "the
specialist who...avoids making small mistakes while moving
toward the grand folly"? And what's the rush about making a
living? What did Buckminster Fuller say, "the true business
of people should be to...think about whatever it was they
were thinking before somebody came along and told them they
had to earn a living."

Then in reply I would think, "So you want to be a medi-
ocre Jack of all Trades and not pursue real excellence in
one, huh? And how far are you gonna take this simple life
thing, anyway? You can't live very well on a shoestring. Remember that night we went down the hill from the Planetarium
into Hollywood for dinner with Howard? Remember he warned
that "not going after the money" would lead to a disaster. He
was always so silly with his joking, but he got dead serious
then, remember?"

The dialogue continued with one mentality saying,
"Money? You're hardly gonna get rich being an astronomer! I
mean look at the job market, you might end up doing something
else, not astrophysics, right? And the other replied, "I
suppose you've got a point. But you don't have much faith in
my mathematical abilities, do you?"

Exchanges like this began once I entertained dropping out of grad school. They slowly grew in number and intensity and after many days came to dominate my being. A decision was needed, I couldn't bear the stress much longer. Finally, after some meditation in a nearby state park's redwoods, my left brain seemingly surrendered to my right. I would withdraw. The next day, October 5, 1973, just three weeks after beginning coursework, I would tell others.

After a troubled sleep back in my Santa Cruz apartment, I awoke to pouring rain. I drove to the campus feeling fairly confident, but in walking from the parking lot to my destination--Natural Sciences Building II--I began to sense the monumental nature of the step I was about to take. The whole rest of my life would hinge on this decision, I knew it. The doubts crept in as the internal dialogue heated up again.

I couldn't deal with it. As I climbed into the momentary security of an empty elevator, pushed the button for the fourth floor and the door closed, I burst into tears. I was losing the courage to go see Dr. Brock and tell him--but the elevator was carrying me to my fate. I stopped it on the third floor, got out and went back down the stairs drying my eyes. Then somewhere in my head I thought, "You haven't cried like this in public for years...you're not a small boy. Get it together. You're on your own now. It's your life to make or break. You can't hold someone's hand any longer!"

I did get it together. Dr. Brock was very understanding. I later realized that my frontal brain had made the decision. The next few months would be a difficult, but full of inner growth, transition period. The decision I had made was always with me. I would relive that elevator trip again and again.

IV. CHANGING DIRECTION

The longer one pursues an increasingly narrow specialized course, the harder it is to begin again in a new direction. If one can gradually redefine goals in terms of both the old and new, and slowly, where appropriate, phase out the old in favor of the new, the transition will be easier.

In Santa Cruz, that rainy fall of 1973, I realized this. I set out to pick up the pieces of my break with the past and assemble something new.

Immediately leaving was out of the question. It would financially hurt my room-mate, and besides, I didn't know what to do. I needed time to think and perhaps make some

money. I accepted a half-time temporary position as a research assistant for Dr. Herman Bigelow, a world famous
astronomer and past president of the International Astronomical Union. With more time to think, a plan for the
future gradually emerged. I would return to UCLA and tie
together my academic loose ends in a way that would make me
more employable.

So late in the afternoon, the day before Thanksgiving,
1973, I said goodbye to the redwood-forested mountains, ocean
vistas, and community of good people. I headed south for the
smog, lights, concrete, and anonymity of Los Angeles.

Within three weeks of my badly over-loaded VW's arrival
in Los Angeles, I found a $100/month North Hollywood apart-
ment and employment. First, I worked as a door to door can-
vasser for the Environmental Alert Group. I lasted three
weeks--my psyche was ill-suited for such fund-raising. After
a month's unemployment during which my savings evaporated, I
got a job as an electronic parts salesman.

Two months later, I left this for the Physics Dept. at
UCLA , where I resumed being a grad student and found employment as a teaching assistant. As for future plans, I had
tentatively settled on getting an M.S. degree in physics, a
secondary teaching credential, and a rural life somewhere
teaching school. I had to get out of Los Angeles.

That someone living alone in a cramped apartment with
anonymous, noisy neighbors a thin wall away, in a metropolis
of millions of people--who to survive must deaden and desens-
itize themselves to all of the sensory inputs which threaten
to overload their circuitry--would not be joyously happy
should not be startling.

I managed to spend most of that summer out of the city.
First, I worked at Thacher School in Ojai, California as a
teaching assistant at a summer science program for gifted
high school students. Later, I toured western U.S. national
parks with a friend. At Thacher I met Annie, a brilliant,
honey-haired 16 year old from wealthy San Marino, California.
She shared my disdain for the Southern California rat race
and its materialism.

With the start of the 1974-75 academic year at UCLA, I
began bicycling to classes from a $165/month apartment in
nearby Belair. I preferred this to battling rush hour and
crowded freeways in commuting to school from the San Fernando
valley. Having received a prestigious Chancellor's Intern

fellowship, I didn't have to work to support myself. This
made the year somewhat more leisurely. I frequently made
trips over to San Marino to see Annie, who was finishing her
senior year of high school. As the year progressed, my future
plans gradually became intertwined with hers. By June, 1975,
I had worked out a scheme to partly escape Los Angeles a bit
ahead of schedule.

V. MY WORLDVIEW; PLANNING RESEARCH

My story now comes to a turning point so I pause and
examine my worldview as of mid-1975. Had someone thrust Fig.
#1 (see LETTERS) in my face, and asked me to describe myself
using its worldview themes, I'd have responded like this.

"My worldview is science-based (themes #5 and #6),
moderated by a 'small is beautiful' mentality (embodied by
themes #16, #21, and #23). I share many humanist ideals
(theme #10), but have trouble loving the imperfections I see
in myself and others. I believe I control my own fate (theme
#12). (Perhaps my feelings about free will grew out of
childhood frustration with my mother's passive 'I guess God
must have meant it to be' stance.) I am mildly receptive to
Eastern ideas (theme #7). I am unable to accept the Christian requirement that an individual must unconditionally
accept Jesus as savior to escape hellfire. (What of those
who've never heard of Jesus? What of children brought up in
the Jewish faith?) I do not conceive of God in personal,
moralistic terms (anti-theme #14), so I have no use for the
concepts of sin or salvation. Given my exposure to the cosmic perspective astronomy provides, my worldview is spatially
and temporally broader than most (theme #4). Finally, I
confess that my behavior is often driven by anti-Grabber,
anti-elitist, anti-expansionist, anti-consumerist tendencies
(anti-themes #19, #20, #22, and #26)."

Abandoning Ph.d program and research astrophysicist
career plans left a vacuum in my life. My sense of adventure, of being part of a quest for new knowledge, was admittedly shaken. Gradually however, another educational opportunity and research possibility--in a much different setting
--emerged to fill this need. Let me explain.

Teacher education courses at UCLA exposed me to the educational philosophy of Carl Rogers. Rogers advocated experiential learning: self-initiated, self-evaluated learning
that involves the whole person in a discovery process, a

reaching out to illuminate "the dark area of ignorance". Increasingly, I perceived an area which might be termed "responsible lifestyles for world citizens" as one amenable to worthwhile experiential learning.

In thinking about possible directions such learning might take, from my fuzzy notion of "a simple life in the country", a clearer vision emerged. During some idealist introspection--perhaps triggered by African starvation scenes--I imagined a world built on sharing. Suppose the world's resources and wealth could be divided equally amongst all people. What would it be like living with an equal share?

Had I been a university researcher, I might have written a grant proposal to fund such an investigation. I would have devised a way to quantify "equal share", outlined procedures to be followed (literature searches, field interviews, data gathering), set a time frame for the study, and drawn up a budget. I'd have written some objectives and promised that upon completion, findings would be disseminated by submitting papers to appropriate journals.

I had no desire to conduct the study in this fashion. Since I was looking for an ethical lifestyle--and this shar- ing orientation seemed an obvious starting point--I needed to know how practical it was. To answer that, no ivory tower effort would suffice. I had to <u>know</u> what equal share living would be like--know on a thinking, feeling and doing level that demanded my complete participation.

So it was decided: I would do experimental research as part of an experiential learning study conducted at "The School of Hard Knocks". Although I did not know it then, the study would run ten years , I would eventually quantify "an equal share" and document my experience. It began July 1, 1975, 100 miles north of Los Angeles.

VI. THE EXPERIMENT BEGINS--THE FIRST YEAR

Isla Vista--or IV as residents call it--is a student village of perhaps 15,000 people bordered by the University of California at Santa Barbara (UCSB) campus and the Pacific Ocean. As the 1960s became the 1970s, IV gave the country two powerful images. First, a picture of concerned young people patiently cleaning oil from the feathers of birds unfortunately caught in the great oil slick created by the blowout of a Union Oil Co. well offshore at nearby Coal Point. Second, apparently outraged madmen burning down the

Isla Vista branch of the Bank of America.

When Annie and I moved into a $65/month garage on Sueno Road in IV in late June, 1975, we associated the community with both images in a positive way. Eventually these images were joined in our minds by a third. It was something one encountered when entering IV--a hand-painted sign that somehow made you think of solidarity. It said simply, "Isla Vista--The People--Yes".

When we first inspected the garage living quarters, they seemed a filthy, depressing mess, with only the low rent as a plus. Anticipating having more time than money that summer, we took them anyway. Before moving in, we hauled the junk left by former tenants to the community free box, hosed off the concrete floor, scrubbed and vacuumed.

We spent the summer together growing a vegetable garden, acquiring natural food cooking skills, lounging on the beach, hiking in the mountains, attending IV parties, and reading. For money, we sold unwanted belongings at local swap meets. As summer ended, we took a trip to Northern California.

The trip was inspired by a wild idea that had laid dormant in my head for many years. Now, nourished by visits to the back-to-the-land oriented New World Resources and Supply Co. in IV, and Helen and Scott Nearing's book, Living the Good Life, it firmly took root. The idea was this: why not buy a small piece of land in a naturally beautiful area, set up a self-sufficient homestead, ignore Corporate America, and live happily ever after?

We left IV on a Tuesday in early September and headed first to Yosemite National Park. After some sightseeing there and to the northeast in the Lake Tahoe/Reno area, we swung northwest and began "serious land-hunting". If those realtors had known we had less than $100, they'd not talk to us! Their stories of snow in June and short growing seasons hastened our departure to the southwest.

In the Trinity Mountains, at a gas station in the little town of Hayfork, an incident occurred that marked the trip's highpoint. After filling the VW with regular, I retreated to the bathroom, telling Annie I was "liable to be awhile". I planned to both use the toilet and change my clothes. Having accomplished the latter, I now sat on the former, my dirty pants and wallet resting on the sink, beside and above the toilet. The wallet contained driver's license, various ID cards, a dwindling supply of dollars, and--should some auto

repair mishap threaten to consume this resource--the pre-
caution of a Standard Oil credit card. I did not like using
this. After a few months fling with putting a mostly unde-
cipherable obscenity directed at the large corporation in
place of my signature, I'd stopped using it altogether.

Back in the restroom, I simultaneously flushed the toilet and reached for the pants I'd left laying there. As I
turned them over, my wallet suddenly fell out of the pocket.
In mid-air it did a 180 degree maneuver, one card fell out,
and the otherwise intact wallet landed harmlessly on the
floor. The chosen card, with magnificent timing, was deposited into the flushing toilet and consumed by the sewer
drain before my panic-stricken hand could grab it! When I
emerged from the restroom and encountered Annie, a big grin
covered my face. Inspection of the wallet revealed that the
Standard Oil credit card had been flushed down the toilet!

We breakfasted in Hayfork, then inquired about land.
Acre lots, it seemed, started at around $2000. We left Hay-
fork about ten-thirty. After crossing a few forks of the
Trinity River, following the Mad River, passing through towns
like Mina--population 5, an Indian reservation, and driving
south on gravel for 100 miles through oak-covered mountains,
we emerged in Covelo at 5 p.m. There we talked with our
trip's last realtor.

By Saturday night, we were back in our IV garage. As for
land-hunting conclusions, it seemed summers were too dry in
the Trinity Mountains--water availability and brush fires
were concerns. Farther south, it seemed too expensive.

Back in Isla Vista, money nearly exhausted, our leisurely summertime lifestyle soon changed. School was starting for
us both--Annie's freshmen year at UCSB, my last at UCLA.
Money would be easier to come by. I was slated to be a UCLA
Physics Dept. teaching assistant. I would earn $5200 for the
20 hour/week, nine month long assignment. But there was an
unresolved question: "How could I live 100 miles away from
where I would work and attend grad school?"

That fall quarter, I found the answer: with planning
and willingness to endure a few hassles. I succeeded in
arranging my teaching duties and classes for Tuesdays, Wed-
nesdays, and Thursdays. I made one trip a week to UCLA in my
VW. I spent Tuesday and Wednesday nights parked a few blocks
away on Veteran Avenue asleep in the car's back seat.

This worked for awhile. But as 1975 became 1976--and the

vehicle developed fuel injection problems--the strategy changed. I took buses. Typically, I'd drive to Santa Barbara and catch a greyhound bus at 5 a.m. Tuesday morning. I'd ride it for two and one-half hours, then transfer to a Santa Monica city bus. I'd get to UCLA--Kelty backpack full of clothes and books--around 9 a.m. I'd sleep in my office, or if that proved inconvenient, sometimes in the very lab where I'd teach a class the next morning! Once, I awoke on a lab bench, terrified that I'd overslept and that students were about to discover me!

When not sleeping, teaching, or attending classes, I studied in campus libraries. Sometimes I would put aside physics books and fantasize about escaping the urban rat race. I spent hours tracking down relevant meteorological statistics and other information about "back-to-the-land" areas of interest. Then I'd return to physics. Completing the Los Angeles-based part of the week Thursday afternoon, I'd make transportation connections in reverse fashion and return to Annie and IV by 6 p.m.

Financially, it all worked out rather nicely. Typically, Annie and I lived on $250/month -- including $70 for food, $43 for transportation, $25 for entertainment, and the rest for rent and miscellaneous expenses. Annie's university expenses were covered by scholarship and a Psychology Dept. job as a professor's subject in a hypnosis experiment. Despite fears that my weird schedule would preclude doing a good job as a teaching assistant, when the school year ended in June, students' evaluations earned me a $100 Distinquished Teaching Performance Award from the UCLA Physics Dept!

On the procuring pieces of paper front, Annie had taken half again as many classes as most students would during a freshmen year. When these credits were added to her high school advanced placement credits, she was making rapid progress toward a bachelor's degree in psychology. I now had the master's degree and teaching credential I'd decided was needed before I could opt for a simpler life.

As the summer of 1976 began, we were about to embark on a second land-hunting excursion--this one to the Ozark mountains of Missouri and Arkansas. Given the past year's frugal lifestyle, we had $3,000 for a land purchase.

VII. BUYING LAND IN THE OZARKS

We left Southern California in the late afternoon of

Sunday July 4, 1976--after hanging around to attend Annie's parents' bicentennial party. With its fuel injection problems fixed, the VW required but 45.7 gallons of gasoline and two and one-half days to make the 1694 mile trip to Springfield, Missouri--averaging an impressive 37 miles/gal. Once in this strange city of 150,000 people, we found a motel room and rather nervously made a phone call.

The call was to some people whose names were written on a scrap of paper given us by friends before we left IV. Along with the scrap came a story: Ken and Susie Cotterman once lived in IV. They own 40 acres somewhere in the southern Missouri Ozarks and live in Springfield. Maybe they can help you....Now, feeling a little unsure of ourselves so far away from home in the southwest corner of Missouri, we hoped so.

Ken and Susie were feeling homesick and welcomed visitors--even strangers--from their old California stomping ground. It turned out--rather amazingly--that Ken and I had gone to the same rather large high school (one year apart)! After establishing this bond, and with subsequent interaction revealing similar values and approaches to living, it seemed assured that Ken and Susie would help.

During the next six weeks, Annie and I used the Cotterman house as an operations base in searching the Ozarks for suitable land. First, we traveled east to Willow Springs and spent hours with a realtor we'd corresponded with. Next, south and east took us to Ava--where Ken and Susie's land was. Our third excursion was a longer trip to north-central Arkansas, where we looked at land near Fox and Leslie. Land prices sure beat those in northern California: here $2000 might buy not one but ten acres!

But we found nothing outstanding and headed west to Neverson--where we spent the night at a KOA campground. The next morning we noted the existence of Central Ozarks College as we skirted around the town, and then turned toward the Mulberry National River and the small town of Braselville, population 400. In Braselville, we were surprised to see a natural food store on the town square. Conversation with its owner revealed the existence of "countercultural back-to-the-land" types in the area and the location of a prime swimming hole. There, Annie and I relaxed after meeting with realtors. Heading back to Springfield in the morning, we talked of the natural beauty of the Mulberry River country and vowed to return.

By late July, I decided, 1) I liked the Ozarks and wanted to buy land and build a house there somewhere, and 2) more money was needed to put these plans on a secure financial footing. A brief search landed me a teaching job--at a small rural high school in Exeter, Missouri--an hour's drive southwest of Springfield. With that, Annie decided to return to Isla Vista to finish her bachelor's degree. So by mid-August, we found me a nice $75/month apartment on a 10 acre Cassville, Missouri farm, put Annie on a Greyhound bus back to Los Angeles, and decided to put our relationship and "back-to-the-land" plans on hold for awhile.

My next trip to the Mulberry River country was on a Saturday in early October. After a two and one-half hour drive, I parked on the Braselville town square around 10 a.m. There, I encountered a crowd of 50 to 75 countercultural types--"hippies" some would have called them--milling around near the courthouse and across the street at the movie theater. I hadn't seen such a sight since leaving Isla Vista. I did a little circulating in this unexpected crowd. The gathering was a musical benefit for the Thomas County Conservation Board (TCB)--a group fighting the U.S. Forest Service spraying of herbicides in the nearby National Forest.

Resuming the land quest, I found nothing promising that day. However, 10 days later, an ad in a Strout Realty brochure from the Braselville office caught my eye.

No. 3224   22 acres -- $3300 ... On improved road, close
to town. Springs reported; electricity available.

Shortly thereafter, I explored, fell in love with, and formally offered $3000 in cash for this land. The next day I learned I was to have stewardship over a piece of the Earth.

In the final analysis of Sunday morning, October 17, 1976, I couldn't say no to the vision of the house I'd build beneath the pink maple leaf/patches of blue sky canopy that I saw as I walked through the hardwood-forested upper bench, or to the scenic bluffline that lay up the hill. A couple of days later, after hearing my glowing description of the 22 acres over the phone, Annie likewise couldn't say no to my proposal of marriage.

VIII. MARRIAGE; BUILDING A CABIN; A RETURN WEST

Two and one-half months later, in a church in San Marino, California, after the minister was done saying things like, "Out of the wild exuberance of creation throughout

millions of years, you two have appeared....", Annie and I
began exchanging vows. Our words included "between us a consciousness of humility" and "...the hope that together we
will be able to live as conscientious members in the community of all living creatures on this fragile planet Earth."
After a brief honeymoon in Ojai, where we met, we returned to
our southwest Missouri farm apartment and some record cold
January, 1977 weather. Heavy snows cancelled school for three
weeks and I got an extended vacation.

By February, the severe weather was gone. Annie and I
began weekend camping trips to our Thomas County land. After
giving it a more thorough survey, the axe we got as a wedding
present was used to clear a short access road on the land's
lower bench. There, we selected a location for the small cabin we'd live in while building a big house on the upper
bench. Work on the cabin's foundation had just begun when it
was time for Annie to again board a bus for Santa Barbara and
her last quarter at the university.

During the next two months, I used ancient oak 2 x 4 s
salvaged from an Exeter school building, stones for a floor,
sawmill slabs for siding, and new corrugated steel roofing in
constructing the 10 x 12 foot cabin for but $140. By the end
of May, with teaching duties completed and the cabin about
so, I drove a tired and ailing VW to an IV reunion with
Annie. We remained there until Annie finished school in mid-
June--graduating summa cum laude at age 19!

The following three weeks were spent selling the VW,
buying an old GMC van, and readying for a trip in which we'd
move the bulk of our possessions 1700 miles eastward to
Northwest Arkansas. This would be the final hurdle in what
had so far been an orderly transition to a simpler life. Our
escape from becoming cogs in the corporate state machine
seemed imminent.

IX. MOVING: ON THE ROAD

It took us 11 hot, car-trouble-plagued days to make the
trip east. These were days filled with steaming radiator concerns, a worn distributor, burned out points, a valve job in
Clinton, Oklahoma, the growing realization that our van was
carried twice its rated load, and a succession of cheap mo-
tels. We spent the last night of the trip in a church parking
lot in Clarksville, Arkansas--but a 90 minute drive from our
destination. Earlier we'd attempted the climb into the Ozark

mountains north of town. The van lacked power to take the
first hill. In turning around, the oil pressure light glowed
briefly and I feared the engine was blown.

Sweltering that night inside the van, I began to see our
trip in allegorical terms. Last year, on the country's 200th
birthday, I declared my independence and headed east for the
unknown, the new frontier. The path seemed to have a heart
and I started building a home in the wilderness. But this
year, it was as if something had been alerted to my bid for
freedom. Suddenly forces had been mustered to put down my
rebellion. Instead of a path with heart, there was 1700 miles
of pavement and it was a battleground where my every mile
was contested. The enemy I'd become so obsessed with was this
old General Motors Corporation machine--which I now imagined
to be a manifestation of the corporate state machine itself.

I'd begun the journey home thinking I was the master of
my own fate--now I wasn't sure. At times it seemed like I was
being taken for a ride; wherever it led, I had no choice but
to follow. That machine was the source of our problems and
perhaps abandoning it was the only way home. That was an
option--not a very practical one given all that was riding
with the vehicle. I thought of the abandoned Jalopies that
had once littered the road we'd been traveling, of the broken
hearts, shattered dreams, lost dignity of those depression-
era Arkies and Okies. Although they had been heading west,
and Annie and I east, I knew we shared a common struggle.

While we desperately wanted to be rid of that vehicle
right there in Clarksville, I ended up fixing it. The next
morning I walked to an auto parts store and bought an engine
compression tester for $4. The compression seemed fine. In-
specting the engine, I noticed the points were closed.

Opening the points helped. The van managed to climb the
steep Highway 63 stretch from Clarksville to the Boston
Mountains ridgetop road, Highway 48. This road was fairly
flat all the way to the Highway 21 junction and it gave us no
trouble. The van started missing on the more up and down
Highway 21 stretch--but still it kept on. Finally, we turned
off pavement and--but three and a half miles from home--onto
the gravel road.

Here we encountered more trouble: the van couldn't get
up a short hill. Backing down, we tried again...and again.
Finally, we backed to the top of the previous hill and,
gathering a full head of steam, just pulled ourselves up and

over this troublesome hill. Ten minutes later, the van pulled into our short driveway. A new life and the promised land was in front of us.

Questions & Projects

1. Relate the "new star" of this "bible" to the star in the New Testament. Contrast differences in meaning using fatalism/free will and astrology/astronomy distinctions.
2. Light pollution is quite an issue around major U.S. observatories in the southwest. Characterize it as another "tragedy of the commons" (see LIBERALS). Report on social restraint laws enacted to combat it.
3. "Live in the moment...Go with the flow" is advice followed by someone dominated by which worldview theme(s)?
4. Discuss Fuller's quote and McLuhan's quote as they relate to your own future / career goals.
5. The Voice Dialogue Method⁴is a personal growth tool that allows understanding and accessing numerous sub-personalities that comprise one's psychological being. Contrast dialogues it fosters with this chapter's inner voice dialogue. Relate "sub personalities" to worldview themes.
6. In a fashion similar to the example in the middle of this chapter, describe yourself in terms of worldview themes from Fig. #1 (LETTERS) If those provided are inadequate, supplement them with ones of your own design.
7. Scott Nearing--who died at age 100--had a remarkable life. Report on him and his ideas.
8. The trouble-plagued GM van of the author's journey east is symbolically significant. Discuss.
9. "If they're strong, determined, and lucky, it's possible for poor Americans to exercise freedom--but so many end up as caged birds." Discuss.
10. After reading John Steinbeck's The Grapes of Wrath , use it to characterize the "common struggle" referred to in this chapter.

Notes

1. Gaskin, Ina May, Spiritual Mid-Wifery, The Book Publishing Co., Summertown, TN 1978.
2. Reich, C. The Greening of America, Random House, NY 1970.
3. Wolfe, T. The Electric Kool Aid Acid Test, Bantam, NY 1969
4. Stone, H. & Winkelman, S. Embracing OurSelves --The Voice Dialogue Manual, New World Library, San Rafael, CA 1989.

CHRONICLES

I. OUR LAND--A DESCRIPTION

We own 22 acres of hardwood-forested land. Our house sits on a 100 to 200 foot wide, mostly level bench which lies 2/3 of the way up the southwest side of Lost Mountain. From that fall, 1976 day when I first walked there, I've called it "the upper bench". We own 1200 feet along this upper bench-- the house lies toward its southeast edge.

At an elevation 100 ft. below, the lower bench is not as wide nor as secluded as the upper one, since it's bounded by the county road below. The two benches are linked by a steep, 30 degree slope hillside, where underlying limestone rock occasionally shows itself.

This rock also outcrops in a scenic bluff line, up the hill from the upper bench. Here are sheer cliffs, some with vertical relief approaching 40 feet, impressive rock over- hangs which form sheltered areas, pine and cedar trees trying to compete with dominant hardwoods, wet weather springs, and grayish-white rocks colored in places with browns, oranges, and reds. Over recent geological time, sections of the bluff line have succumbed to weathering and gravity. Thus, along both benches, one sometimes encounters huge, lichen-covered rocks--some as big as pickup trucks.

Numerous breaks in the bluff line provide access to the land above, which climbs steadily at a 20 degree slope and finally levels out near the top of the mountain. This hill- side land lacks the rich soil of the benches. Thus, while black walnut trees are found with the maples, oaks, and hickories on the bench land, above this species is lacking.

In the summer of 1977, travel between the upper and lower benches was by foot, along a steep, 300 feet long hillside trail. This started its climb near the 10 ft. x 12 ft. lower bench cabin--which we moved into on July 16th.

II. SETTLING IN

During our first two weeks we finished the cabin's stone floor, bought kerosene lamps, containers for hauling water, and more Coleman stove fuel to cook on. We cleared small trees and bushes from the area to the cabin's immediate north. We set out a mailbox and got to know our neighbors. On our first trip to nearby Braselville, a "hillbilly" mechanic quickly pinpointed a worn distributor as the van's problem.

He sold us a used distributor and installed it for but $6.

As July ended, we contemplated our financial situation: we had savings of $3400, a house to build, living expenses to meet, and no income. The last difficulty was unexpectedly resolved a few days later. Given the hot, sticky Ozark summer and cleanliness habits based on abundant hot and cold running water, we missed baths and showers. One "go to town" day, we planned bumming a shower in a dorm or gym at the college in Neverson. We had no such luck, but as an afterthought decided to investigate employment possibilities. Four weeks later I began teaching a Monday night astronomy class and Annie a job tutoring students. For the next six years at least one of us would be employed at this two year college.

During August we built an outhouse, attached a wood shed to an outside wall of the cabin, and bought miscellaneous supplies, tools, and equipment--including three large galvanized trash cans. In these we placed some 500 lbs. of bulk food purchased from a natural food co-operative warehouse in Fayetteville. This $180 of food--including wheat, rice, rolled oats, corn, soybeans, peanuts, lentils, split peas, pinto beans, safflower oil, honey, nutritional yeast, and raisins-- would serve as the basis for our meals for the next six months. We bought whole grain and used a hand mill to grind flour or cornmeal as needed.

While we anticipated growing fruits and vegetables, at that time numerous tree stumps, roots, and rocks occupied our 25 ft. by 50 ft. lower bench garden spot. A shovel, pick, mattock, axe, and power puller which locals called a "come along", and lots of patient hard work were needed to eradicate the former. The latter were likewise overcome until late one August afternoon when my pick detected a large rock. Probing established its 8 ft. long by 3 ft. wide by 2 ft. deep nature. Common sense suggested either gardening around it or blasting. I bought three sticks of dynamite, but having no experience with explosives was hesitant to use them. Fortunately, our neighbor Lee, a 62 year old, warm, colorful, jack of all trades hillbilly seemingly offered help.

I tunneled under the huge rock, laid in a stick of dynamite, attached my wires, and positioned a battery detonator inside a 55 gallon drum turned on its side. In there I planned to lay 65 feet away from the intended explosion. After Lee's inspection provided the go-ahead, we crouched together inside the drum and I set off the explosion. But instead of a loud earth-shaking BOOM, there was but a feeble "pop". Lee turned to me and said, "Steve, I could have farted louder than that!"

Before Lee and I could talk about what went wrong, his wife Rene showed up. She needed him for a town trip. After Lee left I told Annie, "If that's all one stick of dynamite does, I'm gonna need a whole case to take care of that boulder!" When I repeated the procedure and laid in my two remaining sticks, my respect for the explosives was considerably diminished. As the second explosion neared, I casually told Annie, who was inside the cabin, of my blasting plans. I suggested she probably wouldn't notice much. Then I stood facing the rock 50 feet away and touched the wires to my detonator. The KA BOOM, shock wave, and rain of small rocks that followed sent me scurrying for cover--my tail between my legs! Still shaking, I opened the cabin door and verified that Annie was alive too and had not died of fright.

The dynamite broke the rock into small fragments, all easily manageable except the largest piece. Lee returned the next day and together we used poles, chains, come alongs, and good ole hillbilly know-how to drag this rock to the garden's edge. Long before accomplishing this, we concluded that only the small blasting cap--not the dynamite--had exploded in the previous day's initial effort!

We planted our garden, hoped for rain, and turned attention elsewhere. We bought a used chainsaw for $60 and an old wood cookstove for $100. We hoped this stove would adequately heat the cabin in winter. But before we cut down more trees, we needed a plan for our intended homestead. We scouted the upper bench for sites for house, garden, orchard, and pasture and by mid-September had settled on an unusual house site. Down the hill from our longest running spring (late September to early July in normal "wet" years), where the hillside met the eastern edge of the bench, lay a huge rock. The rock had a fairly level top side and measured about 20 ft. long, 12 ft. wide, and 8 ft. high.

Our plan was to build the house on and around that rock. This seemed like an easy, low cost way to incorporate lots of thermal mass and earth-tempering into our structure. Access to the upper bench was a big uncertainty. Putting a short temporary road across a neighbor's land was a possibility, as was a much longer, permanent road all on our land. Hand carrying building materials up the trail was also an option--

one I didn't like to think about!

We wanted to build an energy-efficient passive solar house. We didn't want to hand-mix all the concrete one usually employed in such buildings--we certainly couldn't carry all that weight up the hill in a worst case scenario! Using "the rock" seemed like a sensible alternative--but it would complicate our house design.

After the house site was selected, our remaining homestead plans fell into place. By late October, with harvesting in our fairly successful fall garden mostly done, work shifted to the upper bench. After excavating and clearing around the house site, we began cutting trees covering our future orchard and upper garden spot. Given our unfamiliarity with chainsaws and timbering operations, clearing but one acre took several working days. Grapevines--seemingly anchored to everything--complicated matters. By late November, fruit trees had been planted, and work pulling stumps began. Gathering building stone, in preparation for the intended house foundation walls also commenced.

We didn't just work that first summer and fall. We went to social gatherings. We explored the natural environment--backpacking, canoeing, exploring caves, and hunting for ginseng. We became steadily more involved with the environmental activists of the Thomas County Conservation Board (TCB).

Our second winter in the Ozarks was more trying than the first. In contrast to the thermostatically controlled gas furnace, our wood stove demanded constant attention. Cold and snow--on the ground continually beginning January 9th--confined us indoors. Cabin fever plagued us. On February 1st I assessed our finances. During the past six months we spent $982 -- 40 % on food, 30 % on transportation. Our savings had dropped to $3000. The snow cover remained for 23 more days.

III. ENVIRONMENTAL ACTIVISM / BUILDING PLANS

We got a reprieve from the snowy boredom in late February. Representing the TCB and financed by the Sierra Club, we flew to Washington, D.C. and attended a USDA/EPA--sponsored symposium on the use of herbicides in forestry. There we helped found the Citizen's National Forest Coalition, and made friends with people representing organizations having cute names like CATS, GOATS, and HOEDADS. We listened to technical presentations--some damning, some advocating forest use of herbicides like 2,4,5-T. One described the detection of TCDD-dioxin, the lethal contaminant in 2,4,5-T, in nursing mother's milk and beef fat samples taken from sprayed areas. Health risks of using this herbicide included cancer, birth defects, genetic damage, and immune system malfunction.

Later we watched slide presentations on alternative, labor intensive forest management practices. At an evening cocktail party we sold a TCB T-shirt which said "Save Our Natural Forests--People Not Poisons" to an attorney for 2,4,5-T manufacturer Dow Chemical Corp. On a more serious note, we met with the U.S. Forest Service Chief regarding the TCB lawsuit. We also set up an early March meeting in Fayetteville with the EPA Deputy Assistant Administrator for Pesticide Programs. He was reportedly considering issuing an RPAR (Rebuttable Presumption Against Registration) notice for 2,4,5-T. This would submit the herbicide to a complex review process--whose outcome could be banning its use in forestry. We felt personally lobbying him was important.

Back in Arkansas, the TCB / Forest Service legal battle was coming to a head. 45 minute trips to Staymore for meetings and two hour drives to Fayetteville to meet with attorneys were becoming more frequent. By now we had cemented a friendship with Robert Kale, the TCB intellectual leader. Like me, he had a physics background and had similarly traded an astrophysics job for life on an Ozark farm.

Gradually the weather improved. After negotiations with a neighbor, I got permission to drive through his land and haul building materials to the house site until August 1st. I paid another neighbor $20 for some bulldozer work improving this access. As March turned to April, I spent four days tearing down an unwanted part old, part new house. The lumber I salvaged would save us $1000. A friend who worked at a Neverson furniture plant likewise provided recycled building materials he'd rescued from the company's throw-away pile. Especially valued were 50 three foot long ornate hardwood railing posts with only minor cosmetic flaws. All of this, along with 20 sacks of cement and many cubic yards of sand, was stockpiled near the house site. Finally, after months of planning, frustration, and uncertainty, building began.

IV. BUILDING A HOUSE

During the next eight months, I worked physically harder than during any such period in my life. The days started early with breakfast--eaten while sitting on a convenient rock outside the cabin door. After a five minute walk up the trail, any previous work protected from the rain was uncovered, and I began work. Pauses were only for water, to wipe off sweat, or for meals. If I was working alone, Annie would carry a hot lunch or early dinner up the hill to me. Often I would finish late and walk down the trail in near darkness.

Annie and I worked together for the first eight weeks. After some crude surveying, trenches for the footings were dug, and foundation wall construction began. It was a slow process given our hand-mixing of mortar in a trough methods. After six weeks of building with stone, we decided to speed things up. After leveling up what we'd done, we used concrete blocks to complete this 100 ft. perimeter wall. By June 11th, I was ready to begin house framing and Annie to tend our fully-planted garden.

Using hand tools, it took six weeks to frame the two-story 1000 sq. ft. house. To allow the use of additional insulation, I used 2 x 6 s for the wall studs and 2 x 10 s for the cathedral ceiling rafters. Building the house was complicated by its unusual angles. It was built along two main axes: 1) a south-north line for aligning the south wall glazing, and 2) the axis of the massive rock--offset by 30 degrees from due south. Framing the roof-top central area was especially complicated. Here the house "bent" 30 degrees and large operable vents for summer heat exhaust were desired. The solution involved building a distinctive wedge-shaped triangular protuberance which slopes to the west.

In late July, with roof framing completed, some lower siding and plywood subfloor already installed, and a small upstairs deck added, work halted as the August 1st access deadline neared. I spent three days anticipating, buying, and hauling materials we'd need in later construction.

August was occupied with installing corrugated steel roofing, building a stairway, and nailing up remaining lower story siding. As the summer heat grew, so did the realization that moving out of the cramped cabin and into the house was critical to our psychological well being. With the heat intolerable, we'd given up sleeping in the cabin's loft and moved our mattress to the van. After August 1st all our cooking was done on a campfire as our massive cookstove had been moved up the hill.

During the first week of September, I erected a primitive scaffolding and courageously installed siding on the upstairs bedroom. One afternoon before teaching my evening classes, I bought a new mattress, second hand chest of drawers, and a carpet. The next day Annie and I built a bed frame and carried my purchases up the hill. The following day we installed carpet, furniture, and tacked up some old draperies on the bedroom's open interior wall to keep bugs out. Then we settled into our new bedroom and went to sleep. It was September 11, 1978.

During the next few weeks, I finished the siding, built insulated doors, and installed the Kalwall fiberacrylic solar glazing. The weather turned cooler as October began. The rough house shell was completed--we now faced a race with the approaching cold in getting it ready for winter. We began installing fiberglass insulation and six mil thick plastic sheeting to act as a permanent air-infiltration reducing barrier in sealing walls. By October 20th we'd spent over $2400 on the house but still lacked a heating stove and a chimney.

Both these presented problems as they would involve carrying heavy items up the hillside trail. A temporary solution would be to stick a long stovepipe through the roof to serve as a chimney. We rejected that as too dangerous. The alternative was a concrete block, clay flue tile 23 foot high chimney. I estimated materials for it would weigh 2000 lbs.

Shortly thereafter I made the 50 minute long trip to Neverson and returned with flue blocks, tiles, sand, etc. The next day I faced 40 trips up the trail carrying 50 lbs. each trip. My legs have always been strong and I wasn't especially concerned about them failing me. After the first few trips, I was worried about the internal dialogue filling my head as boredom set in. Like so much of life, keeping motivated was the key. I managed to structure my thoughts to include ones of people grinding for 30 years of wage slavery to pay off home mortgages. The trick worked. By the time friends happened by and offered help, I'd made 35 trips.

Annie and I worked for the next four days on the chimney. We produced a straight, solid structure that somehow managed to exit both our first story and the roof between the appropriate joists and rafters. We solved the space heating problem by buying an Ashley heating stove. By removing its cast iron door and top, I managed to carry the rest of it up the trail. Around November 1st we built our first fire in the Ashley and traded our campfires for the wood cookstove.

On Thanksgiving, Ken and Susie drove down from Missouri.

Together we ate a vegetarian meal and planned the Christmastime Southern California trip we'd make in our van to visit family. Privately, I gave thanks that we were warm inside our now completely insulated house and wouldn't have to pay homage to some bank for decades to come.

V. CHALLENGING HERBICIDE USE AND NUCLEAR POWER

We spent 1979 finishing the house interior, restoring our depleted finances, and with environmental battles. At the college, I was teaching two or three classes each semester and Annie now supervised the tutoring program.

As 1978 ended, the EPA had restricted 2,4,5-T use and the TCB / Sierra Club and U.S. Forest Service were negotiating an out of court settlement. In late February 1979, the Forest Service gave in on three of the five contested points. They would not 1) aerially spray any herbicide, 2) use any dioxin-containing herbicide, and 3) convert hardwood forests to grow pine trees. While we knew our fight against clearcutting and for ecologically sound forest management would go on, we nevertheless took time to celebrate. Hundreds turned out for a dusk to dawn TCB victory bash at Staymore.

The TCB meant a lot to many people. A few of us had even affectionately recast the group's straight-laced name into something more personally felt. "Taking Care of Business" was the most popular such appellation, with "The Country's Best" running a close second. Annie and I contributed "This Can't Be"--expressing our frequent feeling of amazement over how loose ends were pulled together despite obstacles....Vehicles broke down. Rivers were too rain swollen to cross, snow covered roads too dangerous. Money for filling the gas tank was hard to come by. Calling meetings on short notice was difficult since most people had no phone. Often those who showed up divided time between participating and child care. Yet, despite it all, the TCB won a battle.

The relaxed, somewhat smug feeling of TCB activists was short-lived. In late March, a Babcock & Wilcox-designed nuclear reactor at the Three Mile Island plant in Pennsylvania suffered a near core meltdown. 250,000 people were evacuated. Within weeks a group of Arkansans, concerned about the Babcock & Wilcox designed reactor at Arkansas Nuclear One near Russellville (65 miles from Braselville), had formed The Dogwood Alliance.

A June 2nd non-violent demonstration and accompanying

acts of civil disobedience at the Arkansas nuclear plant were scheduled. Annie and I mobilized the "Thomas County radicals" and taught two workshops in non-violence training. About 100 people took part in the demonstration, marching through drizzle one mile to the power plant's gate.

We then made a big circle and joined hands. With TV cameras rolling, Annie went to the center of the circle. Drawing upon talent that had won her numerous high school speech and debate tournaments, she delivered a speech that I had written.

> Why is it that we have chosen to spend this Saturday morning sitting in a circle snuggled warmly at the base of this nuclear reactor?...We can help start our nation down the "soft energy path" here in Arkansas by closing down this costly nuclear electricity factory. Our grandchildren will thank us for helping our country decide to make the "hard" nuclear energy path "The Road Not Taken"....The circle we're in emphasizes our commitment to environmentally sane energy options that disrupt natural cycles as little as possible.

As Annie began delivering the concluding "Prayer of Reconciliation", I recalled how a room of Dogwood Alliance leaders had burst into spontaneous, teary-eyed applause after she'd finished reading it to them a few days before. Now as she finished its last sentence, "Let us put aside our past differences and work together to forge a solution to which we can all say a resounding YES!", a hundred voices joined hers.

VI. ALONG THE SOFT ENERGY PATH

The Three Mile Island nuclear accident energized me. After a few months of being somewhat uncomfortably against nuclear technology, I spent the next four years as an activist for soft technologies. Through my involvement in the Dogwood Alliance, I got to know some higher-ups in the newly created Arkansas Dept. of Energy. Its existence was a sign of the times. The country was in the middle of a second oil price escalation/energy crisis and suddenly government funding for appropriate technology projects became available.

Years later I was commissioned to write a book-length report to the public on the results of several such projects in Arkansas. One of the projects I described in this 148 page book was the alternative to the power company that Annie and I opted for.

For three years we lived without electricity. In July, 1980, three panels providing 100 watts of photovoltaic solar electricity were installed, followed by a 200 watt wind-driven generator. With highly energy-efficient 12 volt appliances (Fig. #36) and meager needs, we used an average of just 20 kilowatt-hours per month of electricity during the mid-1980 to mid-1985 era. This is but 1/35 of the U.S. household averge electrical energy consumption!

```
+-------------------------------------------------------------+
|              FIG. #36 OUR 12-VOLT DC APPLIANCES             |
|                                                             |
|  * Five halogen lights. Each delivers light equivalent to   |
|    a 60 watt incandescent bulb yet consumes but 20 watts    |
|    of power. We like the light quality, but the bulbs       |
|    are fragile and require a clean environment.             |
|                                                             |
|  * Six "air-craft type" incandescent directional lights,    |
|    mainly used for reading, these use 12 watts each.        |
|                                                             |
|  * A thermo-electric refrigerator, 1.7 cu. ft capacity      |
|    with thermostat for controlling interior temperature.    |
|    Requires 24 watts power at 70 ° F. ambient temperature.  |
|                                                             |
|  * An AC/DC B & W 12-inch television, uses 15 watts max.    |
|                                                             |
|  * A stereo cassette player / AM-FM radio, 20 watts max.    |
|                                                             |
|  * A kitchen blender, uses 40 watts max.                    |
|                                                             |
|  * A circulating fan, 8 in. dia., 660 CFM, uses 14 watts.   |
|                                                             |
|  * An auto, hand-held vacuum cleaner, uses 108 watts.       |
|                                                             |
|  * A power tool set , includes drill, circular saw, sabre   |
|    saw and sander, each typically uses 180 watts.           |
|                                                             |
|  Besides these 12 volt appliances, a 250 watt frequency-    |
|  controlled inverter converts 12 volt DC into 110 volt AC   |
|  for our microcomputer system and a stereo turntable.       |
|                                                             |
+-------------------------------------------------------------+
```

Although our two and a half year long experiment with windpower ended in March, 1983 when winds estimated at 75 mph slammed into our 100 foot tower and did extensive damage, others benefitted from this learning experience. After receiving a $2550 grant to implement my combination wind / solar electricity system, I approached Richard Randall, a Neverson TV antenna builder, about adapting and installing a tower for a wind generator. He responded enthusiastically and began educating himself about wind systems. In the next few years, he installed the majority of the state's wind-electric systems for dozens of satisfied customers.

Unfortunately, our tower was not built from the heavy duty steel angle iron he soon began using. It could not stand up to high winds like the rest of his installations. Also, I've concluded that our hillside site, 300 feet from the house, is too turbulent for a wind machine.

Shortly after this accident we added more solar panels--by June, 1985 we had six panels supplying 204 watts of electricity. (These are pictured on the book's front cover.) The photovoltaics have performed up to expectations and there have been no problems. They charge a 500 amp-hour (over six kilowatt-hour) deep cycle battery bank storing enough electrical energy to meet our needs for 10 sunless days. In practice, after just a few days of cloudy weather, we curtail appliance use when battery voltage drops. We will go without electricity when voltage drops below 11 volts to prevent damaging them, but have had to do this only twice in the last five years.

We have avoided using noisy gasoline generators to backup our system. To help overcome summertime electricity shortages--or provide added cold food storage space--I installed a 2.5 cubic foot icebox in our kitchen. We sometimes augment the refrigeration our small 12 volt refrigerator provides by purchasing ice--not gasoline--from town. Our Jeep also helps provide backup electricity. Its alternator feeds electricity--which otherwise would be wasted by the car's voltage regulator--into an auxiliary battery.

Besides solar electricity, we use sunshine and energy efficient technology in meeting other household needs. 280 sq. ft. of single glazing on the south wall of our house--coupled with lots of thermal mass and other passive design features--result in an estimated 40 % solar contribution to our winter heating load. The 1000 sq. ft. house is insulated to R-20 in the walls, R-30 in the roof, has double pane east and west wall windows, and south wall moveable insulation.

Unique ventilation, earth-tempering, an overhang, and deciduous trees are summer cooling features. The earth helps cool air, which is pulled through the house by a naturally induced draft. A roof-top false ceiling is removed in summer exposing large roof peak vents where hot air can exit. The house cooling mode works well. During the record setting heat wave of July 1980--when outside temperatures exceeded 100 $^{\circ}$F on 20 of 31 days, the lower levels of the house never got above 79 $^{\circ}$F. This was achieved without the use of a cooling fan--which is now sometimes employed to cool the warmer upstairs on the hottest days.

A passive solar batch water heater, built for $50 using a recycled 30 gallon tank, meets most of our hot water needs for eight months of the year. In winter, when wood and LP gas heat our water, it is drained to prevent freezing.

The annual bill for our household energy costs is around $120--including $65 for LP gas which we cook with, $40 for chainsaw fuel/maintenance, and $15 for ice. We have $2475 invested in our solar electric system--including $1595 in photovoltaic panels, $355 in transmission wire, $225 in batteries, $150 for inverter, and $150 miscellaneous (appliance costs excluded).

A $2550 grant initially financed our wind/solar project. I obtained two other appropriate technology grants through my college employer. In fall 1979 I taught a popular class "Energy and Society". Its success helped me convince administrators to expand the school's energy education commitment. By summer 1980, we had received $50,000 in grant money to install a photovoltaic demonstration project and establish an appropriate technology resource center.

This Energy Center came to include books, periodicals, slide/cassette programs on solar and energy-efficient technologies, building plans, product literature, solar design computer programs, and technical papers. Equipment available for loan included solar siting tools, wind speed and DC kilowatt-hour meters, heat loss detectors, and chimney flue cleaning equipment. A mobile solar teaching lab--dubbed "The Solar Coaster"--aided outreach activities in surrounding communities.

Unfortunately, by July 1983 federal funds to operate The Energy Center were exhausted. Given the Reagan administration's preference for the "hard energy path", attempts to renew it seemed futile. At that time I moved my solar energy activities to the private sector.

VII. 1980-1981: EXCITEMENT AND DIFFICULTIES

I have recounted many years in our back-to-the-land adventure with numbers and technical descriptions--but said little about the human drama involved. Certainly mid-1980 was both an exciting and trying time for us. In July we retired the smelly kerosene lamps, marveled at how bright our house was with electric lighting, enjoyed gulping cold beverages after a trip to the refrigerator, and watching television. Summer brought record heat. Garden plants--and even some natural vegetation--simply dried up.

It must have gotten pretty rough for some wildlife species. Around 7 A.M. one morning I awoke to what sounded like the footsteps of a friend coming to visit...but there was no knock. Puzzled, I went downstairs and looked out the window. There on the porch was a big black bear with its nose inside a compost pail!

I checked the door's lock and immediately summoned a groggy and very pregnant Annie to have a look. Just as she peered out the window, the bear turned, stood upright and looked in the window. For a second, Annie and the bear were nose to nose with only two panes of glass separating them! Recalling that the porch level was two feet below where Annie stood, I realized that the bear was a seven footer. With a swipe of a paw this 300 to 400 lb. beast could have disfigured Annie and possibly entered our house.

Fortunately, it wasn't interested in us. When it finished eating our old food scraps it headed into the woods, first mulling around the orchard for an hour despite my silly efforts to hasten its departure. It took awhile to recover from the shock of seeing this furry visitor. For the next week, it seemed that a bear was lurking behind every bush!

In late August an incident made us reconsider ecological and privacy-based objections to building a road to the house. Annie (very pregnant!) was climbing our trail in twilight and narrowly missed stepping on a copperhead snake! Besides much joy, the birth of our first child, Dayton, a month later also meant new things to carry up the hill. That was another reason for a road. Also, our water supply was inadequate.

We lacked a large water tank to tide us over dry spells.

Leaks defeated one attempt at building a concrete block water tank under our house's crawl space. A large, plastic-lined children's outdoor swimming pool met our storage needs for one year--but it was plagued by contaminants and ultimately by leaks. We needed a road, either to transport a commercially-built tank, or to haul cement, sand, and gravel for building our own.

During the 1980-81 school year I worked full time at the college and climbed the trail daily in all kinds of weather. By the year's end, building a road had gone from a possibility to a priority.

VIII. OVERCOMING DIFFICULTIES / NEW ADDITIONS

During a two week period in late spring, 1981, Sonny Rogers a careful, conscientious, and talented bulldozer operator built a 1/5 mile U-shaped road between our mailbox on the county road and our house. The road climbs a 7 to 10 % grade in linking our lower and upper benches together.

The project was a gamble. Fortunately, Sonny's D5 Caterpillar dozer missed the hidden, ancient bluff line--so no expensive blasting was necessary. Where the bluff was encountered as expected, a ramp was built over it using fill dirt from 1) a sink pond built to control spring run-off, 2) widening the bend in the road, and 3) making a hillside cut just above the intended ramp.

After that, 30 truckloads of gravel were dumped on the road. One truck nearly tipped over on the road's soft shoulder--it took two bulldozers to pull it out. Despite the difficulties, by mid-July, after spending $2000 we had a suitable road. To insure year-round reliable access we bought a four wheel drive 1972 Jeep Wagoneer. Soon those long trips up and down the hillside were made in memory space only.

After the bulldozer left we planted grass to cover scars it had made. For the next 18 months we had no trouble with the road. (Record heavy rains would later trigger a mud slide on the hillside cut. In March 1985, Sonny's bulldozer would return to rescue our Jeep which became trapped in mud and was threatened by new movement in this area.) Our attention turned to water supply improvements.

Three years earlier, Annie and I had dragged a metal bathtub to the bluff above our house where it could catch water from our best spring. Past efforts to store much water for the dry season had failed and every summer we hauled

water from town. In winter, when the spring froze, we
sometimes chopped the huge icicles hanging from the bluff
into manageable chunks, and melted them for water.

Just before Sonny left, he fixed a spot above the house
so that a truck could set a large water tank in place. There
a backhoe was employed to dig a large hole. By the next
year, two 1000 gallon concrete tanks sat in this hole and our
water supply hassles eased.

The fall of 1982 brought four additions to our home.
First, Annie and I refinished an old piano and moved it into
our living room. Second, we sold our old wood cookstove and
bought a combination wood/LP gas stove. We installed a 25
gallon gas bottle and--after five years of building at least
one fire a day to cook on--began cooking on LP gas. Annie's
lack of enthusiasm for chopping stove-wood was excusable: she
was expecting in mid-October.

Feeling uneasy about leaving her alone and isolated during the last month of pregnancy--while I was working in
Neverson--we had a third addition, a phone, installed. The
last and most important addition, our daughter Ruthie, arrived two weeks later in a Fayetteville hospital. When Annie
relates the story of giving birth like a relaxed wild animal
would, it sounds like quite an ad for natural childbirth.
Seven hours later she walked out of the hospital.

IX. GARDENING AND ADDITIONAL FOOD PRODUCTION

1982 was fruitful in another respect--gardening. For the
first time we worked our entire 50 ft. x 100 ft. upper garden, although the strawberry patch we established that year
wasn't ready to bear a crop. We are "old-fashioned" gardeners, using only hand tools and no chemical fertilizers or
pesticides. We do use plenty of compost, manure, and mulch.

That year we kept detailed records of time and money
investments in gardening, as well as produce harvested.
Weatherwise, nature co-operated. Unlike 1980, there was no
prolonged drought. A groundhog who penetrated our "thought to
be varmint proof" fence did some damage. Before we caught him
in August, he devastated our sweet potatoes and soybeans, and
was starting in on the tomatos. Despite hours of destroying
eggs and hand picking, squash bugs finally overwhelmed us and
limited our expected 60 lb. squash harvest to one zucchini
and 15 winter squash. And, just when our cantaloupe and wa-
termelon needed water most, it turned dry in late August.

With these problems, the estimated $650 worth of produce we expected to harvest was limited to about $400 worth. We canned a total of 220 quarts--2/3 of them tomatos and green beans. The rest included spinach, peas, beets, cucumbers, carrots, peppers, and okra. We harvested 85 lbs. of onions, 85 lbs. of potatoes, 45 lbs. of peanuts, 35 heads of broccoli, cauliflower, and brussel sprouts, a few pounds of garlic and sunflower seeds, and all the salad greens and sweet corn we could eat.

In producing this bountiful harvest, we labored around 350 hours--including 50 hours canning and 85 hours in preparing the ground. We spent around $50 that year on seeds, strawberry and raspberry plants, thuricide bacterial spray for cabbage worm control, a soil inoculant for legumes, and rotted hay for mulch. Subtracting this from the $400 garden produce value leaves a net $350. Dividing this by the hours invested, yields a 1982 return of about $1/hour of labor. Such economic reckoning is plagued by intangible costs and benefits that are impossible to quantify. What is exercise, or fresh, pesticide residue free vegetables worth to one's health? What's the satisfaction of picking a ripe red juicy tomato, or seeing your children learn first-hand about where food comes from, worth?

Since 1982, our food production scene has expanded. That spring we loaded the disassembled lower bench cabin walls and roof onto a neighbor's truck and moved them up the hill. Our one-time home was resurrected as a small goat barn and chicken house. I spent a few fall days fencing a pasture, and the following spring we traded a broken down car for two dairy goats, three chickens, and $125 cash. After a twice a day 15 minute milking chore, we soon had a surplus of milk, and Annie began making cheese and yogurt.

The following year, after obtaining a 12 volt blender, Annie began making tofu from commercially grown, organic soybeans. After learning how to put subtle, delicious flavors into this bland, high protein, high calcium, low fat food, we now utilize it in perhaps 2/3 of our main course dinner meals. Annie typically makes six lbs. of tofu in two hours for family use, or 20 lbs. in six hours if friends also want some. Given the $.20/lb. it costs to make, and the $1.40/lb. supermarket price, Annie's labor is worth around $3.50/hour.

Initially, we fed the soy pulp byproduct of tofu-making called okara, to the chickens. Now Annie makes a cultured,

high protein, vitamin B-12 rich, bean cake called tempeh, and
an imitation sausage product from it. Both have a delicious
taste and tempeh is even cheaper to make than tofu. For us,
goat milk products and soy foods offer a better monetary
return for the labor invested than does gardening. These
three food production and processing activities represent the
steps we've taken toward food self-sufficiency.

    We moved to the Ozarks with fantasies of becoming highly
food self-sufficient. Fortunately, we soon met the Taylor
family--who had just won a $10,000 first prize in a maga-
zine's food self-sufficiency competition. This family--two
adults, two teenaged boys--had spent the last five years on
their Ozark farm attempting to produce all their own food.
They succeeded to the extent that their total annual expenses
for food items they couldn't produce themselves were but $20!
That outlay was for salt, vinegar, baking powder, yeast, and
sugar for wine and meat curing.

    In achieving this, the Taylors learned to distinguish
between the "true" cost of food, based on all the energy, raw
materials, and biosphere impacts involved in its production,
and its supermarket price. They would write,

> The "cost of food" is far higher than we imagined. In
> our earlier lives between the paycheck and the super-
> market, we had completely lost sight of what is required
> to provide our basic needs. We get an indication of the
> "cost" in the hours of effort we must now spend to pro-
> cure our food without the aid of non-renewable re-
> sources. We estimate that the four of us now spend 5000
> hours of work per year devoted directly to food pro-
> duction. The same quantity of food could be purchased in
> the supermarket with the pay from 10 hours of work per
> week or 500 hours per year. The food in the supermarket
> was produced with massive expenditures of petroleum for
> energy and for the manufacture of agricultural chemi-
> cals. The earth and the sun have invested monumental
> amounts of energy and resources in producing this petro-
> leum over untold millions of years. By an odd quirk in
> economic history most of this part of the "cost of food"
> doesn't have to be paid at the supermarket checkout.

    Somewhere in working for the last 1/3 to 1/2 of total
food self-sufficiency, I've decided, diminishing returns set
in. Laboring at food production only up to an imagined

optimum level may make more sense.

X. HASSLES AND PROBLEM-SOLVING

Many of our hassles involve extreme weather, old automobiles, and animals. People who live close to nature often suffer during unusual weather unless they are well-prepared. Temperature extremes, ice storms, excessive rain which triggered record flooding and mud slides, drought and high winds have either caused us discomfort or significantly set back homestead operations. Poor rural people--given the gravel roads they drive and their poverty--typically own old, run-down vehicles in constant need of repair. Driving steep, rutted roads is especially hard on tires, brakes, and drive trains. One year we suffered about 20 flat tires; in another, collisions with rocks separated muffler and exhaust pipe on five occasions. Finally, living close to nature means being in close proximity to wild animals, including predators and parasites. Over the years, raccoons have killed our chickens, wild dogs attacked our goats, rabbits and groundhogs ravaged our garden, and snakes, woodrats, and bears threatened us. We are plagued by ticks and chiggers every summer.

Establishing a homestead in a remote area means setting up one's own life support systems. While this can be a satisfying outlet for creativity, with it comes the chore of fixing things when they break down. Having lived with hassles and problems demanding solutions, I've found that a patient constructive attitude is crucial to overcoming them. Recalling past, creative, problem solving successes also helps. Consider the following examples.

Annie and I are both pleased with the functional, efficient workplace our 8 ft. x 14 ft. kitchen is. We have solved the problem of integrating stove, refrigerator, and appliances with double sink, countertop workspace, and kitchen storage with minimum expenditures, the re-use of perfectly functional components, and our own labor. For but $600, we turned an unfinished room into a versatile food preparation and storage facility. From garage sales, auctions and second-hand stores we obtained cabinets, countertops, sink, shelf units and a combination wood / LP gas stove. We bought (at off season discount) our thermoelectric refrigerator and an icebox. Finally, lumber, building materials, plumbing components, and our own labor finished the project.

Our kitchen isn't perfect. Most Americans, accustomed to

a superficial niceness, would find it unattractive. We are
sometimes bothered by space limitations and lack of a freezer
in our thermoelectric / backup icebox refrigeration combination. But until we are convinced that investing the $2000
or more that a large energy-efficient 12 volt refrigerator
would cost is necessary, we'll tolerate minor inconvenience.

Our small bathroom has been similarly designed and furnished. A deep, double sink bought second-hand for $5 serves
not only for personal hygiene, but occasionally for washing
laundry. When water and sunshine are abundant, we dispense
with trips to the laundramat in favor of hand washing and
clothesline. Above the sink is our medicine cabinet--bought
at a garage sale for $1. Our fiberglass bathtub likewise cost
but $8 due to a minor cosmetic defect.

Our bathroom and kitchen contribute raw material for our
garden soil fertility-building compost pile. One furnishes
kitchen food scrap wastes, the other bathroom compost toilet
offerings. Our toilet design was inspired by many things.
First, we considered typical flush toilet / septic tank systems to be water-polluting ecological no-nos, given the por-
ous Ozark limestone soil. Second we saw our own excrement as
a potentially valuable resource. Finally, we sought to minimize monetary outlay.

Our compost toilet consists of a conventional toilet
seat placed over an insect-proof, vented cylindrical metal
can, both of whose ends are open. The bottom of this two foot
long cylinder sits about 1/2 inch above the open top of a ten
gallon can of similar diameter. Resting on the concrete floor
of the crawl space below, this can serves as the waste chamber. To empty it, I open the door which separates the waste
chamber from adjoining cellar. I carry this 50 lb. load out
the cellar door to the compost area near the garden. It begins decomposing in 55 gallon drums. After one year these
drums are emptied into a wooden compost bin-- being appropriately layered with other wastes to insure a rapid transformation into rich garden fertilizer.

Emptying the toilet is a ten minute chore I repeat every
two weeks. After reinstalling the waste can beneath the
metal cylinder, I seal the 1/2 inch gap between the parallel
circular rims with duct tape. We keep an elastic cloth cover
over the upper end of the metal cylinder. This cover is removed with each use of the toilet. These steps have proven
effective in preventing insect entry. We put a scoop of saw-

dust into the toilet with every use and refilling this bath-room sawdust bin completes the toilet emptying chore. This simple compost toilet has worked well in years of odor free use. It was built for a total cost of $25--which includes the cost of four 55 gallon drums for outside decomposition.

Throughout our six room house are scattered unique solutions to various problems. In the kitchen is our fireless cooker--a well-insulated box that houses a cooking pot with a tight-fitting lid and a flat stone. In using it, the pot and stone are briefly heated on the stove. Both are then rapidly transferred to the insulated box--where heat is impressively retained for hours. Such slow cooking not only cuts fuel use dramatically, it improves the taste of certain foods. We use it to cook rice, beans, stews, and to make yogurt.

Besides its south wall glazing, our house has 22 20 in. x 28 in. double pane windows--all (except one) located on east and west walls. To install them we used free hardwood 1 x 2 s discarded from a local furniture manufacturer to hold the panes in place, a desiccant in between the panes to pre-vent condensation, and silicon caulking to seal each window. Having purchased the glass for $.20/ sq. ft., these 22 ener-gy-efficient windows cost but $45 altogether. Most homes employ similarly sized windows which cost $45 or more each! Our windows do not open--nice in winter since additional cracks for air infiltration are eliminated. In summer, vents let the house breathe and exhaust hot air.

In winter, moveable insulation helps us stay warm. A large, homemade thermal curtain covers living room south wall, while lift-in, rigid insulating panels are used up-stairs. Such commercially-made window treatments can be ex-pensive, with some exceeding $18/ sq. ft. Our homemade de-vices typically cost $.30 / sq. ft. They provide an R-value and operation we can live with.

Throughout the heating season we spend five minutes a day operating our moveable insulation. After doing this for six years, we have grown accustomed to it, as we are to numerous other chores our lifestyle involves. A listing of these chores appears in Fig. #37. I consider much of this work good exercise. If I lived a more sedentary life in a city, I'd probably jog, exercise, or diet to stay fit. By naturally integrating activity into everyday life, I avoid such artificial regimen.

```
+----------------------------------------------------------+
|                  FIG. #37    CHORES                      |
|                                                          |
|   * emptying compost toilet                              |
|                                                          |
|   * compost pile maintenance                             |
|                                                          |
|   * moveable insulation operation                        |
|                                                          |
|   * seasonal opening and closing vents                   |
|                                                          |
|   * cutting firewood, stacking in woodshed               |
|                                                          |
|   * emptying wood ashes                                  |
|                                                          |
|   * chimney flue cleaning                                |
|                                                          |
|   * road maintenance (filling ruts, keeping ditches clear) |
|                                                          |
|   * seasonal adjustment of photovoltaic array tilt angle |
|                                                          |
|   * battery bank maintenance                             |
|                                                          |
|   * refrigeration chores: loading ice blocks, draining water |
|       (summer), exposing unit to outdoor cold (winter)   |
|                                                          |
|   * burning combustible trash; recycling glass, metal    |
|                                                          |
|   * cleaning spring water catch tank after heavy rains   |
|                                                          |
|   * seasonal draining, refilling of solar water heater   |
|                                                          |
|   * pointing TV antenna toward channel to improve reception |
|                                                          |
+----------------------------------------------------------+
```

XI. MID-1983 TO MID-1985 / THE EXPERIMENT ENDS

After federal funding for my solar energy education job ran out in July, 1983, we relied on my small solar business for income. This began while I was still working part-time at the college in mid-1982 with a couple of jobs as a solar consultant for a local architect. Eventually I developed and began marketing solar energy educational slide programs and solar design microcomputer software to architects, engineers, and energy educators.

This software, which was technically based on scientific papers from professional solar engineering journals, was originally developed to aid my consulting work. The response to an article I wrote for a leading alternative energy publication resulted in my first sales in spring 1983. A year later, a solar trade publication used the software to evaluate performance of photovoltaic panels and again for active solar collectors in its preparation of industry-wide collector directories. This exposure spurred sales.

Meanwhile, Annie began selling home-made tofu and related soy food products to friends. As I became pre-occupied with writing this book, her income was a timely addition to the family finances.

Some of the most important work we do--both in personal growth and serving the public interest terms--is volunteer work. Thus in October, 1984, I traveled to an Indiana conference on forest management, and in March, 1985, Annie journeyed to Washington D.C. for a symposium on forestry and herbicides. Thereafter, we joined a dozen other TCB members in preparing a 200 page response to a U.S. Forest Service environmental impact statement and forest management plan.

Putting total food self-sufficiency fantasies aside, we now realize that the success of back-to-the-land ventures depends on finding suitable money-generating employment. We care little for money itself, rather it is the livelihood it provides that we seek to maintain through our employment. Ideally, such a job should be so well integrated with one's interests and life, that the usual work / non-work or work / play distinctions become blurred. In earning income and other aspects of our livelihood, we also wish to contribute to planetary well being and play fair.

On June 30, 1985--after spending the day helping an organic farmer friend mulch several acres of blueberries--I realized that our Ecosharing experiment had run 10 years. It was time to evaluate. Monetarily, our annual family income during this decade averaged $2339 per capita--a figure but 10 % above the world per capita annual income for the same period (expressed in similar dollars). Likewise, an energy index (described in GOOD NEWS) which I believe is a representative, first approximation of one's non-renewable resource usage / biosphere impact yields a figure 11 % below

the corresponding world per capita figure over the same 10
year period. (see APPENDIX B and C)

Certainly the last decade has been full of hardship--but
there have also been great rewards. After a decade of ecosharing, do I feel deprived, do I see my family as poverty-
stricken? No--but I suspect many Americans would. I can imagine a visit from affluent Americans and judgements I and
they might make.

XII. POVERTY-STRICKEN OR WELL-OFF ?

Many Americans--citing our meager income over the last
decade--would conclude that our family is very poor and
therefore we are "losers". If they came to visit they'd see
other evidence supporting their contention. They would look
down on the children's mostly hand-me-down or homemade clothing and at my patched jeans. Inside the house they'd see the
living quarters as cramped and be appalled at our relative
lack of interior decorating. "Do you realize that not only is
there no wallpaper, but when they nail up paneling they don't
even hide the nailheads?" one might report. They would find
our black and white television, refrigeration, and wintertime
hot water situations most unsatisfactory. They would view the
carpets as rather filthy and the rest of the house dirty.
When the true nature of our toilet facilities became apparent, they would politely express disbelief and find an excuse
to leave. Our 13 year-old beaten-up vehicle would similarly
be looked down on.

I can argue that we are really quite well off. We have
lots of friends. We own more land than all but a small percentage of Americans, and live with natural beauty that few
American estates can match. Unlike most Americans, our
family--not some bank--owns our house and land, and we don't
owe money to anyone. We have clean air to breathe, clean
water to drink, and can afford to buy food that's free of
chemical pollutants, or take time to produce it. Although the
technology is said to be too expensive for American residen-
tial use, our family has photovoltaic solar electricity. For
the last five years our family--not some utility company--has
owned and controlled this power plant.

Our children always have at least one parent to care for
them, and frequently two. Instead of working 80 hours/week
away from home like many two working parent American families, in the last decade we have averaged but 20 hours/week.

Lately, much of this has been done at home. Our children benefit from this additional time we spend with them. They also have a two-acre, completely fenced mountain bench natural paradise for a backyard and four goats as animal playmates.

Our family library numbers 910 volumes. On the mountain above our house, a 12 ft. x 12 ft. roll-off roof observatory houses my 16 inch reflecting telescope--which sits on a massive equatorial mounting. Along both our benches are scattered dozens of black walnut trees in the 12 to 18 inch diameter range. You'd no doubt realize that, should we need income in our old age, selectively cutting them could yield a nice income. Finally, if I showed you the albums of hundreds of color photographs which document our lives, you'd think "rich family life" rather than "poverty-stricken".

Of course, in comparison to much of the world's population, we are well off. Perhaps to the soft, spoiled, sedentary affluent of the Western world, my chronicles recall an unimaginable, dangerous life of constant hardship and struggle. As hard as our lifestyle seems, our hassles are minor compared to the real life and death struggles of millions of Third World people.

Typically, we have elsewhere to turn where they have none. If garden or other food production schemes fail, there is always the supermarket. If money-making opportunities dry up, there're food stamps. If the house is destroyed, there's property insurance to build it back. If the Jeep won't run, there's the motorcycle or help from friends--instead of walking. If our rugged rural existence proves too difficult, there are temporary living situations available with relatives until city jobs are found. Living on the trash of a throw-away society would be preferable to the marginal existence of many in dirt-poor countries.

These chronicles of what it's like down "the road less traveled by" have provided a look at one family's solution to finding a simple way of living based on fair play. Hopefully, they will prove illustrative of a more general approach to living--based on a philosophy called Ecosharing, which I'll outline shortly.

Questions & Projects

1. Aspects of many subjects are important in designing and building a home. List and discuss.

2. "Ideally, all students should spend a semester involved in building design and construction, and farming / food production activities. The way education occurs and the setting is as important as the subject matter." Discuss.
3. Identify specific ways the Cooks saved energy that normally would be wasted.
4. Could most American families immediately put photovoltaic solar electric panels to use (if they were cheaper)? Why or why not?
5. People who manage land, be they homesteaders or public employees must wrestle with various land use ethical viewpoints. These include 1) "use it for economic gain", 2) "preserve it from development", 3) "use it, but preserve its ecological integrity", and 4) "use it wisely for multiple purposes in a way that conserves affected resources". Provide examples of each drawing on this chapter and elsewhere in this book.
6. How does the Cooks' relationship with food differ from typical American families? Discuss.
7. "Tofu is close to being the ideal food. It is nutritious, versatile, and makes sense." Discuss.
8. Only 20 % of Americans have ever tasted tofu. Go to a natural foods restaurant and taste soy-food dishes if you never have. Discuss.
9. How is a compost pile built? Why is it constructed in this fashion? Report.
10. Make a list of plusses in the Cooks' living situation that others might see as minuses, and vice versa.
11. Do you think the Cooks' lifestyle of the 1975-1985 era was fairly representative of the average world lifestyle (under perfect sharing conditions)? Discuss.
12. How does the Cook's 1975-1985 lifestyle compare to the world per capita average as to number of cars and annual miles driven (the Cooks averaged .42 cars and 4,168 miles per person.) Investigate. Repeat for annual KWH of electricity used per person. (Cooks used 147 KWH per person.)
13. Do you view the Cooks' lifestyle (as described) as representing that of "a poverty-stricken family" or one "materially and spiritually well-off"? Discuss.
14. Discuss the implications of "yes" responses to questions 11. and 13.

GOOD NEWS

I. QUESTIONS ABOUT THE HUMAN FUTURE

Thinking about the human future provokes one immediate question: Ideally, what do we want? Addressing this means resolving various issues. How should people be governed? Who should make the rules and on what should they be based? Must the world be a just and fair place? How much poverty should be tolerated? What consideration should be given to needs of future generations? What rights do other species have? How important is maintaining the long-term integrity of the biosphere? Should humanity plan on colonizing other planets? How a person answers these and similar questions depends on his or her worldview and on how various value judgements are made. After pondering our list of 26 worldview themes (Fig. #1 LETTERS) one grasps the range of possibilities. Consider how those with narrow worldviews might respond.

Desirable types and bases of government (and associated dominating worldview theme #) would include: 1) none or anarchy (#18), 2) theocracy / the Bible / God (#9), 3) authoritarian / blind faith (#15), 4) economically-entrenched oligarchy (#19 and #20), 5) scientifically-entrenched oligarchy (#13 and #20), 6) democracy / education (#10 and #21). Besides traditional, rationally-based ethical theory (#10 and #16), justice might be based on vengeance (#17 and #18), religious morality (#14), economic realities (#19, #22, and #26), or environmental concerns (#23).

Certainly the economic elite (#19 and #20) would tolerate a wealthy few / impoverished masses world more than the struggling populists (#21 and #24). A person with tunnel vision (#3) would not consider future generations' rights; a person caught up in anthropocentrism (#25) would discount other species' rights. Someone possessing global vision (#4) would value both. Those dominated by expansionist tendencies (#22) might envision escaping a crowded, polluted, resource-depleted planet Earth, while others would work to insure its long-term health (#23).

While true believers' crusades (#2) might be driven by dreams of some future utopian world, humble skeptics (#1) would ponder the coming conflicts over values. They would ask two additional questions, "What type of future world can we actually have? and "How do we do it?"

All of these questions--especially the last two--are thought provoking. And--as humanity muddles toward the 21st century and our planetary home increasingly feels the impacts--that concerned, intelligent people are seriously discussing such questions is good news.

But alas, if only we could find that someone who has the best answers to these questions--best answers as far as the future well being of the entire human species and its planetary home is concerned. What characteristics might dominate the personality of such a person? Certainly one would expect to find an empathic love for humanity, a well-developed sense of fair play, and exceptional future vision--besides great wisdom. Suppose such a person--someone whose worldview is dominated by themes #4, #10, #16, and #21, a saviour of mankind--suddenly appears and quickly rises to a prominent place in the family of man. Imagine what this great humanist, this democratic man of the people, would say to the world.

II. THE GREAT HUMANIST RESPONDS

I'm sorry that what I'm going to say must be so structured and intellectual sounding. I wish we could sit on a hillside together, watch our children play, share a meal, listen to some music, and tell stories in a language we all understand. Out of necessity however, I must limit our interaction. I want to involve you in two exercises.

First, imagine you are God (and a personal God!) Imagine your voice is to be heard inside all human heads. Suppose your words will be understood and given importance befitting words of divine origin. Suppose you can say no more than 100 words. What will you say? Here is what I would say.

"Attention. I am speaking to all the Earth's people. As a species you must give up the wild, unrestricted exercise of materialistic freedom of your childhood. You must trade it for a new freedom tempered by responsibility -- responsibility based on playing fair with other people and with your planetary home. You must grow up. As individuals, it is no longer enough to live by The Golden Rule. You must control yourselves. Don't be a burden on your planet's life support systems: don't exceed your fair ecoshare."

Would such commands be obeyed? Perhaps, but without God to guide us could we learn to play fair? How would we do it? What would the rules be and who would make them? How could we get everyone to follow them? How could they be made to seem like something other than rules?

Alas, our task would be easier if humanity had a real collective consciousness--one that each individual was both part of but also separate from, something that would allow each person to perceive that he or she is sharing a home called Earth with the family of man just as naturally as fathers, mothers, sisters, and brothers perceive their family bond. But that day is far in the future. It will dawn only if we start working toward it now.

III. AN ECOSHARING CO-OPERATE / DEFECT CHOICE

Consider a second exercise. You are one of five billion people living on a planet with limited resources and a fragile life support system. Imagine yourself, or any arbitrary human being, paired with another arbitrary person. Suppose neither of you know the identity of the other. Now suppose both the permitted human biosphere impacts and the portion of non-renewable resources deemed permissible for human use have been divided among every pair of humans, with 2 1/2 billion equal shares. If divided in half equally, the ecoshare you and your unknown partner receive will provide for your life support needs and many, if not all, of your higher needs.

It will take planning, efficiency, frugality, hard work, co-operation, and motivation to achieve such self-actualization. Nonetheless with each ecoshare still comes an important promise. The good news is: If we all play fair, if each of us finds our own efficient, simple way of living, we can all be happy. There is room on the lifeboat for everyone. Even if we abolish first class occupancy and put everyone in the spaceship hold, we can all be comfortable.

Before this exercise can continue, there is an important consideration. How will you and your unknown partner choose to divide up the share that was given to you in common. In making this choice, you've no knowledge of what your partner--who will also be deciding--will choose.

There are two choices for each individual to independently make: 1) the "co-operate" with your partner choice, in which you agree to give him or her the same ecoshare as yourself, or 2) the "defect" on your partner choice, in which you grab a large share for yourself and leave nearly nothing for your partner. There are three possible outcomes of this interaction between anonymous human beings over ecoshare allocations: 1) both partners co-operate, 2) one partner co-operates and the other defects or vice versa, and 3) both partners defect.

Some may not like this hypothetical scenario. I pause to consider objections to the imagined exercise of five billion humans voting to co-operate or defect on Ecosharing. OBJECTION #1: Limiting humans to the Earth's resources is unnecessary given their growing access to the rest of the solar system. Your exercise's validity rests on defining a closed system, and your definition is erroneous.
REBUTTAL: Despite talk of eventually colonizing outer space and drawing on the resources of other worlds, such efforts, at least for the next century, perhaps much longer, will have no real effect on the predicament of the average human being. The high energy and monetary costs per pound (now $4000/lb.) of material transported between Earth and space will preclude massive colonization in the near future.

Not only must the potentially beneficial utilization of lunar or other celestial raw materials be considered, but also potential space-related disasters. Encounters with malfunctioning rockets carrying radioactive materials, large meteoroids, small asteroids, comets or unusual solar disturbances could wreak havoc.

Each of these possible positive and negative perturbations of the closed terrestrial system has some finite probability of happening. These probabilities are very small, so such possibilities are discounted. As far as you and the next few generations of your offspring are concerned, you are part of a closed system. During this "closed system" era, non-renewable resource use will have to be limited.
OBJECTION #2: Many people may choose not to participate because they see themselves as Americans, Germans, Russians, Chinese, etc. and not as world citizens.
REBUTTAL: Scientists have identified a biological species called Homo Sapiens. All people belong to this natural group, independent of any artificial divisions into smaller groups.
OBJECTION #3: This is an exercise in "human chauvinism" lacking in respect for other species and grounded in Anthropocentrism (worldview theme #25).
REBUTTAL: I think one must acknowledge the reality of human supremacy among species. We alone are capable of forever wiping out all life on the planet. Yet with this recently acquired capability has come new wisdom. W. Jackson Davis summarizes it well.[1]

> Ecology has revealed the intrinsic logic of karma and
> the Golden Rule: what we do unto nature, we do unto
> ourselves as well. We are in a position to understand
> that we do not control nature: we are nature, and it is
> us. There is no separation: all is one, propelled
> through different physical forms in space-time by na-
> ture's omnipresent cycles.

Biosphere impacts can be equated with "what we do unto nature". Such impacts are to be limited in appreciation of
this ecological corollary of the Golden Rule.
OBJECTION #4: How can <u>all</u> humans be informed of this
choice they must make?
OBJECTION #5: Those who are informed will surely ask,
"How is this ecoshare to be measured?" Won't this be an
impossible question to answer as not all impacts or resources
are, or ever will be, fully known?

These information and measurement objections underscore
the need to restructure our exercise. To overcome these
difficulties let us employ a 1st approximation index to gauge
individual biosphere impact/resources use: money. Employing
money for this has advantages and disadvantages. The concept
of money is universally understood and measures of it often
roughly correlate with biosphere impact / resource use.
Unfortunately, seldom do product prices reflect manufacturing, transportation, use and disposal environmental costs.
Putting economic activity on a sustainable footing will
require "pay as you go" pricing that includes hidden costs.
In such a world, monetary expenditures would provide a more
suitable index for our exercise.

Pragmatically re-orienting our exercise, imagine we ask
five billion humans this: "Suppose meaningful work opportunities are available. You can earn a global average annual
per capita income, one that will continue indefinitely as
long as your productive work contributing to human and
planetary well being continues. <u>All</u> humans are being offered
this chance. You can accept the work and the average salary
and thereby co-operate with your fellow humans, or you can
decline and thus defect from this movement toward human
solidarity and fair play. What is your choice, to co-operate
or defect?"

Many will smile at hearing the "modest proposal" this
question raises and perhaps even seem sympathetic to it. They
feel no need to answer themselves as surely only a wildly

idealistic visionary would imagine all humans could participate in such an exercise. To make clear my serious intent,
consider another pragmatic move: pairing the participants in
this Prisoner's Dilemma game (see LIBERALS) in a special way.

Suppose we pair humanity by individual income, composing
each pair of one "rich" person and one "poor" person. Doing
this preserves the validity of our exercise and simplifies
carrying it out, since we now only have to question one of
the individuals in the pair. A review of Fig. #21 from
NUMBERS & CYCLES tells us there's no practical reason why the
poor member of the pair should even be questioned. The
question to be asked might be the equivalent of, "Would you
co-operate and accept 12 times your current income?" All who
understood would co-operate.

So practically we need only ask the question of people
whose income exceeds the per capita world average. Our information problem is simplified because these people can more
easily be reached with education to aid decision-making. This
Ecosharing education might consist of two parts: 1) arguments for defection (what follows might be advanced by a
libertarian--see LAW), and 2) arguments for co-operation.

IV. ARGUMENTS FOR CO-OPERATION AND DEFECTION

I urge you to make your decision on this Ecosharing
issue only after fairly and rationally considering the
arguments of both sides. If, after I've finished generally
describing the choice you must make, you say "yes" to co-
operation, you may want to work out the ramifications yourself. Later, I'll go over my own rules for responsible living, for playing fair, in some detail. If you like them,
they're yours too. If you don't, refine them or formulate
your own. But remember, a globally aware, ethical person's
guidelines are fair to everyone else. And applying The
Principle of Greatest General Good isn't easy.

ARGUMENT FOR DEFECTION

Pursuing your own happiness--maximizing pleasures, minimizing pain--comes naturally to you, not self-sacrificing
for others. Pursuing your own needs insures you are master--
no one's pulling your strings. Just make sure that--in looking out for yourself--you don't forcibly interfere with other
people's rights.

Making money is what spurs people to produce more and
wealth is created in this way. Don't retreat from acquiring

money and wealth--see it as evidence of your own superior productive ability.

The impractical sharing constraint would create a monotonous, drab society in which innovation is stifled and people are lazy. Equality, instead of producing universal material well being, will lead to uniform poverty. Economic growth will halt. As <u>Wealth and Poverty</u> author George Gilder points out,[2]

> An economy can continue to grow only if its profits are constantly joined with entrepreneurial knowledge and control. Divorce the financial profits from the learning process or from investment control and the economy stagnates.

Freedom-loving Americans used to a high standard of living will not tolerate Ecosharing proposal restrictions on acquisition of property and wealth. They know that private property insures freedom and view inequality as a necessary byproduct of economic growth. In fact, according to a 1990 poll published in <u>American Enterprise</u> magazine, only 29 % of Americans agreed with the statement, "It is the responsibility of the government to reduce the differences in income between people with high incomes and those with low incomes".

Americans view capping wealth proposals as unacceptable assaults on their freedom and standard of living. The wealthy will fight those who will otherwise steal from them. Socialistic efforts to redistribute wealth will be dangerously destabilizing and--like past attempts--doomed to fail.

REBUTTAL TO DEFECTION ARGUMENT

Those embracing the Libertarian philosophy behind this argument constantly interfere with the rights of others. Valuing private property rights, they are champions of multinational corporations. Multinationals' economic exploitation and dominance of poor people in under-developed regions, pollution of air, water, and food chains, and lobbying against the public interest, all represent massive interference with individual rights.

Libertarians fail to perceive the corporate-government marriage inherent in the term corporate state. Hazel Henderson[3] notes that Libertarians are confused "over the role of corporate power parading under the guise of private property and free enterprise" and myopic "about corporate abuse of the power of accumulated property and the Fourteenth

Amendment-based interpretations of corporations as persons, but with only rights--not the concomitant duties that real persons also are bound by".

Libertarian thinking has been shaped by those living in large cities. As such it is contrary to a fundamental law of village based culture--what Richard Crutchfield calls "the village ethic of mutual help" and sees at its heart The Golden Rule.

As for Ecosharing, the income constraint says nothing about the redistribution of existing wealth and neither will the promised Ecosharing objectives. There simply will be no stealing. There will be a realization that a world in which a few earn vastly more than the rest-- not through any greater effort (indeed people who live off interest and investment income put forth much less effort)--is unjust and full of unnecessary suffering. The suffering must halt. Under Ecosharing, the halt will come gradually as the old Grabber mentality is replaced by a worldview based on fair play, sharing, and restraint.

While the poll you cite indicates only 29 % of Americans want the government intervening to redress personal income inequalities, over 60 % of Britans and West Germans and over 80 % of Austrians and Italians favored such action.

George Gilder also writes,[5]

> Capitalism works because the people who create wealth
> are rewarded with the right and burden of reinvesting
> it.

Ecosharing will not challenge this right. It will add to the burden by demanding that reinvestment be consistent with some broad guidelines (to be spelled out in the Ecosharing objectives). Creation of wealth for the benefit of society will be encouraged; an individual's selfish reveling in it will not.

The economic system that Ecosharing will produce will hardly be socialism, but it will not be capitalism either. Instead, a system that combines the best features of the old, competing, antagonistic ideologies--and asks them to live together in the same economic house--will evolve. The best model for this is the small, but steadily growing, worldwide co-operative economics model.

As the 21st century approaches, as the planet effectively shrinks under the onslaught of new technology to become an electronic global village, the old co-operative economics can be slightly recast. According to The International

Co-operative Alliance[6]

> The primary hypothesis of co-operation is that the con-
> sumers are everybody, and that all the machinery of
> industry and organization of society should be for them.
> When this supremacy of interest is brought to pass, it
> is found that the consumers have become the pro-
> ducers, and that the interests of producer and consumer
> are one.

Now, "everybody" can mean truly that: all humans.

ARGUMENT FOR CO-OPERATION

First I formalize two assumptions.

ASSUMPTION #1: I am a human being.

ASSUMPTION #2: For planning my future behavior purposes, I acknowledge that the Earth is a closed system.

Now for the crucial assumptions regarding equality.

ASSUMPTION #3: All new borne human beings are endowed, not only with their own unique gifts, but with roughly equal innate potential for leading happy lives and contributing to the well being and happiness of others.

ASSUMPTION #4: Given this equal innate potential, all humans should have a roughly equal opportunity to pursue their own happiness and contribute to planetary well being.

If you do not accept these assumptions then you must think that some humans are better than others and deserve better treatment. What right do you have to say someone is better than somebody else? What criteria do you use in making this judgement? Wouldn't any such criteria be based on incomplete knowledge and therefore arbitrary? If you don't think so, perhaps you are an all-knowing being and have all the answers? If you don't claim to be God, and still reject these assumptions, then your positions on equality and sharing--issues at the heart of human ethics--must be based on something other than reason.

You may want better treatment for yourself and will be unable to accept these equality assumptions. The reason for your defection will be selfishness. There is nothing wrong with this position as long as you acknowledge it and can live with its consequences. Some people may view your defection as interfering with their own opportunity for a decent life. Living with how they express their disappointment at your defection may prove unsettling. Defecting may not be in your own long-term interest.

With your acceptance of these four assumptions, I shall

proceed. Human infants are totally dependent on those caring for them. Inadequate care precludes a child's proper development and realization of potential. If the "equal opportunity" you desire for them is to be more than an empty phrase, it must be practically backed by the continuing economic provisions necessary to meet the child's life support and higher needs. If the opportunities are to be "roughly equal" then these continuing economic provisions, i.e. income, must be roughly equal. How can it be otherwise? If you had an income typical of the poor quarter of humanity, could you really expect your child to have an opportunity equal that of a child born in the rich 15 % of humanity, where per capita income is 62 times as great?

Assumptions #3 and #4, with their emphasis on the continuing process of new human creation, are necessarily concerned with the future. So I assume your desire for "equal opportunity" is not arbitrarily limited to babies born next year, or in the next decade, but in general holds for infants born at any time in the future? You'd like to see a baby born tomorrow have an opportunity roughly equal to that which a baby today has, right?

To insure this, the economic provisions available for tomorrow's children must roughly equal today's. In a closed system with both renewable and finite resources, non-renewable resource usage must be limited so that some are left for future closed system era children. The closed system also dictates that wastes generated in meeting today's needs don't damage Earth's biosphere and impair ability to meet future needs. By necessity, this means limiting biosphere impacts to those which can be tolerated without long-term damage.

If you accept these arguments, you've logically arrived at a decision to co-operate on Ecosharing. If not, be sure you understand the reason behind your defection.

REBUTTAL TO CO-OPERATION ARGUMENT

Most people, I suspect, will rationally or irrationally opt for selfishness and escape the conclusion you force them to. Since most people haven't considered "the virtue of selfishness", your pompous comments seem designed to make them feel guilty. Shame on you!

V. BEFORE YOU VOTE / ECOSHARING OBJECTIVES

Our imagined exercise and subsequent discussion ties voting to co-operate to advocating roughly equivalent eco-

```
+-----------------------------------------------------------------+
|             FIG. #38  THE SHAKERTOWN PLEDGE[7]                   |
|                                                                 |
|   Recognizing that the Earth and the fulness thereof is         |
|   a gift from our gracious God, and that we are called          |
|   to cherish, nurture, and provide loving stewardship           |
|   for the Earth's resources; and recognizing that life          |
|   itself is a gift, and a call to responsibility, joy,          |
|   and celebration, I make the following declarations:           |
|                                                                 |
|   1) I declare myself to be a world citizen.                    |
|                                                                 |
|   2) I commit myself to lead an ecologically sound life.        |
|                                                                 |
|   3) I commit myself to lead a life of creative simpli-         |
|      city and to share my personal wealth with the              |
|      world's poor.                                              |
|                                                                 |
|   4) I commit myself to join with others in reshaping           |
|      institutions in order to bring about a more just           |
|      global society in which each person has full access        |
|      to the needed resources for their physical,                |
|      emotional, intellectual, and spiritual growth.             |
|                                                                 |
|   5) I commit myself to occupational accountability, and        |
|      in so doing I will seek to avoid the creation of           |
|      products which cause harm to others.                       |
|                                                                 |
|   6) I affirm the gift of my body, and commit myself to         |
|      its proper nourishment and physical well being.            |
|                                                                 |
|   7) I commit myself to examine continually my relations        |
|      with others, and to attempt to relate honestly,            |
|      morally, and lovingly to those around me.                  |
|                                                                 |
|   8) I commit myself to personal renewal through,               |
|      prayer, meditation, and study.                             |
|                                                                 |
|   9) I commit myself to responsible participation in a          |
|      community of faith.                                         |
|                                                                 |
+-----------------------------------------------------------------+
```

share allocation for all. While some see this as a worthy long-term goal, its short-term implementation is impractical. Initially, voting to co-operate should be equated with vowing to "control yourself". Individuals must use global vision to define this restraint in personally meaningful ways that can be practically implemented.

Preliminary to voting, education that helps to clearly distinguish choices is necessary. Before you vote, contrast defection and co-operation-based lifestyles and the global implications of your choice. In GRABBERS (Fig. #26) and here in Fig.#38, examples of ethical codes behind defection and co-operation are presented.

Subjective language in ethical codes leaves them open to one's interpretation of the behavior involved. For example, just as some Christians debate what is and isn't a sin, what's an "ecologically sound life" to one person, may not be to another. In formulating co-operation "rules to live by", some language must necessarily be left in subjective form, but some can be quantified or otherwise be made more precise. In this form, such guidelines enable people to readily assess their success or failure in following them. (This approach has limitations: much that is important in life is impossible to quantify or measure.)

Consider what co-operation means to me by examining the ethical code I have constructed. I envision co-operators governing their lives by the spirit of the Shakertown Pledge and the rigor of the Ecosharing objectives which follow.

These 13 objectives have been divided into three groups according to their emphasis. For a large number of people to live peacefully and happily on a sustained long-term basis, 1) sharing, 2) efficiency, and 3) responsible individual decision-making objectives are needed. Out of necessity, individual actions must be based on one's relationship to the larger body--whether it be household, community, or global village--rather than just self-interest.

The six sharing objectives are the foundation on which Ecosharing, a philosophy of moderation and enoughness, is based. They are summarized in Fig.#39--where each objective is concerned with regulating a certain variable.

VI. #1 FOOD, #2 WATER

DISCUSSION--OBJECTIVE #1

A basic minimum individual food share is not specified. Instead the specified minimum income and energy consumption should enable meeting minimal dietary calorie and protein intake requirements. To overcome inequalities in the world per capita dietary protein distribution, and promote efficient resource utilization, an "individual dietary protein

```
+------------------------------------------------------------------+
|            FIG. #39  THE SHARING OBJECTIVES                      |
|                                                                  |
|     In living my life on our fragile planet, in                  |
|  consideration of both my own rights and the rights of           |
|  others (including future generations and other species),        |
|  I feel entitled to the basic minimum value (where               |
|  specified) of each of the provisions below, but promise         |
|  to limit my share so that I don't exceed the specified          |
|  maximum value.                                                  |
```

	Provision	Units	Min.	Max.	Notes
#1	Food	protein impact index	--	$F_o=10$	APPENDIX A FIG. #40
#2	Water	gallons/day	5	$W_o=50$	household water[8]
#3	Income	U.S. \$/year	$I_o/4$	$10{\times}I_o/4$	I_o = ave. annual world per capita income
#4	Land	acres/person	--	$L_o=6.1$	
#5	Children	# per couple	1	2	
#6	Energy	MBTU/year	$E_o/3$	$10{\times}E_o/3$	E_o = ave. annual world per capita permitted energy use see text, APPENDIX C

```
+------------------------------------------------------------------+
```

impact index" F has been invented and a limiting maximum value for this index F_o established. In determining F, three factors are considered: 1) how much useable protein is yielded by a given land area devoted to this type of food production, 2) the fossil fuel energy required to produce a given

amount of protein, and 3) the amount of grain fed to animals
to produce a given amount of protein. Clearly maximizing
protein yield/acre, while minimizing fossil fuel usage and
grain fed to animals, would be desirable shifts in world food
production.

F can loosely be thought of as a measure of how high on
the food chain one is eating. To determine its value, an
individual estimates the extent to which various protein
sources contribute to his or her protein intake. Using the
various protein source impact indices in Fig. #40, a weighted
average calculation can compute F (APPENDIX A).

FIG. #40 PROTEIN IMPACT INDEX[9,10]

Food Item	Useable Protein/Acre (Soybeans=1)	Fossil Fuel Energy (Cal/ Cal-protein)	lbs.grain to lbs.protein	Indiv. Impact Index
feedlot beef	17.8	78	16	37
milk/cheese	4.3	36	(1)	14
pork	(6)	35	(6)	16
beef-average	15.9	56	(12)	30
broilers	(3)	22	3	11
eggs	4.6	13	3	7
range beef	(8)	10	NA	9
corn	1.7	3.6	1	2.1
wheat	2.6	3.4	1	2.3
beans/legumes	1.9	3.4	1	2.1
rice	1.3	(4.5)	1	2.3
soybeans	1	2.0	1	1.3
fish-fert.pond	(7.7)	NA	1	4.3
fish-grain fed & supplement	(3.1)	NA	1.7	2.4

Note: numbers in parentheses are estimates;
NA=not available or not applicable

In Fig. #40, note a protein source's impact index is an
average of each number in columns #2, #3, and #4. Protein
yield/ acre is relative to soybeans, which at 356 lbs. of
useable protein per acre is the most protein efficient way to
use land. Feedlot cattle supported by grain grown on 17.8
acres would produce the same useable protein as one acre of

soybeans. Similarly, to produce a calorie of protein in the form of feedlot meat requires 78 calories of fossil fuel energy inputs. Every pound of meat produced in this manner requires 16 pounds of grain as feed. Averaging these three values for feedlot beef yields the protein impact index of column #5, i.e. 37.

The limiting value of F, $F_0 = 10$, was arrived at by establishing limits for the three individual components (APPENDIX A). Clearly an exclusive feedlot beef diet would exceed this permissible limit. In general, exceeding F_0 means one's diet is supporting an inefficient utilization of land, excessive fossil fuel subsidies, and excessive protein loss in intermediate plant to animal food chain conversion steps.

Although not included in Fig. #40, consumption of fish (non-fish farm) and wild game should be limited to levels that will insure sustained yields. Since such fishing yields a worldwide average of 31 lbs. (live weight) per capita per year, and in many areas (for many species) overfishing is a problem, wild fish consumption should not exceed this amount. The fish in Fig. #40 refer to aquaculture--not wild fish. These now compose 12 % of all fish eaten.

The numbers in Fig. #40 are applicable to American con-sumers--but clearly the particular values depend on the exact circumstances of food production. Adjusting these numbers to fit individual situations may be needed.

DISCUSSION--OBJECTIVE #2

Water consumption per person ranges from extremes of but 1.25 gal/day in Madagascar to over 130 gal/day among the af-fluent. While the lower extreme barely meets metabolic re-quirements, the upper extreme reflects enormous waste. This objective adopts upper and lower per capita household water usage limits within these extremes. Meeting the maximum value $W_0 = 50$ gallons/day per person will require the installa-tion of water efficient appliances--including water-conserv-ing toilets, flow restrictors, more efficient dishwashers, washing machines, etc. in many U.S. households. These im-provements, which should pay for themselves in a few months to four years time through lower water, sewer, and energy bills, should reduce American household water usage by 1/3. In areas with long-term water deficits, or in times of drought, using the indicated maximum amount may be excessive.

VII. #3 INCOME, #4 LAND, #5 CHILDREN

DISCUSSION--OBJECTIVE #3

World data on individual incomes is very poor. In estimating a nation's per capita income, the $ GNP per capita is typically used. But national income and GNP are not the same. (GNP less capital consumption allowance, less indirect business taxes, less statistical discrepancies equals national income.) For the U.S., national income typically equals 5/6 of GNP. We assume this relationship holds throughout the world--clearly an off the wall assumption but data is lacking to do much better!

As 1990 began, the value of I_0, the world per capita annual average income, was around $3000 in current U.S. dollars. Thus a family of four would be limited to an annual income of $10/4 \times 4$ people $\times \$3000$/person $= \$30,000$ if they sought to comply with this objective.

Living within this income constraint may be difficult for some Americans. Initially, it may be impossible for households of one or two members in urban areas due to high housing costs. In a rural setting--or as part of an extended family/larger household, abiding by it will be much easier. As to the monetary mechanics of attaining the desired income limit, households which otherwise would earn far more will either: 1) have certain household members relinquish their paying jobs or cut back the hours they work , or 2) give their excess earnings to those in need. Households lacking the means of reaching the $1/4 \times I_0$ minimum income would be logical recipients of either vacated jobs or excess income. In return for any monetary transfers, recipients would be expected to engage in "sweat equity"--such as child care, work for volunteer organizations, in subsistence agriculture, or other activities which benefit society.

This objective specifies an upper to lower permissible income ratio of ten. Guaranteed minimum and (especially!) an upper limit on income are anathema to those embracing "The Expansionist Worldview" (theme # 22)--including most economists. Herman Daly is one of the few prominent economists who endorses such limits. Integrating something similar to "Sustainable Worldview" (theme #23) into his worldview, Daly advocates a steady state economy. He writes[11]

> The idea of minimum and maximum limits on income is not
> central to my definition of the steady state. But it's
> important in the interest of justice, and I think it's
> essential to community. Community really can not

tolerate unlimited inequality. And without justice and
community there can be no steady state economy.
...Plato thought that the richest citizens ought to be
four times as wealthy as the poorest. I don't know where
he got that number; I would suggest maybe 10 times.
Where do I get that number? Well, there is some
empirical evidence for it. In the civil service, the
ratio of the highest level to the lowest is about 10 to
one. Same in the military. Same in the university.

Daly's comments refer to the U.S. economic scene. At least
one not so small U.S. corporation--Ben & Jerry's Homemade,
Inc.--with 1988 ice cream sales of $45 million, already has
adopted maximum and minimum income limitations.

DISCUSSION--OBJECTIVE #4

Figuring an ethical upper limit on individual land
ownership is straightforward. The planet's total land surface
area--excluding oceans but including ice-covered polar re-
gions--is 32 billion acres. Simply dividing this number by
the world population gives L_0. Currently L_0=6.1 acres/person,
a value which will decrease as population grows. Where more
land is needed for agricultural operations, the smaller holdings of many workers can be combined to create larger tracts.

DISCUSSION--OBJECTIVE #5

By limiting the numbers of new human beings, that an
individual has joined with a partner in conceiving and that
have, or are expected to, become adult individuals, future
resources and biosphere impacts can be regulated. Some, most
notably in the Chinese government, feel this number should be
one, not two. Indeed, where population pressures are great, a
family's having two children may be excessive.

VIII. #6 ENERGY
DISCUSSION--OBJECTIVE #6

Generally speaking, an individual will perturb the biosphere from its natural condition in direct proportion to his
or her energy use. These impacts will generally be greater
for non-renewable energy use--which causes air, water,
thermal and radiation pollution problems and is linked to the
atmospheric buildup of carbon dioxide and acid rain.

While renewable energy use is both sustainable and has
fewer impacts than non-renewable energy, where such energy is
concentrated there can nevertheless be problems. Large hydro-

electric dams and square miles of solar collector arrays clearly disrupt river and desert ecosystems in numerous ways.

Resource depletion and biosphere impact problems can be minimized by employing small, renewable decentralized power. This strategy, with its rooftop solar collectors, wood stoves, small wind and hydro electricity generators--in conjunction with passive solar architecture and energy conservation--is the "soft energy path".

In assessing energy use impact (because of measurement difficulties and in view of their relatively benign nature), an individual's small, decentralized renewable energy use will not be counted. The calculation of the individual energy impact index E has two parts. First, E_H, which specifies average annual household energy use per person (including transportation) is figured, and second E_N, which denotes an individual's indirect share of the nation's average annual non-household energy use. E_H can be found exactly--usually from utility bills or other records of fuel used. E_N will be estimated, using relative income and energy usage to gauge the extent of participation in the non-household sectors of the national energy economy. E is found by adding E_H and E_N; the units of all three variables are MBTU/person per year (1 MBTU =one million BTUs) (see APPENDIX C).

Both upper and lower individual energy impact limits are specified in terms of E_0, the worldwide per capita annual permitted energy use, in MBTU/person-year. Because the current level of global fossil fuel burning (264 quadrillion BTUs/year = 50 MBTU/person-year) results in excessive carbon (5.7 billion tons/year) and sulfur (over 100 million tons /year) emissions and greenhouse / acid rain concerns, in setting E_0, fossil fuel energy use must be reduced. EPA findings suggest that a 50 % reduction in such energy use, along with technical fixes, can reduce global carbon emissions to 2 billion tons / year. At this rate, it's believed atmospheric carbon dioxide levels will stabilize at current levels. Renewable energy use will not be restricted but steps must be taken to insure biomass energy utilization is truly sustainable. Current global renewable energy use is around 15 MBTU/ person-year.[12]

We find E_0 by summing the permitted per person global fossil fuel burning--132 quadrillion BTUs/year divided by the world's population in billions--and the average renewable energy use per person. Currently, E_0 = 25 + 15 = 40 MBTU /

person-year. Unless the growth rate for per capita renewable energy use exceeds the population growth rate, E_0 will fall.

What is the minimum energy usage needed for a satisfactory human life? Around 4 MBTU/person-year is required in the form of food to satisfy basic human metabolic needs. Village agrarian draft animal farming-based lifestyles require 15 to 20 MBTU/person-year. On the high end, energy efficient Japan uses energy at a 130 MBTU/ person-year rate. Note the U.S. figure of 328 MBTU/person-year implies each person employs 82 "energy slaves".

Upper and lower limits are set within these extremes by applying (as for income constraints) factors to E_0. Meeting the 130 MBTU/person-year upper limit constraint of objective #6 will necessitate American lifestyle changes and an energy-efficient restructuring of the economy.

Since part of this index is pegged to income, following the dictates of objective #3 will be an important step toward compliance. Complying individuals will have found energy-efficient and renewable energy-based solutions to household and transportation energy needs. Due to availability of mass transit in urban areas, city dwellers may have an advantage over rural people in minimizing transportation energy use. Climate and availability of solar, wood, or other renewable resources are variables which will affect the feasibility of individuals abiding by objective #6.

IX. EQUITY VS. EFFICIENCY TRADEOFFS

Two of the six sharing objectives, those regulating income and energy, are especially important. Their constraints designate economic/environmental impact middle-ground where the bulk of the world's population should be operating.

Despite these sharing constraints, much economic growth is still possible. However, with total centralized, non-renewable energy use held at current levels, such growth will have to come from efficiency gains and renewable energy.

The sharing objectives can be thought of in terms of equity and the practical lifestyle guidelines they suggest, i.e. the next three objectives, in terms of efficiency. Finding acceptable equity vs. efficiency tradeoffs is a very real part of societal problem solving. As Harvard scholar Daniel Bell notes,[13]

> The question of equity and efficiency is the problem of
> balance between the "economizing mode" of the

society--the doctrine of productivity, or the effort to
achieve increased output at lesser cost--and the social
criteria of non-economic values. In another sense, it is
also the question of balance between present and
future: how much does the present generation have to
forego (in consumption) to insure a higher rate of
capital stock for future generations? And conversely,
how much of the exhaustible resources can the present
generation use up at the expense of the next generations?

The Ecosharing objectives involve sharing between current and
future peoples in such a way that 1) the overall suffering of
humanity is minimized; 2) the integrity of the Earth's biosphere is maintained indefinitely.

While the discussion of the first six objectives has
clearly involved the "economizing mode", equity considerations have been paramount. Before considering the efficiency
objectives, note the classification of the 13 objectives into
three categories is not a perfect one. Objectives placed in
one category may have aspects relevant to another.

X. THE EFFICIENCY OBJECTIVES: #7, #8, AND #9

The three efficiency objectives are shown in Fig. #41.

DISCUSSION--OBJECTIVE #7

This objective and objective #1 are related. Together,
they provide a means for globally maximizing long-term
individual health and well being while minimizing monetary
outlay for food and medical services. Besides its sharing
ethical component, eating lower on the food chain will generally be less expensive and, assuming one learns how to
obtain adequate protein from plant sources, more nutritious
than meat centered diets.

The seven components of "America's Experimental Diet"
can be thought of as poor health traps to avoid. Certainly
this experimental diet is different from the diet that
millions of years of evolutionary development designed the
human body to handle. The human mouth, teeth, and digestive
tract are similar to those of vegetable and fruit-eating
mammals and relatively unlike those of carnivores.

Certainly modern Americans, with some 80 plus "energy
slaves" working for them, get little exercise when compared
to their nomadic, pre-historic counterparts. Given this last
trap, the energy limitations imposed by objective #6 can be

seen as contributing to good health. Those using far less
household and transportation energy, generally get more
exercise from walking, bicycling, chopping wood, gardening,
washing and drying clothes the old-fashioned way, and many

```
+-------------------------------------------------------------+
|            FIG. #41  THE EFFICIENCY OBJECTIVES              |
|                                                             |
|                      Objective #7                           |
|   In recognizing the need for my body's proper nourishment  |
|   and maintenance, I will avoid the dangerous excesses      |
|   of "America's Experimental Diet"14:                       |
|       1) Too much total fat and cholesterol from animal-    |
|          based foods                                        |
|       2) Too much sugar                                     |
|       3) Too much salt                                      |
|       4) Too little fiber                                   |
|       5) Too much alcohol                                   |
|       6) Too many food additive, antibiotic, and           |
|          pesticide residues                                 |
|       7) Too many calories and not enough exercise          |
|                                                             |
|                                                             |
|                      Objective #8                           |
|   I will construct my solutions to the everyday problems    |
|   involved in meeting individual, household, and community  |
|   needs, on a foundation of rational methodology,           |
|   creative simplicity, the spirit of co-operation,          |
|   functionality, and soft technology.                       |
|                                                             |
|                                                             |
|                      Objective #9                           |
|   I will not attempt to have something today unless I       |
|   can do so without contracting a monetary or ecological    |
|   debt against tomorrow.                                    |
+-------------------------------------------------------------+
```

other chores. A simple, low on the food chain diet will also
have less biosphere impact--using less fossil fuel energy,
water, and topsoil--than a more typically American diet.

DISCUSSION--OBJECTIVE #8

To clarify the rather subjective wording of this
objective, some problem solving dos and don'ts are presented.
The best solutions will be those which:
1) are based on the real process of sizing up the problem,
collecting relevant information and resources, formulating,
testing, and refining various solutions, and then finalizing

a best solution. This approach is preferable to irrational
reliance on convention, authority, peer pressure, or the
advice of pushers--whose motives seldom involve your welfare,
2) optimize real quality of life benefits while minimizing
long-term biosphere and resource impacts and monetary costs,
3) solve two or more problems simultaneously or recycle the
liabilities of wastes or discards into useful assets,
4) involve mutually advantageous labor trades or barter
between individuals, if a "do it yourself" prescription is
not appropriate,
5) are entirely functional and unconcerned with superficial
appearances, pleasing outsider's tastes, fashion or status,
6) and employ "soft", appropriate technologies, rather than
"hard", polluting, corporate-controlled ones.

DISCUSSION--OBJECTIVE #9

This third and final efficiency objective is seemingly
set squarely in the "economizing mode", yet it too has a
sharing aspect. At first glance, it simply advises against
credit cards, buying on the installment plan, home mortgages,
and budget deficits. While many view this position as dangerously radical, it is actually highly conservative since it
embraces abstinence and saving, major components of the old
Protestant work ethic.

At the household level, this objective insures that
limited income will pay for real goods or productive labor--
not the interest charges of capitalists living on the sweat
and toil of others. Such a monetary policy can be critically
important to a household economy since 50 to 70 % of the
money ultimately spent in buying a typical American home will
go for interest charges. In "household ecology" terms, this
objective has personal or family health ramifications. Dietary practices or jobs which provide short-term pleasures or
monetary benefits, but carry long-term health hazards are to
be avoided. The policy of continual maintenance of the infrastructure of the household economy--whether it involves
interpersonal relationships, health, education, soil fertility, water quality, shelter or vehicle repairs--will maximize
long-term household quality of living.

XI. DECISION-MAKING OBJECTIVES #10-#13

While human society has become incredibly complex and
seldom amenable to black and white characterizations, the

individual decision to buy, make, or do something ultimately
is one of choosing between "yes" and "no". Human history is
the aggregate of quadrillions of individual "yeses" and
"nos". Unfortunately, with nuclear weapons poised for mass
destruction, civilization could abruptly end after but a few
mouths say "yes" to war and "no" to peace. Assuming humanity
can avert nuclear disaster, an "aggregate yes/no mix" that
will minimize suffering and result in a sustainable society--
not "overshoot and collapse"--must be found. The need for
responsible decision-making has never been greater.

If humanity is to trade childish, environmentally reck-
less behavior that perpetuates injustices for a sustainable,
just society, a co-operation movement must be built. To insure that co-operators are not successfully co-opted or in-
vaded by the defector message, decision-making guidelines are
needed. These appear in Fig. #42. A look at these objectives
underscores the ultimate foundation for a sustainable society: a continuing affirmation of co-operation, both in individual decisions and in feedback given to others.

DISCUSSION--OBJECTIVES #10 - #13

Objectives #10 and #11 prohibit a co-operator's production or consumption of products which are 1) dangerous to
workers producing them or consumers using them, 2) not really
needed, and 3) associated with improper disposal of dangerous
waste byproducts. Before such decisions can be made, individuals need accurate background information from people whose
own self-interest does not distort what they furnish. Eventually, in a "global co-operative economy", where the producers and consumers have the same interests, applying these
objectives will be considerably simplified.

The questions in objective #12 are important. They demand "thinking globally before acting locally" and also encourage practicing a variation of the Golden Rule with all
humans: "I will/wouldn't do this because I would/wouldn't
want everyone else to do it."

Objective #13 announces that policy of co-operation will
not be unconditional. Defectors will be pressured with confrontations, demonstrations, and boycotts if they persist in
defection. When they begin co-operating, the societal pressure will cease. The need for such reciprocal treatment is
one lesson from Prisoner's Dilemma game theory (LIBERALS).
By tempering their co-operation with this negative feedback,
co-operators are adopting a program reminiscent of the TIT

for TAT strategy.

+---+
| FIG. #42 THE RESPONSIBLE DECISION-MAKING OBJECTIVES |
| |
| Objective #10 |
| In my role as a producer of goods or services, or in my |
| employment by others to do this, I will not take part |
| in production activities which can harm people or cause |
| unnecessary resource depletion and biosphere impacts. |
| |
| Objective #11 |
| In my role as a consumer of goods and services, I will |
| boycott those producers whose activities can harm people |
| or cause unnecessary resource depletion and biosphere |
| impacts. |
| |
| Objective #12 |
| As a basis for determining what not to take part in |
| producing or what goods and services to boycott, I will |
| ask myself two questions: 1) Is this part of the |
| solution--keeping in mind the best solutions as in |
| Objective #8--or part of the problem? 2) What would |
| happen if all human beings were to make the same |
| production or consumption decision? (note application |
| of the Principle of Universality) |
| |
| Objective #13 |
| While my participation in human economy will be based on |
| co-operation, I will not idly stand by while activities |
| of other producers and consumers cause misery, waste |
| resources and the biosphere. Instead, I will provide |
| these defectors with feedback on how I view their |
| actions. Where possible, I will join others in pressur- |
| ing these individuals and institutions to change their |
| behavior. |
+---+

XII. MORE GOOD NEWS

Objectives #8 and #12 provide a foundation for an eco-logical approach to problem-solving. Out of such an approach comes more good news--as Donella Meadows observes in the following article.

Problems Interconnected--So Are Solutions, by Donella Meadows

One of the favorite maxims of environmentalists is that
Everything is Connected to Everything Else. That idea is
usually delivered with a heavy charge of negativity--if you
do something stupid in one place, it will lead to bigger
problems somewhere else, or horrible disasters sometime in
the future. Your ecological misdemeanors will come back to
haunt you.

Environmentalists like to collect examples of Awful
Interconnections, some of which you've surely heard:

Buy a fast-food hamburger and you will create a demand
for cheap beef, which will be produced in Central American
pastures, which will be created by chopping down tropical
forests, which are the wintering grounds of the songbirds
that glorify your summer and eat your mosquitoes. You will
also contribute to poverty in Central America, which will
encourage communist movements, which will have to be opposed,
which will require constant funding from Congress, which will
necessitate frequent speeches from the President, interrupt-
ing your favorite prime-time TV programs.

Build a dam on a river and you will stop the annual
flood of nutrients that fertilizes the downstream soil; you
will reduce the source of food for the fish populations in
the estuary, thereby bankrupting the fishing fleet; your
reservoir will flood historic monuments, prime topsoils, and
endangered species; you will so alter groundwater levels that
harmful metals will be leached out of the soil and become
lodged in the bones of your children.

Buy a fast food hamburger packed in a foam-plastic
container (hamburgers are sources of many ecological disaster
stories), and you will release chlorofluorocarbons that will
wipe out the ozone layer, thereby allowing the sun's ultraviolet rays to penetrate, thereby frying most terrestrial
forms of life. If the hamburger is wrapped not in foam but in
paper and cardboard, you will contribute to the destruction
of northern forests, which are slowly dying anyway from acid
rain from the coal-fired electric plants needed for the ugly
roadside signs that attracted you to the hamburger joint in
the first place!

The way it is usually told, the message Everything is
Connected to Everything Else is not fun to hear. It is
intended to cause repentance and reformation. More often, of
course, it causes guilt, fear, and an uncontrollable urge to

avoid environmentalists.

What we are rarely told is that solutions are as inter-connected as problems. One good environmental action can send us waves of good effects as impressive as the chain of disasters that results from environmental evil.

Take energy efficiency, for example. That doesn't mean deprivation of creature comforts; it means insulating houses, driving cars with better mileage, and plugging in appliances that deliver the same service for less electricity. Amory Lovins of the Rocky Mountain Institute says we could reduce electricity use by 70 % with already-proven and currently-economic efficiency measures. We could cut our $430 billion annual energy bill in half just by being as efficient as Japan and West Germany are.

Energy efficiency is a solution to economic problems--it cuts costs to homes, businesses and government. But look at all the other problems it solves. It could allow us to shut down every nuclear power plant in the country, eliminating the need for heroic financing, political hassle, evacuation planning, the disposal of undisposable wastes, and the bureaucracy of the Nuclear Regulatory Commission. It could free us from dependence on Persian Gulf oil and from involve-ment in Persian Gulf wars. It would do wonders for our trade and budget deficits. It would improve the air quality of our cities and go a long way toward solving the problems of acid rain and global climate change.

Recycling is another favorite environmental solution--a solution to the problem of where to put the garbage. It also reduces groundwater contamination from leaking landfills and air pollution from incinerators. It provides paper, metals, glass, plastics, rubber, oils and other raw materials for a host of businesses. It slows the depletion of forests and mines, and reduces pollution from smelters, oil refineries, paper mills, and plastics factories. It saves a lot of ener-gy, and therefore contributes to all the good interconnec-tions listed in the previous paragraph.

Organic farming, practiced successfully by tens of thousands of farmers in this country, can cut a farmer's costs, helping to save the family farm and reducing the need for billions of dollars of farm subsidy. The use of fewer hazardous chemicals improves the health of farm workers and animals, reduces contamination of groundwater and lakes, restores wildlife populations, and eliminates the need for *polluting chemical factories. It saves energy (half the energy used for agriculture goes into the manufacture of fertilizer). Returning organic wastes to the land reduces soil erosion, improves water retention, slows siltation by downstream reservoirs, and reduces urban garbage.*

Many of these environmental solutions are considered "uneconomical", but that is because the economics have been figured only for most short-term and close-in links of the chains. If we calculated the effects on the whole system, we'd see that the wages of environmental sin may be deadly, but the wages of environmental good sense can be enormous.

Everything is connected to everything else on this planet. That can be good news as well as bad.

Questions & Projects

1. Answer the initial "Questions About the Human Future". Relate responses to components of your worldview.
2. Classical liberals in America won't like the imagined co-operate / defect on Ecosharing voting exercise involving all humans. Why not? (see LIBERALS)
3. Media magnate and Better World Society founder Ted Turner's counterpart to The Ecosharing Objectives are his "Ten Voluntary Initiatives". Report on this and other examples of environmental ethical codes.
4. As 1990 began, a) U.S. gasoline prices were 1/4 to 1/2 those in Europe, and b) Japan was buying old growth trees from the Tongass National Forest in Alaska for $1 to $2 per tree. Discuss and provide similar examples.
5. That the critical parameters of the Ecosharing Objectives vary with conditions underscores their utilitarian nature. Moralistic approaches involve absolute, rigidly fixed laws. Discuss.
6. Using the example of APPENDIX A to guide you, calculate your dietary protein impact index F based on a typical day's meals. How high on the food chain are you eating?
7. Compare the value of F listed in Fig. #40 with the real value for a) garbage, table scrap fed backyard chickens, b) Chinese pigs subsisting on cotton leaves, corn stalks, rice husks, water hyacinths, and peanut hulls.
8. "Caps on income destroy what is perhaps the strongest feature of the free enterprise system: the powerful motivation that dreams of wealth provide." Discuss.
9. Ben & Jerry's Homemade Inc.'s director of retail

operations dislikes the company's five to one income ratio and $84,240 salary cap. "I'm materialistic...I'm an expert at what I do. I've trained for years...I don't think the five to one ratio recognizes that." Discuss.

10. Walmart founder and largest stockholder Sam Walton (and his family) are worth $14 billion. George Gilder argues that because Walton's real wealth resides in intangibles like his marketing prowess, his company's reputation for constant growth, and his workers' loyalty, that he is "essentially powerless to redistribute his wealth". A co-operative economist says nonsense and suggests Walton turn his stock over to his 270,000 employees. Discuss.

11. Avis is one major U.S. corporation owned by its employees. Find other examples and report on the viability of this arrangement.

12. Should laws limit couples in overpopulated countries to one or two children? Discuss in light of the Chinese experience. Should similar restrictions apply to affluent population stabilized countries? How does one's worldview influence responses? Discuss.

13. Report on significant differences in energy efficiency between the U.S. and Japanese economies.

14. Solid state compact fluorescent light bulbs typically produce the same light output as incandescent bulbs, but use only 1/4 the electricity. Obtain data on initial costs & lifetimes of both bulbs, and your $/KWH electricity cost. Then survey your home or school building and compute long-term monetary and energy savings that could be realized by switching to more efficient lighting.

15. Suppose you had to abide by the Ecosharing objectives, how would your career plans or current lifestyle change? What does that tell you? Discuss.

16. Should an Ecosharing ethic (roughly equal ecoshares for all) be a long-term goal for humanity? Discuss.

17. A developing country's leader responds to U.S. pleas for a halt to his government's subsidy of deforestation with, "You've already cut your virgin timber and become rich. What right do you have to tell us we can't do likewise?" Answer his question from a global citizen viewpoint. Is this more effective than answering as a U.S. citizen?

18. Provide examples supporting the following. "The more removed (either in time or distance) the consequences of a decision are, the less importance we are likely to

attach to them."
19. Following Donella Meadows' examples, construct a wave of good resulting from people shifting from meat-based to vegetarian / low-on-the-food chain diets.

Notes

1. Davis, W.J. The Seventh Year: Industrial Civilization in Transition , Norton, NY 1979.
2. Gilder, G. "Tied to the Masts of Their Fortunes", Forbes , October 24, 1988.
3. Henderson, H., Politics of the Solar Age , Anchor / Doubleday, NY 1981.
4. Crutchfield, R. op cit.
5. Gilder op cit.
6. address: 11 Upper Grosvenor St., London, England.
7. from Finnerty, A. D. No More Plastic Jesus , Orbis Books, New York 1977 (in paperbook, E.P. Dutton, New York 1978) Appendix A of Finnerty's book defines "What It Would Mean To Take The Shakertown Pledge" and Appendix B answers commonly asked questions about it. The Pledge grew out of a 1973 meeting of religious program directors at a restored Shaker village in Kentucky. Grassroots efforts publicizing The Pledge, and encouraging people to govern their lives by its message, contributed to the voluntary simplicity movement that swept America in the later 1970s. While familiar with The Pledge, the author discovered Finnerty's book only as he finished writing this book. This book's Ecosharing Objectives nicely pick up where Finnerty left off in his "Toward a Just World Standard of Living" chapter.
8. includes toilet flushing, bathing, laundry and dish washing, drinking, cooking, personal hygiene, etc.
9. based on work by David Pimenthal--see his book Food, Energy, and Future Society and "Energy and Land Constraints in Food Protein Production", Science , November 21, 1975
10. Moore-Lappe, F. Diet for a Small Planet, Ballantine, NY, 1982.
11. from New Options , November 30, 1987
12. Energy data in this paragraph based on UN Energy Statistics Yearbook, and State of the World 1990
13. Bell, op cit.
14. Moore-Lappe, op cit.

DREAMS

I. FUTURES #1 & #2 : SENIOR CITIZENS OF 2089

In this chapter we look at several future worlds and scenarios (numbered for discussion purposes). We begin with Donella Meadows' jump 100 years into the future--where two possible future worlds are contrasted.

Senior Citizens of 2089, by Donella Meadows

Ann Landers ran a tribute recently to today's senior citizens, who have survived a lifetime of change.

She pointed out that they were here before the Pill, penicillin, plastic, and pantyhose, before television, Xerox, ball point pens. Before tape recorders, much less CD players, before the 40-hour week, co-ed dormitories, computers. They have gone through a lot. They have adjusted to great trans-formations.

Peggy Streit, the editor of "World Development Forum" was prompted by that tribute to think about the senior citizens 100 years from now. What changes will they witness? Her imaginings were not cheerful:

* FUTURE #1 *

"They will be the ones who were here before the seas rose to flood coastal plains around the world; before the Panama Canal was silted up; before the headwaters of the Nile became a trickle; before the AIDS epidemic decimated cities on three continents.

"They were around when the Amazon forests were something you could visit rather than read about in history books; when venturesome travelers could still see gorillas, elephants, sea turtles, and bald eagles; when only a handful of lakes had gone lifeless; when sunbathing was fashionable and not fatal; when Los Angeles was a megalopolis with swimming pools, irrigated lawns, and free drinking water.

"They will remember when the USA and USSR--then called superpowers--still thought the name of the global game was ideology, not ecology.

"Those senior citizens, if they are not extinguished in a nuclear winter, may have to be an even hardier bunch than their ancestors of 1989. Unless, that is, nations heed their scientists and begin soon a massive, concerted effort to save their fragile planet."

That vision of a dismal future is a common one these days, and understandably so. An ecologically deranged Earth is at the end of the path our current world is hotly pursuing. The reason for describing it, as Peggy Streit has done, is to try to whip up some political will, some intention NOT to travel in that direction.

The trouble with such descriptions, though, is that they may stimulate not will but denial. They only point out the way NOT to go. Political will is more readily summoned for a way forward to a desirable future. We need to imagine not only a desolated world 100 years from now, but also one that has achieved sustainability, peace, and justice.

So here's the beginning of another possible tribute to the senior citizens of 2089. I invite you to add to it.

* FUTURE #2 *

The elders of 2089 were here before the cities were regreened, when the streets were still unsafe and when people choked on pollution. They themselves helped to reclaim waste spaces, build up topsoil, and plant trees. They witnessed the harnessing of solar energy and the phasing out of polluting machines powered by coal, oil, and nuclear reactions.

They can remember when people actually tried to control pests by spraying poisons over the whole countryside. They helped pioneer the agricultural revolution that produced high yields using elegant natural controls instead of toxic chemicals.

They think back with disbelief on the times of their parents, when people tossed away mountains of paper, metal, and plastic and then went to great expense to wrest more from the soils and rocks of the earth. They remember learning how to recycle; some of them were enriched by investing early in the great materials recycling industry.

They were the first generation to think of the societal implications when they chose the number of children they would have--and they had two at most. They were also the first generation with whom society worked wholeheartedly to assure the sustenance, the health care, and the first class education of every one of their children.

These elders saw with their own eyes the teams of tree-planters reclaiming the deserts and reversing the greenhouse effect. They saw the Amazon forests regenerate and streams everywhere begin to flow clear. They remember the news reports when, one by one, the populations of gorillas, elephants, bald eagles began to rise again.

They are the last generation to have experienced what it

*was like when much of the human race was hungry and desperate
--when great areas of the world were poor, oppressed and angry. They are profoundly grateful that they can now travel
anywhere and find sufficiency, stability, warmth,and welcome.
They remember living under the terrifying shadow of
nuclear war. They also remember the historic day when the
last nuclear weapons were dismantled and people everywhere
turned out in the greatest celebration the world has ever
seen. They love to tell stories of that day. They say their
lives have been great, but that was the greatest day of all.*

II. FUTURE #3 -- AMERICA

Describing imagined future human utopias is not as difficult as creating a reasonable scenario detailing how that
world comes about. The future that follows builds on Meadows'
Future #2--filling in gaps and imagining "how-it-happened".

* FUTURE #3 *

As Americans increasingly perceive the morally, economically, and environmentally bankrupt condition of their
land, public outrage with the Grabber politicians grows.
Shortly before the turn of the century--after massive voter
registration drives--they "throw the rascals out".

Perhaps what triggered a legislative response from the
new Administration was the report of a presidential commission on "Restoring American Economic and Environmental
Health--With Justice for All". The task force majority summary concludes, "Most American businesses avoid long-term
projects and planning. They have learned the market undervalues this and have seen firms with short-term profit-
seeking orientations prosper. America does not prosper from
this stance. The rewarding of these corporations--along with
environmentally and socially irresponsible ones--must halt."

The task force minority report echoes this sentiment and
calls for Green Tax legislation. The tax would cover hidden
environmental costs and make prices reflect "true costs". One
member even argues for maximum and minimum income limits
legislation. Under public pressure, the nation's media are
forced into discussions of this long taboo subject.

Spurred by passage of The Corporate Responsibility Act,
a grassroots effort to legislate a new, balanced media viewpoint arises. Behind the movement are millions of Americans
who still believe in fair play and "telling it like it is",
including schoolteachers and religious leaders. The latter

seek to balance network portrayal of unethical, violent lifestyles with glimpses of "other-oriented" actions. The effort culminates with passage of The Media Education / Fairness Act. This promises to both revolutionize education and counter the shaping of Americans into consumerists.

Among other things, the legislation requires networks to provide at least six hours/day of educational programming. Whereas 1980s TV programs were cut from the Lifestyles of the Rich and Famous, Wheel of Fortune, Dynasty, Dallas , conspicuous consumption / mindless comedy/ sex / violence mold, the new century brings much different offerings. Three especially popular programs are Fighting for Nature, Lifestyles for a Sustainable World, and Sister Cities.

Fighting for Nature features dramatizations of the real life struggles to protect the integrity of the natural environment. Lifestyles shows healthy alternatives to a corporate existence. The program depicts people during more with less. Many watch it because the simple lives portrayed are rich in human relationships. To the millions of "prisoners" caught up in dead-end jobs and "the pursuit of loneliness", the freedom they see on the screen is captivating. Sister Cities--based on a movement to pair and transfer aid from "haves" to "have-nots"--documents cultures interacting to help each other.

As the 21st century begins, America is changing in ways that promote face-to-face, humanized interactions. The media re-orientation and growing feelings of belonging to a community are transforming the nation. Money is now less important; family, friends, helping, and learning, more important.

Eventually, after American heads saturate with "fair play as part of a team" as they once were with "going after the big bucks", legislation is passed to cap personal income and energy use. This is somewhat anti-climactic, as a majority already abides by the legislated constraints. While those who create wealth that benefits everyone are looked up to, enormous societal pressures fall on money-grabbing law breakers indulging in lavish excesses.

Growing renewable energy utilization and preventive medicine / ecological consciousness culminates with Green Tax legislation. America becomes a healthier place to live. With personal income capped, everyone's money goes farther because there are few "ripoffs". Time formerly spent making money is now freed up. Children are getting more attention. Education is now a life-long pursuit for many. With shorter work weeks and democratic workplaces, work-induced stress is declining.

American institutions have been transformed. At many corporations, owners and workers are the same people. As the meaning of national security changes, the military helps with environmental cleanup of federal facilities and repairing highway and public services infrastructure. Utility companies have become energy-efficiency promoters. Engineering is flourishing, as American "ingenuity"--freed from creating consumer demand or planned obsolescence--is now working at "doing more with less". After decades of decline, family farms are coming back, as sustainable agriculture replaces petro-chemical based agribusiness operations.

III. FUTURE #3 -- THE WORLD

The new leadership in Washington--citing friendly relations with the Soviet Union--reduces the armed forces and massively cuts weapons outlays. Yet, recognizing new threats, national security expenditures remain near former levels. The threats are Third World poverty, ecological decline and hopelessness. U.S. leaders meet these threats with a good neighbor orientation and begin cultivating world community.

A near panic atmosphere precedes an important first step. Working through the UN and in conjunction with international monetary organizations, the U.S. helps resolve the Third World debt crisis and avert a collapse of the global financial system. An international agreement wipes out about $1 trillion in indebtedness. Banks are compensated with money shifted from defense contracts and investment trust shares. These funds are established with monies that otherwise would go for interest payments. Instead, capital is kept inside the debtor country and used for projects to benefit the poor.

In many countries one of the first projects undertaken is to implement or expand family planning programs. Many Third World leaders had been impressed by estimates that such programs undertaken in the 1970 - 1985 era had reduced world population by 130 million and saved $175 billion in food, shelter, clothing, health care and education. Sadly, but $500 million / year had been available for such efforts--only 1/8 of what was needed to provide family planning to all who wanted it throughout the world. Lack of funding had plagued many programs aimed at improving the plight of the world's poor. But now the money is available. It's spent on education and attitudinal / appropriate technology fixes--

which is to become a common problem-solving approach.

European economic unification in 1992 contributed to an important attitude change sweeping the affluent world early in the new century: growing numbers of people overcome national allegiance and see themselves as global citizens. Given this shift, in the decades to follow western surpluses and charitable contributions, along with technical assistance and knowhow, increasingly flow to the developing world.

By the mid-21st century a typical Third World village-- home to 500 to 1000 people--can be characterized as follows. Besides a marketplace, the village contains a medical clinic and school/library--both of which provide free services. Nearby is the communications center, where low power TV station, earth satellite receiver, phone and computer services are based. Spreading out from the village square, household dwellings and gardens dot the adjacent countryside.

Transportation needs are predominantly met by bicycle-- some with solar/rechargeable battery powered assist motors-- and small automobile--some electric, some biofuel powered. The latter average 80 to 100 miles / gallon and typically run on locally produced ethyl alcohol. Such technology is quite old. By the late 1980s several manufacturers had produced prototypes of such fuel efficient vehicles. One large country--Brazil--met nearly half of its auto fuel needs with crop-derived alcohol. Now, with help from biotechnologists, certain problems involving inefficient land and energy utilization in making ethanol have been overcome. Both food protein and fuel alcohol can now be obtained from the same crop.

Likewise, problems once facing the widespread use of renewable electricity have been overcome. Before the rich world's defector to co-operator transition, the prospects for this happening did not look promising. Less than a human lifetime ago, in 1985, a senior UN energy advisor's sad article appeared in the journal <u>Photovoltaics</u> <u>International</u> . There he outlined the electricity needs of one billion people in small, isolated villages. He estimated a need for 60,000 to 70,000 peak megawatts of solar electricity and sought to interest multinational corporations in investing in Third World photovoltaic (PV) manufacturing plants.

The article[1], featuring pictures of village doctors performing operations by kerosene lamp light, ended
the profit motive alone is what drives the private
sector and encourages competition. But what is

the harm if the PV industries of the developed countries
also earn an invisible dividend in the form of gratitude
of millions of voiceless people in the Third World?
These people who live half of their limited life spans
in utter darkness and, in drought-affected countries,
whose cattle perish, not in search of food, but in
search of water. Isn't it tragic that while the scorch-
ing sun shines over their heads and there is sub-soil
water under their feet, the people and their cattle
should be allowed to die just because PV pumping systems
are "too costly"? In such situations, there is no power
which is more costly than no power at all.

Decades later, villages are typically served by PV systems of 60 to 70 kilowatt peak capacity. This solar electric
/ superconducting flywheel storage setup, lights buildings,
homes, and streets, pumps drinking and irrigation water, re-
charges batteries in bicycles--besides powering the village
medical, educational, and communications facilities.

Despite the description of a typical village, there is
no such thing. Individual villages differ depending on location and cultural heritage. Personal income in the old affluent world still exceeds that of the once undeveloped
world--not by a factor of 60 to 70 like a human lifetime ago-
-but by a factor of 3 to 4. The technologies used to provide
life support services and other needs vary with location. In
areas near an established utility grid, small photovoltaic
installations give way to larger, more centralized hydroelectric, wind, or solar thermal power plants. Homes and buildings are passive solar, energy efficient structures. The
technology employed is that most appropriate for local con-
ditions--climate, socioeconomic, cultural. Projects typically
employ local resources--materials, labor, know-how.

Cultural heritages have been preserved in building the
global village. There are still some regional antagonisms--
which even rarely erupt in military skirmishes. But world
military expenditures as percentage of gross world product
are only 1/1000 of peak levels of the 1990s. Generally, the
world seems to be enjoying an outbreak of peace.

As human society has become more synergistic, aggression
has steadily diminished. Some psychologists attribute this
decline, not just to material sharing and economic justice,
but also to "cerebral sharing". Increasingly, human worldviews tolerantly integrate opposing tendencies resulting in

moderate, balanced behavior. Human qualities once labeled "male" or "female" have been integrated. Men and women have been freed from past pressures of acting "masculine" or "feminine". Excessive pride and macho aggression that once led to wars are now restrained by humbling tendencies.

IV. FREEDOM, LIBERALS, AND THE FUTURE

In the central portion of this book, we examined the players and trends behind five general paths down which the future might head. Futures #2 and #3 are decentralized ones built on an environmental ethic, soft technology, attitudinal fixes, and co-operation. In Future #3, this co-operation is only possible after legislation weakens the impact of those pushing envy and conspicuous consumption, and society has been restructured to promote more face to face interactions with a future. In this world, electronic media and social pressure are used to encourage people to control themselves and put public interest first, and self interest second.

With individual income limited, corporate needs to self-ishly guard technological secrets diminishes, as do individual desires for patent protection. Technology becomes more like science: information is freely exchanged. As priorities shift, corporate structures evolve into new urban villages.

In this scenario, legislated restrictions on individual freedom (i.e. social restraint fixes) are not as great as other scenarios might demand. Caps on individual income and energy use will be disturbing to some liberals. The restriction is only on income for one's personal use. Income beyond this can be directed--as individuals see fit--to socially responsible endeavors or to those in need. In this respect it is preferable to progressive income tax schemes with steep taxation rates applied--where government taxation sometimes is used for purposes the individual disapproves of.

Futures dominated by hard technology, the corporate state, and lifeboat ethics, could involve greater restriction of individual freedom. Without long range planning and pre-paration, crowding, poverty, resource shortages, climatic change and ecosystem collapse may trigger social unrest. As the gap between "haves" and "have nots" widens, affluent countries may be continually plagued by "have not" terrorism. Some sectors of modern technological society--where computer control and end use are separated by hundreds of miles--are increasingly dependent on vast power grid and communications networks. In that respect, they are "brittle" and vulnerable to terroristic disruption. In desperate situations, governments may respond with authoritarian coercive measures.

In contrast to Future #3, one can imagine futures where goals are similar but methods more "heavy-handed". A world of rational individuals--pushed a bit toward a "Family of Man / Other People Orientation" and imbued with global vision-- might evolve in the direction outlined in Future #3. Unfortunately, many who view the world in terms of greedy, sometimes hateful, individuals clinging to irrational beliefs and following self-serving, short-term oriented corporate state leaders, can't imagine it. Without a positive vision of the future, we may end up with something quite different. Consider the following (shorter) "heavy-handed" future scenarios.

V. HEAVY-HANDED FUTURES #4, #5, AND #6

Imagine futures in which "destroy nuclear weapons" and "world solidarity" movements result in the formation of a world government. At first, this entity is little more than a loose confederation of nations having jurisdiction only over the global commons of oceans, atmosphere, and unsettled polar areas. Cultural and political diversity is maintained. But a mid 21st century crisis necessitates the global government become more authoritarian and exercise real power.

* FUTURE #4 : HALTING POPULATION GROWTH *

Progress has been made in solving many of the world's problems with one glaring exception: population growth is excessive. This is straining food supplies and frustrating efforts to eradicate poverty and minimize ecological disruption. Fortunately, a world government planning team is recommending action to solve this problem.

Their plan calls for globally regulating reproductive rights by requiring all males--before they reach age 10--be given reversible vasectomies.[2] The procedure--which became technically feasible in the early 21st century--involves implanting an electronically controlled bypass valve in the seminal fluid duct. Before a child can be fathered, a license must be secured. Then, coded electronic pulses reorient the valve restoring seminal flow to its original route.

In this manner, a limit of one child per couple will be enforced. After protests, people are assured that the limit will be increased to two once the current crisis eases.

* FUTURE #5 : GENETIC BASED ETHICS *

Late in the 21st century, world leaders are looking for a long-term solution to the "getting people to be good" problem. Past approaches are fraught with problems. Belief in a judgemental God has eroded, "the market system" creates instability, the constant coercion of a central authoritarian state is unacceptable to liberals, and electronic media propaganda can be tuned out. From a meeting of top scientists and humanists, two technology-based solutions emerge: the genetic approach and the AI (=artificial intelligence) approach. Society is wracked by furious debate over which to implement. Liberals don't like either, but eventually side with those favoring the human genetic engineering effort...

In the decades following the turn of the century completion of the human genetic makeup map (CONCEPTS), geneticists had established the genes responsible for altruism, aggression, and certain types of learning ability. Unlike remedying some diseases--where but a single defective gene is fixed--improving fetuses with respect to altruism, aggression and learning, required manipulating several genes.

Proponents maintained that a combination of encouraging "the freedom to choose responsibility", and continual, steady, worldwide introduction of the desired traits into new individuals would, as genetically-engineered infants grew to adults, insure long-term stability. Opponents of this "super race" program (as they called it), attacked it for three reasons: 1) it was irreversible thus extremely dangerous, 2) too many unknowns still plagued efforts to translate (inherent) genotype into (expressed) phenotype when complex behaviors were involved, and 3) it would take decades before the "super race" would dominant the human scene.

* FUTURE #6 : AI BASED ETHICS *

"Super race" opponents embraced a plan they described in terms of creating a human collective consciousness. Critics branded it "mind control".

Promoters described a "goddess" that would live in every head. They named her GAIA for Goddess Artificial Intelligence program A--the last A signifying this would be the first of a steadily improving creation. The plan called for fitting a tiny piece of microprocessing/memory hardware into a person's tooth and a sensor into a fingertip. In this way every human would interface with the global village communication grid, the world of economic transactions, and a super-computer based collective consciousness software program.

"Input" to GAIA could be actual speech, subvocalization, or fingertip scanning. A pleasant speaking voice--which individuals could select themselves--would provide "output". The goddess would help people maintain a "Family of Man / Other People Orientation" and global vision. Built into her would be state of the art human understanding of atmospheric, hydrologic, geologic, soil, agricultural, forestry, wildlife, plant community, and human life support systems. Using this with inter-related systems dynamics models and files of one's past activities, GAIA would supplement self-interest-based decision-making by taking other humans and the Earth's biosphere into consideration. Not only would she police individual behavior and make certain obligations known, she would also function as teacher, doctor, counselor, therapist, or just a good, caring friend who's always there.

Always there, that is, unless you decide to turn her off. After liberals' fulminations about "not being able to escape Big Brother", technologists agreed to this provision.

VI. THE AI / GLOBAL BRAIN SOLUTION--PRO AND CON

The heavy-handed future scenarios involve controversy sure to stir emotions and require weighing conflicting values. Consider one of them--Future #6--and the arguments that might be advanced today "for" and "against" the future creation of something like GAIA. Already, mention of such possibilities appear in serious journals. Consider the comments in a <u>Futurist</u> Sept/Oct 1989 article by Joseph Pelton, "Telepower--The Emerging Global Brain".

> Well into the 21st century, there can even be hope for the building of a true global consciousness and ultimately for the emergence of a "global brain". Eventually, we may see the emergence of a new human species...a species with a more global consciousness and more empathic links to the rest of the species. The true mystery is whether this new "species" will be derived from humans, from bioengineering, from machines, or from another telepower source.

THE ARGUMENT FOR GAIA

While the individual letter acronym gives GAIA one meaning, there is another. In classical times Gaia was the Greek Earth goddess. More recently, the word has received attention as part of British scientist James Lovelock's, "The Gaia Hypothesis". According to this idea, our whole planet functions as a single self-regulating organism. Seemingly adrift without a steersman, Lovelock wondered, "To what extent is our collective intelligence also part of Gaia?" and "Do we as a species constitute a Gaian nervous system and brain which can consciously anticipate environmental change?"

The GAIA program will provide that steersman. It will allow humanity to perceive itself both as a whole and a collection of parts. The day will have dawned when individual self interest will be regulated by direct communication with an entity representing a collective human consciousness.

When you rely on GAIA, rest assured she will always guide you in a way that minimizes suffering and maximizes happiness on a long-term planetary basis. You'll be able to switch her off and take full responsibility for your actions. Seldom will anyone do this: GAIA will be such a helpful friend--besides it would hurt her "feelings".

Unlike television, which was in living rooms before people knew what they were saddled with, GAIA will be introduced only after decades of planning and public debate. Uppermost in everyone's mind will be avoiding an Orwellian "Big Brother" creation. GAIA will be preferable to what we have now by default: people worshipping Orwell's money god with the encouragement of media pushers!

It may always be necessary to perfect the GAIA program as dictated by user feedback and better understanding of complex systems. However, as years pass the changes will be fewer. Once the software reaches certain levels of modeling accuracy and human satisfaction, the need for human government institutions will lessen.

After years of living with GAIA, many will forget that she is a computer program. For them, she will be the empathy-concerned, other-oriented part of their own consciousness. To others, she will be a benevolent goddess. Just as primitive man perhaps relied on internal bicameral voices for guidance, so will these future individuals. Humanity will have come full circle. But its childhood will be over. It will have outgrown the dangerous, out of control, excessively self-interest based behavior of its youth.

THE ARGUMENT AGAINST GAIA

So-called "shallow ecologists" may support GAIA --if they abandon freedom-based liberal traditions. No one else will. These people arrogantly think that humanity can someday understand nature completely. This is impossible: nature is incredibly complex. The technologists' real goal is control of people and nature. "Deep Ecologists" believe that humans should work with nature--not attempt to control it. Attempts at control never turn out as planned.

In the last two decades, scientists have begun exploring why detailed predictions of a complex system's future behavior may be impossible. Lumped together, the results of such investigations are now called chaos theory.[3] In short, non-linear effects and sensitivity to initial conditions may make predictions coming from an extraordinarily complex model like GAIA worthless. (Chaos scientists refer to "The Butterfly Effect" in which a butterfly flapping its wings in Peking conceivably (admittedly not likely) could trigger a major storm over New York weeks later!)

Suppose seemingly fundamental limitations can be overcome and useful models developed. Mere contemplation of something like GAIA raises all sorts of questions. Who will program her? Could an adequate job ever be done? Wouldn't any programming team represent a mind-boggling, freedom-threatening concentration of power? Wouldn't such people effectively be playing God with humanity?

Supposing its successful implementation, GAIA would represent the ultimate technological fix: a solution to one manifestation of human imperfection--greed. This solution would be anathema to humanists who love people for what they are--faults and all. The technologists' control of people that GAIA represents would destroy spontaneity and joyful diversity of free expression. It would squeeze life out of people and replace it with something monotonous, rigid, and artificial. Creating GAIA would be a step toward a future where there is little difference between people and machines.

Instead of more technology-based mechanical gods, we need attitudinal fixes that ultimately produce a world of self-actualized people. Utopia--whether it be Ecotopia, Eupsychia, or whatever--results when humans make choices which promote planetary health, well being, and harmony. Helping people make these choices begins with education.

VII. MY FONDEST DREAM

Since childhood I've been interested in other worlds. When I was seven years old, my father took me to a Burbank shoe store and bought me a pair of "U.S. Keds" tennis shoes. As a bonus I got a free "U.S. Keds Map of Outer Space". This colorful map excited my imagination. It also puzzled me.

Between the orbits of Venus and Earth, the mapmakers placed a comet, with long slender, arching tail. Although a particular comet was not specified, I later supposed this to be Halley's Comet--last seen in 1910. Before 1958 ended, I was dreaming of that comet and its next coming in 1986.

Dayton turned five in late September, 1985. As a birthday present I agreed to take him up the hill for some stargazing through "the big telescope". So a few weeks later, one clear, moonless night, I spent an evening showing him Saturn, Jupiter, star clusters, nebulae, galaxies, double stars, and teaching him constellations. The last object we viewed, well after midnight, was a faint fuzzy patch low in the eastern sky in the Taurus-Gemini region.

Of all we saw that night, this decidedly unimpressive object was actually the closest thing to us--at a mere 150 million miles away. After I rolled back the observatory roof and put the telescope to bed, we started down the hill. I told Dayton to remember that last thing we'd seen. "It's moving closer to us and the sun. In a few months it should be quite a sight!" I explained. Back home, instead of reading him a bedtime story, I gave him an account of why the comet we'd seen was named for Sir Edmund Halley.

I had quite a dream that night. It was the summer of 2061. I had returned home after a few weeks absence. My wife was curious about the important job I'd taken on. We talked about my work, then she told me we'd been invited to Grandpa's for the evening. "How is Dayton doing these days?" I wondered. The story she related was not entirely unexpected.

It seemed this 81 year old man was being charged with renewed vigor and enthusiasm for living as Halley's Comet drew steadily closer to a second coming in his life. Now that it was nearly visible with a small telescope, he was reportedly bubbling with child-like excitement. My wife didn't understand what all the fuss was about and speculated that the old man was succumbing to senility.

"I don't think so!" I responded. "Many years ago he tried to tell me what Halley's Comet meant to him and his dad. For Dayton, seeing the comet again is like keeping faith with his father, although I don't really understand why. Maybe we can get him to talk about it..."

Despite some far-off thunder, I insisted we walk up the
mountain to Grandma & Grandpa's, instead of driving. My five
year old son Stephen always loves visiting his great grandparents. Quickly overcoming initial tendencies to cling to
his home-at-last Daddy, he ran on ahead. Three year old JoAnn
preferred to let Daddy carry her up the hill.

After dinner, the kids played out back for a few minutes. Soon Stephen was asking Dayton about the telescope,
which was set up on the patio. "That telescope is nearly 100
years old--it belonged to my daddy. He bought it with money
earned from delivering newspapers when he was 13 years old--
back in 1964. When I was about your age, we watched Halley's
Comet with it from the upstairs deck of the old house." he
replied, then asked, "Do you like it?"

The small boy answered affirmatively and the old man
continued. "Well, someday it'll be yours provided you keep
the faith and put it to good use. The stars can teach you a
great deal: about natural cycles, about your relationship to
the universe, about how your mind works, about where you came
from and where you're going. Remember too, how much it meant
to your great grandpa to see Halley's comet both at the beginning and at the end of his life..."

"When will I get to see it?" the five year old asked.
I had been listening to their conversation and now joined in.
"Could be tonight. Look, those clouds are breaking up."

Sure enough, about three hours later, we spotted the
faint comet in the ancient telescope. Grandpa's hearing was
half gone, his sense of smell completely gone, but his eyes
were still remarkably sharp. He peered through the eyepiece
and saw his childhood friend--looking much the same as when
he'd first met her. He took several minutes and got a good
long look. He wasn't looking as much as remembering...

For a moment he was in his daddy's arms again, descend-
ing the ladder that once hung from the colored bluff below
the observatory and the solar cell platform. He heard his
long dead father's voice telling him about Sir Edmund Halley
and his mother's voice reading him Winnie the Pooh stories
while he snuggled under the covers.

Dayton looked at the night sky, then turned back to the
eyepiece. When I last saw you, he thought, the humans you
passed by on your sunward plunge were divided. While an
affluent minority acted like spoiled children playing King of
the Mountain, most were involved in an all too real life and

death struggle--which sometimes ended in painful cries. Compounding the human failure to share and help those in need, all people lived as hostages of nuclear terror.

My parents, he thought, and a relative few like them, banded together and resisted the Grabber tidal wave and the corporate state steamroller. When most Americans were concerned with only what their next paycheck would buy, my parents dared to think of the atmosphere's integrity during the next few decades, forests several hundred years in the future, and human gene pools thousands of years hence.

He again thought about his father. 76 years ago the man was in his prime--working on that holy book. What his Eco-sharing philosophy prescribed as the antidote for an ailing humanity could be summarized in two words: "fair play", or as a command, "play fair!" He dared hope that one individual of five billion could matter, and planned accordingly--just as he hoped that someday his son would again see Halley's Comet.

And there it was! Three human generations later, again passing by the small planet as it had since before the dawn of recorded history. He had grown up, and, defying all odds, so too had humanity. His father had dared to "teach your children" and the old man knew that they'd responded. The planet the comet flew by was not a lifeless wasteland--or even threatened with becoming one. Remarkably, it was a world of compassion, sharing, and solidarity--a global village.

Soon he became too blurry-eyed to look. He backed away from the eyepiece and urged his five year old grandson to "take a look". The old man was lost in thoughts however. He paid no attention to the logistics of the small boy's eyes finding the eyepiece--and I stepped in to help.

Questions & Projects

1. Two books that have taken detailed looks at imagined futures are Edward Bellamy's <u>Looking</u> <u>Backward</u> --an 1887 account of the last century from a year 2000 perspective, and Arthur C. Clarke's 1961 <u>Profiles</u> <u>of</u> <u>the</u> <u>Future.</u> Compare the book's predictions with realities.

2. "A computer/modem/FAX work at home movement could spur urban to rural population shift and help make American society less de-humanized and anonymous." Discuss.

3. How might a Green Tax work? Before reporting on this, investigate a) Iowa's taxation of fertilizers and pesticides to pay associated hidden environmental costs[4], and

b) carbon tax proposals to combat global warming.
4. Report on long-term transportation alternatives.
5. In 1970 Issac Asimov wrote, "Perhaps by experimenting on a very limited scale, we may stumble across ways of producing human beings with far greater wisdom than ourselves, and to these, we may hand over the task of improving the human race as a whole." Discuss.
6. Which of the Future scenarios-- #4, #5, or #6 --is the most disturbing to you. Why?
7. Would someone embracing worldview theme #20 or #21 feel more comfortable with the GAIA proposal? Discuss.
8. It is said that, "The whispers of conscience are seldom heard over the shouts of self-interest." How would GAIA rectify this?
9. "The future creation of something like GAIA and its eventual life inside human heads is quite a price to pay for a perfect world." Discuss.
10. GAIA is an outrageous proposal--the author advances such a radical plan only to make taking action against those now monopolizing the media look reasonable. Discuss.
11. The American Association for the Advancement of Science's Project 2061 derives its name from the date of the next appearance of Halley's Comet. The most ambitious goal of this educational reform effort is <u>Science</u> for <u>All</u> <u>Americans</u> --itself the title of a 1989 Project 2061 report on scientific literacy goals. Obtain a copy of this report[5] and contrast its learning objectives with those of Fig. #2 (LETTERS).
12. Is the 76 year interval between appearances of Halley's Comet a) too long, b) too short, or c) about the right time interval for long-range human planning? Discuss.
13. "As a society, we need to dream of the future world we desire and work for it--otherwise we'll not end up with the future of our choice, but the future by default". Discuss.

Notes

1. Usmani, I.H., <u>Photovoltaics</u> <u>International,</u> February 1985.
2. Leo Bowman, Ark. Tech University contributed this idea.
3. Gleick, J. <u>Chaos</u> , Viking, NY 1987.
4. Reganold, J. et al "Sustainable Agriculture" <u>Scientific</u> <u>American,</u> June 1990
5. AAAS, 1333 H Street, NW, Washington, D.C. 20005

REVELATIONS

I. INNER CONFLICT OVER ENDING THE BOOK

Once I became convinced that humanity needed a new "holy book" (INSPIRATION), my whole being mobilized and I began writing in earnest. I worked with the type of sustained motivation and self-discipline that I'd always suspected I was capable of summoning, but had never actually done so. I didn't understand what was driving me, but I yielded to it completely. Why?--because it felt right.

But after many months of work things changed. I became uncomfortable in the role of "Messiah". And what type of ending would I write? These doubts led to inner conflict.

There were three participants in this inner tug of war. First, my rational, analytical, one-at-a-time left brain perspective, was skeptical of the book's supposed divine inspiration. He saw writing as pulling words out of his cerebral storage and sequentially chaining them together in a way that was both interesting and accessible to others. He would occasionally go along with the other two voices and proceed as if something bigger was behind the literary effort, but he felt certain he was in control.

My intuitive, all-at-once, timeless, spatially-oriented right brain felt otherwise. She--the third entity who helped her express herself perceived this second voice as more feminine than masculine--argued that there was no need to create an ending to "the movie". Instead, she planned to ascertain what the ending was through other channels. Dreaming, meditation, fasting, listening to music and other natural methods of altering one's consciousness might all be involved. She could glimpse the ending only if her analytical partner, who lived in the same "house", co-operated. First, the mental background noise that he produced had to be reduced. Second, her perceptions were meaningless without his analysis.

This co-operation was only possible when he suspended the skepticism that said "it isn't" and proceeded as if "it is". Lately, this had been easier to do. Perhaps those fringe physicists' ideas on human consciousness were influencing him. One of these guys claims[1] "the future is more important than the past in determining the present" and that time is an illusion.

Finally, my frontal brain manager, administrator, and decision-maker was there to arbitrate and integrate. During

writing it usually ignored the right hemisphere worldview
input in favor of the left brain skill the activity demanded.
But now the right brain's creativity was needed.

    I couldn't write anymore--I had to get outdoors. There's
a part of my head that sometimes won't let me write. So, I'm
out here, with my tape recorder, sitting amongst the hardwoods right below the great colored bluff. Although spring is
about over, there's still a little waterfall plunging down
the face of the bluff, where four months ago I heard huge
icicles crashing down. But now it's warm. The sun is peeking
out from behind billowy clouds. I can't write with this
dialogue going on inside my head. I'm hearing these voices...

RB/FB: You're scared of becoming the Messiah!

LB: I'm not God or Jesus--I can't become the Messiah!

RB/FB: You became the Messiah once: during a peak experience
        many years ago.

FB: She's right. It was May 10, 1975 at a Hollywood theater.
        Annie and I were there to see the rock opera <u>Tommy</u>--in
        which a deaf, dumb, and blind boy is awakened to his
        hidden potentialities, becomes a self-actualized leader
        and then a Messiah. Remember getting high from the music
        and the story and merging with the reality on the screen?
        Remember leaving the theater feeling like a resurrected
        Tommy?

RB/FB: And now here you are--backing away from the ultimate
        growth possibility--the highest high!

LB: I can't do it. It's blasphemous, arrogant--who do you
        think I am? Leave me alone. I'll figure something else
        out for the ending.

RB/FB: You've come part of the way. You've accepted Maslow's
        challenge[2]: "If you do not aspire to write the great
        new classic, who will?" And you've gotten to the
        decisive turning point in your classic--but suddenly
        you've come down with what Maslow described[3] as a bad
        case of "The Jonah Complex": "We are generally afraid
        to become that which we can glimpse in our most per-
        fect moments." That's why we're having this conflict.

LB: I don't like it. You're involving me in this cosmic
        consciousness stuff--and patterning the whole experience,
        not after a Blake, Emerson, Whitman, but after a Messiah.
        And that ending--I don't want to die! And I'm puzzled.
        You referred to my death, what happens to you?

RB/FB: Look, I'm not sure. But I'm surprised! You said...
FB: You need to tone down your arguments and begin co-
operating. We all share this cerebral house together. If
we can't get along, we'll be a psychological wreck.

II. A STRANGE DREAM AND A PEAK EXPERIENCE

For the next two weeks, I fasted and meditated. I also
had strange dreams--as if my right brain was trying to provide information otherwise inaccessible. The last dream helped bring this period to a climactic end. For the previous few
nights, I had been reading Charlotte's Web to the children...

That night she dreamed she was Charlotte--sometimes a
spider and sometimes a person--you know how dreams are? She
wasn't at home--perhaps she was in Los Angeles. She was desperately trying to save her friend Wilbur--sometimes a pig
and sometimes a faceless person--from a premature death. The
plan was to construct a web with an important message in it--
one that would save Wilbur. To make it happen she needed the
help of a reluctant co-operator: Templeton--sometimes a rat
and sometimes a nearly forgotten yuppie friend--you know how
dreams are? Just then, Templeton returned carrying a newspaper clipping and a word he shared with Charlotte. The word
was 'Humble'...[4]

The next morning I told Annie about it. "It wasn't an
ordinary dream--it was powerful. I don't know what it means,
but somehow I'm to be involved in some miracle and then...",
my voice trailed off, "I'll die." I paused--noted Annie's
startled look--and concluded, "Perhaps a part of me will live
on after this death."
Despite her initial reaction, Annie seemed to dismiss my
dream as nonsense and went over to turn on the television.
"I'm headed up the mountain." I announced. My departure was
interrupted by a TV minister who was talking about "the end
time" and the present world situation. "We should be listening as never before for the shout from on high" this voice of
authority was telling his electronic congregation.
"I forgot it was Sunday," Annie said, switching off the
television. "Be careful, Steve. You're in a weakened state,"
she cautioned.
I reached the great bluff and sat pondering the sun's
illumination of its subtle browns, oranges, and reds. After

awhile, I got up and climbed the metal ladder--which years
earlier I'd anchored with cable to a less imposing extremity
of the great rock wall. This lead me up to the solar cell
platform and roll-off roof observatory. These are monuments,
I thought, along with the house I built, to my dreams and
highest aspirations.

I rested peacefully under a white oak at the edge of the
woods. I could see the valley below, the vast Boston Mountains stretching to the west, and the blue sky. Occasionally,
a red-tailed hawk or turkey buzzard would sail over me. I sat
soaking up the inspiring sight and feeling free.

I'd spent much of the last two weeks thinking about
cosmic consciousness. How did Bucke phrase it?[5]

> The trait that distinguishes these people from other men
> is this: Their spiritual eyes have been opened and they
> have seen...

I'd been lost in a self-centered quest for enlightenment.
But today was different. Given last night's dream, I planned
to resume being my other-oriented self. "Tonight, I will
break my fast," I decided.

The last two weeks had been a mistake. I'm usually quick
to recognize the true nature of certain silliness that some
in the so-called New Age movement get caught up in. I know
that mantric chanting involves nothing more than summoning up
the Collective Cognitive Imperative worldview. I looked over
at my observatory and thought of all the times I'd corrected
people who confused astronomy and astrology. My gaze came to
rest on the 204 crystalline silicon solar cells that supply
electricity to my house. I contrasted the well understood
physics of this technology with the mysterious occultism of
New Agers pushing the supposed spiritual powers of crystals
and "healing stones". But on cosmic consciousness I apparently had been duped. On this skeptical note, I lay back,
cleared away a few acorns, and went to sleep.

I awoke feeling weak but relaxed. It was late afternoon
and the sun was dropping to the west. My resting place was no
longer in shade and the sun dazzled my eyes. I took shelter
against the back of a huge rock. When I looked up I was
facing the solar cells.

I recalled pictures of photovoltaic installations at
work in Third World villages...Then other scenes came to
mind...In an African village doctors performed an operation
by kerosene lamp light...In Haiti, people left their village

in the morning, walked 2 1/2 miles to the nearest water, and then staggered back lugging the heavy five gallon bucket of water...And of hundreds of millions of the world's hungry.

I visualized children wasting away and parents who loved them unable to do anything. Overcome by this tragedy I saw so clearly in my mind's eye, I begged the parents to hug their children and tell them it would be alright. It would be alright--I would make it alright?

It wouldn't be alright and my empathic "big picture" view was soon blurred with tears. I cried, burying my head in my hands, for several minutes. As I cried I imagined that I was washing away what I deemed responsible for the sorry sights I'd seen. My tears were dissolving all the world's greed and envy...When it was gone there would be a liberating joyousness as people came together...

After this emotional outpouring I was spent and remaining tension flowed from my body. I surrendered to this discharge process and lapsed deeper and deeper into a state of passive yogic tranquility. Then suddenly, perhaps after the noise that's me fell below a critical value, some threshold was crossed and there, like a lightning flash that lights up the whole sky, was the underlying signal...This undifferentiated light was within me. My whole being was filled with joy. This was the cosmic ocean, the Kingdom of Heaven, Paradise.

Then, within this fundamental wholeness, I resolved granular structure. Upon sensing this, I was sailing, my nervous system resonating with every pulsation, with every ebb and flow, every throbbing... I dwelled there for only a few seconds but somehow tasted forever...Then it was over. My eyes had been opened.

What happened next?--I must have gone to sleep again. I awoke to an orangish-red sunset and Annie sitting next to me. It seemed she'd heard my cries and shouts and climbed the mountain to investigate.

III. NARCISSISM

Within days of this peak experience I resumed writing. And one day, after visiting "The World of Narcissism", how to end the book was resolved--not without trauma...

The "World of Narcissism" is down the block from that shop with the prominent sign "Have the Time of Your Life !", here in The Reality Marketplace. I should tell you why I went in there, and then came here to this familiar bench. I'm here

to meet with the professor--nearly a year has passed since we
last sat here and talked. His voice has often filled my head,
but today I must meet him face to face. I've got important
questions to ask and need his advice on ending the book.

As for my reasons for going into that shop, I'm concerned about a growing arrogance within me. This wasn't to be
"my book", it was to be bigger than me--that was the initial
motivation. But this project has demanded nearly all my energy and all my "stick-with-it-ness". I must admit that, on
occasion, the "other-oriented" motivational approach has been
shelved in favor of selfish inducements. During these times,
I fear that I too am caught up in narcissism.

Once narcissism meant something like self-love, caused
by staring too long at one's reflection. Today, it's become a
complex, misunderstood and controversial word. Erich Fromm,
in The Heart of Man , describes narcissists in terms of
"vanity", "self-admiration", "self-satisfaction", and "self-
glorification" and sees such asocial behavior as the anti-
thesis of brotherhood--something hindering co-operation.

Christopher Lasch, in The Culture of Narcissism ,
restores an original clinical psychoanalytical dimension to
the word. He chides Fromm for "eagerness to sermonize about
the blessings of brotherly love", and suggests that narcissism has more in common with self-hatred rather than self-
admiration. Lasch sees the era's self-preoccupation as a desperate hunt for "...the feeling, the momentary illusion of
personal well being, health, and psychic security." He argues
that in today's society "self approval depends on public recognition and acclaim...Today men seek the kind of approval
that applauds not their actions but their personal attributes." Lasch sees pathological narcissists as defensively
striving for grandiose perfection to ward off self-hatred,
and believing that any badness negates the goodness.

IV. MY WORLDVIEW STRETCHED BEYOND ITS LIMITS

I was fairly certain the professor would meet me, but
unprepared for how long I'd have to wait. I'd finished my
lunch and was contemplating spending more time in the "Human
Consciousness Mall" when I saw him approaching. For a second,
just before he spoke, he seemed to resemble the minister from
my Sunday school days--Mr. Godwin. But that recollection was
so vague, I quickly let it pass. We exchanged greetings and
soon got down to business.

"As I see it," he advised, "you can choose the ending from the family of humble, actually possible futures, or you can select it from the narcissist, boldly speculative, nearly impossible futures of self-glorification. It's a difficult choice: there are good arguments for either ending. The former ending, I suspect, is thematically needed to counter the "have the time of your life" mentality which you despise and in keeping with your "small is beautiful" orientation. Yet the latter ending might sell more books and get your message to more people. What would be the harm in it? Most psychologists agree that everyone needs a little narcissism."

"I've heard those arguments," I replied, "people can use a little narcissism because it enhances their survival prospects. But survival is exactly why I don't want to become some superstar martyr. I much prefer life as it was before my inspiration, to living and dying as some celebrity guru."

From him I sought specific suggestions or plots to develop for the ending, but he kept urging me to embrace the role of Messiah. As our conversation continued I became increasingly disillusioned. Finally, I grew irritated and blew off steam, saying, "Sometimes, I'm sure you don't tell me anything I don't already know, and that I'm being fooled."

"How's that?" he demanded.

"You know we're not talking about the _real_ ending," I replied, "Only the fictional ending I'll write. I think you purposely blur reality and fiction."

He looked surprised, but immediately defended himself. "The ending will be fictional, but it will have a reality all its own. You always plan your future ahead of time, then work to make it turn out that way--right?"

"I once thought so," I answered, "but this time the real ending is out of my hands isn't it? Has somebody else written it and I'm just waiting to act it out--is that it?"

I could tell he felt pressed for answers. Finally he said, "No and yes. All possible endings have been written, but it's within your power to select the one you want."

I continued to probe. "So, if I really wanted to be The Messiah at the head of a powerful ideological army that would break the Grabber grip on society, and everywhere free the caged birds and rescue those crying for help, I could do it?"

He hesitated, then replied, "Yes, I told you I'm on a special assignment with the highest possible authorization."

By now, I was unable to contain my skepticism. "So you

can perform magic, ah...do miracles?"

He appeared startled by my tone, but after a searching
look at me, answered, "We like to think of it in terms of
selecting events of otherwise extraordinary low probability."

I guess these revelations stretched my worldview beyond
its limits, given what happened next. My personality began to
disintegrate. The next thing I knew, my left brain was doing
the talking...

LB: Wait a minute! You're asking me to believe in something I
don't understand and can't imagine how it might work--I
can't. In fact, the only sense I can make of this conversation is that some part of my brain needs you and has
conjured you up. I'm hallucinating you!

Before the professor could say anything, I flung my
right arm through him and he was gone--vanished! But that was
not the end of the conversation.

RB/FB: Damn you! Look what you've done! You've destroyed him
--he'll never be back!

LB: You don't understand: your imaginary friend was never
there to begin with. I just broke the trance you were in.

The bickering continued. My head ached. I feared a nervous breakdown But it didn't happen--Annie came to my psychological rescue.

Over many hours she related stories of where her right
brain had taken her. I'd heard most of them before--still the
therapy worked. She persuaded me to accept what she had concluded: A given reality can sometimes be fitted to a rational
cause and effect framework, and at other times be experienced
as totally irrational, acausal, mysterious, defying description. But having it both ways simultaneously isn't possible.
After recalling the old physicist in "The Quantum Reality
Mall", I grudgingly conceded the point.

I had valiantly tried to find Truth--to sit with God.
But my bench was an illusion: there was no solid ground. And
without my "ally" from The Reality Marketplace, my becoming
"The Messiah" was beyond the realm of possibility...

...Or was it? Somewhere inside me is a creature full of
Shining Purity narcisstly seeking grandiose perfection.
This true believer cerebrally co-exists with someone so
schooled in complexities that he trusts only in realities
he's encountered, experiences he's had. These two could not
agree on a single ending to this book. Thus I have provided
shortened versions of what each wanted to be the ending.

V. THE IMAGINED COMING OF THE PLANETARY MESSIAH

The children are quiet. Annie is asleep next to me as
I drive home from an extraordinary gathering at Staymore.
A week ago, I'd agreed to a meeting--supposedly a question /
answer session for friends who had read my book. Instead,
I've presided over a bizarre circus--already being called the
initial worship service of The First Church of Ecosharing.

If the 'sermon' I delivered had a theme, it was "live
simply so that others may simply live". 'Scripture readings'
were from the book of GRABBERS, chapter two verse 19 (the
Grabber Ten Commandments in the form of the 23rd Psalm), and
from the book of GOOD NEWS, chapter five verse five (The
Shakertown Pledge). The congregation accompanied a local band
singing Jethro Tull's "Hymn 42", the Eagles' "Last Resort",
the traditional "We Shall Overcome", the Who's "I'm Free",
John Lennon's "Imagine", and The Live Aid for Africa theme
"We Are the World". For 'communion' we moved outside and sat
in a circle around a bonfire. While some wanted to hastily
improvise a Native American sweat lodge, we settled on
listening to some shamanic drumming.

During this interlude, I couldn't resist fooling 'em
with some chemistry magic (luminol-based) I'd brought along
for such an occasion. Unfortunately, after my 'trick' but
before I could "set 'em straight", I was interrupted by
unexpected commotion. Later Annie told me that many spoke of
my aura and psycho-kinetic powers. She said four or five
people want to be "my disciples".

With all the craziness, the service ended in a surprisingly reverent fashion. Everyone joined hands for my concluding "Prayer of Reconciliation"...

All eyes were on me. There in the center of the circle,
my whole being seemed to radiate--although it was just my
shirt reflecting light from the fire. Then I looked at them
and said simply, "Let us pray."

"We are but a drop in the sea of humanity aboard Spaceship Earth. How can our being possibly affect the ship's life
support systems and insure a safer journey for our children?
Our only hope rests with reaching other passengers and alert-
ing them to the crisis looming ahead. Help these people see
us as more than troublemakers. Help them see that ultimate
technological tools bring the ultimate responsibility: we are
all caretakers of this planet, its destiny is in our hands.
Give our political and technological leaders the insight to

see the eternity of the whole interwoven picture--not
fragmented glimpses of its bits and pieces. Give each of us
strength to take personal responsibility for our actions--
weeding out life threatening ones and cultivating the life-
nurturing ones. Help us forge a collective conscience and
give it the strength and unity to say "NO" to myopic solutions based on short-term economics. Let us put aside our
past differences and work together to forge a solution to
which we can all say a resounding 'YES !' "

    Perhaps it was triggered by the impassioned rising in-
tensity of my voice, or by memories of the demonstration long
ago, or both, but as I spoke that last word of the prayer,
100 voices spontaneously resonated with mine. This was no
ordinary "Amen", that somehow made one think of all the heavy
immovable inertia of the status quo. Instead it immediately
provoked thoughts of the new age, the possibilities, the
people--yes! It was a "Yes!" given as if in response to a
challenge...Perhaps those in the circle imagined they were
giving their verdict on Ecosharing, their answer to "Will you
join us as a co-operator?"

VI. IS THE MESSIAH DEAD?

    As I write, the 1990s have begun. Recall (CHRONICLES) my
family's 10 year long Ecosharing experiment ended in mid-
1985. I do not want to confuse your conception of global
average ecoshare living with particulars of my post Ecosharing experiment life. Suffice it to say my lifestyle is
no longer that of "an average world citizen". It is more
like that of millions of other frugal, rural Americans.
There is little of a "Survival Oriented" (theme #24) mentality left in my head.

    Yet when I receive letters, drawings, and photos from
the Third World children (two girls) I sponsor through Plan
International USA (formerly Foster Parents Plan), it all
comes back. 10 year old Bungania lives with her parents, two
brothers and sister in South Sulawesi, Indonesia. Her home is
a 20 ft. by 24 ft. wood stilt house with nipa leaf roof and
bamboo walls. Five year old Dorcas lives with her family in a
one room, kerosene lamp lit, mud and stick hut with a sheet
iron roof near Jacmel, Haiti. I shall never forget showing my
daughter Ruthie their pictures and telling her about our
family's new relationship with these two girls.

    Is the Ecosharing Messiah dead? Has he succumbed to the

temptations of affluent living ? I don't think so. My commitment to social change is as strong as ever. My values have
changed little; my commitment to Ecosharing philosophy has
not wavered. Someday, I hope to again live "an average world
citizen" / fair ecoshare type lifestyle.

Five years of part-time work on this book, a university
teaching job along with other circumstances and obligations
have suppressed "messianic" activities once anticipated. Its
publication and subsequent use in educational activities will
go a long way toward a resurrection. I'll know when the "true
believer" is reasserting himself. One of my children will ask
an important question. In response I'll say, "Gee, I don't
know. Let's see what Coming of Age in the Global Village says
about that!" Together we'll open it and start reading.

Questions & Projects

1. Relate "the future is more important than the past in
   determining the present" to teleology (see GENESIS).
2. Extend the dream episode's Charlotte/Templeton interaction
   by reading the relevant conversation in Charlotte's Web.
   Discuss the significance of "web" and "Fair" to the dream.
3. What powers do some New Agers attribute to crystals and
   why? Critique from the viewpoint of a rational person
   whose worldview is dominated by a) theme #6, b) theme #7.
4. Some New Agers believe that children choose their parents.
   Why might such a belief be viewed with alarm by those
   compassionately trying to aid the Third World's poor?
5. Consult Bucke's book on cosmic consciousness and report on
   historical figures who had such peak experiences.
6. Discuss what prompted "the cosmic consciousness episode"
   in terms of coming face to face with greedy technologists.
7. Associate the opinions below with particular worldviews
   and discuss. a) "Embrace the god-like in yourself. Jesus,
   the Buddha, Confucious, and all the great prophets have
   already returned. They are there inside you. You need
   merely let go, overcome your fear, and let them shine
   through you." b) "I don't appreciate the way you make
   Jesus look like a fable. I don't believe the theory of
   evolution: we come from the creator and that's God.
   Someday you will find out about God: 'Every knee shall bow
   and every tongue confess that Jesus Christ is Lord'."
   c) "Maybe a person doesn't have a soul of his own, only a
   piece of a big soul." (to paraphrase what Tom Joad tells

his mother in The Grapes of Wrath)   d) "If (humanity is)
to survive we must somehow face the problems...with all of
the intellectual capacity and rationality at our disposal.
We are lost if we pin our hopes instead on pseudoscientific speculation or on the murky occult beliefs of
past millennia."[6]   e) "...The hand of God is the promise
of my own...the spirit of God is the brother of my own...
All the men ever born are also my brothers, and the women
my sisters and lovers..." (from Whitman's Song of Myself).

8. Discuss "the killing of the ex-theology professor" and
"the cosmic consciousness episode" in terms of inner
conflict related to fitting God into one's worldview.

9. Did you or someone you know have "an imaginary friend"
playmate as a child? What do psychologists say regarding
the prevalence and origin of this phenomenon? Discuss.

10. "Unlike real heroes, celebrities are narcissists".
Discuss.

11. Contrast the Staymore 'church service' with typical
Christian church services.

12. Any self-styled Messiah eventually faces the frustration/
inaction of "the extrapolation to infinity syndrome". This
leads to an "if I can't change the world quickly, I won't
try to change it at all" stance. Discuss.

13. Obtain literature from private donation supported
organizations assisting children in poor countries (like
Plan International USA). Report on these efforts.

14. Use the two photos on the cover to summarize the book's
most important themes for someone who hasn't read it.

15. How much of a "holy book", a "bible for the family of
man" has this book turned out to be? Recall question 13.
in LETTERS and discuss.

Notes

1. Wolfe, F.A. StarWave , MacMillian, NY 1984

2. Maslow, A. "Neurosis as a Failure of Personal Growth",
Humanitas , 1967.

3. Maslow, A. Motivation and Personality, Harper & Row,
NY, 1954.

4. White, E.B. Charlotte's Web , Harper & Row, NY

5. Bucke, R.M. Cosmic Consciousness , University Books,
NY, 1901

6. ed. Abell, G. & Singer, B. Science and the Paranormal,
Charles Scribner's Sons, New York, 1981.

A.I. DETERMINING YOUR DIETARY PROTEIN IMPACT INDEX

Step 1: Determine an "average" daily menu for you or your family.

Step 2: Translate this menu into grams of useable protein per major protein source (see Fig.#40 GOOD NEWS)

Step 3: Add up all the useable protein to get total useable protein.

Step 4: Divide each amount in step 2 by the total amount in Step 3, rounding to the nearest thousandth. For each major protein source, you now have the fraction it contributes to your total useable protein.

Step 5: For each major protein source consumed, multiply the individual impact index (Fig. #40) by the fractional amount for it you computed in the previous step, rounding to the nearest tenth.

Step 6: Add together all of the values computed in step 5. This is your individual or household dietary protein impact index. (If < F_o=10, you are in compliance with Objective #1.)

Example: I performed a protein analysis of our household by picking two days of typical meals to produce an "average" daily menu.

+--+
| FIG. #43 PROTEIN IMPACT INDEX--SAMPLE CALCULATION |

Protein Source	Useable Protein, g	fractional contribution	impact index	impact index contribution
milk/cheese	45	.347	14	4.9
tofu(soybeans)	13.2	.102	1.3	.1
rice	25.9	.200	2.3	.5
eggs	24	.185	7	1.3
wheat	9.6	.074	2.3	.2
other grain	6	.046	2.1	.1
peanuts(legumes)	6	.046	2.3	.1
Total	129.7 g	1		7.2

+--+

Step 1: Breakfast--1 cup milk, 2/3 cup rolled oats, 4 eggs
   Lunch--2 peanut butter sandwiches, 2 grilled cheese sandwiches
        (all sandwiches on whole wheat bread), 2 cups milk
   Dinner--2 cups milk, 7 oz. tofu, 5/6 cup uncooked rice
        (cooked as part of "Savory Rice" meal)

Step 2: The values in col. 2 of Fig. #43 were computed.
i.e. for milk/cheese, total milk = 1 + 2 + 2 = 5 cup x 7 g/cup = 35 g
each grilled cheese sandwich has 1 oz.cheese,x 2 = 2 oz. x 5g/oz = 10 g
        adding, 35 + 10 = 45 g

Step 3: 45 + 13.2 + 25.9 + 24 + 9.6 + 6 + 6 = 129.7 g

Step 4: The values in col. 3 of Fig. #43 were computed.
i.e. for milk/cheese, 45 g / 129.7 g = .347 (= 34.7 %) is the contribution of milk/cheese to the total protein.

Step 5: First, Fig. #40 is consulted and individual impact indices are listed as in col. 4. Next, values in col. 3 & 4 are multiplied = col.5
        i.e. for milk / cheese, .347 x 14 = 4.9

step 6: 4.9 + .1 + .5 + 1.3 + .2 + .1 + .1 = 7.2

Note 7.2 is less than 10 so objective #1 is satisfied. Suppose, instead of a roughly 30 % contribution from rice and tofu, we had consumed beef and chicken--say, 20 % beef contribution to protein, 10 % chicken. With this change, the impact index is 13.7, too high to satisfy objective.

A. II. ESTABLISHING F_o

I shall use information about the world food production and dietary scene to establish three individual maximum levels of protein impact--corresponding to the measures in col. 2, col. 3, and col. 4 of Fig. #40 (GOOD NEWS). These values will then be averaged to obtain F_o.

a) Protein/acre Efficiency Index

Consider how much plant protein could theoretically be produced on the 3.6 billion acres of land available for cultivation. Refer to Fig. #40. If it were all planted in soybeans yielding 356 lbs. useable protein per acre, then calculation shows that 338.4 grams/day per

person is potentially available. How does this compare to what is
actually produced? Considering the data in Fig. #44, this comparison
can be made. Undoubtedly, there are significant amounts of plant protein not included in this tabulation. Both to allow for this--and to
make the numbers easier to handle--I round the total weight of plant
protein and useable plant protein up to 2000 MMT and 120 MMT.

FIG. #44 TOTAL WORLD USEABLE PROTEIN^2			
Plant protein	millions metric tons	useable protein conversion factor	millions tons
wheat	489.7	.09	44.1
oats	45.9	.09	4.1
corn	346.8	.04	13.9
barley	170.4	.06	10.2
rice	448.9	.05	22.4
soybeans	79.7	.20	15.9
potatoes	291	.012	3.5
	-------		-------
	1872.4		114.1
Animal Protein			
grazing animals	105	.17	17.9
grain-fed animals	143	.17	24.3
fish	74	.15	11.1
	-----		--------
	322		53.3

     In computing the per capita protein available, we divide the 120
MMT by 2 to account for the 50 % of it which is fed to animals worldwide, leaving 60 MMT. Add to that amount the grain-fed animal protein,
i.e. 60 + 24.4 = 84.3 MMT. Spreading that over the human population
yields 48.5 grams of useable protein/day per person. This is the
useable protein that the cultivated land actually produces. (I am
treating grazing land and land under cultivation differently.) Comparing the theoretically available 338.4 to the actual 48.5, a roughly 7.0
to 1 ratio is computed. Given the observation that a significant portion of the human population is malnourished, a cultivated land utilization that is any less efficient in terms of useable protein/acre
cannot be justified. Note that if all grain was fed to people instead
of 50 % to animals, then 120 MMT rather than 84.3 MMT would be avai-
lable--42 % more. (The protein/acre efficiency would improve to 4.9)
b) Fossil Fuel Energy per Protein Production
     This measure was included in Fig. #40 as a weighting factor--not
just to gauge actual non-renewable energy use, but also other biosphere
impacts. As one eats higher on the modern human food chain, soil loss,
water consumption, pesticide and other agricultural pollution impacts
climb accordingly. To establish an appropriate limit for this index,
note that American per capita energy use is about five times the world
average. The energy-intensive American feedlot beef way of producing
protein, requiring 78 calories of energy input per calorie of protein
produced, is typical of a wasteful and environmentally abusive system.
If maximum energy inputs and associated impacts could be reduced by a
factor of five, i.e. limiting the fossil fuel energy index to 78/5 =
15.6, then perhaps such protein production impacts would be acceptable.
c) Plant to Animal Conversion Ratio
     Recall a net useable protein loss of 35.7 MMT (from 120 MMT to
84.3 MMT) due to feeding grain to animals. This resulted from 50 % of
the 2000 MMT of plant protein, or 1000 MMT fed to animals to yield 143
MMT (see Fig. #44). Note that 1000 / 143 = 7, reflecting 7 lbs. grain/

1 lb. meat ave. conversion ratio. Again, since too many are malnourished, no higher conversion ratio can be justified. If plant to animal
protein conversion became more efficient, less protein would be lost.
For example, if a 3 to 1, not 7 to 1, average prevailed, with the same
grain fed to animals, useable protein declines from 120 to 116.3 MMT.
d) Arriving at F_o
     Collecting the three individual maximum levels of protein impact--
established in a), b), and c) above--and averaging yields,
     F_o = 7.0 + 15.6 + 7.0 = 29.6 / 3 = 9.9 (I round this to 10)

B. THE ECOSHARING EXPERIMENT--MONETARY DATA

     Fig. #45 provides the mid-1975 to mid-1985 monetary history of my
family. All dollar amounts represent actual earnings and the incomes
are gross amounts before taxes. During this decade we were assessed
roughly $7,000 in income and social security taxes. We also received
government benefits of approximately the same amount in the form of
unemployment compensation, WIC, food stamps, and tax credits (energy
and earned income credits). Because the taxes paid roughly equalled the
benefits received, I have not included these in Fig. #45. On June 30,
1985 our savings totalled around $2300, our net worth was $30,000 to
$35,000. We were receiving no government benefits and had no debts.

```
+----------------------------------------------------------------------+
|      FIG. #45  ECOSHARING EXPERIMENT--MONETARY HISTORY                |
|                # in      Steve's    Annie's   interest    total       |
|             household    income     income     income     income     |
|   July-                     $          $          $          $        |
|   Dec 1975    2           1700         0          5         1705      |
|       1976    2           6725        800        35         7560      |
|       1977    2           4055        850       100         5005      |
|       1978    2           1094       2376         6         3456      |
|       1979    2           3076       5060        19         8155      |
|       1980    2.8         8373       3136       111        11620      |
|       1981    3          11408         0        331        11739      |
|       1982    3.7         6588         0        390         6978      |
|       1983    4           5226         0        274         5550      |
|       1984    4           3870         0        340         4210      |
|   Jan -                                                               |
|   June 1985   4            310        295       130          735      |
|            -------------------------------------------------          |
|     Totals  2.85        $52425     $12497     $1741       $66663      |
+----------------------------------------------------------------------+
```

     During this decade our annual household income averaged $6,666.
Dividing this by the average 2.85 household members, yields an average
annual per capita income of $2,339.

C. I. CALCULATING YOUR ENERGY IMPACT INDEX

     To determine compliance with Objective #6, calculation of E is
necessary. The formula needed is
     eqn. 1 $E = E_H + E_N$
     where E_H = average annual household energy (including
                transportation) per person
           E_N = the individual share of the national average
                annual non-household energy use
I shall discuss calculation of each of these values and do an example.
a) Calculating E_H
Step 1: List all energy sources (omit renewable, decentralized) you use
for household or transportation needs. Col. 1 of Fig. #46 lists the
various possibilities. This can be used as a worksheet for your
calculation. Note provisions for use of public transportation.
Step 2: For each of these, record the amount used during the past year.
Old utility bills, fuel purchase receipts, travel records, etc. will be
needed. Pay attention to the units each amount is measured in. You need
these amounts in the units indicated in col. 2 Fig. #46, put them in
col. 3. (For the record, the $ costs of each fuel or energy source

can be entered in col. 6 of the worksheet.)

```
+-------------------------------------------------------------------+
|   FIG. #46  WORKSHEET FOR HOUSEHOLD ENERGY E_H CALCULATION         |
```

Source / Units	Your Amount	Unit/ MBTU	Your MBTUs	Your $ Cost	Notes
Natural Gas Cuft		975			
Electricity[3] KWH		95			
Heating Oil Gal		7.25			
Coal lbs		75			
LP Gas Gal		10.35			
Gasoline Gal		8			
Air Travel--round trips/person		.0833			
Intercity Bus/Train round trips/person		2.5			
Intracity Bus/Train round trips/person		15			
Totals	XX	XX			

Step 3: Divide the amount in col. 3 by the conversion factor in col. 4 and record this quotient in col. 5.
Step 4: Add together the entries in col.5. If you are doing this calculation for a household or more than one person, divide your result by the appropriate number of people. The result is E_H, expressed in MBTU/person per year (recall 1 MBTU = 1,000,000 BTU).
b) Calculating E_N
     Whereas E_H measures the energy in the household and personal transportation sector which one directly uses and pays for, E_N measures one's indirect use of energy in other (commercial, industrial, etc.) sectors. Everyone who buys products, enjoys public and commercial services, makes use of the national infrastructure of highways, water systems, sewer and sanitation facilities, and so on, benefits from these hidden energy subsidies.. It may seem impossible to fairly assess individual shares of this national, non-household, non-personal transportation energy. Perhaps just assuming everyone uses an equal share is the best approach? Actually, we can do better than that.
     We improve on that equal share model by making two observations. First, the more money a person spends, generally the more energy use he or she is responsible for. The greater one's share of the monetary economy, the greater one's share of the energy economy. When you spend money you either are paying for a hidden energy cost or supporting others' energy consumption. While this is generally true, we can improve any model based on it. So second, we observe that if people meet their own household and transportation energy needs frugally and efficiently, their indirect participation in the rest of the energy economy will generally reflect that orientation.
     The model employed for assessing an individual's share of the national energy economy, E_N, factors in both of the above concerns.
          eqn. 2 $E_N = W1 \times W2 \times (1-f) \times E_{ave}$ (national average)
where   eqn. 3 $W1$ = (your income/national per capita income)
          eqn. 4 $W2$ = (your E_H / national per capita E_H)
and f=fraction used in the household/personal transportation sectors

The $(1-f) \times E_{ave}$ represents the equal share starting point. W1 and W2 are the correction factors used to improve the model.

C. II. EXAMPLE: ECOSHARING EXPERIMENT--ENERGY HISTORY

To illustrate the process, I'll calculate my family's average energy impact index E for the ten-year mid-1975 to mid-1985 period.

a) Calculation of E_H

Using the worksheet format provided, my completed worksheet appears in Fig. #47. Summing col. 5 gives 1111.1 MBTU/ household for 10 years. Dividing by 10 years and the average 2.85 household members (see APPENDIX B), yields E_H=39.0 MBTU/person-year.

FIG. #47 ECOSHARING EXPERIMENT--ENERGY HISTORY

Source / Units	Your Amount	Unit/ MBTU	Your MBTUs	Your $ Cost	Notes
Natural Gas Cuft	22000	975	22.6	50	1975-77
Electricity KWH	3000	95	31.6	100	1975-77
Heating Oil Gal		7.25			
Coal lbs		75			
LP Gas Gal	162.5	10.35	15.7	160	1982-85
Gasoline Gal	7295	8	911.9	7295	118800 mi
Air Travel--round trips/person	10	.0833	120	1000	
Intercity Bus/Train round trips/person	20	2.5	8	250	1975-77
Intracity Bus/Train round trips/person	20	15	1.3	50	1975-77
Totals	XX	XX	1111.1	$ 8905	1975-85

b) Calculation of E_N

For the ten-year period indicated, the pertinent average values to put into equations 2, 3, and 4 are:

	my household	U.S. average value
annual income/ person, $/year	2339	9580
E_H, MBTU/person-yr	39.0	121.4
f		.37
E_{ave} (nation), MBTU/person-yr		328

Putting these into eqn. 3 yields: W1 = 2339/9580 = .244, and into eqn. 4 gives W2 = 39.0/121.4 = .321. Using these in eqn.2 gives E_N= .244 × .321 × (1-.37) × 328 = 16.2 MBTU/person-yr.

c) Calculation of E

Using eqn. 1, E = 39.0 + 16.2 = 55.2 MBTU/person-year.

Notes

1. consult tables in Moore-Lappe, F. Diet for a Small Planet, Ballantine, NY, 1982
2. 1983-84 data from The Foreign Agricultural Service, USDA except for potatoes (National Geographic, May, 1982), and fish (State of the World 1985) useable protein conversion factors from Moore-Lappe.
3. this calculation includes energy wasted at the power plant in the typically 30 to 40 % efficient conversion to electricity.